KW-222-326

Universal Screening in Educational Settings

SCHOOL PSYCHOLOGY BOOK SERIES

Health-Related Disorders in Children and Adolescents: A Guidebook for Understanding and Educating
   Edited by LeAdelle Phelps

Enhancing Relationships Between Children and Teachers
   Robert C. Pianta

Working With Parents of Aggressive Children: A Practitioner's Guide
   Timothy A. Cavell

Empowered Families, Successful Children: Early Intervention Programs That Work
   Susan Epps and Barbara J. Jackson

School-Based Mental Health Services: Creating Comprehensive and Culturally Specific Programs
   Bonnie Kaul Nastasi, Rachel Bernstein Moore, and Kristen M. Varjas

Working With Parents of Noncompliant Children: A Guide to Evidence-Based Parent Training for Practitioners and Students
   Mark D. Shriver and Keith D. Allen

Behavioral Interventions in Schools: Evidence-Based Positive Strategies
   Edited by Angeleque Akin-Little, Steven G. Little, Melissa A. Bray, and Thomas J. Kehle

Healthy Eating in Schools: Evidence-Based Interventions to Help Kids Thrive
   Catherine P. Cook-Cottone, Evelyn Tribole, and Tracy L. Tylka

Treatment Integrity: A Foundation for Evidence-Based Practice in Applied Psychology
   Edited by Lisa M. Hagermoser Sanetti and Thomas R. Kratochwill

Assessing Bilingual Children in Context: An Integrated Approach
   Edited by Amanda B. Clinton

Universal Screening in Educational Settings: Evidence-Based Decision Making for Schools
   Edited by Ryan J. Kettler, Todd A. Glover, Craig A. Albers, and Kelly A. Feeney-Kettler

Universal Screening in Educational Settings

Evidence-Based Decision Making for Schools

Edited by **Ryan J. Kettler, Todd A. Glover, Craig A. Albers, and Kelly A. Feeney-Kettler**

American Psychological Association • Washington, DC

Copyright © 2014 by the American Psychological Association. All rights reserved. Except as permitted under the United States Copyright Act of 1976, no part of this publication may be reproduced or distributed in any form or by any means, including, but not limited to, the process of scanning and digitization, or stored in a database or retrieval system, without the prior written permission of the publisher.

Published by
American Psychological Association
750 First Street, NE
Washington, DC 20002
www.apa.org

To order
APA Order Department
P.O. Box 92984
Washington, DC 20090-2984
Tel: (800) 374-2721; Direct: (202) 336-5510
Fax: (202) 336-5502; TDD/TTY: (202) 336-6123
Online: www.apa.org/pubs/books
E-mail: order@apa.org

In the U.K., Europe, Africa, and the Middle East, copies may be ordered from
American Psychological Association
3 Henrietta Street
Covent Garden, London
WC2E 8LU England

Typeset in Goudy by Circle Graphics, Inc., Columbia, MD

Printer: United Book Press, Baltimore, MD
Cover Designer: Mercury Publishing Services, Rockville, MD

The opinions and statements published are the responsibility of the authors, and such opinions and statements do not necessarily represent the policies of the American Psychological Association.

Library of Congress Cataloging-in-Publication Data

Kettler, Ryan J.
  Universal screening in educational setting : evidence-based decision making for schools / Ryan J. Kettler, Todd A. Glover, Craig A. Albers, and Kelly A. Feeney-Kettler.
    pages ; cm. — (School psychology book series)
  Includes bibliographical references and index.
  ISBN-13: 978-1-4338-1550-8
  ISBN-10: 1-4338-1550-8
1. Educational tests and measurements—Evaluation. 2. Education—Evaluation. 3. Educational psychology. 4. Learning disabled children—Identification. 5. Language arts—Evaluation. 6. English language—Study and teaching—Foreign speakers—Evaluation. 7. Mathematics—Study and teaching—Evaluation. I. Title.
  LB3051.K365 2014
  371.26—dc23

                                2013020746

British Library Cataloguing-in-Publication Data

A CIP record is available from the British Library.

Printed in the United States of America
First Edition

http://dx.doi.org/10.1037/14316-000

CONTENTS

Contributors .... *vii*

Series Foreword .... *ix*

Acknowledgments .... *xi*

Chapter 1.   An Introduction to Universal Screening
in Educational Settings 3
Ryan J. Kettler, Todd A. Glover, Craig A. Albers,
and Kelly A. Feeney-Kettler

I. Universal Screening Within Educational Models **17**

Chapter 2.   Screening Within a Multitiered Early Prevention
Model: Using Assessment to Inform Instruction
and Promote Students' Response to Intervention 19
Danielle M. Parisi, Tanya Ihlo, and Todd A. Glover

Chapter 3.   Multiple-Gating Approaches in Universal Screening
Within School and Community Settings 47
Hill M. Walker, Jason W. Small, Herbert H. Severson,
John R. Seeley, and Edward G. Feil

II. Developing, Evaluating, and Implementing Screening.................... 77

Chapter 4.   Developing and Evaluating Screening Systems:
Practical and Psychometric Considerations................... 79
Theodore J. Christ and Peter M. Nelson

Chapter 5.   Screening as Innovation:
Implementation Challenges...................................... 111
*Susan G. Forman, Tzivia R. Jofen,
and Audrey R. Lubin*

III. Content-Specific Screening 139

Chapter 6.   Early Childhood Literacy Screening............................ 141
*Scott R. McConnell, Tracy A. Bradfield,
and Alisha K. Wackerle-Hollman*

Chapter 7.   Screening for Early Reading Skills: Using Data
to Guide Resources and Instruction............................ 171
*Matthew K. Burns, Katherine Haegele,
and Shawna Petersen-Brown*

Chapter 8.   Mathematics Screening Measures
for the Primary Grades 199
Ben Clarke, Kelly Haymond, and Russell Gersten

Chapter 9.   Broadband Screening of Academic
and Social Behavior 223
*James C. DiPerna, Catherine G. Bailey,
and Christopher Anthony*

Chapter 10.   Behavioral and Mental Health Screening 249
*Randy W. Kamphaus, Cecil R. Reynolds,
and Bridget V. Dever*

Chapter 11.   Universal Screening of English Language Learners:
Language Proficiency and Literacy............................. 275
Craig A. Albers and Paige L. Mission

Index 305

About the Editors... 319

CONTRIBUTORS

Craig A. Albers, PhD, University of Wisconsin–Madison
Christopher Anthony, MEd, The Pennsylvania State University, University Park
Catherine G. Bailey, PhD, Montgomery County Schools, Greensboro, NC
Tracy A. Bradfield, PhD, University of Minnesota, Minneapolis
Matthew K. Burns, PhD, University of Minnesota, Minneapolis
Theodore J. Christ, PhD, University of Minnesota, Minneapolis
Ben Clarke, PhD, University of Oregon, Eugene
Bridget V. Dever, PhD, Lehigh University, Bethlehem, PA
James C. DiPerna, PhD, The Pennsylvania State University, University Park
Kelly A. Feeney-Kettler, PhD, FKK Consulting, Basking Ridge, NJ
Edward G. Feil, PhD, Oregon Research Institute, Eugene
Susan G. Forman, PhD, Rutgers, The State University of New Jersey, Piscataway
Russell Gersten, PhD, Instructional Research Group, Los Alamitos, CA
Todd A. Glover, PhD, University of Nebraska–Lincoln
Katherine Haegele, MA, University of Minnesota, Minneapolis
Kelly Haymond, MA, Instructional Research Group, Los Alamitos, CA
Tanya Ihlo, PhD, University of Nebraska–Lincoln

Tzivia R. Jofen, MS, Rutgers, The State University of New Jersey, Piscataway
Randy W. Kamphaus, PhD, Georgia State University, Atlanta
Ryan J. Kettler, PhD, Rutgers, The State University of New Jersey, Piscataway
Audrey R. Lubin, BA, Rutgers, The State University of New Jersey, Piscataway
Scott R. McConnell, PhD, University of Minnesota, Minneapolis
Paige L. Mission, MS, University of Wisconsin–Madison
Peter M. Nelson, MA, University of Minnesota, Minneapolis
Danielle M. Parisi, PhD, Amplify Education, Brooklyn, NY
Shawna Petersen-Brown, PhD, University of Minnesota, Minneapolis
Cecil R. Reynolds, PhD, Texas A&M University, College Station
John R. Seeley, PhD, Oregon Research Institute, Eugene
Herbert H. Severson, PhD, Oregon Research Institute, Eugene
Jason W. Small, BA, Oregon Research Institute, Eugene
Alisha K. Wackerle-Hollman, PhD, University of Minnesota, Minneapolis
Hill M. Walker, PhD, University of Oregon, Eugene

SERIES FOREWORD

Outside of their homes, children spend more time in schools than in any other settings. From tragedies such as Sandy Hook and Columbine to more hopeful developments such as the movement toward improved mental health, physical health, and academic achievement, there is an ongoing need for high-quality writing that explains how children, families, and communities associated with schools worldwide can be supported through the application of sound psychological research, theory, and practice.

Thus, for the past several years the American Psychological Association (APA) Books and APA Division 16 (School Psychology) have partnered to produce the School Psychology Book Series. The mission of this series is to increase the visibility of psychological science, practice, and policy for children and adolescents in schools and communities. The result has been a strong collection of scholarly work that appeals not only to psychologists but also to individuals from all fields who have reason to seek and use what psychology has to offer in schools.

Many individuals have made significant contributions to the School Psychology Book Series. First, we would like to acknowledge the dedication of past series editors: Sandra L. Christensen, Jan Hughes, R. Steve McCallum,

LeAdelle Phelps, Susan Sheridan, and Christopher H. Skinner. We extend special thanks to David McIntosh for his dedicated service as series editor on this volume as well as on previous volumes in the series. Second, we would like to acknowledge the outstanding editorial vision of the scholars who have edited or authored books for the series. The work of these scholars has significantly advanced psychological science and practice for children and adolescents worldwide.

We welcome your comments about this volume and other topics you would like to see explored in this series. To share your thoughts, please visit the Division 16 website at www.apadivisions.org/division-16.

Linda A. Reddy, PhD
Series Editor

ACKNOWLEDGMENTS

We must first thank each of the contributing authors, who graciously agreed to share their knowledge, endured our multiple requests, and ultimately advanced our understanding of universal screening. We also extend our gratitude to our graduate students, project assistants, support staff, and mentors, each of whom contributed in various ways to bringing this book to fruition. Most important, we acknowledge the understanding and patience our families demonstrated while we worked on this project.

Ryan and Kelly thank Austin Joseph Kettler for providing the inspiration to work toward a better future.

Todd thanks Maya and Michaela for their daily inspiration and Alec and Anne for their ongoing support.

Craig thanks Michele, Madeline, Anabelle, Calysta, and Keelan Albers for their unending support.

Universal Screening in Educational Settings

1

AN INTRODUCTION TO UNIVERSAL SCREENING IN EDUCATIONAL SETTINGS

RYAN J. KETTLER, TODD A. GLOVER, CRAIG A. ALBERS, AND KELLY A. FEENEY-KETTLER

Screening is not a new concept. During the 7th century B.C., Sparta was a dominant Greek city-state, renowned for its focus on military training. All male infants who were eligible for Spartan citizenship were bathed in wine by their mothers as a test of strength. Those who survived were examined by the Gerousea, a council of elders, for signs of physical or mental defects or general weakness. Children who displayed signs of defect or weakness were thrown into a chasm of Mount Taygetus.

Around the beginning of the 20th century A.D., the French government asked Alfred Binet to develop a method for identifying children with mental retardation. In 1905, he collaborated with Theodore Simon to develop the 30-item Binet–Simon scale, the first iteration of the Stanford–Binet scale that

The editors wish to express gratitude to Anna Braverman, Melissa A. Palladino, Jennifer C. Rodriguez, and Lindsey P. Zahra for their able research assistance in developing this chapter.

http://dx.doi.org/10.1037/14316-001
Universal Screening in Educational Settings: Evidence-Based Decision Making for Schools, R. J. Kettler, T. A. Glover, C. A. Albers, and K. A. Feeney-Kettler (Editors)
Copyright © 2014 by the American Psychological Association. All rights reserved.

remains one of today's most popular measures of intelligence. The original scale involved a wide range of tasks, including comparison of two weights, verbal definition of known objects, and paper cutting.

In 1921, the Swiss psychiatrist Hermann Rorschach published *Psychodiagnostik*, a monograph that included the results of case studies on patients with mental health disorders, as well as 10 cards with inkblots that would serve as the basis for the Rorschach test. Rorschach had observed that people with schizophrenia expressed very different perceptions than did people from the general population. Soon thereafter psychologists began using the Rorschach inkblot test as a general personality test and indicator of mental health difficulties, a practice that continues to this day.

The aforementioned and many other examples of screening have existed throughout history. Traditionally, the practice of screening has involved the use of brief assessments with a group to identify individuals who are at risk or may be at risk of future difficulties. Screening procedures continue to be common practice in various disciplines, including medicine, social and behavioral sciences, the military, and criminal justice.

SCREENING IN EDUCATION

Screening is also prominent in educational settings, in which it often focuses on academics, behavior, emotional functioning, and physical health. Screening in educational settings may occur in the format of timed tests of narrow academic skills, teacher ratings against grade-level expectations, student self-report of symptoms, or any one of a multitude of other forms. Some forms of screening are practiced in nearly all schools, but the prevalence and level of formality are extremely variable. Screening decisions are made informally any time a child study team meets and identifies students who are struggling academically or behaviorally. If all students in a population (e.g., one grade level of a school) are considered in such a meeting, the screening is universal. To the extent that scores from a common source or sources of data are considered for all students (e.g., all students' scores on a test, behavioral referral records), the decisions made by the child study team are more likely to be consistent (i.e., reliable) and lead to identification of opportunities for preventive intervention. If the screening process is further specified, for example, including guidelines for making decisions from the screening data, it may be considered a screening system. Such a system may include multiple stages or gates of assessment through which students progress, with the assessment becoming progressively more thorough at each stage. At the most formal end of the spectrum, the system may include directions for training implementers and for storing and communicating results, as well as for assigning interventions and monitoring their effectiveness.

Although screening historically has focused on the identification of shortcomings presumed to exist within individuals (e.g., learning disabilities, behavioral difficulties), a contemporary conceptualization is that screening identifies cases in which the match between the student and the learning environment is suboptimal, leading to a plan of action for addressing health, behavioral, or skill needs. Behavioral and skill-based screening are now commonly used to identify (a) the presence of symptoms that predict future behavioral or academic problems, and (b) opportunities for future practices to prevent or remediate difficulties. Within this context, screening is not used to label a problem but instead to create an opportunity for change.

Within school settings, there is a strong and compelling empirical justification for the use of screening to identify (and subsequently address) academic and behavioral difficulties as early as possible. Unfortunately, students whose academic and behavioral needs are not met early often experience significant and enduring consequences. For example, without appropriate intervention, Francis, Shaywitz, Stuebing, Shaywitz, and Fletcher (1996) found that 74% of students with reading difficulties in third grade continued to have trouble reading in high school. Likewise, children with behavioral difficulties at an early age have an increased risk for school maladjustment and antisocial activity (e.g., Schofield, Bierman, Heinrichs, & Nix, 2008). Childhood behavioral difficulties have been associated with increased academic difficulties (Reinke, Herman, Petras, & Ialongo, 2008) and high school dropout (Vitaro, Brendgen, Larose, & Tremblay, 2005). Thus, early identification of difficulties is crucial, so that educators can better address students' needs before they manifest into more pervasive problems.

Screening Within a Multitiered Response-to-Intervention Framework

Recent attention to the early detection and prevention of academic and behavioral difficulties has resulted in increased use of screening as part of a multitiered, response-to-intervention (RTI) approach to service delivery in schools. According to this approach, core instruction and programs (Tier 1) are designed for the majority of students (at least 80% of students), additional secondary-level support (Tier 2) is provided to students whose needs are not addressed by primary practices (about 15% of students), and intensive individualized interventions (Tier 3) are provided to students with additional needs (about 5% of students). Within this framework, screening is used to identify students who may benefit from additional intervention to better address academic or behavioral concerns, as well as to determine whether core programs meet the majority of students' needs. Accordingly, screening data are vital to make the decisions necessary to support students at each level of the service-delivery system (e.g., Glover, 2010; Walker & Shinn, 2002).

Increased Policy Emphasis on Screening

Several key legislative and political developments have promoted the use of screening within a prevention-focused framework in schools. In 2001, Congress passed the No Child Left Behind Act (NCLB, 2001), which recommended that universal screening systems for reading be adopted to help identify low-achieving students not performing at levels consistent with high academic standards. Soon thereafter, a report from the National Research Council (NRC; Donovan & Cross, 2002) recommended that states utilize universal screening methods for reading and behavioral problems to improve the early identification of students at risk for academic difficulties. The report indicated that universal screening was a critical component in remedying such problems as disproportionate minority representation in special education and the gap between academic assessment and intervention. The NRC recommended that multitier universal screening procedures, developed with input from large-scale research centers, be implemented at a federal level. Furthermore, the reauthorization of the Individuals With Disabilities Education Improvement Act (IDEIA, 2004) permitted that referrals to special education be made based on failure to respond to intervention, rather than on traditional discrepancy model criteria. Accordingly, screening was identified as a critical component of an RTI model because it is needed to identify students for whom preventive interventions are appropriate. Such policy changes dramatically have increased the emphasis on universal screening in U.S. schools.

A Comprehensive Definition of Screening

With increased attention to prevention-focused service delivery in schools, several definitions of *screening* have emerged that take into account the function of assessment as it relates to instruction and student assistance. The American Educational Research Association, the American Psychological Association, and the National Council on Measurement in Education (1999) jointly define a *screening test* as "a test that is used to make broad categorizations of examinees as a first step in selection decisions or diagnostic processes" (p. 182). Although this definition depicts screening as an important step along a continuum from identification to diagnosis to intervention, it does not conceptualize screening within a larger framework of early prevention. The National Center on Response to Intervention (2012), with a focus on supports for school-age children, expands on this definition by describing screening as a process that

> involves brief assessments that are valid, reliable, and evidence-based. They are conducted with all students or targeted groups of students to identify students who are at-risk of academic failure and, therefore, likely to need additional or alternative forms of instruction to supplement the conventional general education approach.

Although both of these definitions help to illustrate a function of screening, a broader conceptualization of screening in educational settings includes applications for systems-level considerations. As such, we define *screening* as the use of a test or other evidence to make broad categorizations of examinees to (a) identify which students would benefit from preventive interventions and (b) determine whether school-based instructional or behavioral assistance are meeting students' needs. Accordingly, screening involves brief assessments conducted with all students (i.e., universal screening) or with targeted groups of students to identify individuals who are at risk for future difficulties as well as to evaluate existing practices. Students identified as at risk (based on established criteria or benchmarks) may benefit from preventive interventions used in addition to existing practices. For example, a third-grade student who is identified as at risk for a reading difficulty might benefit from participation in a reading group with intensive direct instruction and increased opportunities for reading practice and performance feedback. When a large proportion of students within a school setting (e.g., more than 20% of students in a classroom) are identified as at risk for a problem, existing school-based instructional or behavioral supports may need to be adjusted or replaced to better meet student needs. In such cases, evaluation and alteration of both instructional practices and the overall curriculum may be warranted. For example, a third-grade classroom with 40% of students identified as at risk for reading difficulties would not only require intervention for students who are struggling but also likely would benefit from reexamination of the general reading curriculum and current instructional practices.

It is important to consider screening as a process for informing educators about students' academic or behavioral needs. Although screening traditionally has been used to identify deficits, disabilities, or problems, more recent applications focus on determining which practices are needed to address student concerns. Consistent with this perspective, the editors strongly support recent efforts to replace characterizations of child-centered deficits with a focus instead on student needs. In discussing the screening process and student outcomes, it is critical that educators use language that depicts a concern for specific preventive intervention practices (e.g., a need for support with phonics or computation skills), rather than labeling the students themselves (e.g., "behavior kids" or "Tier 2 kids").

SCREENING TERMINOLOGY

Given an emergent literature on screening, it is important to consider several key terms related to the validation and use of screening tools. In education, screening takes place whenever a relatively brief assessment method is used with a group of students for the purpose of identifying instructional or behavioral needs and opportunities for preventive intervention. A benefit of screening is that relatively small difficulties or predictive factors can be identified before they grow more problematic and difficult to treat; when this happens, there is an opportunity to help students. Identifying such opportunities involves distinguishing between students who need assistance and those who do not. Only by accurately making this distinction can screening benefit children who need help, both by identifying behavioral and skill needs and by ensuring that much needed instructional and intervention resources are not spread too thin.

Predictive Validity of Screening

As the profile of universal screening in the schools has been raised in the past decade, so too has the profile of a class of indices that are used to define screening decisions. Conditional probability analyses (also known as sensitivity–specificity or diagnostic accuracy analyses) are useful for characterizing the predictive validity of screening systems (i.e., their accuracy in predicting future outcomes) because they reflect the dichotomous nature of screening decisions (i.e., whether a child is at risk for a difficulty, which in turn would indicate an opportunity for preventive intervention). This dichotomy, which characterizes both the screening decision (made based on data from the screening instrument) and reality (which never truly can be known but is the condition the screening instrument is designed to predict), yields four possible categories: a true positive, a false positive, a false negative, or a true negative. Each screening case fits into one and only one of these categories. Of these four categories, a false negative generally is considered to be the worst possible outcome because it represents a student in need of assistance who is not identified by the screening system (Ikeda, Neesen, & Witt, 2008). From these categories, a number of indices pertaining to the predictive validity of a screening system can be calculated, including the following: sensitivity (the likelihood that a screening test will correctly identify as at risk a child who truly is at risk), specificity (the likelihood that a screening test will correctly identify as not at risk a child who truly is not at risk), positive predictive value (PPV; the likelihood that a child identified as at risk truly is at risk), and negative predictive value (NPV; the likelihood that a child identified as not at risk truly is not at risk). Table 1.1 depicts

TABLE 1.1
Conditional Probability Framework

| Screening result | Reality (defined by established measure) | | Total |
	At risk	Not at risk	
At risk	a (true positives)	b (false positives)	a + b
Not at risk	c (false negatives)	d (true negatives)	c + d
Total	a + c	b + d	a + b + c + d

Note. Sensitivity = [a / (a + c)], specificity = [d / (b + d)], positive predictive value = [a / (a + b)], negative predictive value = [d / (c + d)], base rate = [(a + c) / (a + b + c + d)], and hit rate = [(a + d) / (a + b + c + d)]. From "Screening Systems and Decision-Making at the Preschool Level: Application of a Comprehensive Validity Framework," by R. J. Kettler and K. A. Feeney-Kettler, 2011, *Psychology in the Schools, 48,* p. 436. Copyright 2011 by Wiley-Blackwell. Adapted with permission.

the conditional probability framework between a screening instrument and reality. In research and evaluation, an established measure or collection of measures is used as a proxy for reality.

Because all four of the aforementioned indices are related mathematically, it is critical to consider them together when evaluating a screening system; developmental decisions and sample characteristics that maximize one index are likely to reduce another (Kettler, 2011). One example of a developmental decision is the setting of the cut score, or the rule indicating which students are at risk versus not at risk. If the cut score is moved in the direction of identifying more students as at risk, the screening system becomes more sensitive but less specific. If the cut score is moved in the direction of identifying fewer students at risk, the system becomes less sensitive but more specific. One example of a sample characteristic that affects conditional probability indices is the base rate, or the prevalence of the difficulty in the sample, as defined by the established measure. Finally, it is helpful to consider the hit rate of a screening system because it reflects the likelihood that the results of a screening test are true regardless of whether the finding is positive or negative.

The values for each of these indices have a theoretical range from .00 to 1.00, with higher values indicating more accurate screening results. Each screening instrument should be evaluated based on the screening decision's own unique criteria for acceptable values of conditional probability indices, based on the relative cost of a false positive versus a false negative as well as on the base rate of the need for preventive intervention in the user's population (Kettler & Feeney-Kettler, 2011). In general, indices equal to or exceeding .80 but less than 1.00 can be considered high and indicative of screening systems that are working well. This is a good criterion to use across indices if the relative cost of a false positive and a false negative is equal, and if the base rate of need for intervention is around .50. Indices equal to or exceeding .60, but not exceeding .80, can be considered moderate; such indices are acceptable under many circumstances. Indices equal to or exceeding .40, but not exceeding .60, can be considered low but also might be acceptable under some circumstances. For example, these values might be acceptable for specificity and PPV in a situation in which a false-positive case is not very costly compared with a false-negative case, such as in the first stage of multistage screening for a reading difficulty. A false positive would result in one additional student being considered at the second stage of assessment, but a false negative would result in a student in need of preventive intervention not receiving it until possible identification during the next screening cycle. In this example, later stages of screening would be expected to be more specific and to have greater PPV compared with earlier stages. Conversely, indices in the high range for sensitivity and NPV would be required in all stages, because false negative cases (i.e., students at risk for reading difficulties not being identified) would be relatively costly. The base rate of the need for intervention in a sample also affects the PPV and NPV. Attaining high PPV is difficult when the base rate is low, and attaining high NPV is difficult when the base rate is high. Any indices that do not exceed .40 are very low and may indicate that a screening system is not ideal for the population and purpose for which it is being tested. Table 1.2 summarizes these ranges of conditional probability values and provides examples of circumstances under which each might be acceptable.

A number of other indices also are used to evaluate the reliability and validity of screening systems. For a thorough review, the reader is directed to Chapter 4 in this volume.

Screening as Formative Assessment

Universal screening often is conducted as part of a formative assessment process. Formative assessments are designed to yield information to assist educators with adjusting instruction, intervention, and other services during their provision. (Summative assessments, by contrast, are designed to provide evaluative information when services are completed.) Formative assessment data are used to make immediate instructional decisions.

Universal screening systems are suited uniquely for formative assessment, given their primary characteristics and core features, which include (a) suitability for multiple administrations throughout an academic year, (b) provision of data regarding student progress that can be used to make instructional or curricular changes, (c) quick and easy administration requirements, and (d) design for strong predictive validity properties. Thus, universal screening assists in identifying which students are or are not in need of additional assistance as well as in determining whether existing curricula and instructional practices are meeting students' needs. As such, screening

TABLE 1.2
Ranges of Conditional Probability Index Values and Potential Conditions for Each to Be Acceptable or Required

Range	Label	Sensitivity	Specificity	PPV	NPV
.00 ≤ Index < .40	Very low	Not acceptable	Not acceptable	Not acceptable	Not acceptable
.40 ≤ Index < .60	Low	May be acceptable when FPs are more costly	May be acceptable when FNs are more costly	May be acceptable when the base rate is low	May be acceptable when the base rate is high
.60 ≤ Index < .80	Moderate	May be acceptable when the costs of FPs and FNs are equal	May be acceptable when the costs of FPs and FNs are equal	May be acceptable when the base rate is around .50	May be acceptable when the base rate is around .50
.80 ≤ Index < 1.00	High	May be required when FNs are more costly	May be required when FPs are more costly	May be required when the base rate is high	May be required when the base rate is low

Note. PPV = positive predictive value; NPV = negative predictive value; FP = false positive; FN = false negative. From "Screening Systems and Decision-Making at the Preschool Level: Application of a Comprehensive Validity Framework," by R. J. Kettler and K. A. Feeney-Kettler, 2011, *Psychology in the Schools, 48*, p. 437. Copyright 2011 by Wiley-Blackwell. Adapted with permission.

data serves an important function in school- or classwide planning by informing decisions about practices and curriculum that are working for students as well as by identifying additional supports that may be needed within the educational setting.

THE CURRENT VOLUME: EVIDENCE-BASED DECISION MAKING FOR SCHOOLS

Throughout this book, the chapter authors have defined key aspects of universal screening. Each chapter focuses on techniques that can be used to accurately identify the need for preventive interventions that address individual students' needs, as well as the efficacy of core programs. Chapter authors discuss the use of screening data and the systematic analysis of needs and available services to improve student experiences, along with other outcomes for schools. This book is composed of chapters from experts in educational psychology, who were recruited to assist the editors in relaying information about the appropriate selection and implementation of universal screening procedures as well as the current state of screening research.

Key Questions Addressed

In the past decade, the number of screening systems marketed to schools has increased substantially, while guidance in determining their technical quality and usefulness has been slow to follow. School psychologists and other assessment professionals in education need to know the best strategies for selecting (or developing), implementing, and interpreting screening systems to meet their various early identification needs. This book addresses many pertinent questions, including the following:

1. Under what circumstances is a screening system needed or helpful?
2. How does one select or develop the correct screening system?
3. What factor does the educational environment play in universal screening?
4. How is screening different for different types of problems?
5. Is screening different within special populations (e.g., early childhood, children with intellectual disabilities, English language learners)?
6. How should screening systems be evaluated?
7. What do the various quality indicators (e.g., reliability, validity, sensitivity) mean?
8. What is the relationship between screening and RTI?

These and other questions are answered in this book in a manner that is dually grounded in rigorous research and real-world practicality. The 2007 special issue of the *Journal of School Psychology* dedicated to universal screening, in which Glover and Albers (2007) proposed a framework for evaluating universal screening procedures, was a guide to the current text. Consistent with the Glover and Albers's (2007) framework, much of the content contained within this book addresses issues relating to the *appropriateness* (e.g., compatibility with local needs, alignment with constructs of interest, support both theoretically and empirically), *technical adequacy* (in terms of norms, reliability, and validity evidence), and *usability* (e.g., feasibility, acceptability) of universal screening procedures. Additionally, multiple measurement perspectives, including classical test theory and item response theory, are included in discussions within this text.

Although the chapter authors have established expertise in their own content areas and in screening methodology, relevant practical implications of screening are emphasized throughout the book. Where appropriate, comparative analyses of available instruments are presented, and case studies are used to illustrate conceptual issues. Authors frequently provide lists and other organizers for considerations pertaining to educational screening situations. This book truly is intended to be helpful and intriguing for a diverse readership, all of whom are stakeholders in educational screening.

Intended Readers

A number of professionals—school psychologists, social workers, speech and language pathologists, principals and other school administrators, licensed counselors, psychiatrists, physicians, nurses, state assessment leaders, test developers, special education leaders and advocates, classroom teachers, and assessment researchers, among others—should find this book a valuable addition to their libraries. This book also has potential for use in graduate training programs in school psychology as well as in educational psychology, special education, and educational policy studies. Readers will (a) gain an appreciation of the multitude of issues that surround screening choices, (b) learn to critically examine and select or develop the appropriate system for their setting and situation, and (c) appreciate which attributes of screening are domain specific (e.g., academic, behavioral) versus which attributes are broadly applicable.

Content Foci

Although the editors have included some outstanding conceptual information in this book, we have focused on keeping the text informative and helpful for situations that arise every day in educational settings. All of the chapter authors agreed and strove to meet this requirement. A number of commercially available screening systems are described in the text, but it is always for the purposes of illustrating concepts and letting the readership know what is available. Chapter authors have remained objective in addressing instruments that they developed, as evidenced by describing each instrument's strengths and weaknesses, and by including alternate measures where appropriate. This book includes screening topics in the academic–educational and mental health–behavioral domains, both of which are highly pertinent in schools. We did not include information on health screening, which also occurs in schools, but is more isolated in terms of the personnel and process. The reader is directed to *Screening: Evidence and Practice* (Raffle & Muir Gray, 2007) for information specific to health screening. Likewise, although many of our chapters address behavioral screening, this book is not a prescriptive guide for selecting and implementing such a system. The reader is directed to *Systematic Screenings of Behavior to Support Instruction: From Preschool to High School* (Lane, Menzies, Oakes, & Kalberg, 2012) for such a guide. Lastly, this book truly focuses on screening by addressing only short measures and efficient systems, rather than more time-intensive measures that have been used for diagnosis or classification purposes.

Following this introductory chapter, the book begins with two chapters on how universal screening fits within educational models. Chapter 2 contextualizes screening issues within the framework with which it is most often associated in schools: RTI. Chapter 3 addresses considerations around multiple-gate screening, a process that involves multiple steps and assessment procedures. Part II, "Developing, Evaluating, and Implementing Screening," includes two chapters that describe technical considerations regarding screening instruments. Chapter 4 reviews the psychometric characteristics on which screening systems should be developed and evaluated. Chapter 5 examines the challenges of implementing screening systems as innovations in schools. The chapters that follow in Part III, "Content-Specific Screening," are defined by the domains on which they focus. Chapter 6, Chapter 7, and Chapter 8 address considerations and available instruments for screening in early literacy, reading, and mathematics, respectively. Chapter 9 addresses the unique concept of screening for academics and behavior together, and Chapter 10 addresses issues and options for behavioral and mental health screening. The final chapter, Chapter 11, addresses the unique considerations pertaining to screening within populations of English language learners.

The editors believe that anyone who is a stakeholder in the educational screening process will read this book and find guidance. Experts, including chapter authors, do not *always* agree with one another (nor do editors, for that matter). That said, researchers and practitioners continue to advance wonderful theoretical and practical work related to screening in educational settings. We have come a long way since bathing infants in wine as a test of strength! *Universal Screening in Educational Settings: Evidence-Based Decision Making for Schools* brings together current knowledge and work in screening for critical consumption; we hope that in doing so this book functions to advance the field of universal screening in education.

REFERENCES

American Educational Research Association, American Psychological Association, & National Council on Measurement in Education. (1999). *Standards for educational and psychological testing*. Washington, DC: Author.

Donovan, M. S., & Cross, C. T. (2002). *Minority students in special and gifted education*. Washington, DC: National Academy Press.

Francis, D. J., Shaywitz, S. E., Stuebing, K. K., Shaywitz, B. A., & Fletcher, J. M. (1996). Developmental lag versus deficit models of reading disability: A longitudinal, individual growth curves analysis. *Journal of Educational Psychology, 88*(1), 3–17. doi:10.1037/0022-0663.88.1.3

Glover, T. A. (2010). Key RTI service delivery components: Considerations for research-informed practice. In T. A. Glover & S. Vaughn (Eds.), *The promise of Response to Intervention: Evaluating current science and practice* (pp. 7–22). New York, NY: Guilford Press.

Glover, T. A., & Albers, C. A. (2007). Considerations for evaluating universal screening assessments. *Journal of School Psychology, 45*, 117–135. doi:10.1016/j.jsp.2006.05.005

Ikeda, M. J., Neesen, E., & Witt, J. C. (2008). Best practices in universal screening. In A. Thomas & J. Grimes (Eds.), *Best practices in school psychology V*, (pp. 103–114). Bethesda, MD: National Association of School Psychologists.

Individuals With Disabilities Education Improvement Act of 2004. Pub. L., 108–446, 118 Stat. 2647.

Kettler, R. J. (2011). Computer-based screening for the new modified alternate assessment. *Journal of Psychoeducational Assessment, 29*(1), 3–13. doi:10.1177/0734282910370804

Kettler, R. J., & Feeney-Kettler, K. A. (2011). Screening systems and decision-making at the preschool level: Application of a comprehensive validity framework. *Psychology in the Schools, 48*, 430–441. doi:10.1002/pits.20565

Lane, K. L., Menzies, H. M., Oakes, W. P., & Kalberg, J. R. (2012). *Systematic screenings of behavior to support instruction: From preschool to high school*. New York, NY: Guilford Press.

National Center on Response to Intervention. (2012). Retrieved from http://www.rti4success.org

No Child Left Behind Act of 2001, Pub. L. No. 107-110, § 115, Stat. 1425 (2002).

Raffle, A. E., & Muir Gray, J. A. (2007). *Screening: Evidence and practice*. New York, NY: Oxford University Press. doi:10.1093/acprof:oso/9780199214495.001.0001

Reinke, W. M., Herman, K. C., Petras, H., & Ialongo, N. S. (2008). Empirically derived subtypes of child academic and behavior problems: Co-occurrence and distal outcomes. *Journal of Abnormal Child Psychology, 36*, 759–770. doi:10.1007/s10802-007-9208-2

Schofield, H. T., Bierman, K. L., Heinrichs, B., & Nix, R. L. (2008). Predicting early sexual activity with behavior problems exhibited at school entry and in early adolescence. *Journal of Abnormal Child Psychology, 36*, 1175–1188. doi:10.1007/s10802-008-9252-6

Vitaro, F., Brendgen, M., Larose, S., & Tremblay, R. E. (2005). Kindergarten disruptive behaviors, protective factors, and educational achievement by early adulthood. *Journal of Educational Psychology, 97*, 617–629. doi:10.1037/0022-0663.97.4.617

Walker, H. M., & Shinn, M. R. (2002). Structuring school-based interventions to achieve integrated primary, secondary, and tertiary prevention goals for safe and effective schools. In M. R. Shinn, H. M. Walker, & G. Stoner (Eds.), *Interventions for academic and behavior problems II: Preventive and remedial approaches* (pp. 1–25). Bethesda, MD: National Association of School Psychologists.

I

UNIVERSAL SCREENING WITHIN EDUCATIONAL MODELS

2

SCREENING WITHIN A MULTITIERED EARLY PREVENTION MODEL: USING ASSESSMENT TO INFORM INSTRUCTION AND PROMOTE STUDENTS' RESPONSE TO INTERVENTION

DANIELLE M. PARISI, TANYA IHLO, AND TODD A. GLOVER

Identifying and remediating academic and behavioral difficulties early is crucial for promoting students' success. Without appropriate instruction and intervention, early academic and behavioral difficulties contribute to ongoing problems in school and later life. The influence of early academic difficulties has been well researched, especially in the area of reading. For example, Francis, Shaywitz, Stuebing, Shaywitz, and Fletcher (1996) noted that without appropriate intervention, the majority (74%) of students with reading difficulties in early elementary grades continue to have significant reading problems by the time they reach high school. Poor reading skills also are correlated with a lack of motivation to read, and this relationship is established early (Morgan, Fuchs, Compton, Cordray, & Fuchs, 2008). Furthermore, the long-term outcomes for students who are struggling readers are daunting; struggling readers are at high risk for academic failure and school dropout (e.g., Juel, 1988; Walker & Shinn, 2002).

http://dx.doi.org/10.1037/14316-002
Universal Screening in Educational Settings: Evidence-Based Decision Making for Schools, R. J. Kettler, T. A. Glover, C. A. Albers, and K. A. Feeney-Kettler (Editors)
Copyright © 2014 by the American Psychological Association. All rights reserved.

Fortunately, recent developments in the use of early screening tools and prevention-focused models of service delivery enable educators to meet students' needs early, before more pervasive problems emerge. With these developments, many schools have begun to adopt a response-to-intervention (RTI) approach for promoting early prevention and intervention via multiple tiers of academic and behavioral support.

RTI provides a framework for both the provision of evidence-based instruction for all students as well as the ongoing measurement of student performance. The purpose of an RTI approach to service delivery is to improve instruction and educational outcomes for *all* students. Within a multitiered, RTI framework, students are provided with evidence-based instruction and reliable and valid data are used to make decisions about whether instruction is meeting students' needs. Core instruction is provided using a curriculum that addresses the needs of most students (Tier 1), additional intervention is provided for those requiring supplementary support (Tier 2), and more intensive and individualized interventions are provided for students who continue to demonstrate significant needs (Tier 3). At its foundation, RTI includes measuring the performance of all students and basing educational decisions regarding curriculum, instruction, and intervention intensity on student data. Thus, screening is integral to any RTI approach.

This chapter describes screening within the context of a multitiered RTI model. First, a justification is presented for the use of screening to guide instructional and intervention decisions. Several practical considerations then are posited for integrating screening within school settings. A case example is provided next, followed by an assessment of the state of screening research and future recommendations for advancing research and practice.

ROLE OF SCREENING IN MAKING HIGH-QUALITY INSTRUCTIONAL DECISIONS IN A MULTITIERED MODEL

In multitiered RTI models, data are used for multiple purposes—screening of all students to determine whether they are on track to becoming successful readers, skill diagnosis to determine specific targets for instruction and intervention, progress monitoring to ensure that interventions are meeting students' needs, and measurement of overall outcomes for groups of students (Witt, Elliott, Daly, Gresham, & Kramer, 1998). Screening is the first step in data collection and analysis in a multitiered, RTI model. It involves assessing an entire population of students to determine (a) whether core instruction meets the majority of students' needs or whether changes to instruction for all students are required and (b) whether follow-up assessment and more intensive intervention supports may be needed for students experiencing difficulties. The skills measured via screening are basic and the assessments are brief and easy to administer. Screening data are used to identify which students may be at risk for academic problems without instruction and intervention that is more intensive than what typically is provided in the general education classroom.

Although earlier conceptualizations of screening focused primarily on identifying deficits, disabilities, or disorders, contemporary approaches focus on identifying which instructional practices are needed to prevent future difficulties for students. Screening is now regarded as a tool to guide systems-level instructional planning and evaluation across the entire continuum of tiered instructional supports and to make district- and schoolwide decisions about the effectiveness of supports for all students (Simmons et al., 2002). Screening data are used to identify areas in which instruction for all students (Tier 1) needs to be improved and, once these changes have been made, to identify students in need of more intensive instructional supports (Tiers 2 and 3).

Several considerations are crucial for schools interested in integrating screening practices into a multitiered RTI model. This chapter includes an overview of these considerations and current research on screening for RTI and offers guidelines and worked examples for educators interested in developing and implementing schoolwide screening for the purpose of improving instruction for all students.

CONSIDERATIONS FOR INTEGRATING SCREENING INTO A MULTITIERED MODEL OF SERVICE DELIVERY

Screening is the cornerstone for successful implementation of an effective multitiered model of service delivery. Screening data are used to guide the implementation of effective instructional supports. Although many schools have begun *collecting* screening data, several considerations are important for *using* these data in an effective and efficient decision-making process geared toward improving academic outcomes for all students.

Systematic planning and school leadership are critical to the successful implementation of universal screening within schools. For screening to make an impact in guiding practices and improving student outcomes, school leaders must be willing and able to integrate screening into a continuous planning and implementation process that takes into account core school programs and individual and groups of students' response to instruction and intervention. Accordingly, school personnel must use accurate data as part of their planning process to inform and guide ongoing changes to programs and student intervention supports. To promote successful integration of screening in schools, it is important for stakeholders to take into account key considerations, common pitfalls, and potential professional development needs related to (a) the investment of school staff in a process of continuous improvement, (b) school leadership, (c) the selection of screening tools, and (d) required actions and procedures for effective use of data.

Investment in Continuous Improvement

Regardless of whether an entire school or only a select team leads the charge of schoolwide data-based decision making, it is important for all stakeholders to appreciate the need to use data to improve instructional practices continuously. Although screening data often are collected on all students within a school, few schools successfully integrate systematic and regular data-based decision making into a consistent planning process. Schools frequently adopt an identification and placement strategy, whereby students whose screening scores fall within various categories of risk (e.g., benchmark, strategic, intensive) are assigned to different types of services (e.g., reading group, special education, Title 1). Unfortunately, few schools make use of screening to evaluate the impact of and need for changes to core school programs and interventions.

For screening to make a difference in guiding school practices and in improving student outcomes, schools must invest in a system of continuous improvement that involves using data to determine (a) whether core programs are effective in meeting the majority of students' needs, (b) which individual students are in need of more intensive instructional supports, and (c) whether intervention programs are meeting the needs of the groups and individual students receiving them. Within this system of continuous improvement, schools take individual student data seriously, retaining only those practices that result in positive data-based outcomes. Core programs are altered when the majority (e.g., 80%; Walker & Shinn, 2002) of students' needs are not met, and interventions are adjusted when groups or individual student performance is not improving at a rate that will allow them to reach designated data-based goals (Hintze & Marcotte, 2010). According to this approach, schools regularly evaluate the impact of programs and interventions on all students, engage in instructional and intervention planning, and make ongoing changes to meet data-identified needs.

Screening serves an important function within a system of continuous improvement. It is used to identify whether core programs require adaptations to effectively meet the needs of the majority of students or whether additional interventions are needed. In addition, screening data are used at regular intervals, along with more frequently collected progress monitoring data, to determine whether students who are experiencing difficulties would benefit from a change in instruction or intervention. To effectively make use of screening data, schools are required to commit to using data-based indicators of student performance as a primary source of information about instructional and intervention needs.

Professional Development Considerations

Although many school personnel are familiar with assessments conducted for the purpose of examining outcomes, they are often unfamiliar with the use of data for planning supports and for identifying students who may be struggling in an effort to prevent future difficulties. School stakeholders may benefit from professional development that focuses on the use of a multitiered model of supports and the important role of screening data in identifying struggling students early so support can be provided to prevent future difficulties. Additionally, school personnel may benefit from opportunities to discuss the purposes of various types of assessments (i.e., screening, progress monitoring, diagnostics, outcome measures) used within a multitiered model of student support and which type of judgments can and cannot be made from various assessment tools.

Common Pitfalls

Unfortunately, schools frequently encounter difficulties in integrating screening into an effective model for continuous improvement. Three common pitfalls are among the various obstacles that schools encounter.

- *Pitfall 1: Schools collect but do not use screening data systematically with all students.* It is not uncommon for schools to collect data that never are used or are considered only for select students. To address this pitfall, it is important that school personnel understand (a) how to interpret screening outcomes for groups (e.g., entire grade levels and classrooms) and individual students and (b) the relationship between screening outcomes and various instructional–intervention needs. Although schools may devote considerable resources to training personnel to administer and score screening data, use of that data requires a full understanding of how to interpret the data to select instructional programs and interventions that can address identified needs. Because screening instruments often are designed to provide a general indication of which students are potentially at risk, school personnel also must understand how to conduct follow-up survey-level or diagnostic assessments to determine how best to individualize instruction and intervention. Training in the adaptation of instruction and intervention based on data-identified needs is a vital prerequisite to adopting and using screening in schools.

- *Pitfall 2: Schools use screening data to identify the need for additional intervention, regardless of whether the majority of students are responding to core programs.* When schools disregard the efficacy of core programs, they shift significant resources away from more efficient foundational instruction to time-intensive Tier 2 and 3 supports. Although it is crucial to utilize interventions, schools often do not have resources to maintain Tier 2 and 3 supports over time for a large number of students. To address this pitfall, it is important that schools first make adjustments to core programs when screening data indicate that the majority of students' needs are not met (e.g., core programs typically should meet the needs of at least 80% of students). Doing so decreases the need for extensive intervention (Hintze & Marcotte, 2010; Walker & Shinn, 2002).

- *Pitfall 3: Schools are inconsistent in the use of data-based decisions.* Schools do not always make consistent use of screening data. Effective use of screening within a continuous planning process requires equitably responding to all students' data-identified needs. When schools begin to make exceptions or change data-based decision criteria for select students, students miss much-needed supports. To address this pitfall, school personnel must be willing and able to develop, adopt, and regularly make use of predetermined data-based decision rules for service delivery. By applying data-based decisions consistently, schools optimize opportunities for all students to be successful.

Careful consideration of these three common pitfalls is especially important as stakeholders integrate screening into a continuous planning process. By engaging in an ongoing cycle of assessment, planning, implementation, and evaluation for all students across all levels of instructional supports, schools are able to regularly adapt instruction and intervention to promote student success.

School Leadership and Planning for Systems-Level Decision Making

Although it is important for all school personnel to understand the role of screening in a continuous improvement process, strong leadership is critical at the school level to plan, oversee, and hold staff accountable for the implementation of a multitiered model of service delivery, including screening. The most effective form of building-level leadership involves a team that shares responsibilities and brings a range of expertise and experience across the general and special education continuum of services. Typically, the team provides direction in selecting the schoolwide screening tools, analyzing school-level data, planning and guiding the implementation of systems-level instructional changes based on the data, providing professional development to staff, updating and involving staff in the screening and decision-making process, and allocating resources for instructional supports across tiers. Thus, it is crucial for team members to possess expertise in data interpretation and use, problem solving and instructional planning for students with varying instructional and behavioral needs, implementation of professional development and consultation, and organizational leadership.

The team should include a building-level administrator who can make decisions about the allocation of time, staff, and other resources based on the data. By including representatives from general and special education, teams are better able to create a true continuum of instructional supports across all tiers of the multitiered system. It is also important to include members proficient in the use of data for decision making who understand the purpose and goals of conducting screening assessment. By understanding how the use of screening data can be used to align existing school practices and initiatives within the context of the multitiered model, team members are better able to make decisions about how to effectively and efficiently serve all students. Team members also must be able to effectively communicate with the entire school staff and provide professional development to build the capacity to integrate screening data use into everyday practice.

Common Pitfalls

Many schools have found screening implementation difficult when engaging in the following practices pertaining to leadership and team member participation.

- *Pitfall 1: Leadership team does not include regular involvement of an administrator.* When a team meets regularly and makes decisions without the involvement and support of an administrator, it is often difficult to allocate resources and enforce decisions as needed. Furthermore, if the administrator does not advocate the practice and hold all staff members accountable, staff members who are not a part of the leadership team may be less likely to buy into the collection and use of screening data.
- *Pitfall 2: Leadership team does not include adequate representation of members with complementary expertise and decision-making ability.* To successfully lead the implementation of schoolwide screening data collection and use, the team must include members with

complementary expertise and decision-making ability. Schools that attempt to implement a data-based decision-making system without the involvement of general education staff may limit screening and data-based decision making only to special education for struggling students. Because high-quality general education instruction provides the foundation for the multitiered system of supports, these schools are unable to successfully implement RTI and meet the needs of all learners. Schools that exclude special education staff create systems in which special education remains a separate component of the service delivery puzzle (i.e., supports provided through special education resources are not considered part of the continuum of supports and thus are not analyzed and aligned to the rest of the system). Without someone who is proficient in data use, a team has difficulty analyzing and interpreting data to make meaningful and accurate instructional decisions.

- *Pitfall 3: Leadership team waits for consensus before fully using the data to make decisions.* Often, not all staff will be committed to a process of collecting and using screening data and implementing a multitiered model of service delivery. Much of the literature on implementation of multitiered service delivery calls for a level of at least 80% buy-in for implementation to be effective (e.g., Sugai & Horner, 2002). This high level of buy-in may be difficult to achieve, and insisting on a level of 80% buy-in and spending valuable time on consensus building alone can result in the delay of implementation of evidence-based practices. Schools risk spending too much time building consensus when they could be spending that time collecting data, interpreting data, and using the data to make change. Many schools have found that they can initiate screening with well below 80% buy-in and that buy-in for implementation is increased when data on the need for improvement in schoolwide instruction and resulting improved student-level data are presented. School teams are most effective when they create a culture of shared ownership for improved school-level academic outcomes for all students, which may increase buy-in over time.

Screening Tool Selection

One of the key functions of the leadership team is to carefully select tools for screening data collection. As Glover and Albers (2007) noted, it is important for school personnel to investigate whether a screening instrument is appropriate, technically adequate, and usable for its intended purpose. Too often, school personnel adopt screening measures based on advertised research support or claims about their utility in identifying students in need of intervention. Although general information provided by developers may be useful for making initial decisions about school fit, it also is critical to explore whether specific tools are compatible with a school's service delivery approach. Accordingly, school personnel should investigate (a) whether the timing and frequency of screening tool administration and the screening outcomes will be sufficient for identifying instructional and intervention needs, (b) whether the format and content of the tool have been validated in previous research, and (c) whether the measured constructs are relevant to areas of concern and important for future academic success.

Unfortunately, many schools fail to systematically use collected screening data. To safeguard against gathering data that are of limited utility in guiding service delivery, school personnel should address several critical questions:

1. *Has the instrument been designed and validated for the purpose of screening?* Although many instruments are useful for measuring skills or behaviors, instruments vary in their appropriateness for use as screeners, diagnostic tools, or measures of achievement. As described in Chapter 4 of this volume, screening instruments typically are evaluated for their utility in predicting students who are potentially at risk and who subsequently may experience difficulties. Predictive validity is especially important within a multitiered model of prevention, given the emphasis on the early identification of students' needs (Jenkins, Hudson, & Johnson, 2007).

2. *Do the measured indicators (e.g., skills, behaviors) align with service delivery needs in the school? If so, are the indicators specific enough to determine whether students are meeting benchmark expectations or are in need of additional instruction or intervention?* If screening indicators are not directly related to service delivery needs, then they may be of limited value in informing instruction or intervention planning decisions. For example, it is unlikely that an early reading screener designed to measure comprehension would be useful for discerning students' acquisition of early phonics or phonological awareness skills. Because the acquisition of phonics and phonologic awareness skills is critical for successful comprehension, measured indicators may need to also address those target areas. By selecting screening instruments with content aligned to specific practices, schools maximize opportunities to use data to inform decisions about appropriate instructional supports.

3. *Is the timing and frequency of administration appropriate for identifying instructional or intervention needs?* It is important to consider whether a screening instrument can be administered at times that are appropriate for informing core program implementation and additional intervention needs. If an assessment cannot be administered at appropriate intervals for making educational decisions, it will not likely be of value to school personnel. Typically, within a multitiered prevention model, schools should be able to administer a screening assessment at least three times during an academic year to appropriately determine whether core programs are serving the majority of students' needs and which students may benefit from further intervention (Hintze & Marcotte, 2010).

In addition to considering a screening tool's appropriateness, it is also important to consider its technical adequacy. An extensive discussion of the psychometrics of screeners is provided by Christ and Nelson in Chapter 4 of this volume and is beyond the scope of this chapter. As Christ and Nelson and others (Glover & Albers, 2007) have noted, given the need to repeatedly and accurately measure student performance, it is important to consider traditional indicators of reliability (both internally across items and between multiple forms and administrations) and validity (internally, based on factor analyses or analyses of item discrimination, differential item functioning, or item-total test or subtest correlations; and concurrently, as depicted by a measure's relationship with other similar measures). Because school personnel commonly rely on published benchmarks, cut scores, or normative performance levels to make screening decisions, it is also essential to assess the recency, representativeness, and sample size of an instrument's norms (Glover & Albers, 2007; Salvia & Ysseldyke, 2004). Among the many psychometric indicators for screening assessments used within a multitiered service delivery model, however, an instrument's predictive validity or classification accuracy is perhaps its most important attribute. As noted in Chapter 4 of this volume, classification accuracy (as depicted by an instrument's sensitivity, specificity, and positive and negative predictive values) is an indication of the instrument's ability to distinguish between those who will and will not experience future difficulties in a targeted domain. Given the focus on prevention within a multitiered model, the accurate identification of students who may later experience difficulties (i.e., predictive or classification validity) is paramount. School personnel, in selecting screening instruments, should investigate all published psychometric indices, with special attention to the instruments' predictive validity or classification accuracy.

Finally, as Glover and Albers (2007) contended, it is important to consider a screening instrument's usability within a specified school setting. The logistics and cost of collecting and managing the data must be feasible. Because school personnel collect and manage data on all students within a multitiered model, it is important to consider any necessary specialized training or data management skills required to make use of screening outcomes. Personnel also must be able to appreciate the value of the selected screening instrument in informing instruction and intervention. Furthermore, the screener should yield interpretable outcomes with clearly defined applications for instruction or intervention decisions.

Required Actions and Procedures for Successful Use of Screening Data

In addition to building a leadership team and selecting screening tools, schools must consider several key actions and procedures for integrating screening into their schoolwide processes. The school leadership team must determine how the assessments will be administered and scored and how the resulting data will be managed so that all staff members have access to the data as soon as possible. It is important for schools to maintain a screening data collection plan that addresses the following issues.

Data Collection

Screening data should be collected with enough frequency to inform educational decisions. Typically this takes place in the fall, winter, and spring of every year for all students (Ikeda, Neesen, & Witt, 2008). It often is recommended that the data be collected during a 2-week window at each time point so that students' data is comparable and easily managed. It is also beneficial to collect the data within equal intervals (i.e., 16 weeks between fall and winter data collection and 16 weeks between winter and spring data collection) so that growth across each time period can be compared easily.

Administration and Scoring

There are many approaches to collecting screening data. Each school must determine which option works best for their staff and resources (Harn, 2000). In some schools, individual classroom teachers collect their own screening data. When teachers administer and score assessments for their students during independent work time, they are provided with immediate insight into current skill levels. They may find it difficult to be objective, however, given their investment in the academic progress of their students. Furthermore, this approach can significantly disrupt instructional time.

Another approach involves grade-level teachers assessing an entire grade level while another adult supervises students. Although this allows teachers to assess some of their own students, it can disrupt instructional time.

Finally, many schools utilize a schoolwide team composed of educational assistants, specials teachers, specialists (e.g., counselors, school psychologists, speech pathologists), and any other staff members with flexible schedules and responsibilities to assess an entire school. Teachers bring entire classrooms to a common location (e.g., the library), or the team travels from classroom to classroom administering assessments in hallways or other rooms nearby. This procedure can be efficient; depending on the number of data collectors, an entire classroom can be assessed in minutes. This approach also helps to create a culture of shared responsibility for student academic achievement.

Although computer-based and group-administered screening tools are available to assess select skills, individually administered screening assessments often have the best psychometric support for their use in predicting students' skill needs, especially in the area of reading. Computer-based and group-administered assessments allow for more students to be assessed at one time. Schools also must consider the availability and location of computers, however, as well as who will monitor administration of such screeners. Schools should consider their resources and needs when selecting a method for collecting screening data. Whichever approach schools take, it is important to document the plan to save time and effort in preparing for data collection.

Professional Development Considerations

Although screening assessment administration and scoring may seem intuitive (and schools may be inclined to elect a single person to teach others to use the assessments), careful training is required to ensure that scores obtained are reliable.

All data collectors should be provided with accurate and in-depth initial training in administration and scoring according to standardized procedures. This training also should be provided to teachers and other staff members who will need to interpret and implement subsequent instructional changes based on the data. The training activities should include a description of standardized procedures, modeling of these procedures, and multiple opportunities for participants to practice. Before or during administration and scoring, it is important to train staff in the use of procedures for conducting reliability checks and checks of fidelity to standardized procedures. To promote reliable administration, it is also important to provide booster training sessions before each data collection period (e.g., fall, winter, and spring). Furthermore, it is crucial for the school leadership team to develop a plan for training new staff on the measures at the beginning of every school year and at various points during the year when and if new staff are hired.

Data Management

To effectively make use of student data, schoolwide teams must utilize an organizational system. This typically involves selecting a data management tool. Many universal screening tools (e.g., AIMSweb, Dynamic Indicators of Basic Early Literacy Skills [DIBELS]) are accompanied by an online, web-based management system that includes reporting and graphing options to assist educators in making data-based decisions at the school, grade, classroom, and individual student levels. For other screening approaches, the team must develop its own method for storing data and generating reports and graphs.

Regardless of the approach, schoolwide teams must determine who will enter and have access to data, and how reports and graphs will be generated within a timeline that allows for immediate instructional changes. Typically, schoolwide teams, grade-level teams, and individual teachers all analyze data and thus require access. Specialists who work with specific students also require access to data. Many schools have found that having an individual or small team of people who can access and generate reports and graphs is beneficial for reducing data entry errors and ensuring that staff members receive reports in a timely manner. Schools may give all members access to the data system so that they can analyze the data whenever they choose.

Data Review

It is important that the leadership team allocate time to meet immediately after data are collected and reports are generated to ensure that they have sufficient time to make instructional decisions. Grade-level teams need time to meet to make decisions about instruction across an entire grade and individual classrooms. Teachers and specialists also need to meet about shared students to determine whether the instruction being provided is meeting students' individual needs. Typically, schools utilize common planning periods for grade-level teachers or early dismissal on a weekly or monthly basis for planning time. It often is helpful if scheduled meeting times are integrated into written schoolwide policies and procedures. This allocated and protected time will increase the likelihood that the screening data are used for decision making.

Data-Based Instructional Changes

To ensure that high-quality instruction is provided equitably for all students, it is important to develop and implement objective data-based decision rules across all tiers of the multitiered system (Kaminski, Cummings, Powell-Smith, & Good, 2008). To help increase the accuracy of assessments, it is crucial for school teams to make a systematic plan for validating screening data for any child who falls below a predetermined cut point and who may be in need of intervention. Data can be validated by administering an alternate form of the assessment or by collecting additional data using other assessments, work samples, and teacher observation.

Systematic decision rules for Tier 1 are used to make changes to core instruction for all students. Data on the implementation of core instruction are consulted to determine whether the program is being implemented as designed. If a majority of students are below the benchmark or predetermined cut scores, a plan for improving core instruction is developed and enacted.

Once it is determined that core instruction is implemented as designed and that classwide instruction is effective for an acceptable proportion of students (typically at least 80%), decision rules then are applied to identify individual students whose scores are below a set point and are in need of intervention. Once the data have been validated, students receive an intervention that matches data-identified needs. The decision rules for selecting interventions typically include criteria for using screening data along with skill diagnostic data to match the interventions to students' skill needs. Because the focus of instruction changes across grade levels, the decision rules may need to be different at each grade level. For example, kindergarten students may not be placed into an intervention until the second quarter or second semester of school to provide an opportunity for students to learn school routines. An example of a decision rule template is included in Figure 2.1.

Once interventions are provided, screening and progress monitoring data can be used to analyze the systems that are in place. Growth over time and level of performance for groups and individual students receiving intervention supports can be reviewed to determine intervention effectiveness.

After analyzing data and deciding that instructional modifications are needed, teachers then make use of a library of tools to provide a continuum of instructional supports for students. They deliver primary instruction utilizing a comprehensive, research-based program. Supplemental programs also often are used to enhance the core instruction as determined by the screening data. For Tier 2 or 3 interventions, schools use research-based intervention programs that vary in the intensity of delivery and content covered based on students' needs.

Professional Development Considerations

It is important that professional development for interpreting screening data include a clearly defined process with examples from schools that successfully have used the process. One common approach incudes a four-step problem-solving process. Teams first address the question, "What is our current situation?" by using various screening data reports to create a data

Tier 1 Decision Rules

<u>**Identifying Students Who *May* Need Support**</u>

Assessment Data Used: _____(i.e., universal screening data)

Criteria: _____ (e.g., all students who do not meet benchmark *may* need additional support)

<u>**Validating or Confirming Data**</u>

How are data validated or confirmed before Tier 2 intervention supports?

☐ Data are consistent across time (e.g., scores obtained on multiple occasions reveal a deficit).

- A minimum of ____ data points are collected within _____ (time period)
- Assessment measure(s) used: _____

☐ Data are consistent across measures or data are consistent with work samples and teacher observation (e.g., multiple measures reveal deficient performance).

- Measures used: _____

*Be sure the team has checked for the following:
- o   Fidelity check data (ensure strong Tier 1 instruction)
- o   Performance of identified student(s) is discrepant from classroom peers. If most of the students in the class or grade are performing low, be sure plan is in place to strengthen core
  - Measures used: _____

<u>**Making Tier 1 Decisions** (How is level of support determined?)</u>

Grade level	Criteria (category or score) on screening or validation data on which assessment or combination of assessments	Level or type of support
	Well above benchmark: _____	Receive Tier 1 instruction and enhancement activities
	Meets benchmark in all areas on screening	Receive Tier 1 instruction with regular benchmark assessment
	Barely meets benchmark: _____ *or* Barely did not meet benchmark: _____	Receive Tier 1 instruction with _____ (e.g., monthly) progress monitoring
	Barely did not meet benchmark: _____ *or* Performing at _____ or below on measure of _____	Receive Tier 2 instruction _____ with _____ progress monitoring

Figure 2.1. Decision-rule template. Schools can use this template to develop their own decision rules.

profile. They address the second question "Why do we have the data that we have?" by analyzing current practices in their schools and identifying areas of need. To address the third question, "What are our goals and what strategies will we use to achieve them?" teams determine the research and data-based goals they would like to achieve as well as the instructional approaches they will use to attain those goals. Finally, schools address the fourth question, "Is instruction or intervention effective for students?" by evaluating the percentage of students that meet established expectations on measured skills.

Use of Screening Data at a Systems Level to Plan, Implement, and Evaluate Programming. Screening data often are underutilized as a tool for evaluating effectiveness of core instructional supports for all students. It is important that professional development for using screening data at a systems level focus on the use of a data profile to examine the effectiveness of the system of supports for all students. Typically, schools assess (a) the proportion of students meeting benchmark expectations, (b) the proportion of students remaining at benchmark over time, and (c) the normative growth of all students across the year.

Regardless of whether schools use an online data system or another approach for managing and analyzing data, it is important for school teams to provide training in the use of reports for decision making.

Use of Screening at an Individual Level to Provide Data-Based Intervention Delivery. Screening data provide a powerful tool for identifying student needs early so schools can provide supports to prevent future concerns. To ensure equitable treatment for all students, it is critical that professional development for the leadership teams focus on (a) determining which data to include in decision making and (b) creating effective decision rules for determining who may need additional support, how to validate the need for support, and how to determine next steps (i.e., collect additional assessment or match students to intervention).

Common Pitfalls

Unfortunately, schools encounter difficulties in integrating screening into schoolwide practices. Two common pitfalls are among obstacles that schools encounter.

- *Pitfall 1: Lack of standardization of data collection and decision protocols.* Schools do not always make use of consistent, standardized data collection and decision protocols. Without accurate and comprehensive documentation of these procedures, the implementation of screening data collection, analysis, and use for instructional decision making likely will be implemented inconsistently. To address this pitfall, decisions and actions must be documented clearly in screening data collection and decision rule plans.
- *Pitfall 2: Inadequate time to conduct data-based decisions.* Another common pitfall is lack of time allocation for data entry and review by teams. Educators need the time to review the data to carefully and effectively make decisions about groups and individual students. To address this pitfall, it is important that

leadership teams set aside time for decision making and ensure that data entry is coordinated with time for reviewing and discussing data and making plans for instructional changes.

USING SCREENING DATA WITHIN A MULTITIERED MODEL OF SUPPORTS FOR READING: THE STORY OF RUEBEN ELEMENTARY SCHOOL

Implementation of multitiered models of supports in schools involves an ongoing process of analyzing data and making decisions to adapt and change practices to meet the needs of students. The use of screening data is a critical component of this process. Screening data can be used to identify needs at a systems level and monitor progress of systems-level changes as well as to identify individual student needs. To help illustrate this process, we follow a school for 4 years through its process of using screening data to make decisions at the schoolwide level and its development of procedures for using screening data to identify individual students in need of intervention.

Rueben Elementary School Background

Rueben Elementary School has 375 students in kindergarten through sixth grade. An administrator from the school learned about RTI and was interested in beginning implementation. He decided to have a leadership team participate in a professional development series focused on development and implementation of a multitiered model. This team included the administrator, the speech pathologist, a first-grade teacher, the teacher of students who are English language learners (ELLs), a fourth-grade teacher, and a Title I reading specialist. It was charged with the responsibility of facilitating implementation of the multitiered system of supports and reviewing data on a regular basis to make decisions about the system.

The training series focused on helping districts and schools use a systematic planning process to develop, implement, and refine their multitiered systems of support. Within the planning process, teams created a data profile to help develop a picture of the "current situation" and then analyzed their practices to determine what contributed to their data. On the basis of that analysis of current practices, the team identified aspects of the multitiered model that were not in place and developed and implemented a plan to include them. Finally, the team evaluated whether they actually implemented the plan and whether the changes affected student data.

Screening Plan at Rueben Elementary

As a first step in the training, teams learned about the importance of implementing a clear plan for conducting screening that specifies a process for initial and booster training on the administration and scoring of the screening measure to ensure accurate data are available for decision making within a multitiered system of support. Before participation in the training, Rueben Elementary had been collecting screening data for 3 years, but it had not been using the data to make decisions. The team realized they had not been collecting data at similar time points from year to year, and the data collectors had not received updated training. As a result, the team developed a screening plan that described the screening assessment selected (i.e., DIBELS) and provided assessment windows within which the screening would be conducted each year (the first 2 weeks of the school year; 16 weeks before the mid-year, 2-week window; and another 16 weeks before the end-of-year, 2-week window). The plan also provided guidelines for who would collect data, who required professional development, how the data would be collected and entered in an electronic data system, how reliability of the data collection would be measured, and how the data would be presented to the team and the school staff for decision making.

The leadership team decided a team approach would be used to conduct the assessments at each screening period. The assessment team—including the school psychologist, speech pathologist, Title I teacher, and a paraprofessional—traveled from one classroom to the next to conduct the assessments. The leadership team felt it was important for classroom teachers to also be a part of the assessment team to increase buy-in and the likelihood that they would understand the data and utilize it for decision making in the classroom. To enable teachers to be a member of the assessment team, the administrator either hired substitutes or reorganized paraprofessionals' time to cover the teachers' classrooms.

The assessment team members received refresher training on administration and scoring of the DIBELS screening measures. The professional development included didactic training in the purpose of screening assessments, foundations for the particular measures used, and procedures for standardized administration and scoring of the measures. Participants received multiple opportunities to practice administering and scoring the assessments by viewing and scoring videotaped administrations and administering the assessment to other participants acting as students. The leadership team then planned to provide booster training each fall that would focus on any updates to the measures and additional opportunities for practice.

Reliability checks were collected at each screening period (fall, winter, spring) through shadow scoring. Shadow scoring involved one person administering the assessment with a student while a second person completed a checklist to assess adherence to standardized administration procedures and scored the assessment to assess the reliability of scoring. Those administering assessments were required to meet or exceed an interrater reliability of 95%.

Using Screening Data Within a Systematic Planning Process

The leadership team at Rueben Elementary School used their screening data within the systematic problem-solving process previously described. The leadership team was responsible for working through the process but was careful to ensure that all teachers were informed and aware of how screening data were to be used and why decisions were being made. Screening data were presented and analyzed with all staff members.

Presenting Screening Data

The leadership team from Rueben attended a training at which they received assistance with the development of a data profile to share with school staff. Although they had been collecting data for years, the school had not examined the data closely for decision making. The school staff members were aware of consistently low percentages of students meeting benchmarks on the screening measures and low achievement on end-of-year outcome measures. Although they had set yearly goals to increase student reading scores on their continuous improvement plan (CIP), their data looked the same year after year.

Although successful implementation of a multitiered model of supports requires that educators possess a desire to alter practices when data indicate a need, it was more common for staff at Rueben Elementary to generate explanations for data outcomes rather than take ownership for the data and recognize a need for change. The staff explained that they had a difficult group of students in certain years and that a change in demographics produced an increasing number of ELLs who were not able to meet benchmarks on the assessments.

Rueben's leadership team compiled a data profile that reported the proportion of students at each grade level meeting benchmarks (disaggregated by subgroup), cross-year data examining student scores over time, and the odds of struggling students meeting benchmarks within a year. The data profile also included the proportions of students who maintained benchmark expectations between the beginning of the year and the middle or end of the year (an indication of the effectiveness of core instruction at maintaining students' performance) and proportions of students who transitioned from below benchmark performance at the beginning of the year to meeting benchmarks (by the middle or end of the year).

The leadership team presented these data to the school staff and discussed implications about supports for students at Rueben Elementary. Because the data indicated that low percentages of students were meeting benchmarks year after year at every grade level, it became clear to the team and to the school staff that there was no evidence that the problems at this school were due to "bad classes." The data also indicated that it was not only the ELL students who were not performing well. At some grade levels, there were higher percentages of ELL students who were meeting benchmarks than non-ELL students. Finally, the data indicated that many students at benchmark at the beginning of the year were no longer meeting benchmarks in the middle or end of the year (e.g., 52.3% of first-grade students at benchmark in the fall no longer met benchmark levels in the winter). The leadership team and school staff realized the data indicated a need for change to the instruction provided for *all* students. A noticeable sense of urgency emerged among the staff and administration.

When the leadership team first began their journey, they expected that training in development of a multitiered model of supports would generate ideas for new interventions to provide to students who were struggling. The data indicated, however, that if they were to provide intervention for all students not meeting benchmark expectations, they would need to intervene with at least 50% of students in their school. This was not feasible given the high level of resources that it would require. Even if the resources were available to provide that level of support, it did not seem to be an efficient approach to the leadership team from Rueben, especially because students at fall benchmarks did not continue to reach benchmarks at later points in the year. The team theorized that even if the students receiving intervention improved enough to discontinue it, they then would have a new group of students in need of intervention (i.e., those who had been meeting benchmarks, but who did not continue to do so because of ineffective core instruction). They hypothesized that this would create a "revolving door" of intervention that would not truly be effective at preventing further reading difficulties for students. The leadership team from Rueben knew something needed to be done to affect instructional supports for *all* students.

Examining Current Reading Practices

Once there was agreement about a need for change, the leadership team began asking, "What change is needed?" A common pitfall among schools with data indicating persistently low student performance is to begin to immediately develop action steps without analyzing the current situation. The leadership team at Rueben Elementary realized that even though they had been setting goals and developing action steps on their CIP for years, their approach was not working for the students in their school. The leadership team needed to attend professional development to help them to begin to answer the question "Why do we have the data that we have?"

To begin the analysis, the school had to examine current core practices. Through training, the team examined their core instructional materials for coverage of essential content needed to teach students to become strong readers (e.g., the presence of a research-based, systematic scope and sequence of skills) and the presence of effective instructional methods (e.g., explicit instruction that includes effective modeling, ample opportunities for student practice, and immediate corrective and affirmative feedback to ensure teaching to mastery). They also observed classrooms to monitor the level of fidelity to the current core program materials, to determine the amount of time devoted to reading instruction, and to examine teacher practices for grouping to provide differentiated instruction in their classrooms.

The leadership team examined the information from their analysis and discovered that although they adopted a core reading program 6 years earlier, most of the teachers were not implementing it as intended. Some teachers were using portions of the program and others were not using it at all. Core reading time consisted of mostly whole-group instruction with very little differentiation to address individual student needs.

Development and Implementation of a Systems-Level Plan

Following their analysis of the current reading practices at Rueben Elementary, the leadership team developed several hypotheses for the consistently low percentages of students meeting benchmark expectations on their screening measures. They hypothesized that their findings were the result of low fidelity of core program implementation, a lack of differentiated instruction, and weak core program materials. The team explored the possibility of adopting a new core reading program. They hypothesized that even if they improved fidelity, the original outdated core program would not cover content necessary to teach reading, did not include explicit instructional techniques, and did not provide sufficient materials to help support differentiation of core instruction in the classroom. They sought professional development for navigating the adoption of a new program. The training provided the team with information about how to review research to evaluate the effectiveness of core programs and how to identify whether programs cover critical skills and use effective instructional practices. With training assistance, the team identified and requested research on potential core reading programs to investigate and requested research on all of the programs. They narrowed the selection to two programs and reviewed each using two widely available tools: *A Consumer's Guide to Analyzing a Core Reading Program* (University of Oregon) and *Guidelines for Evaluating a Comprehensive Core Reading Program* (Florida Center for Reading Research).

Rueben adopted a research-based program and committed to implementing all pieces of the program with fidelity. Before the first year of implementation of the new program, all teachers received training from the publisher on the use of the instructional materials. The team also developed a fidelity checklist to examine implementation of the program and to identify areas in which the teachers may need additional support with implementation.

Evaluating the Systems-Level Plan

Rueben Elementary continued to collect screening data three times per year, and the leadership team and the school staff continued to review the data after each data collection period. After implementing the new core reading program with high fidelity for a year and a half, the leadership team and staff examined the screening data and felt they were unsatisfied with a lack of progress in changing their data. Everyone at Rueben Elementary recognized that even with an effective change, results may take time. The team decided, however, to recycle through the strategic planning process and conduct another analysis of core reading practices because they felt they should have seen additional improvement in the data.

Recycling Through the Systematic Planning Process

Using screening data to identify areas of need and then further analyzing those needs to change instruction opened a new dialogue about reading at Rueben. Although the teachers honored their commitment to implement the new core reading program with fidelity, they were frustrated with a lack of change in student data. In selecting a new core program, the leadership team realized that all programs had areas of strength and weakness. On the basis of a lack of change in the screening data and teacher frustration, the team decided to provide the teachers with an opportunity to further examine the program and develop a plan for strengthening it.

Grade-level teams (i.e., kindergarten through first-grade teachers, second- and third-grade teachers, and fourth- to sixth-grade teachers) attended training that focused on necessary components of core instruction, including its content and instructional methods. They then examined their own materials and instructional methods to identify "holes" in the program. The teachers discovered during the training that many of them did not have experience with delivering explicit instruction, and the program did not provide examples of how to do so. In addition, they discovered that (a) there were insufficient opportunities for students to practice newly taught skills, (b) there were no procedures for correcting student errors, and (c) there were too many activities included in a lesson to complete within their 90-minute core reading block.

To address the "holes" in their core reading program, the school staff began participating in an intensive professional development series focused on the delivery of explicit instruction and a process for identifying which activities within the core program lessons were critical (and which could be skipped if time did not allow for their completion). They integrated what they learned into their fidelity checks for core program implementation.

The leadership team continued to examine screening and fidelity data with the school staff and to monitor change in student data after participating in professional development to strengthen the newly implemented program. Although less than 80% of students were still meeting benchmark expectations at each grade level, select grade levels were closer to this goal. The leadership team at Rueben also closely reviewed the progress for students who were struggling the most (i.e., students scoring in the intensive range on the DIBELS who were at risk of not meeting future benchmarks). Only a small percentage of students in the intensive range made enough progress to change their risk status. The team realized that improving core instruction alone would not meet the needs of all students, so they continued to build the multitiered model for their school.

Using Screening Data to Identify Individual Students in Need of Additional Instructional Support

After using screening data at the systems level and developing and enacting a plan for strengthening core instruction, the leadership team from Rueben then needed to shift their focus to using screening data to identify student needs and begin planning the intervention system. The team attended professional development focused on the importance of using clear, written decision rules with screening data to determine which students may be in need of intervention supports. Before the team could apply decision rules to identify students, they had to determine which intervention supports were available and whether those implementing the interventions had been trained properly trained. The team developed an intervention inventory that included all of the interventions available at the school, who was trained in the interventions, for which grade levels each intervention was appropriate, and the skill focus for each intervention. The team verified that they had interventions that covered each of the critical reading skills.

The next step in development of Rueben's decision rule plan was to identify a cutoff point for determining which students *may* need intervention support. The team at Rueben decided to use DIBELS benchmarks as cutoffs for this purpose. As described, the team then developed a procedure for validating the screening data. The Rueben team decided to validate the screening data across time by collecting two additional data points within a 3-week time period, using DIBELS progress monitoring probes. Students whose scores were stable and consistently below benchmark levels then were identified to receive intervention supports. This process for validating student screening data was only required after the first screening period following development of the decision rules. After that initial time, validation was completed only for students who previously had met benchmark cutoffs but were no longer doing so. For students receiving intervention, progress monitoring data provided the necessary information about the need for continued intervention.

To implement decision rules, determine student intervention needs, and review student data at each grade level, the team at Rueben decided to meet immediately following each screening period (i.e., in the fall, winter, and spring). For the initial implementation of decision rules, the team created a list of students for whom additional data were required for validation; they conducted the additional assessments during a 3-week window following their meeting. The team then met again to review the validation data and determine student intervention needs. Although the screening data were helpful for identifying which students needed intervention supports and for identifying a general area of concern (e.g., phonemic awareness, phonics) for younger students, the data did not provide all of the information needed. So, the team enacted a plan to (a) obtain additional data when necessary to determine how to best match students to interventions and (b) collect progress monitoring data to review student progress in the future.

Next Steps for Rueben Elementary

At present, Rueben Elementary has only just begun the journey of implementing a multitiered model to support student needs. They continue to use screening data on a regular basis to make decisions about the overall effectiveness of their system of support and to identify students in need of intervention. The leadership team continues to use a strategic planning process to build and refine aspects of their multitiered model based on needs indicated by the data.

STATE OF THE SCIENCE AND FUTURE NEEDS FOR ADVANCING RESEARCH AND PRACTICE

This chapter outlines crucial considerations, current research, and case examples for utilizing screening within a multitiered RTI model. Over the past decade, there has been significant growth in the empirical literature on the use of screening within a multitiered prevention model. Despite this increase in research, screening and multitiered service delivery in school settings still is in its infancy. Additional investigations are needed to determine how to best implement screening and provide supports that lead to positive student outcomes. Although the field likely would benefit from research in a variety of domains, there are several pressing needs for further investigation.

First, given the importance of early prevention and the identification of students potentially at risk within a multitiered service delivery model, ongoing research comparing the predictive validity of various screening approaches is needed. Within the field of school psychology and special education, an emerging database of studies is examining the predictive validity and classification accuracy of select screening measures (e.g., Hintze, Ryan, & Stoner, 2003; Jenkins et al., 2007; National Center on Response to Intervention, 2012). These studies have focused on evaluating the predictive accuracy or relationships between screening outcomes and students' subsequent performance on a variety of criterion measures. For example, John Hintze, Joseph Jenkins, and others (e.g., Hintze et al., 2003; Jenkins et al., 2007; National Center on Response to Intervention, 2012) have investigated the accuracy of various screening approaches in predicting students who later experience difficulties on select achievement measures. Others have used logistic regression to link specific screening scores to subsequent achievement outcomes aligned with local standards (e.g., Burns & Gibbons, 2008).

Despite the emerging database of studies on screening instruments, differences in research approaches prevent investigators and practitioners from making direct comparisons between measures to determine their appropriateness in various settings. Regardless of the content area, there is little consensus about which criterion measures are best for validation studies (Glover & Albers, 2007; Jenkins et al., 2007). Without the application of common criterion indicators or research methods, it is impossible to compare screening instruments with respect to their predictive validity in multitiered prevention models. Although educational stakeholders may perceive local indicators to be highly relevant, additional efforts are needed to make comparisons between screening measures utilizing equivalent approaches and criteria.

Second, although there have been numerous investigations of reading screening instruments for multitiered service delivery, screening approaches for other content areas are beginning to emerge (e.g., for screening for mathematics, see Chapter 8 in this volume; for writing, see DeLa Paz, Espin, & McMaster, 2010; and for behavior, see Chapter 3 in this volume). Unlike with reading, very little is known about which specific indicators best predict later difficulties in various content domains. Given the importance of early identification and prevention within a multitiered service delivery model, additional work is needed to identify which skills or behaviors are most predictive of students' risk or need for instruction or intervention at various service-delivery levels.

Third, although screening is integral to early prevention within a multitiered service delivery approach, little is known about the long-term costs and benefits of screening implementation. With its origins in public health (e.g., Walker & Shinn, 2002), multitiered screening and accompanying supports are expected to yield long-term benefits to both individuals and their surrounding communities (e.g., reduced service delivery load time over time; reduced learning difficulties; ultimately, less dire life outcomes) that outweigh the costs of their implementation. Such benefits, however, have never been studied systematically. Investigations of the actual immediate and long-term societal outcomes associated with screening and subsequent multitiered service delivery will be useful for determining the true extent of the impact of various practices.

Finally, additional research on professional development is sorely needed. Within a multitiered service delivery model, little is known about the impact of various professional development approaches on teachers' implementation of screening and subsequent data-based service delivery and student outcomes. Several researchers, including the present authors, are currently involved in ongoing evaluations of the impact of professional development activities on (a) teachers' knowledge, (b) the implementation of screening and data-based decision making and intervention delivery, and (c) resulting student achievement. Additional direct comparisons of the impact of various professional development approaches on teacher implementation and student outcomes are needed to determine how to best ensure that teachers are able to implement screening and multitiered service delivery with fidelity and with documented benefits to students.

REFERENCES

Burns, M. K., & Gibbons, K. (2008). *Response to intervention implementation in elementary and secondary schools: Procedures to assure scientific-based practices.* New York, NY: Routledge.

DeLa Paz, S., Espin, C., & McMaster, K. L. (2010). RTI in writing: Implementing evidence-based interventions and evaluating the effects for individual students. In T. A. Glover & S. Vaughn (Eds.), *The promise of response to intervention: Evaluating current science and practice* (pp. 204–238). New York, NY: Guilford Press.

Francis, D. J., Shaywitz, S. E., Stuebing, K. K., Shaywitz, B. A., & Fletcher, J. M. (1996). Developmental lag versus deficit models of reading disability: A longitudinal, individual growth curves analysis. *Journal of Educational Psychology, 88,* 3–17. doi:10.1037/0022-0663.88.1.3

Glover, T. A., & Albers, C. A. (2007). Considerations for evaluating universal screening assessments. *Journal of School Psychology, 45,* 117–135. doi:10.1016/j. jsp.2006.05.005

Harn, B. (2000). Approaches and considerations of collecting schoolwide early literacy and reading performance data. Retrieved from http://oregonreadingfirst. uoregon.edu/downloads/assessment/data_collection.pdf

Hintze, J. M., & Marcotte, A. M. (2010). Student assessment and data-based decision making. In T. A. Glover & S. Vaughn (Eds.), *The promise of response to intervention: Evaluating current science and practice* (pp. 57–77). New York, NY: Guilford Press.

Hintze, J. M., Ryan, A. L., & Stoner, G. (2003). Concurrent validity and diagnostic accuracy of the Dynamic Indicators of Basic Early Literacy Skills and the Comprehensive Test of Phonological Processing. *School Psychology Review, 32,* 541–556.

Ikeda, M., Neesen, N., & Witt, J. C. (2008). Best practices in universal screening. In A. Thomas & J. Grimes (Eds.), *Best practices in school psychology V* (pp. 103–114). Bethesda, MD: National Association of School Psychologists.

Jenkins, J. R., Hudson, R. F., & Johnson, E. S. (2007). Screening for at-risk readers in a response to intervention framework. *School Psychology Review, 36,* 582–600.

Juel, C. (1988). Learning to read and write: A longitudinal study of 54 children from first through fourth grades. *Journal of Educational Psychology, 80,* 437–447. doi:10.1037/0022-0663.80.4.437

Kaminski, R., Cummings, K. D., Powell-Smith, K. D., & Good, R. H. (2008). Best practices in using Dynamic Indicators of Basic Early Literacy Skills (DIBELS) for formative assessment and evaluation. In A. Thomas & J. Grimes (Eds.), *Best Practices in School Psychology V.* (pp. 1181–1204). Bethesda, MD: The National Association of School Psychologists.

Morgan, P. L., Fuchs, D., Compton, D. L., Cordray, D. S., & Fuchs, L. S. (2008). Does early reading failure decrease children's reading motivation? *Journal of Learning Disabilities, 41,* 387–404. doi:10.1177/0022219408321112

National Center on Response to Intervention. (2012). *Screening tools chart.* Retrieved from http://www.rti4success.org/screeningTools

Salvia, J., & Ysseldyke, J. E. (2004). *Assessment in special and inclusive education* (9th ed.). Boston, MA: Houghton Mifflin.

Simmons, D. C., Kame'enui, E. J., Good, R. H., Harn, B. A., Cole, C., & Braun, D. (2002). Building, implementing, and sustaining a beginning reading improvement model school by school and lessons learned. In M. R. Shinn, G. Stoner, & H. M. Walker (Eds.), *Interventions for academic and behavior problems II: Preventive and remedial approaches* (pp. 403–432). Bethesda, MD: National Association of School Psychologists.

Sugai, G., & Horner, R. (2002). The evolution of discipline practices: School-wide positive behavior supports. *Child and Family Behavior Therapy, 24,* 23–50. doi:10.1300/J019v24n01_03

Walker, H. M., & Shinn, M. R. (2002). Structuring school-based interventions to achieve integrated primary, secondary, and tertiary prevention goals for safe and effective schools. In M. R. Shinn, H. M. Walker, & G. Stoner (Eds.), *Interventions for academic and behavior problems II: Preventive and remedial approaches* (pp. 1–25). Bethesda, MD: National Association of School Psychologists.

Witt, J. C., Elliott, S. N., Daly, E. J., III, Gresham, F. M., & Kramer, J. J. (1998). *Assessment of special needs and at-risk students* (2nd ed.). Madison, WI: Brown and Benchmark.

3

MULTIPLE-GATING APPROACHES IN UNIVERSAL SCREENING WITHIN SCHOOL AND COMMUNITY SETTINGS

HILL M. WALKER, JASON W. SMALL, HERBERT H. SEVERSON,
JOHN R. SEELEY, AND EDWARD G. FEIL

This chapter focuses on the use of multiple-gating procedures to screen and identify students who may be at risk for developing, or who already manifest, serious learning and behavioral challenges within school settings that are appropriate target areas for prevention. Multiple gating refers to a generic process involving multiple assessments that cost efficiently identify a subset of individuals from a larger pool of target participants with a combination of methods and measures generally arranged in sequential order. Merrell (1999) has defined multiple gating as a best practice in assessment that uses multiple sources, often within multiple contexts (home vs. school), in the screening of students having behavioral, social, and emotional challenges. Multiple-gating approaches to screening, as a rule, have proven superior to single occasion assessments using a single measure (Kilgus, Chafouleas, Riley-Tillman, & Welsh, 2012). The addition of each assessment gate or stage

http://dx.doi.org/10.1037/14316-003
Universal Screening in Educational Settings: Evidence-Based Decision Making for Schools, R. J. Kettler,
T. A. Glover, C. A. Albers, and K. A. Feeney-Kettler (Editors)
Copyright © 2014 by the American Psychological Association. All rights reserved.

within an integrated, multiple-gating model is designed to increase the accuracy of screening while focusing more intensive measurements on a smaller number of targeted individuals.

This chapter describes and illustrates the range of multiple-gating applications that have been reported in the literature over the past several decades. The major topics dealt with are (a) definition and critical features of multiple gating; (b) procedural variations in multiple-gating applications across disciplines and contexts; (c) multiple gating and the increase in demand for cost-efficient, brief, and accurate screening instruments that are intervention sensitive; (d) some methodological issues in the use of multiple-gating procedures; (e) case studies of successful multiple-gating applications within school systems; (f) emerging web-based assessment technology and use of multiple gating; (g) lessons learned and recommendations for how and when to use multiple-gating procedures; and (h) concluding remarks.

DEFINITION AND CRITICAL FEATURES OF MULTIPLE GATING

Multiple-gating approaches for screening were introduced by Cronbach and Gleser (1965) and have since been adapted for use in numerous domains or areas, including personnel selection, delinquency, mental health, and youth behavior in school, family, and community contexts (Loeber, Dishion, & Patterson, 1984; Merrell, 1999; Walker & Severson, 1990). The basic logic of multiple gating is that a large population is sorted or narrowed down through a series of sequential assessments, called gates or stages, so that by the final gate there is a strong likelihood that those individuals who survive each screening stage manifest the condition being screened for. Survival means that one is ruled in for the condition rather than ruled out, which is the case for most of the individuals being screened. After the final assessment gate, those who "survive" (i.e., meet its exit or passing criteria) are very likely to have the condition and be in need of referral for additional evaluations and access to intervention supports and services.

One of the major goals of multiple gating is cost efficiency. That is, assessment resources are conserved through use of gate 1 universal screening procedures that allow each individual to have an equal chance to be identified for the condition. When a broad scan, such as informal teacher evaluation and nominations of students likely to have the screened-for condition or attribute (i.e., the gate 1), is used, universal screening of large numbers of students can be accomplished quickly. This process, however, is highly dependent on the accuracy of the teacher's judgment of student characteristics and is perhaps the most important of the assessment stages within a multiple-gating model. The teacher (or other social agent such as a parent) must have a thorough understanding of the behavioral characteristic that is being screened if the gate 1 screening is to work as envisioned.

Charlebois, Leblanc, Gagnon, and Larivee (1994) identified a lack of precision in the early stages of multiple-gating approaches as being a threat to the integrity of the whole screening process. There also has been substantial commentary on potential bias (and thus likely error) in teacher judgments of student behavior and performance. Such limitations would be especially problematic in the initial stage of universal screening. When teachers are asked to make judgments about these student dimensions, based on clearly specified criteria, their judgments generally meet acceptable standards of accuracy (see Gerber & Semmel, 1984). Each screening stage of a multiple-gating process generally involves a qualitatively different measure, so that a multimethod and, usually, multi-informant assessment process is implemented. These measures become more complex and labor intensive as one moves through the sequential assessment gates, but they are applied to a smaller and smaller number of those individuals who survive each gate. The multiple application of the same screening measure at different time points has been referred to occasionally as multiple gating, but this is an incorrect use of the term.

Figure 3.1 illustrates the structure of the multiple-gating process for the Systematic Screening for Behavior Disorders (SSBD) screening procedure (Walker & Severson, 1990).[1] A pool of elementary-age, general education students is screened in gate 1 using teacher nominations in relation to separate, standardized definitions of externalizing and internalizing behavioral dimensions. Teachers nominate lists of their students whose characteristic behavior patterns most closely match either an externalizing or an internalizing dimension. They then rank order each list according to how closely students' behavior patterns match each definition. The top-three-ranked students from each list move to screening gate 2, in which they are evaluated with brief behavior rating (BBR) scales, which are frequency based, along with a 33-item checklist of critical events indicators that assesses low-base-rate but highly intensive behavioral episodes (e.g., hallucinates, tries to seriously injure another student, displays inappropriate sexual behavior). Those students who exceed normative criteria, based on cutoff points established from a national norm sample of 4,400 cases on the gate 2 SSBD measures, meet the screening exit criteria and are moved to gate 3, where they are observed systematically by professionally trained observers in classroom and playground settings.

Classroom observations focus on academic engagement, and playground observations focus on the student's social behavior with peers. The stage 3

[1]The revised, updated second edition of the SSBD will be published by Pacific Northwest Publishing Company located in Eugene, Oregon, in late summer 2013. The revised SSBD will be part of the Screening, Identification, and Monitoring System (SIMS), which is a comprehensive assessment system for behavioral problems and social–emotional need consisting of multiple products.

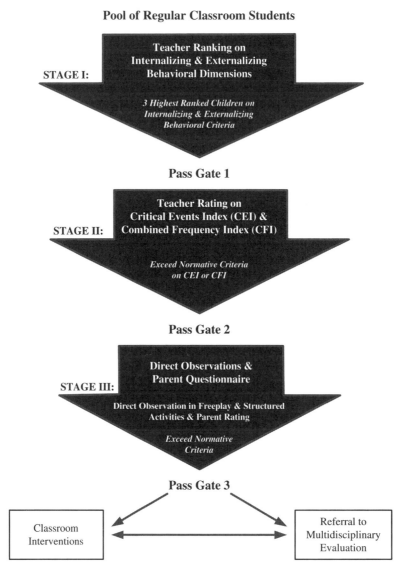

Pool of Regular Classroom Students

STAGE I: **Teacher Ranking on Internalizing & Externalizing Behavioral Dimensions**

3 Highest Ranked Children on Internalizing & Externalizing Behavioral Criteria

Pass Gate 1

STAGE II: **Teacher Rating on Critical Events Index (CEI) & Combined Frequency Index (CFI)**

Exceed Normative Criteria on CEI or CFI

Pass Gate 2

STAGE III: **Direct Observations & Parent Questionnaire**

Direct Observation in Freeplay & Structured Activities & Parent Rating

Exceed Normative Criteria

Pass Gate 3

Classroom Interventions ←→ Referral to Multidisciplinary Evaluation

Figure 3.1. Multiple-gating process used by the systematic screening of behavior disorders. From "Early Screening Project: Identifying Preschool Children With Adjustment Problems," by E. Feil, H. Severson, and H. Walker, 1994, *The Oregon Conference Monograph, Vol. 6.* Copyright 1994 by E. Feil, H. Severson, and H. Walker. Adapted with permission.

observational measure of academic engaged time (AET) specifically assesses the amount of time a student is actively engaged (i.e., attending to tasks, seeking assistance as needed, interacting appropriately, and listening attentively) in structured and unstructured academically focused classroom activities. The stage 3 observation of peer social behavior (PSB) assesses the quality, amount, and nature of student–peer social interactions (i.e., social engagement, participation, parallel play, alone time) in free play contexts. Both AET and PSB provide a direct measure of a student's behavioral adjustment and can be used to partially verify gate 1 and 2 teacher rankings. They are also useful in facilitating comparison to normative levels for students meeting stage 2 eligibility criteria.

These two observation codes have been normed on a national sample of 1,300 cases. The students meeting gate 3 exit criteria then are referred for additional evaluation, an archival records review, and possible intervention. The SSBD typically identifies one to two students per classroom who qualify on the externalizing dimension and one student for every two to three classrooms who qualifies on the internalizing dimension.

Multiple-gating approaches, as a rule, involve a *dimensional* rather than a *categorical* approach to screening in which individuals can be ordered along a severity dimension on the basis of behavioral profiles within each of the sequential and integrated screening stages (Merrell, 2010). Being able to array the survivors of a multiple-gating process along such a severity dimension can have important implications for treatment and placement decisions. This capacity is one of several critically important features missing from the federal definition of emotional disturbance used to certify behaviorally at-risk students as eligible for mandated services (Walker, Yell, & Murray, in press).

When designed and implemented appropriately, multiple-gating procedures can be applied to a variety of assessment tasks in school and nonschool contexts (e.g., selecting at-risk students in kindergarten or Grade 1 who will need secondary and tertiary prevention supports and services early in their school careers, identifying later school dropout students in middle schools, or predicting likely recidivists among a population of incarcerated juvenile offenders). Multiple gating can substantially improve the quality of clinical and educational decision making. It is an accurate and cost-efficient procedure when implemented with integrity.

PROCEDURAL VARIATIONS IN MULTIPLE-GATING APPLICATIONS ACROSS DISCIPLINES AND CONTEXTS

Over the past several decades, the use of multiple-gating approaches has ramped up substantially within the areas of antisocial behavior, delinquency, mental health, and education. A number of published studies have illustrated interesting variations on the application of this screening technique. Some of these variations are described in the following examples to illustrate the range and diversity of these applications.

One of the most important demonstrations of multiple gating was reported in an early study by Loeber et al. (1984). These investigators designed and evaluated a multistage procedure to screen delinquent from nondelinquent youths using a sample of 12- to 16-year-old boys ($N = 102$). The base rate of official delinquency of the population in which the study was conducted was 16.33%. Loeber et al.'s multiple-gating procedure consisted of three increasingly more expensive and sequential assessments. These were (a) teacher ratings in school at gate 1, (b) parent telephone report of conduct problems at home at gate 2, and (c) an interview with the study's youths and parents about family management practices at gate 3. Results showed that each successive screening gate improved the positive predictive value from 24.5% to 56.3% when official delinquency status was verified from court records. Impressively, the three-stage screening procedure correctly classified 88.2% of the full sample with an overall improvement of 86.6% over the chance level of recovery. Loeber et al. estimated that their multiple-gating procedure was 58% less expensive than a single-stage screening procedure.

Lochman and the Conduct Problems Prevention Research Group (1995) evaluated a three-stage multiple-gating procedure applied to a sample of 382 students selected at entry into first grade. The goal in the study was to predict which of these students would experience behavior challenges over the course of the next year. The screening procedure consisted of (a) teacher ratings at gate 1 on the 14-item Teacher Observation of Classroom Adaption—Revised scale (Werthamer-Larsson, Kellam, & Wheeler, 1991); (b) parent responses, via in-person interviews or telephone contacts, to 24 items measuring externalizing symptoms drawn from existing scales published in the literature at gate 2; and (c) a 22-item questionnaire that measured parents' self-reports of their disciplinary practices at gate 3. Using a series of regression analyses, Lochman and the Conduct Problems Prevention Research Group found the teacher and parent screening process to be relatively effective in predicting student behavior status during first grade. The rate of problem behavior was 3.5 times higher for the identified high-risk group than the low-risk group. The gate 2 parent screen added a small but statistically significant improvement to the prediction of externalizing behavioral outcomes at the end of first grade. The parenting practices questionnaire, however, added nothing to the two-step, teacher and parenting screens or to their use in combination. The study's specificity (.70) and sensitivity (only .50) placed logical constraints on use of the screening procedure in identifying child behavior problems for prevention and early intervention.

McConaughy and Achenbach (1989) illustrated the application of their model of multiaxial, empirically based assessment within a multiple-gating context. The focus of their study was a seriously emotionally disturbed child identified under the auspices of the Education of All Handicapped Children Act (P.L. 94-142). Their gating procedure involved initial parent ratings of the child's behavior, teacher ratings at school, and direct observations recorded in classroom, recess, and playground settings. The empirical, standardized measures were supplemented with clinical interviews and psychoeducational testing in a three-phase multiple-gating procedure. Results of the study supported the application of this approach as a combined assessment and intervention planning procedure for general use with behaviorally at-risk students.

August, Realmuto, Crosby, and MacDonald (1995) used a multiple-gating procedure to screen 7,231 children attending suburban elementary schools. The goal in the study was to identify, early in their school careers, children who were at elevated risk for challenging behavior of an externalizing nature. Measures of cross-setting disruptive behavior and parent discipline practices were administered in sequential fashion to screen this large population. The convergent validity of the respective gating measures was confirmed by significant correlations with a series of adjustment constructs. Analyses of covariance performed between positive screens, negative screens, and low-risk comparison children at each screening gate supported the discriminant validity of the screening procedure. Regression analyses indicated that the gating measures predicted diagnostic ratings of attention-deficit/hyperactivity disorder and oppositional deviant disorder 18 months later. The best predictors of high-risk group membership were measures of family process, poor communication and weak parental involvement, poor maternal coping skills, and parental external locus of control.

Kilgus et al. (2012) evaluated the direct behavior rating (DBR) scales as screeners, wherein general education teachers were trained to systematically observe and then rate students' behavior on multiple occasions along the three dimensions of *academic engagement, disruptive behavior, and compliance*. In this procedure, the teacher estimates, using a scale ranging from 0 to 100, the degree to which the student being rated manifests the observed characteristic or target behavior during the immediately preceding observation period. DBR scales differ from typical parent or teacher rating scales, in that they are considered by their developers to be a direct performance measure that does not require the indirect, more retrospective inferences that are characteristic of commonly used rating scales. The study also investigated the diagnostic accuracy of DBR scales when administered within a single dimension rating context versus a multiple dimension rating context. Although the latter context was referred to as a multiple-gating procedure, it did not employ the sequential stage assessments of multiple gating. Rather, the multiple dimensions (academic engagement, disruptive behavior, compliance) were rated in a single stage. Results of the study indicated moderate to strong associations between DBR scales and the criterion measures used (the Behavioral and Emotion Screening and Social Skills Improvement Teacher Rating Systems; see Elliott & Gresham, 2007; Kamphaus et al., 2007). Kilgus et al. also found that single-stage, single-dimensional DBR scales had low specificity when compared with multiple-dimensional ratings and that multiple-dimensional assessments resulted in more correct decisions (for a discussion of this issue, see Bennett et al., 1999). Kilgus et al. concluded that multiple dimension rating approaches are the most well balanced and accurate, because they require documentation of risk across multiple areas or domains. Given their findings of high false-positive rates associated with the use of DBR scales, they recommended that schools consider using a multimethod, multiple-gating process to allow for confirmation of screening outcomes from each individual screening procedure.

Finally, for the past 15 years, Duerr Evaluation Resources Inc. of Chico, California, has used the Walker–McConnell Scale of Social Competence and School Adjustment (W-MC; Walker & McConnell, 1995) to screen, identify, and assess program outcomes of primary grade students under auspices of the California Mental Health Department's Early Mental Health Initiative (EMHI). Under state authorizing legislation, the department funds local educational agencies via competitive grants to provide early intervention and prevention services for primary grade students who experience social–behavioral adjustment challenges in school. In the 2006–2007 school year, this program was operating in 438 elementary schools located in 83 school districts throughout the state.

The contractor designed and implemented a multiple-gating approach to screening and identification in which a subset of W-MC scale items ($N = 19$) was used as a universal screener. These items had been selected from analysis of the full-scale item pool and were those that had higher factor loadings on the first factor and lower loadings on the remaining two factors (see Duerr Evaluation Resources, 2007). Those students who met or exceeded cutoff points on the screener then were rated by their teachers on the full scale, consisting of 43 items divided into three domains: *teacher-preferred social behavior, peer-preferred social behavior,* and *school adjustment.* Final identification and selection for the EMHI was based on full-scale W-MC scores. At the end of the 12- to 15-week EMHI intervention, the full-scale W-MC was readministered to assess program outcomes.

Duerr Evaluation Resources Inc. has reported it has a pre–post database on the full-scale W-MC of more than 150,000 cases. In the 2006–2007 school year, 15,829 participants were rated by their teachers on the W-MC scale.

Typically, 70–75% of students show noticeable and statistically significant improvement on the W-MC from pre- to postassessments. All three subscales proved sensitive to the 12- to 15-week EMHI intervention, with participating students showing, on average, a 12-point percentile gain in their overall social–behavioral adjustment status (see Duerr Evaluation Resources, 2007).

Annual evaluation reports of the EMHI program are provided to the California Mental Health Department by the contractor. In these reports, the 19-item initial screener followed by full-scale W-MC administration at pre– and post–time points proved to be an effective multiple-gating approach for selecting appropriate EMHI candidates and assessing their program outcomes. Strong relationships typically were found between assessments using the 19-item screener and the full-scale W-MC.

These studies provide examples of the largely successful use of multiple-gating procedures across disciplines and within multiple contexts. Their great appeal, as noted, has to do with the cost efficiencies they are capable of producing along with the increase in discriminant power as additional gates come into play. The confirmatory function of these sequential gates has substantial value in reducing false positives and their associated mislabeling, unnecessary expenditure of intervention resources, inaccurate recommendations for specialized placements, and possible stigma. In our view, the most rigorous and convincing criterion measures for validating multiple-gating approaches are longitudinal outcomes recorded over substantial time periods (i.e., across years) in which screened populations are followed up and assessed as to their behavioral adjustment and status (see Charlebois et al., 1994; Lochman & the Conduct Problems Prevention Research Group, 1995). Such longitudinal studies provide rigorous tests of the efficacy of multiple-gating approaches.

MULTIPLE GATING AND THE INCREASED DEMAND FOR BRIEF, COST-EFFICIENT, ACCURATE INSTRUMENTS THAT ARE INTERVENTION SENSITIVE

During the past decade, professional consumers have searched for instruments and procedures with which to screen, identify, diagnose, and evaluate outcomes for students who are perceived to be behaviorally at risk to themselves or others. Teachers and many parents are now much more resistant to completing checklists and rating scales having 100-plus items. The current burdens on teachers are barely manageable given the rapid increases in class sizes and reductions in school funding, yet the demand for data-based approaches to much school decision making, along with continuing accountability pressures, is unabated. These pressures have stimulated some excellent development work in the area of BBR scales consisting of very few items (e.g., generally 12 or less). Responses by the professional community to these pressures include the work of Chafouleas, Volpe, Gresham, and Cook (2010) with DBR scales; the work of Gresham et al. (2010) to identify change-sensitive items for the progress monitoring of social behavior; and the research of Lane and colleagues (Lane, Menzies, Oakes, & Kalberg, 2012; Lane, Oakes et al., 2012) to establish the psychometric integrity and utility of the Drummond seven-item scale to identify externalizing, antisocial students. Each of these instruments would be appropriate as a first screening gate in a multiple-gating approach, and some have demonstrated sensitivity to change as a function of intervention (see Gresham et al., 2010). The emergence of the positive behavior intervention and supports (PBIS) approach to school intervention and its three-tiered, delivery framework have created an enormous appetite for screening and progress monitoring tools that are brief, efficient, and sensitive. Only recently have tools and procedures for measuring social behavior within a three-tiered context that parallel progress monitoring procedures for academic performance become available.

These described advances in assessment would fit well into the prevention and early intervention paradigm now being promoted by many experts in school-based mental health. For example, Levitt, Saka, Romanelli, and Hoagwood (2007) have advocated establishing a comprehensive mental health system within schooling contexts that consists of parallel *multitiered assessment approaches* and *multitiered intervention approaches*. Their assessment approach is based on the universal screening of all students followed by Tier 2 and 3 assessments, as appropriate, to rule out or reduce false positives and thoroughly assess for risk factors, presence of disorder, and treatment need. In their comprehensive approach, a multiple-gating screening process could be implemented within an assessment context, within an intervention context, or in some combination of the two. Ideally, the screening process would operate seamlessly within a larger, coordinated system of prevention and early intervention of mental health challenges of K–12 students.

Gresham (2005) has conceptualized an alternative means of identifying emotionally or behaviorally challenged students with a response-to-intervention (RTI) approach that is a multiple-gating process applied to interventions. It assumes that certain students will not respond satisfactorily to a well-implemented universal intervention and will select themselves out of the student pool as needing additional instruction, assistance, or support. A subset of these students will require intensive indicated supports and services at a tertiary level of intervention. This framework has been adapted successfully to school settings in programs using the Institute of Medicine's prevention classification of primary, secondary, and tertiary levels involving, respectively, universal, selected, and indicated intervention approaches (Sugai & Horner, 2002; Walker et al., 1996).

To date, professionals seem to have been generally frustrated in their ability (a) to identify students at a universal level of intervention (i.e., gate 1) who will require Tier 2 and 3 services and (b) to appropriately determine when students should move between levels in this three-tiered system. Gresham (2005) reviewed four approaches that have been proposed for making these decisions, involving *visual inspection of data, reliable changes in behavior, changes on social impact measures,* and *social validation.* The strategies Gresham has provided for implementing each of these approaches have not resonated with professionals working in PBIS and other contexts, perhaps because of the perception that they are too burdensome to implement and because of insufficient information about how to implement and aggregate their outcomes. The development and implementation of BBR scales that allow frequent, low-cost monitoring of student behavior appear to be especially appropriate in addressing the decisions described previously.

The advances in BBR scales have the potential to make multiple-gating approaches to solving some complex screening–monitoring tasks an effective reality. The extent to which they will be incorporated into PBIS-type approaches in the future remains to be demonstrated.

SOME METHODOLOGICAL ISSUES IN THE USE OF MULTIPLE-GATING PROCEDURES

Multiple gating rests on the assumptions that (a) large numbers of individuals can be screened inexpensively and efficiently, (b) each succeeding gate confirms outcomes of the previous screening gate and increases the overall discriminant power of the approach, and (c) those individuals who survive all screening gates are most likely to have or be at elevated risk for the screened-for condition or characteristic (Merrell, 1999). Some of the most salient methodological issues relating to multiple-gating approaches have to do with (a) the selection of gate 1 instruments and procedures to allow universal screening, (b) the need to identify adequate criterion measures for validating the discriminant and predictive validity of screening systems, (c) policy and practice decision making around acceptable ratios of false-positive and false-negative outcomes of screening, (d) the role of BBR scales in multiple-gating approaches, (e) the need to take severity into account in multiple-gating approaches, and (f) the need to account for developmental factors and their relationship to multiple-gating screening.

As noted, Charlebois et al. (1994) have made the case that multiple-gating approaches often suffer from a lack of definitional precision at the initial screening gate in that the rating scale predictor variables, often used at this stage, are too molar to accurately predict a criterion variable, such as delinquency, recidivism, school dropout, or achievement. Lochman and the Conduct Problems Prevention Research Group (1995) have argued that multiple gating is especially vulnerable to biased raters at the initial screening gate. When such is the case, biased raters are more likely to prematurely remove an individual from the risk pool who thereby would not be available to the second-step screening raters. Gate 1 of a multiple-gating process is arguably the most important, because it drives outcomes of the remaining gates and affects the integrity of the screening process. Careful definition and administration of gate 1 assessments thus is of paramount importance. In constructing the SSBD, Walker and Severson (1990) spent more time designing and testing the gate 1 definitions of externalizing and internalizing dimensions than any other component of the system, because teacher nomination and rank ordering of students on these dimensions were the only means of discriminating externalizers and internalizers from each other and from the remaining students. Achieving definitional clarity for the internalizing dimension was especially difficult, because the overlap of internalizing behavioral characteristics with normative student behavior is greater and because internalizing behavior is less salient for teachers. Thus, more attention to carefully selecting and precisely defining the predictor variables that make up the initial screening gate in developing multiple-gating systems may be required.

The criterion measures for confirming and validating results of a multiple-gating screening process also should be carefully selected and precisely defined. Although well defined and systematically recorded by the web-based, school-wide information system, the use of office discipline referrals (ODRs) as an evaluation metric and criterion variable for judging the efficacy of PBIS interventions has been quite controversial (Nelson, Benner, Reid, Epstein, & Currin, 2002). Many professionals consider ODRs to be too crude and molar to be used as a screener and too influenced by a host of school variables (e.g., administrative pressures not to refer students for behavioral infractions) to serve as an adequate criterion measure of PBIS outcomes. Screening to predict the likelihood of an individual committing a violent act at some future point is even more fraught with challenges of definition, measurement, and lack of precision. As noted, the ultimate test of a predictor variable for inclusion in a screening system is that, over time, it allows for detection of those who scored high on the initial screener and were determined longitudinally to have met the criterion. As an example, researchers at the Oregon Social Learning Center have designed and replicated a process that allows for the precise identification of future recidivists among two samples of approximately 800 delinquents. These predictor variables, any three of which will allow for such future recidivist detection, are as follows: (a) has been a client of child protection, (b) has or is receiving special education services, (c) showed an early severe pattern of antisocial behavior, (d) has experienced a family tragedy (death, divorce, family disruption–trauma), or (e) mother or father has ever been arrested. These predictors, which are highly efficient screeners, were culled from large numbers of adjudicated youths' records and served as a model for how to identify and define predictor variables that can be used for screening and diagnostic purposes.

Other potential criterion measures are referral to mental health services or to alternative placement settings, school failure and dropout, and school suspensions and expulsions (Walker, Severson, & Seeley, 2010). Criterion variable assessments can be far removed in time from the occurrence of the predictors, as in the case of Charlebois et al. (1994; 5 years) and Hawkins, Catalano, Kosterman, Abbott, and Hill (1999; 9 years). The ability to predict outcomes across so many years and to do so efficiently and accurately, as in the case of the Oregon Social Learning study of adolescent recidivists, is unusual. We believe more careful attention should be devoted, as Charlebois et al. have recommended, to both predictor screening variables and criterion variables that are used to validate the screening–identification process within multiple-gating approaches.

The literature in our field is filled with numerous debates about the relative risks associated with false positives and false negatives in screening–identification paradigms. Few issues spur more controversy or disagreement among professionals than this one. The stakes with regard to undesirable consequences are obviously higher when false negatives occur in, say, suicide or cancer screening, as opposed to academic performance or behavioral adjustment in school. False negatives in the latter cases, although serious, are not life threatening. It has been interesting to watch U.S. government efforts of late to discourage breast cancer and prostate cancer screening within certain age parameters, primarily due to the costs of such screening and the high rates of false positives that ultimately prove to be expensive. One difficulty with this cost-cutting, public health initiative is that evidence-based medical policy occurs at a population level and the practice of medicine occurs at an individual level. So, the individual who thinks she or he does not have cancer, takes this advice, and forgoes screening may end up later with advanced, untreatable cancer—a true false negative. This argument generally turns on the costs and unnecessary treatments associated with false positives cast against the deleterious effects of a false-negative outcome. We also should note the trade-offs that occur in using the "and" and "or" rules in serial screening approaches. Multiple gating inherently involves the and rule across screening stages. As Seeley, Stice, and Rohde (2009) have demonstrated, the and rule maximizes specificity and predictive value, whereas the or rule does the opposite. Hence, multiple-gating procedures help to maximize statistical power for prevention trials of low-base-rate behavioral events by increasing the positive predictive value, but they do so at the expense of reduced sensitivity. (Guidelines for acceptable values of conditional probability indices in screening are provided in Chapter 1 of this volume.)

So what is the correct answer regarding a false positive–false negative ratio? Loeber et al. (1984), in their classic study of multiple gating with delinquents, suggested the end result of a multiple-gating procedure should be a sensitivity of 50% or greater, indicating that the majority of actual delinquents are identified. Seeley, in Walker, Severson, and Seeley (2010), has advocated the use of receiver operating characteristic (ROC) analysis procedures in the evaluation of screeners and in the estimation of a preferred balance between specificity and sensitivity of the instrument (see Hsiao, Bartko, & Potter, 1989; Murphy et al., 1987). The ROC curve also provides an overview of the screener's overall performance. In general, areas under the curve that are above .95 indicate an excellent screener, those above .90 indicate a good screener, and those above .75 indicate an acceptable screener. When grappling with this complex issue, one has to consider the stakes involved in relation to the goals of screening, the ratio of false positives and negatives, and the contexts and population with which one is working. Another possible limitation of this approach may be that it penalizes a screener who does not perform well across a range of cut scores but performs adequately or well at a specific cut score.

The recent advances in assessment methodology that have produced BBR scales, especially when combined with the emerging use of web-based technology to deliver them, have important implications for the design of multiple-gating approaches. The precision, cost efficiency, and consumer acceptance of these scales likely will be enhanced when they are delivered via web technology. Their collective impact on screening systems of the future may be substantial. The BBR scales of Chafouleas et al. (2010), those of Gresham et al. (2010), the seven-item antisocial screener of Drummond (recently revised and expanded by Lane, Menzies, et al., 2012), and the work of Marquez and Yeaton (in press) on the development of a web-based progress monitoring tool (PMT) are all seminal contributions to the advancement of screening efforts (see the section on multiple gating and emerging technology). Each of these screeners, if predictive of appropriate criterion variables, likely could serve as appropriate gate 1 or gate 2 screening instruments within a multiple-gating model. They already are being used efficiently and successfully as single-stage screening assessments (see Lane, Menzies, et al., 2012).

The need to take severity into account in multiple-gating systems was discussed by Charlebois et al. (2010) nearly two decades ago in their seminal work on multiple gating and the longitudinal prediction of antisocial behavior patterns in boys. They suggested the following criteria to establish a severity index in the realm of antisocial behavior: *early onset, display of problematic behavior in multiple settings, number of coexisting disorders,* and *form or pattern of disorders such as proactive versus reactive aggression.* Lochman and the Conduct Problems Prevention Research Group (1995) used a two-step gating procedure that required evidence of problematic behavior in both school and home settings—a rigorous test of severity by most accounts. In our randomized controlled trial of the First Step early intervention program, we developed an SSBD index that allowed for the ordering of externalizers along a severity dimension. The focus of many behavioral assessment systems is to use a dimensional assessment process to derive categorical status for screened students (e.g., as emotionally disturbed or socially maladjusted). This approach, although required by federal legislation in the identification of students with emotional or behavioral disorders (EBD), generally is not considered to be a best practice in the field. The procedure for identifying students as emotionally disturbed to qualify for mandated services follows this exact approach; it is based on a medical model of diagnostic verification of a specific category of disability (Maag & Katsiyannis, 2008). Being able instead to order students along a severity dimension (e.g., externalizing and internalizing) or on other appropriate indices would enable better decision making in identification, in allocating intervention resources, and in determining the order in which students should receive intervention services along with appropriate dosage levels.

There is a clear need for research to identify effective predictors—for use in screening approaches—at different points on the developmental spectrum, as they likely will show change over the long term. The SSBD is a case in point. We developed the Early Screening Project (Walker, Severson, & Feil, 1995) several years after publication of the SSBD, when it became apparent that a preschool version of the screener was needed. In 2008, Caldarella, Young, Richardson, Young, and Young published a study demonstrating acceptable usage, psychometrics, and staff acceptance of the adapted SSBD at middle and high schools. Thus, three variations of this screening system were necessary to cover the preschool through high school age-grade range. Carefully assessing developmental factors and taking them into account in defining the age ranges in which their use is appropriate are of great importance in designing multiple-gating systems.

These are but a sampling of the many methodological issues that can be raised about multiple-gating approaches to screening. In our experience, however, they are among the most salient. Particularly within school contexts, they moderate the efficiency, power, accuracy, and consumer acceptance of the use of these approaches.

CASE STUDY: INSTITUTIONAL USE OF THE SSBD TO IMPLEMENT A COURT-ORDERED SCREENING–IDENTIFICATION PROCESS

The following case study is an example of the SSBD being used within an RTI-PBIS context and well illustrates this type of SSBD application. Naquin and D'Atrio of the University of New Orleans (UNO) integrated the SSBD screening system into a larger assessment battery that provides multiple information sources on the impact of their pupil assistance model (PAM) in addressing the needs and challenges of behaviorally at-risk students and their teachers. This court-ordered initiative was prompted by a continuing failure of a Louisiana school district to adequately screen, identify, place, and serve students with and at risk for EBD within general education settings. The SSBD fulfilled a number of purposes in this multiyear process, including (a) serving as a child find screening process, (b) providing a template for developing staff training regimens for participating schools, and (c) evaluating outcomes. A more detailed description of this work was provided by Walker, Severson, Naquin, et al. (2010).

Description of the School District Court-Mandated Site

The participating school district was a local education agency in the Greater New Orleans region and forms the largest metropolitan area in Louisiana. According to the U.S. Census Bureau, as of July 1, 2007, the Greater New Orleans population was 704,010. At that time, the population in the community served by the school district was reported to be 423,520 people based on approximately 98% of the population reported by the U.S. Census in 2000. In addition to being the largest metropolitan area, the education agency is the state's largest school district.

The district consists of 88 schools with K–12 student enrollment of approximately 45,000 students. At the time of the study, student enrollment was composed of 33% White and 67% minority students; 61.9% of the students participated in the free or reduced-cost lunch program. The racial makeup of the parish (community) that the district serves is 69.82% White, 22.86% Black or African American, 0.45% Native American, 3.09% Asian, 0.03% Pacific Islander, 2.03% from other races, and 1.72% from two or more races. A total of 7.12% of the population was Hispanic or Latino. The district is recognized as having the largest limited-English-proficient student population in Louisiana, with more than 2,500 students eligible for services. These students represent more than 68 countries with 52 spoken languages. There are 36 nonpublic schools located in the district that serve an additional 18,883 students from the community.

Background of the Corrective Action Plan Initiative

The PAM team at UNO began providing staff development and consultation services in the district's participating elementary schools in 2000. By 2003, the PAM team began to focus consultative services on the implementation of an intervention model. At that time, services were provided in 10 identified "vanguard" schools, and assistance focused on the identification of students needing intervention in the areas of reading and mathematics. Implementation of the current PAM/RTI-PBIS model was facilitated by the issuance of a corrective action plan (CAP) that resulted from monitoring of the district conducted by the Louisiana Department of Education during 2005. In the mediated settlement agreement, the administrators of the CAP identified nine areas in need of remediation and improvement.

The settlement agreement specified that the district "develop, devise, and implement an effective positive behavioral intervention and support program for all students." The stated intent of implementing such a program was to indirectly increase the access that students with EBD would have to the general education setting. Thus, a PBIS model and the associated training initiatives recommended by the Louisiana Department of Education were adopted for the entire school district.

A key provision in the CAP pertained to students having EBD. This provision required that alternative methods be developed to handle behavior and discipline concerns of students with EBD and that behavior management methods other than school suspensions and expulsions be used to manage student behavior. This goal also focused on how the provisions of student individual education plans were to be developed and implemented.

The CAP initiative provided considerable leverage for the investigators' use of the PAM model in meeting the various elements of the court's mandate and settlement with the school district. The role of the SSBD in this process is described in the following section.

Using the SSBD Procedure to Identify Students With EBD

The SSBD procedure provides a cost-efficient means for the PAM team to accurately screen and identify students with emotional and behavioral problems. It also identifies forms of student behavior that teachers request in-service training and technical assistance to remedy.

2006–2007 SSBD Screenings

During the 2006–2007 school year, the SSBD was used to screen general education students in Grades 1–5 in all 53 elementary schools within the district. Of the students included in the screenings, 49.3% were African

American, 33.7% were Caucasian, and 17.0% were distributed across an Other category. For the first year of screening with the SSBD, the PAM team conducted all screenings in the 53 elementary schools. This team was composed of master's and doctoral-level staff with a primary background or certification as an educational diagnostician or a school psychologist. All screening staff had at least 30 hours of graduate coursework in assessment and diagnostic methods.

In January 2007, training was conducted with the 53 elementary school academic and behavioral intervention teams regarding the utilization and philosophy behind the use of the SSBD, the administration of the SSBD, and the scoring and interpretation of data. During the second semester of the 2006–2007 school year, SSBD screenings were conducted at each school either in a faculty meeting (typically 1–1.5 hour) or in grade-level meetings (i.e., during teacher planning periods). To assist the school system, UNO personnel collected all gate 1 and gate 2 protocols. SSBD gate 2 protocols were scored and data were entered into a Microsoft Excel spreadsheet for each school. The Excel spreadsheet for each school included a summary page of all SSBD data for the school and summaries of at-risk students according to name, teacher, grade, and critical events index (CEI) checklist score. Finally, each spreadsheet included a grade-by-grade roster of all students who were either nominated or considered to be behaviorally at risk. Spreadsheets were disseminated to schools by members of the UNO PAM team, and results were discussed with school administrators and members of the academic and behavioral intervention team.

Of the 22,101 students screened in the spring of 2007, 3,488 were nominated by their teachers (approximately 15.8% of all students screened) for further screening with SSBD gate 2 measures (i.e., the CEI checklist and brief adaptive and maladaptive rating scales). Across the 53 schools, the percentage of students nominated ranged from 3.7% to 34.3% of the pool of general education students screened. Of those students nominated, 1,533 were determined to be at risk according to the SSBD criteria and cutoff scores. The percentage of at-risk students ranged from 1.3% to 14.6% of those screened, which was 6.9% of the total student population. Of the 1,533 identified at-risk students, 71.7% were male and 28.3% were female; 66.6% of the at-risk students were externalizers and 33.4% were internalizers. These statistics are consistent with findings reported by Walker and Severson (1990) for the SSBD standardization data.

2007–2008 SSBD Screenings

In the fall of 2007, district-level pupil appraisal staff members, including educational diagnosticians, school psychologists, and social workers, were trained in procedures for administering, scoring, and interpreting data on the SSBD. For the second year of behavioral screening, pupil appraisal staff assisted the UNO PAM team in the administration of the SSBD in the 53 participating elementary schools. To enhance the likelihood that administration procedures would be implemented with procedural integrity, each member of the pupil appraisal team was given a coach card (developed by the PAM investigators) that outlined the step-by-step administration of the SSBD. During the 2007–2008 school year, SSBD screenings began in mid-October, and data for most schools were collected by the end of November. PAM personnel collected gate 1 and gate 2 protocols, and data were entered into spreadsheets as during the 2006–2007 school year.

Spreadsheets for the SSBD data collected during the second year of CAP-mandated screening were expanded and refined. More descriptive and demographic data were provided on the school summary sheet, and two pages were added to each file. UNO staff developed an SSBD item analysis process that provided a frequency count for each of the 33 items on the CEI of the SSBD according to gender and grade. Each time one of the 33 CEI items was checked by a teacher, it was tallied on the item analysis sheet. Each tally was placed in a box that specified the grade of the student, whether the behavioral item was produced by a male or female student, and whether the student was an externalizer or internalizer. This process was followed for all protocols received from each school.

A similar format was used to analyze scores on the adaptive and maladaptive behavior scales. The adaptive behavior scale of the SSBD assesses the frequency of behaviors that are considered to be socially desirable and appropriate to the classroom. Each of the 12 items on this scale is assigned a score ranging from 1 to 5, depending on frequency of occurrence. A score of 1 indicates that the student never exhibits the behavior in question, and a rating of 5 indicates that the student frequently exhibits the behavior. Students can receive a maximum score of 60 on the adaptive behavior scale, with higher scores indicating that students frequently exhibit socially desirable or appropriate forms of expected classroom behavior.

For the item analysis procedure of these scales, a tally was kept for an item on the adaptive behavior scale that received a score of 1 or 2, indicating that a student never or seldom exhibited that desired behavior. Tallies were entered into boxes that specified student grade, gender, and identification as an externalizer or internalizer. On the maladaptive behavior scale, students were rated on 11 items according to the frequency with which they exhibited undesirable behaviors. Student ratings range from 1 to 5, with 1 representing "never" and 5 representing "frequently." Students can receive a maximum score of 55 on the maladaptive scale, with higher scores indicating that students frequently exhibit inappropriate or socially undesirable behaviors. For the item analysis, a tally was developed for an item on the maladaptive behavior scale if a student was assigned a score of 3 or higher. Each tally was entered into boxes that again specified student grade, gender, and identification as an externalizer or internalizer.

As noted, the item analysis procedure was developed by the UNO PAM team to assist with the specification of areas of concern identified within each school. Positive behavior support teams were able to utilize data from the item analysis to more accurately develop schoolwide staff training plans for each participating school. Information from the item analyses for the adaptive and maladaptive behavior scales also was used to guide social skills training in areas needing more intensive attention. By using the item analysis results, administrators and members of the CAP implementation teams were able to obtain information (per teacher report) about specific behaviors or areas in their respective schools as well as subgroups of students needing more focused intervention. The item analysis for the CEI provided information about the behaviors most frequently reported by teachers to be seriously problematic (e.g., "Ignores teacher warnings"). Further examination of the item analysis results also provided information about whether intervention should be directed toward a specific grade level, gender, or at-risk subgroup (e.g., externalizer or internalizer).

An additional component pertaining to administration of the SSBD in 2007–2008 was the manner in which information from three flagged items on the CEI was handled. Discussion between PAM personnel and district administrators led to a determination that Items 18, 22, and 24 required mandatory reporting by the school administration and UNO personnel if checked off by a teacher. These items refer to the presence or evidence of a student having suicidal (or death-related) thoughts and the suspicion of a student having been either physically or sexually abused. The district decided that if a protocol was found to have a check by any of the three items, a report was to be made immediately to the school principal.

During the 2007–2008 school year, the SSBD was used to screen 16,634 students in Grades 1–5. Five of the sixth-grade classes were included. Of the total number of students screened, 3,521 (approximately 21% of the screened population) were nominated for gate 2 assessments by general education teachers. Of those students nominated, 1,299 were determined to be behaviorally at risk based on their SSBD gate 2 profiles. Across the 53 schools, the percentage of students nominated ranged from 5.1% to 33.8% and the percentage of students judged to be at risk in each school ranged from 2.0% to 21.7%. Overall, 7.8% of all students screened were at risk as compared with 6.9% of all students in the previous school year. The percentages of boys and girls identified as at risk were identical to the percentages identified during the first year of screening (i.e., 71.7% boys, 28.3% girls). The distributions of externalizers and internalizers were quite similar (i.e., 66.6% externalizers, 33.4% internalizers).

The SSBD proved to be a highly efficient screening procedure in the CAP-PAM initiative within the participating school district. Its use ensured that all students in the district's participating elementary schools and classrooms were afforded an equal chance to be identified for social–behavioral challenges (a) that put their school success and adjustment at risk; (b) that are important target areas for prevention; and (c) that could qualify them for access to needed interventions, supports, and services. The process was not unusually burdensome given the size of the student populations screened across school years, as only the first two screening gates of the SSBD were used; the optional third screening gate, involving in vivo observations recorded in classroom and playground settings, was not used. The PAM investigators' use of item analysis of gate 2 instrument results was novel. It proved especially valuable in helping to identify specific behavioral areas, on a school-by-school basis, in which teachers wished to improve their skill levels through staff development training and technical assistance.

EMERGING WEB-BASED ASSESSMENT TECHNOLOGY AND MULTIPLE GATING

The authors of the SSBD recently concluded a 1-year, Phase I Small Business Innovation Research grant developing a prototype, web-based version of the SSBD (Grant 1R43HD062096-01A2). To our knowledge, this was one of the first applications of web-based assessment technology to a multiple-gating system designed for universal screening. Surveys of previous users and nonusers of the SSBD procedure overwhelmingly endorsed the need for such a web-based screening system. Advantages of this type of screener include (a) ease and efficiency of use; (b) reduction in errors of administration, scoring, and aggregation of screening data; (c) automated calculation and reporting of screening results; (d) rapid feedback to users; (e) the development of new and expanded norms for screening gates 1 and 2 as the system is implemented; (f) a search and analysis function for the types of behavioral challenges reported over time and by site; (g) administrative monitoring and supervision of the screening process; (h) use as a tool in progress monitoring within an RTI-PBIS framework; and (i) increased consumer satisfaction. The web-based SSBD prototype was evaluated by samples of teachers in Indiana and Oregon; it received positive ratings from users regarding its feasibility and acceptance. Research is being planned to investigate the technical features and psychometric characteristics of this web prototype. We see the web-based screening system as a cost-effective way to expand the application of regular, annual screenings of students in the elementary grades.

Marquez and Yeaton (in press) developed the PMT, a web-based system that allows universal screening for social and academically related forms of classroom behavior considered critically important for school success. The PMT contains a 12-item screener that allows teachers to simultaneously evaluate and rate all students, item by item, on the degree to which they display acceptable levels of target behaviors according to the following scale: (a) at mastery, (b) needs improvement, and (c) cause for concern. The PMT screening items also allow for progress monitoring over time of individual student performance on specific target skills by applying a Likert-type scaling dimension to the target behaviors that are rated by teachers as *cause for concern* during universal screening, Teachers can monitor the student's performance several times a week by assigning a rating ranging from 1 (*Resisting*) to 6 (*Responding*) to reflect their evaluation of the target student's performance.

Although not designed as a multiple-gating screener, the PMT and its 12-item skills inventory can easily accommodate a number of multiple gates or assessment stages and types of data. The PMT's software allows for the integration of the PMT's engine, scaling methodology, and instrumentation into a functional online software application. The PMT software development process relied on an iterative approach, known as Agile, that breaks software development tasks into small increments with short development time frames. The PMT provides significant online user support in the form of online tutorials, which include (a) training in the student rating process, (b) an overview of the PMT and its components, and instructions on (c) how to set up a class, (d) how to progress monitor, and (e) how to use graphs for decision making. The PMT also contains a help desk, a frequently asked questions feature, and print instruction sheets. The PMT is undergoing continuing testing and evaluation for the functions of universal screening, progress monitoring, and analysis of classroom behavior patterns.

We anticipate a rapid expansion in web-based and online approaches to screening and progress monitoring over the next few years. Although much is expected of these applications, substantial research will be required to establish their superiority over existing forms and methods of screening. At the very least, they should provide greater ease of use, cost efficiency, and acceptance by consumers.

LESSONS LEARNED AND RECOMMENDATIONS FOR HOW AND WHEN TO USE MULTIPLE-GATING PROCEDURES

A number of important lessons have emerged from our work in this study and in subsequent studies utilizing the SSBD to identify behaviorally at-risk students. In the current environment of shrinking budgets and limited resources, adherence to the recommended SSBD scoring procedures is preferable, especially in real-world schooling contexts in which students are being identified for special education services. For research purposes, we have combined the SSBD exit criteria with a severity ranking and have begun to incorporate teacher preference into the identification procedure. We suggest that project staff not only describe why one student has been targeted over another but also involve teachers in the decision-making process from the beginning and target a student based on teacher preference in cases in which multiple students meet full inclusion criteria and present similar severity levels. A participatory approach to student identification can create an open and shared understanding of the screening process and simultaneously strengthen a teacher's commitment to evidence-based programming and the promotion of related program outcomes.

The following example illustrates how we have dealt with teacher preference issues in a large-scale randomized controlled trial (Walker et al., 2009). We initially screened general education classrooms and applied strict SSBD exit criteria. The students who met full exit criteria were then rank ordered and recruited in order based on the severity of their externalizing behavior. In some classrooms, students who met full exit criteria often had similar raw scores on the CEI, maladaptive behavior index, and adaptive behavior index. In these cases, we incorporated teacher preference into our severity ranking procedure to identify the student to be targeted for inclusion in the study. We have found that when a discrepancy exists between who the teacher nominates as first-ranked at gate 1 and who ultimately is identified and targeted for study inclusion after application of gate 2 exit criteria and severity ranking procedures, this discrepancy can lead to increased frustration and reduced buy-in from the teacher. This phenomenon can negatively affect the teacher's overall motivation, quality of implementation efforts, and expectations regarding the individual student's capacity for change. To address this issue, we suggest, the screening process should be clearly explained to teachers from the outset, including explanation not only of gate 1 and 2 procedures but also of how students pass through gate 2 and why one student might be targeted over another. This discussion should be framed within the theoretical framework of the screening tool and the proposed intervention.

Whenever possible, it is recommended that teachers receive training in how the multiple-gating process works, what they can expect from it, and why it is being conducted. As a rule, this training can be combined with the actual screening process. It typically takes just over 1 hour for teachers in a school to screen their students through gates 1 and 2. In a 1.5- to 2-hour after-school meeting, the school staff can receive training in the SSBD procedures and also conduct the screening. The PAM investigators found, as we have, that such training is associated with higher quality ratings and fewer implementation issues and challenges.

During the gate 1 teacher nomination process, a teacher may subjectively prioritize certain student behaviors over others. Administration of gate 2 scales, however, encourages the teacher to assess each student systematically on a set of research-validated items that spans a broad array of specific areas for preventive intervention. Thus, at gate 1, a teacher may nominate a student who (a) may not be eligible at gate 2 or (b) may not benefit most from the services being offered from a specific evidence-based program. If, for example, a teacher nominates a student at gate 1 whom she or he considers as at risk due to factors outside the classroom context or due to behaviors that do not fall into the externalizing behavior domain of the SSBD, the student might score in the normative range on the SSBD gate 2 scales and thus be deemed ineligible for participation or services. Also, if students are being targeted to receive a behavioral intervention focused on reducing challenging behavior and promoting social competence, a student who is nominated at gate 1 for behaviors or environmental factors outside the scope of the intervention is unlikely to benefit from the services being offered in the classroom.

We recommend that multiple-gating procedures be conducted three times annually to (a) adequately identify students who have behavioral issues and may be in need of referral or exposure to pre-referral intervention procedures, (b) detect students whose behavioral levels may have deteriorated over time, and (c) screen for new students during the school year who may be in need of supports and services. General education teachers should have at least 5–6 weeks of exposure to their students before being asked to conduct a classwide screening. A second screening around January and a third during March or early April would be optimal.

As is well known, the underservice of students with emotional and behavioral challenges in general education schooling contexts continues to be highly problematic. Teachers are especially unlikely to refer struggling students at rates that match prevalence of these challenges in the K–12 population, which is conservatively estimated at 5–7% (Forness, Kim, & Walker, 2012). Universal screening that can be accomplished efficiently and accurately is an important solution to this problem, but it should be embedded within a three-tiered intervention framework, such as PBIS, or be an integral component of a comprehensive prevention–intervention approach, such as that recommended by Levitt et al. (2007). School staff and administrators are reluctant to positively screen for students for whom they do not see existing and viable treatment, referral, placement, or accommodation options. The enabling features of universal screening regarding the prevention and remediation of both social–behavioral and academic challenges have to be a key element of school-based advocacy and promotion of their use.

Finally, the issue of using in vivo behavioral observations as a third screening gate in systems such as the SSBD has become problematic. This is a lightly used, third-stage option within the SSBD procedure, even though the AET and PSB codes are technically adequate, relatively easy to use, and nationally normed. It appears that the time pressures on school personnel who would be charged with conducting AET and PSB are too intense to justify the perceived benefit of doing so. This is unfortunate, but it appears to be a normative practice. We recommend that, at the very least, an archival records search or a functional behavioral assessment be conducted for all students who meet exit criteria for SSBD screening gate 2. The PBIS approach has developed effective and accepted methods for conducting both of these assessment procedures (Horner et al., 2009).

CONCLUSION

The current interest levels in proactive, universal screening systems and outcomes surpass anything we have seen in the past three decades. Whatever the reasons for it, this strong interest is regarded as a positive development in our field because it allows for the initiation of effective prevention approaches wherein advances in early intervention can be implemented and coordinated across appropriate agencies. The dual screening–intervention model described by Levitt et al. (2007) holds great potential for improving school-based, mental health outcomes if it can be operationalized and delivered in a way that is acceptable to schools. The content of the material in this volume focuses on advances in screening and identification methods that will substantially improve our ability to accomplish more timely and effective approaches to prevention.

Plans are in place to revise the SSBD gate 2 measures and to expand and update the normative database on them. We plan to retain the brief adaptive behavior rating scale in gate 2 but also to develop two brief scales that would target, respectively, externalizing and internalizing behavioral dimensions directly. In its current form, the differentiation of externalizing from internalizing students occurs only in screening gate 1. We anticipate that these more targeted BBR scales will allow for better discrimination of students representing these two behavioral dimensions and will have greater relevance in matching the results of assessment to the task of intervention planning.

Some careful work is needed to align available screening and assessment methods with each of the three tiers within an RTI-type model. So far, satisfactory achievement of this goal remains elusive as to feasibility and efficacy. Although not designed or conceptualized for use in an RTI-type context, the SSBD has the potential to partially address this issue. There are five possible applications for its use within an RTI context: (a) as universal screening to identify students who likely will require Tier 2 and 3 supports;

(b) as assessments for monitoring performance within tiers and determining when to move to a different tier; (c) as an information source for designing interventions; (d) as a vehicle for planning staff training based on analysis of gate 2 behavior ratings; and (e) as one outcome measure of schoolwide interventions (Walker, Severson, & Seeley, 2010). The work of Gresham et al. (2010) on this issue seems especially promising in blending teacher judgments with progress monitoring of student social behavior that supports academic performance and social skills.

It will be interesting to see how the practice and methodology of screening develop over the next few years. Given the impressive work on developing BBR scales and the emergent use of computer technology in assessment that have occurred over the past decade, we believe that multiple-gating screening approaches are an especially useful vehicle for incorporating these exciting innovations and maximizing their value.

REFERENCES

August, G. J., Realmuto, G., Crosby, R., & MacDonald, A. (1995). Community-based multiple-gate screening of children at risk for conduct disorder. *Journal of Abnormal Child Psychology, 23*, 521–544. doi:10.1007/BF01447212

Bennett, K. J., Lipman, E. L., Brown, S., Racine, Y., Boyle, M. H., & Offord, D. R. (1999). Predicting conduct problems: Can high-risk children be identified in kindergarten and Grade 1? *Journal of Consulting and Clinical Psychology, 67*, 470–480. doi:10.1037/0022-006X.67.4.470

Caldarella, P., Young, E., Richardson, M., Young, B., & Young, K. (2008). Validation of the Systematic Screening for Behavior Disorders in middle and junior high school. *Journal of Emotional and Behavioral Disorders, 16*, 105–117. doi:10.1177/1063426607313121

Chafouleas, S., Volpe, R., Gresham, F., & Cook, C. (2010). School-based behavioral assessment within problem-solving models: Current status and future directions. *School Psychology Review, 39*, 343–349.

Charlebois, M., Leblanc, M., Gagnon, C., & Larivee, S. (1994). Methodological issues in multiple-gating screening procedures for antisocial behaviors in elementary students. *Remedial and Special Education, 15*, 44–54. doi:10.1177/074193259401500107

Cronbach, L. J., & Gleser, G. C. (1965). *Psychological tests and personnel decisions* (2nd ed.). Urbana: University of Illinois Press.

Duerr Evaluation Resources. (2007). *Early mental health initiative statewide evaluation report for 2006/07*. Chico, CA: Author.

Elliott, S., & Gresham, F. (2007). *Social skills improvement system: Intervention guide*. Bloomington, MN: Pearson Assessments.

Forness, S., Kim, J., & Walker, H. (2012). Prevalence of students with EBD: Impact on general education. *Beyond Behavior, 21*(2), 3–10.

Gerber, M., & Semmel, M. (1984). Teacher as imperfect test: Reconceptualizing the referral process. *Educational Psychologist, 19,* 137–148. doi:10.1080/00461528409529290

Gresham, F. (2005). Response to intervention: An alternative means of identifying students as emotionally disturbed. *Education and Treatment of Children, 28,* 328–344.

Gresham, F., Cook, C., Collins, T., Dart, E., Rasetshwane, K., Truelson, E., & Grant, S. (2010). Developing a change-sensitive brief behavior rating scale as a progress monitoring tool for social behavior: An example using the Social Skills Rating System—Teacher Form. *School Psychology Review, 39,* 364–379.

Hawkins, J. D., Catalano, R., Kosterman, R., Abbott, R., & Hill, K. (1999). Preventing adolescent health-risk behaviors by strengthening protection during childhood. *Archives of Pediatrics and Adolescent Medicine, 153,* 226–234. doi:10.1001/archpedi.153.3.226

Horner, R., Sugai, G., Smolkowski, K., Eber, L., Nakasato, J., Todd, A. W., & Esperanza, J. (2009). A randomized, wait-list controlled trial assessing school-wide positive behavior support in elementary schools. *Journal of Positive Behavior Interventions, 11,* 133–144. doi:10.1177/1098300709332067

Hsiao, J. K., Bartko, J., & Potter, W. (1989). Diagnosing diagnoses: Receiver operating characteristic methods and psychiatry. *Archives of General Psychiatry, 46,* 664–667. doi:10.1001/archpsyc.1989.01810070090014

Kamphaus, R., Thorpe, J., Winsor, A., Kroncke, A., Dowdy, E., & VanDeventer, M. (2007). Development and predictive validity of a teacher screener for child behavioral and emotional problems at school. *Educational and Psychological Measurement, 67,* 342–356. doi:10.1177/00131644070670021001

Kilgus, S. P., Chafouleas, S. M., Riley-Tillman, T. C., & Welsh, M. (2012). Direct behavior rating scales as screeners: A preliminary investigation of diagnostic accuracy in elementary school. *School Psychology Quarterly, 27,* 41–50. doi:10.1037/a0027150

Lane, K., Menzies, H., Oakes, W., & Kalberg, J. (2012). *Systematic screenings of behavior to support instruction: From preschool to high school.* New York, NY: Guilford Press.

Lane, K., Oakes, W., Harris, P., Menzies, H., Cox, M., & Lambert, W. (2012). Initial evidence for the reliability and validity of the Student Risk Screening Scale for internalizing and externalizing behaviors at the elementary level. *Behavioral Disorders, 37,* 99–122.

Levitt, J., Saka, N., Romanelli, L., & Hoagwood, K. (2007). Early identification of mental health problems in schools: The status of instrumentation. *Journal of School Psychology, 45,* 163–191. doi:10.1016/j.jsp.2006.11.005

Lochman, J. E., & the Conduct Problems Prevention Research Group. (1995). Screening of child behavior problems for prevention programs at school entry.

Journal of Consulting and Clinical Psychology, 63, 549–559. doi:10.1037/0022-006X.63.4.549

Loeber, R., Dishion, T. J., & Patterson, G. R. (1984). Multiple gating: A multistage assessment procedure for identifying youths at risk for delinquency. *Research in Crime and Delinquency, 21*, 7–32. doi:10.1177/0022427884021001002

Maag, J. W., & Katsiyannis, A. (2008). The medical model to block eligibility for students with EBD: A response-to-intervention alternative. *Behavioral Disorders, 33*, 184–194.

Marquez, B., & Yeaton, P. (in press). Progress monitoring methods and tools for behavioral performance. In H. Walker & F. Gresham (Eds.), *Handbook of research in emotional and behavioral disorders*. New York, NY: Guilford Press.

McConaughy, S., & Achenbach, T. (1989). Empirically-based assessment of serious emotional disturbance. *Journal of School Psychology, 27*, 91–117. doi:10.1016/0022-4405(89)90035-6

Merrell, K. (1999). *Behavioral, social, and emotional assessment of children and adolescents*. Mahwah, NJ: Erlbaum.

Merrell, K. (2010). Better methods, better solutions: Developments in school-based behavioral assessment. *School Psychology Review, 39*, 422–426.

Murphy, J. M., Burwick, D., Weinstein, M., Boris, J., Budman, S., & Klerman, G. (1987). Performance of screening and diagnostic tests: Application of receiver operating characteristics analysis. *Archives of General Psychiatry, 44*, 550–555. doi:10.1001/archpsyc.1987.01800180068011

Nelson, R., Benner, G., Reid, R., Epstein, M., & Currin, D. (2002). The convergent validity of office discipline referrals with the CBCL-TRF. *Journal of Emotional and Behavioral Disorders, 10*, 181–188. doi:10.1177/10634266020100030601

Seeley, J. R., Stice, E., & Rohde, P. (2009). Screening for depression prevention: Identifying adolescent girls at high risk for future depression. *Journal of Abnormal Psychology, 118*, 161–170. doi:10.1037/a0014741

Sugai, G., & Horner, R. (2002). The evolution of discipline practices: School-wide positive behavior supports. *Child and Family Behavior Therapy, 24*, 23–50. doi:10.1300/J019v24n01_03

Walker, H., Horner, R., Sugai, G., Bullis, M., Sprague, J., Bricker, D., & Kaufman, M. (1996). Integrated approaches to preventing school antisocial behavior. *Journal of Emotional and Behavioral Disorders, 4*, 194–209. doi:10.1177/106342669600400401

Walker, H., & McConnell, S. (1995). *The Walker–McConnell Scale of Social Competence and School Adjustment*. San Diego, CA: Singular.

Walker, H., Seeley, J., Small, J., Severson, H., Graham, B., Feil, E., . . . Forness, S. (2009). A randomized controlled trial of the First Step to Success early intervention: Demonstration of program efficacy outcomes within a diverse urban school district. *Journal of Emotional and Behavioral Disorders, 17*, 197–212. doi:10.1177/1063426609341645

Walker, H., & Severson, H. (1990). *The Systematic Screening for Behavior Disorders (SSBD) procedure*. Longmont, CO: Sopris West.

Walker, H., Severson, H., & Feil, E. (1995). *The Early Screening Project: A proven child-find process*. Longmont, CO: Sopris West.

Walker, H., Severson, H., Naquin, G., D'Atrio, C., Feil, E., Hawken, L., & Sabey, C. (2010). Implementing universal screening systems within an RTI-PBS context. In B. Doll, W. Pfohl, & J. Yoon (Eds.), *Handbook of youth prevention science* (pp. 96–120). New York, NY: Routledge.

Walker, H., Severson, H., & Seeley, J. (2010). Universal, school-based screening for the early detection of behavioral problems contributing to later destructive outcomes. In M. Shinn & H. Walker (Eds.), *Interventions for achievement and behavior problem in a three-tier model including RTI* (pp. 677–702). Bethesda, MD: National Association of School Psychologists.

Walker, H., Yell, M., & Murray, C. (in press). Identifying EBD students in the context of schooling using the federal definition of ED definition: Where we've been, where we are, and where we need to go. In P. Garner, J. Kauffman, & J. Elliott (Eds.), *The handbook of emotional and behavioural difficulties*. Thousand Oaks, CA: Sage.

Werthamer-Larsson, L., Kellam, S., & Wheeler, L. (1991). Effects of first-grade classroom environment on shy behavior, aggressive behavior, and concentration problems. *American Journal of Community Psychology, 19*, 585–602. doi:10.1007/BF00937993

II

DEVELOPING, EVALUATING, AND IMPLEMENTING SCREENING

4

DEVELOPING AND EVALUATING SCREENING SYSTEMS: PRACTICAL AND PSYCHOMETRIC CONSIDERATIONS

THEODORE J. CHRIST AND PETER M. NELSON

This chapter provides a brief and applied summary of the psychometric foundations for screening in schools. According to the *Standards for Educational and Psychological Testing*, a screening assessment "is used to make broad categorizations of examinees as a first step in selection decisions or diagnostic processes" (the *Standards*; American Educational Research Association, American Psychological Association, & National Council on Measurement in Education [AERA, APA, & NCME], 1999, p. 182; for other definitions, see Chapter 1, this volume).

Reasons to use school-based assessments vary widely. With the increased use of school-based problem solving, it is beneficial to consider screening assessments as a means for accurate problem identification (Bransford & Stein, 1984; Deno, 1995, 2005). In general, a problem exists when there is a discrepancy between what is expected and what is observed. In schools, both formal and informal procedures are used to screen for potential problems.

http://dx.doi.org/10.1037/14316-004
Universal Screening in Educational Settings: Evidence-Based Decision Making for Schools, R. J. Kettler, T. A. Glover, C. A. Albers, and K. A. Feeney-Kettler (Editors)
Copyright © 2014 by the American Psychological Association. All rights reserved.

Parents, teachers, administrators, and a variety of school-based specialists have expectations for students. They informally observe students and attend to discrepancies between what they expect and what is observed. Student performances that violate those expectations trigger the perception of a problem. For example, a teacher might notice that Timmy does not know his letters in first grade and this is atypical or that Margaret bites her peers when engaged in conflict. More experienced teachers develop internal norms that are refined through repeated interactions and observations of children. Student performances that diverge from these norms are more likely to draw the attention of the teacher. Consequently, many students are referred for services or further observations on the basis of one or more persons' perception of a problem.

Historically, person-based perception was the primary method to screen for a variety of problems, including physical health, mental health, and educational health; however, formal screenings for the most salient problems have developed substantially over the past 100 years. In education, this work began in France with Alfred Binet, who developed the Binet scales to identify students with significant cognitive delays (Binet & Simon, 1905, 1908). In the 21st century, educational research includes a broad array of formal assessments. For our purposes in this chapter, formal assessments are those with technical documentation, which the user can review and evaluate to predict the quality of assessment outcomes. Informal assessments are those without technical documentation. Both formal and informal assessments are observations of behavior within a particular situation. It is from these observations that professionals in education derive an inference. In both cases, they often begin with a narrow sample of behavioral observations to infer broader conclusions. It is difficult to know the value of those conclusions, but quality assessment data allow them to derive and refine their inferences.

An inference is a conclusion derived from an incomplete set of information. It is difficult to discern the quality of such conclusions, because there is a leap from what is observed directly to what is inferred or concluded. This is particularly true for screening assessments in education. Although people use intuition to make many decisions in life, most agree that formal assessments—such as reliable and valid screening assessments—improve the quality of educational decisions. All assessments are imperfect, and it is certain that at least some inferences derived from formal assessment data will be wrong; however, an adequate review of the technical documentation that accompanies formal assessments should provide sufficient information to estimate the quality of data and resulting conclusions.

Ultimately, professionals in education must use screening data to make larger inferences regarding student ability and future performance. This is not a task to be taken lightly. We must be confident that the instruments we use for screening purposes are technically viable and that the resulting inferences are appropriate given the content of the instrument. The following sections discuss several critical components that guide test creation, but readers should note the direct correspondence between what is expected of those who create tests and what is expected of those who evaluate those tests for use in schools. To effectively evaluate, we must be familiar with appropriate instrumentation procedures.

The field of psychometrics is dedicated to the science of developing and evaluating formal assessments. It can be fairly technical at times, as you will experience in the latter sections of this chapter, but it is worthwhile to ensure that high-quality assessments are used for screening and that both inferences and decisions are supported by the intended purpose and available evidence for the assessment. To promote clarity, this chapter begins with an overview of test selection that provides a structure to the technical components that contribute to the credibility of screening assessments. It is critical for consumers to accurately judge the limitations and strengths of existing screening assessments. Thus, the remainder of the chapter explores relevant theories and components of test development, providing sufficient background for those tasked with selecting and evaluating screening assessments.

TEST REVIEW AND SELECTION

The material that is relevant for test review is extensive. Thus, the review of screening instruments might divide the process into two phases: initial review and thorough review. The initial search and review are guided by the following questions: (a) What is the purpose and domain of the assessment? (b) Who is qualified for administration and scoring (and what training is necessary)? (c) Who are the students with whom the assessment is used, and which assessments are most relevant for the population (age, grade, ethnicity, disabilities/abilities)? (d) Is group or individual administration preferred? (e) What resources are necessary to implement the test? and (f) Is there technical documentation? Tests that do not meet the purpose, require too many resources, have limited relevance to your student population, or lack technical documentation can be dismissed without further review.

There are a variety of useful sources for test reviews. Many journals print reviews, and a number of online resources are available, such as the Buros Institute's *Mental Measurements Yearbook* (http://buros.unl.edu) and the National Center on Response to Intervention (http://www.rti4success. org). Such reviews are useful for both experts and nonexperts, but they should be used only to inform the initial review.

A more thorough review should follow the initial review. This requires some basic knowledge of psychometrics; in particular, it requires a familiarity with the test development process, prevailing psychometric models, and test validation. What follows is a brief description of the test development process and the technical documentation that test users should expect from test developers. Standard procedures for test development serve as a framework for test evaluation. Last, we summarize this information into a checklist that can be used by consumers to evaluate screening assessments (see Table 4.1).

TABLE 4.1
Checklist for Psychometric Review of Screeners

General criteria for review	Present?
1 Overview and purpose of the assessment	
Philosophical and theoretical basis	☐
Rationale for application as a screener	☐
Theoretical content model	☐
Theoretical psychometric model	☐
Eligible population of examiners	☐
Eligible population of examinees	☐
2 Description of the assessment	
Content definition	☐
Test specification (blueprint)	☐
Methods for item development and review (bias, relevance and completeness)	☐
Test design	☐
Test assembly	☐
Administration procedures	☐
3 Technical characteristics	
Field-testing design	☐
Participant group for field-testing	☐
Test theory for analysis	☐
Item statistics (difficulties, discrimination, point-by-serial or theta domains, subdomains)	☐
Test statistics	☐
Reliability	☐
Standard error of measurement	☐
Linking or equating (alternate tests, forms)	☐
4 Validation	
Content validity	☐
Criterion validity	☐
Group comparisons (evaluate diversity and bias)	☐
Coherent argument for validation	☐
5 Score reporting	
Score reporting	☐
Relative and absolute interpretation of scores	☐
Standard setting	☐
Decision statistics	☐
6 Supporting references	

DEVELOPMENT AND DOCUMENTATION
OF MEASURES FOR SCREENING

Substantial guidance for evaluating a test is provided in the *Standards* (AERA et al., 1999)—and especially within the chapter on supporting documentation for tests—with useful interpretations and extrapolations published in the professional literature (Buckendahl & Plake, 2006; Linn, 2006). The nature and purpose of documentation should support an independent evaluation by those responsible for test selection (Standards 6.2, 6.15) about the "nature and quality of the tests, the resulting scores, and the interpretations based on the test scores" (AERA et al., 1999, p. 67). Such materials include technical manuals, reports, user guides, and stimulus materials. Those materials should provide clarity as to the content (6.2) along with appropriate uses for the test and resulting test scores. At a minimum, documentation includes descriptions of eligible examiners (6.7) and examinee populations (6.4), appropriate and inappropriate applications and interpretations of test scores (6.3, 6.8, 6.10), and supporting validity and reliability evidence (6.6). Specific evidence and justification are necessary to support any proposed cut scores, benchmarks, or normative interpretations.

Test Development: 12 Steps

Downing (2006) provided a 12-step process for test development, which is described in substantial detail in the edited text *Handbook of Test Development* (Downing & Haladyna, 2006). Other detailed and useful information can be found in the fourth edition of *Educational Measurement* (Brennan, 2006).

The first four steps in test development represent the critical beginning to establish the foundation and direction for all other activities. Step 1 is to devise the overall plan that defines the purpose and direction for development. This includes the intended use along with the psychometric model for development and scoring. In Step 2, the content definition must emerge. This definition often will result from a systematic analysis of the domain (e.g., scope and sequence of curricula) and available standards, along with the judgment of subject matter experts. The content definition will define the breadth of the assessment. In Step 3, the test specifications or blueprint is developed to detail all of the major test characteristics. Characteristics include test and item format, content balance (items per subdomain or standard), number of items on each test, cognitive classification system (Bloom's or Webb's taxonomy), type of stimuli (textual, pictorial), item scoring rules (binary, weighted, partial credit), and methods for test interpretation (norm or criterion referenced). In Step 4, item development defines the item formats (open response, multiple choice) and item writing specifications. Item writing should include thorough training for item writers and a review process for issues of content, cognitive classification, bias, and diversity.

Once the purpose, domains, and items are defined, it is time for Step 5, test design and assembly. The form and complexity of this step will depend on whether the intent (as defined in Step 1) is to develop a single assessment or multiple parallel assessments as well as on whether the intent is to develop paper-and-pencil assessments or computer-based assessments (adaptive or nonadaptive). The process and product are largely defined by the test specifications (developed in Step 3). This step also addresses issues of content balancing, item-type balancing, format, font, and the like. In the case of adaptive testing, the method of dynamic item selection and test construction is operationalized; the process might include the use of item response theory (IRT), steps, staging, branching, testlets, or content balancing. Steps 6 and 7 are test production and administration, respectively. Standardization is operationalized and field-tested, often for the first time, based on previously defined test specifications. The conditions for standardization are a critical aspect of validity and must be well defined.

Steps 8 and 9 are scoring responses and standard setting, respectively. Scoring often is straightforward with multiple-choice scanned or computer-based administrations; however, scoring can get rather complex if there are constructed or performance-type responses. It is necessary to develop and systematically evaluate the accuracy, consistency, and validity of scoring routines. The required evidence increases when the methods for scoring require more skills or are less objective. At a minimum, item analysis is carried out to provide evidence of the distribution of item responses with raw and scaled scores, item difficulties, interitem relationships, and item-to-total-score relationships. This is also the point at which linking and equating studies, which are used in many operational tests, are conducted or validated. In addition, many assessments require some cut scores, which require standard setting. That is, the test development process must address the question, "How much skill or ability defines passing?" The primary methods are those of relative and absolute standard setting. The relative method establishes a cut score, which is based on an analysis of the distribution of scores in a sample or population, so that 80% of students might be expected to pass, for example. The absolute method establishes a cut score based on analyses by content experts as to the knowledge—or types of items—that examinees should master, or it is based on an analysis of examinee performances who are at defined points in the scale (e.g., borderline, close to passing, clearly not passing, clearly passing).

Step 10 is reporting examination results, which must be done to promote valid interpretations and use of test scores. Test developers typically provide a context for interpretation, which should include definitions of purpose and domain along with a confidence interval for each reported score. Moreover, the mechanisms for score reporting should ensure that the information is both accurate and timely for the intended use. Step 11 is item banking. Items are expensive to develop and field test. It is common to value well-developed individual test items at $300 to $1,000 each. Test items often can be reused to establish alternate forms or alternate tests, and most operational testing programs have a bank of items for ongoing use. Finally, Step 12 develops and finalizes the technical report. The report includes a description of the development process, administration and scoring requirements, reporting procedures, interpretive guidelines, test analysis, and evaluation. Evaluation includes evidence for reliability and validity for the proposed use of the test.

Modified and Alternate Assessments

Technical documentation should depict the target population of examinees and define the appropriateness for use with various student groups (e.g., English language learners or children with disabilities; AERA et al., 1999; Becker & Pomplun, 2006). If relevant, documentation might provide a continuum of options to promote participation of all or most students. Such a continuum of options spans the standard test stimuli and procedures with and without defined accommodations (e.g., enlarged print), nonstandard modified stimuli and procedures, and alternate assessment options. Guidelines for the comparability and possible aggregation of scores across forms and populations should be provided. In addition, validity evidence is necessary to support interpretation and use of the modified and alternate forms of the test.

Test Documentation: Six Chapters

It should be apparent that effective item and test development is a resource and time-intensive process. Thus, it is critical for test developers to document relevant work and establish clear documentation for consumers— especially consumers familiar with effective test development. In general, the documentation for a test should faithfully and thoroughly represent the 12-step procedures and outcomes. The technical documentation might be organized to include approximately six chapters (Buckendahl & Plake, 2006). Chapter 1 presents an overview and purpose of the assessment, which defines the philosophical and theoretical basis for the assessment along with intended target population of examiners and examinees. Chapter 2 presents a description of the assessment to summarize the test development process: content definition, test specifications and blueprint, item development (review, field-testing, selection), and test design and assembly. Chapter 3 summarizes the technical characteristics, such as the target population and sampling methods, item and test statistics, scaling, equating and linking descriptions, and reliability information. Chapter 4 presents the evidence and argument for validity, which defines the content, criterion validity, group comparisons (diversity and bias), decision statistics (decision accuracy), standard setting and cut scores, and other related evidence. Chapter 5 summarizes score reporting, such as the types of scores and interpretive guidelines. Finally, Chapter 6 should provide supporting references used to bolster various claims throughout (Becker & Pomplun, 2006; Buckendahl & Plake, 2006).

Table 4.1 includes a useful checklist for the evaluation of screening assessments. In Table 4.1, the general criteria for review are outlined in a manner commensurate with typical technical documentation. The utility of the checklist is largely dependent on the degree to which readers grasp some of the more technical components of this chapter. Although previous subsections were intended to provide the big picture for test development, the remaining discussion expands on the concepts of test development and documentation to provide sufficient background for evaluation. Again, although a checklist is useful for evaluation, consumers should be familiar with the basic theories and psychometric concepts presented in technical manuals. A working knowledge of the concepts discussed in these sections is requisite for the effective evaluation of screening assessments.

RELEVANT PSYCHOMETRIC THEORIES

Psychometrics is a theoretically oriented science dedicated to the study of measurement procedures and outcomes. Three prevailing psychometric theories include classical test theory (CTT), generalizability theory (GT), and IRT. Closely related is validity theory. The most central models related to each theory are presented and briefly discussed in the following section. Appropriate interpretation of specific screening assessments and the resulting inferences imposes some understanding of the underlying psychometric theory. Strengths and weaknesses are associated with the common theories that guide test development, and it is helpful to recognize these characteristics when evaluating screening assessments.

Latent Trait and Theory

The role of the latent trait is important in psychometric theory. A latent trait is a semihidden characteristic of an individual that explains—or causes—a person's performance on relevant tasks. Intelligence and domain-specific abilities (e.g., reading and math) are good examples of latent traits.

The magnitude of a person's math ability might be inferred or estimated from observations of that person's performance on a variety of tasks. Assessments are developed to optimize the selection and arrangement of tasks and scoring systems to best estimate the state of a student's math ability at the time of assessment.

In the case of screening, each student's ability in the particular domain (e.g., math) is fixed when the screener is administered. The use of the term *ability*—or latent trait—does not suggest in any way that general intelligence, reading, or math abilities are fixed. Ability is malleable and is influenced by instruction. In the context of psychometrics, traits reference an underlying pattern of performances on related tasks at a particular point in time. The level of a student's ability presumably will influence performance on the screener at the time of assessments. Students with lower abilities will receive lower scores, and students with higher abilities will receive higher scores. Although this generally holds true, there is an imperfect relationship between student performance on a particular test administration and the level of the latent trait. Student performance on a particular test or item is the manifestation of an underlying trait. As such, observable student performances are described as a *manifest variable*, and the underlying trait is described as a *latent variable*. The first is observed directly and the latter is inferred. Latent trait theory is the foundation for CTT, GT, and IRT, which are described in turn in the following sections. A basic understanding of these theories provides the framework to consider the technical adequacy of screening tools. Many subtleties and variations of the concepts have been described. What follows is intended as a generic introduction.

Classical Test Theory

CTT was the foundation for most psychometric work in the first three quarters of the 20th century. The tenets of CTT were established by Spearman (1904, 1907, 1913), who proposed that the outcomes from educational and psychological measurements are test and sample dependent. This means that measurement outcomes depend on both the context of measurement (e.g., difficulty of test items) and the ability of the individuals who are assessed. This section briefly describes the tenets and implications of CTT.

True Score Model

The first assumption of CTT is that the observed test score is the sum of two theoretical components, the true score and the error score. Within the literature, the observed test score is denoted as X, the true score is denoted as T, and the error score is denoted as E. Using that notation, the true score model is denoted as $X = T + E$. Neither the true nor the error score can be observed directly. Instead, the true score and the error score are theoretical values that are used to explain and analyze the inconsistencies in test scores across repeated measurements with alternate raters, occasions, or forms. Stated another way, the observed scores and estimates of true score substantially depend on the measurement process. True scores across measurement instruments and alternate forms are not necessarily equivalent.

Sample-Dependent Behavior

A test is developed to estimate the true score value for a particular characteristic. For example, curriculum-based measurement in reading (CBM-R) often is described as an indicator of early reading development. Each person has an underlying ability (or skill set) to rapidly decode words in connected text. That characteristic is demonstrated and assessed within the specific conditions of a CBM-R test (specific observation) and is extrapolated to the student's reading ability (broader inference). Thus, CBM-R often operates as a screener for reading ability. Nevertheless, it is erroneous to expect that an individual is likely to receive the same score across test forms unless they are parallel; that is, equivalent in both content and score distribution. In practice, parallel forms are difficult or impossible to achieve. The solution is either to depart from the parallel test assumption and transform the observed test scores onto a common scale (e.g., z scores) or to use one of the common methods to equate alternate forms. In practice, raw scores are used rarely in educational and psychological assessment. Scaled scores, such as standard scores ($M = 100$, $SD = 15$), t scores ($M = 50$, $SD = 10$), and z scores ($M = 0$, $SD = 1$), or some other arbitrary scale (ACT: $M = 21$, $SD = 5$), are much more common.

Just as estimates of true score depend on the sample of items that make up a test, estimates of item and test characteristics depend on the sample of examinees. Item characteristics, such as item difficulty and proportion correct, depend on the performance of the sample group. Test characteristics, such as the mean, variance, and reliability, are also sample dependent. Moreover, CTT has a limited flexibility to evaluate items independently of a fixed test. The majority of analysis and procedures have been developed to evaluate test outcomes and not particular items. Of primary concern for consumers is the lack of specificity associated with the error term in CTT. It is likely that differences in test content and administration context will influence students' scores, but the error associated with these differences is not partitioned to allow for more detailed consideration of the appropriateness of the assessment for any given context.

Generalizability Theory

GT is a more flexible extension of CTT that defines each behavior sample (i.e., student response or behavior) as a potential estimate of the universe score. The language and conception of an observed score are replaced with reference to *observations*, or samples of behavior. The universe score is distinct from the notion of true score (in CTT) because it incorporates alternate nonparallel measures. It is the average level of performance for every admissible observation. The definition of every admissible observation may be broad or narrow, depending on the intended use of assessment data. For example, CBM-R procedures might be used to estimate the universe score on third-grade probes as administered by a school psychologist in a quiet test room. Alternatively, CBM-R procedures might be used to estimate the universe score on second- through fourth-grade curriculum samples that are administered by either a school psychologist or a paraprofessional in the setting of either a classroom or a test room.

The minor shifts in language noted thus far represent more substantial shifts in test theory. The conditions of assessment are not strictly fixed before field-testing and norming. Instead, the potential dimensions for behavior samples and assessment are defined by measurement facets, which can be tinkered with after field-testing to establish the most efficient assessment procedure. These facets define the relationship between particular observations and the universe of generalization and provide valuable information for those interested in using the assessment. In the aforementioned CBM-R example, GT can be used to analyze either the former, more restrictive scenario or the latter, more general scenario. The latter case includes more facets, which are domains of generalization such as probe difficulty, rater, and setting, whose levels might influence the outcomes of assessment.

Many possible CBM-R contexts, or facets, might characterize observations and the corresponding universe of generalization. In fact, the total number of possible observations is too large to observe them all. In general, GT provides a framework for analyzing the accuracy of generalizing one or more observations to estimate the universe score. Moreover, analyses can be conducted to examine the relative influence of multiple facets of measurement or of multiple interpretations of assessment outcomes. This is done with a series of generalizability and dependability studies. A generalizability study (G-study) is used to estimate the proportion of measurement variance associated with the objects of measurement, which are usually people, facets of measurement, relevant interactions, and error. A decision study (D-study) is used to establish the accuracy of generalization from one observed score to the universe of possible scores for an individual (Brennan, 2003). D-studies are used to estimate the accuracy and sufficiency of a test score to estimate the universe score. The universe of generalization can be specified to include any or all of the facets from a G-study.

Item Response Theory

IRT is prominent in contemporary test development. As the name implies, the primary focus of IRT is the item rather than the test. It emerged in the 1950s when Lord observed that a relationship existed between the latent trait of examinees and their performance on individual items (Lord, 1953; Lord & Novick, 1968). As previously described, CTT defines measurement outcomes as being test and sample dependent. In contrast, IRT defines both the latent trait and the difficulty of individual items that make up a test as being on the same scale. The difficulty of an item, therefore, is comparable to the trait of the individual. Put simply, a highly skilled reader is more likely than a less skilled reader to respond correctly to any given item. Moreover, the probability of a correct response on each item is conditional on the trait level of the examinee. For the sake of concision, further discussion is limited to unidimensional dichotomous IRT, which encompasses the most common model. Unidimensional indicates that the construct is singular and not multidimensional. Dichotomous indicates that all items can be scored as correct or incorrect, without partial credit or rating scale–type scoring.

Item Characteristic Curves

The item characteristic curve (ICC) defines the relationship between the latent trait and item responses. That is, the ICC defines the probability of a correct response on a particular item given a particular ability. The probability of a correct response on an item increases with the individual's ability on the trait. Individuals who are low on the trait are more likely to respond incorrectly, whereas individuals who are high on the trait are more likely to respond correctly. The ICC is a continuously increasing function with an S-shaped curve, or ogive (see Figure 4.1).

The ICC is defined differently by one-, two-, and three-parameter models. A one-parameter model defines the item by its difficulty, or the b parameter, which is typically in the range of −4 to 4. That difficulty parameter is on the same scale as ability. This links the ability estimate with item difficulty. In a one-parameter model, the difficulty of the item is the point in the ability range at which there is a 50% chance of a correct response. The upper left panel of Figure 4.1 illustrates ICCs for three items. Both the slopes and the intercepts for the lines are the same across items. The slopes are equal to one and the intercepts approximate zero. The difficulty parameter for Items 1, 2,

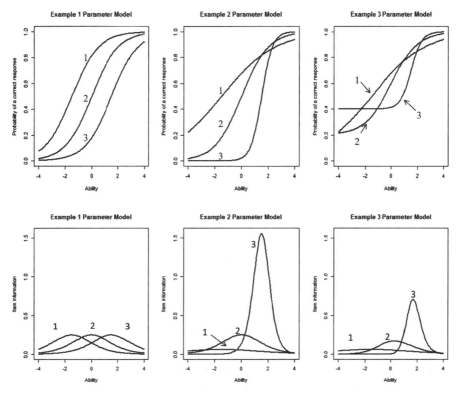

Figure 4.1. Item characteristic curves (top panel) and item information curves (bottom panel).

and 3 are −1.5, 0.0, and 1.5. Students with those respective abilities have a 50% probability of a correct response on the item. As is depicted graphically, the probability of a correct response increases or decreases based on the ability of the examinee. The magnitude of the change in the probability of a correct response is defined by the slope of the ICC.

A two-parameter model provides estimates for difficulty (*b* parameter) and for discrimination (*a* parameter) that are typically in the range of zero to three, with values above approximately one desirable. Common applications of the Rasch model (a special case of a one-parameter model) set difficulty to a value of one for all items, which is consistent with the examples of the one-parameter models described earlier. Discrimination defines the slope of the ICC at the point of the *b* parameter. That is, it defines the steepness of the line toward the middle of the ICC. A steeper slope provides more discrimination and thus more information about students with abilities that approximate the *b* parameter. This is illustrated graphically in the upper middle panel of Figure 4.1. The difficulty parameters for Items 1, 2, and 3 are −1.5, 0.0, and

1.5. The discrimination parameters for those items are 0.5, 1.0, and 1.5. A visual inspection of the ICCs for those items shows that the slope of the ICC, and therefore the discrimination, increases for Items 1, 2, and 3. Thus, Item 3 is the most discriminating item among the examples: Even a small increase in ability would result in a substantial increase in the probability of a correct response.

Finally, a three-parameter model includes difficulty, discrimination, and pseudoguessing, or the c parameter. The pseudoguessing parameter defines the intercept of the ICC, or the chance of a correct response for a person low on the ability scale. This parameter makes sense (to some) for multichoice items, because there is less-than-negligible probability of a correct response for students low on the ability continuum simply because the number of possible choices is limited (e.g., four choices on a multiple-choice exam). The upper right panel of Figure 4.1 illustrates three-parameter ICCs. Item 1 has difficulty, discrimination, and pseudoguessing parameters of 0.5, −1.5, and 0.0 (it is only the limited range of the ability scale that makes the item appear to have a guessing parameter). Item 2 has parameters of 1.0, 0.0, and 0.2, so that students very low on the ability scale (even below −4.0) have a 20% chance of selecting a correct response. Finally, Item 3 has parameters of 2.5, 1.5, and 0.4, so that students low on the scale have a 40% probability of a correct response. Like low slopes, higher pseudoguessing parameters undermine the amount of information that an item provides. There are other models and scenarios, but the models described here cover the vast majority of operational IRT-based testing applications.

Information

The function of each item is characterized by an ICC, and the characteristics defined in the previous section determine the information associated with each item, conditional on ability. Within the context of IRT, information is an extension of reliability in CTT. There is a specific relationship between the ICC and information, which is illustrated in Figure 4.1. Item information is defined and depicted by the item information function (IIF), as illustrated in the bottom panel of Figure 4.1 (note that each IIF aligns with the previously discussed ICCs). The information provided by an item peaks at a point that approximates the difficulty parameter, such that information is conditional on ability. In the case of two- and three-parameter models, items with higher discriminations tend to optimize information. In the case of three-parameter models, items with higher pseudoguessing parameters tend to yield less information at the lower end of the ability continuum.

All items on a test contribute information; however, the information provided by a particular item is maximized at a precise point on the ability continuum. In practice, high-quality items increase the efficiency and precision of computer adaptive testing. This is of particular benefit for screening assessments. Items with known difficulties, favorable discrimination values, and low pseudoguessing parameters increase the amount of information provided, thereby increasing the capability of screening assessments to estimate students' ability. The information on a test is defined and depicted by the test information function (TIF), which is merely the sum of IIF at each point of the ability continuum. Unlike CTT, the concept of information in IRT—as illustrated by the IIF and the TIF—provides critical insight as to the precision of ability estimates across the range that is useful for test construction, selection, and evaluation.

Applications of Test Theories

For consumers, it is most relevant to understand the inherent differences in perspective associated with CTT, GT, and IRT. As mentioned, CTT attributes all variance not associated with true score to error. This means that error associated with different raters, occasions, or administration methods is unaccounted for (it is considered simply as "error"). For measures with clear and specific administration procedures (e.g., CBM), consumers can be somewhat confident that contextual error will be minimized when the screening assessment is administered as intended; however, consumers will not know the relative impact of varying facets of assessment. GT involves a more detailed approach in which the variance associated with varying conditions is measured and accounted for. Thus, test developers who incorporate G- and D-studies may provide important evidence regarding (a) the magnitude of variance-associated important characteristics of the test and (b) the extent to which specific observations may be generalized across conditions.

Despite the extensive use of CTT, IRT has become increasingly prominent. Among other things, measurement outcomes in IRT are not sample or test dependent. The latent trait and the difficulty of individual items that make up a test are on the same scale. Thus, inferences regarding latent traits are tied intrinsically to individual items. Because measurement outcomes are tied to items, the need to establish parallel forms (as in CTT) is not applicable. In addition, the standard error of measurement (discussed in a later section) is not assumed to be constant. Rather, it differs across scores and depends largely on the alignment of the difficulty of items administered and the trait level of the student. It follows, then, that the commonly held notion that longer tests are necessary to obtain more reliable measurement outcomes may not apply. If students are administered items that provide a great deal of information about the intended trait for measurement, a precise estimate is possible from a limited number of items. The potential benefits of this concept are most evident in computer adaptive tests, which often depend on an IRT framework to select items for students in real time (e.g., aReading, STAR, Measures of Academic Progress [MAP]). The benefits of this approach in particular hold special relevance for screening, as it allows for broad estimates of ability in a short period of time.

For the consumer, the brief overview of CTT, GT, and IRT provided in this section highlights important distinctions in test development; however, it should be apparent that the information gleaned from this review is not entirely theoretical. The underlying theory for screening assessments has direct implications for the practical application of those assessments in schools. A general understanding of the benefits and limitations of different psychometric theories is requisite when comparing tests designed for similar purposes.

VALIDATION

> Measurement uses limited samples of behavior to draw general and abstract conclusions about persons or other units (e.g., classes, schools). To *validate* [emphasis added] an interpretation or use of measurements is to evaluate the rationale, or argument, for the claims being made, and this in turn requires a clear statement of the proposed interpretations. . . . Ultimately, the need for validation derives from the scientific and social requirement that public claims and decisions be justified. (Kane, 2006, p. 18)

There are two broad categories of validation. The first is conducted by the developer and is intended to provide evidence for a particular use of a measure. This first type of validation functions as an advocacy role, which guides the development of the assessment and promotes its use for a particular purpose. The second type is conducted by people other than the test developer. The assessment user manual documents the first type of validation. The research literature and published reviews often document the second type of validation. Although the second type of validation is not applicable when the technical documentation for screening assessments is reviewed, it objectively evaluates the plausibility of the proposed uses and interpretations. A thorough review of the evidence includes both types of validation; however, readers should note that the checklist in Table 4.1, as well as the discussion that follows, focuses heavily on the first type of validation. The following subsections address the classical notions of reliability and validity. This discussion is followed by a more comprehensive view of validation presented by Kane (2006).

Classical Notions of Reliability

Reliability evidence is an aspect of validation, because it contributes to the overall argument that test developers must make for the credibility of interpretations associated with the test. Furthermore, in a traditional sense, reliability is a prerequisite for validity: One must be measuring something reliably before there is evidence that one is measuring the right thing. The classical definition of reliability *is the consistency or precision of measurement when it is repeated.* There are four general categories of construct-irrelevant variance, or measurement error. These include (a) natural variation in student performances, (b) variation in the environment where assessments occur, (c) variation associated with processes and methods of assessment, and (d) variation associated with the selection or arrangement of test questions or behavior samples. These extraneous sources of variability in student performances contribute to the unreliability of measurement across time, situations, forms, and the like (Haertel, 2006). Such extraneous variation in student performances is treated as random variation—or measurement–model error—in most test theory. Unexplained variation in student performances is a problem. More extensive application of GT might substantially improve our understanding of test reliability and the influence of various facets; however, this section focuses on classical notions of reliability. Furthermore, classification accuracy and reliability (e.g., whether students are high risk) recently has received substantial attention, especially as it relates to screening (Good, Simmons, & Kame'enui, 2001; Silberglitt & Hintze, 2005) and diagnostic decisions (Macmann & Barnett, 1999). Classification accuracy can be considered relatively distinct from classical notions of reliability. It is addressed more explicitly within the discussion of Kane's (2006) framework for validation, which incorporates aspects of reliability and validity.

The classical notions of reliability include test–retest, alternate form, internal consistency, and interrater-related evidence (Haertel, 2006). Each of these is discussed in more detail in the following sections. All values are reported as the coefficient of reliability or Pearson product–moment correlation (ρ). The magnitude of this coefficient indicates how well the students are rank ordered across forms or conditions. It is typical to expect values of .70 to .80 for screening decisions and .90 for high-stakes decisions. Although those are good guidelines for evaluating whether a test is reliable, the concept of reliability is applied at the time of interpretation with a confidence interval based on the standard error of measurement (*SEM*). Every measure has some imprecision or standard error associated with its score. This was overlooked in the case of CBM-R for decades, but we illustrated that, in the case of CBM-R, reliabilities of .90 to .95 are often still associated with rather large magnitudes of *SEM* and corresponding confidence intervals (Christ & Silberglitt, 2007).

Parallel or *test–retest* reliability typically is derived with alternate administrations of parallel forms or the same form in proximity. It is desirable to use parallel forms, but in cases in which there is a single form, that often will have to suffice. *Alternate form* reliability is related closely to parallel and test–retest reliability. Alternate form reliability is the most desirable estimate when there are multiple forms of an assessment, because it represents different observations of student performances intended to assess the same latent trait. It is important, however, to attend to both the coefficient of reliability and the variation in the distribution of performances (M and SD), so that deviations in difficulty or discrimination are noted. Notwithstanding robust reliability, scaling and equating (i.e., establishing equivalence among scores on different forms) are often necessary to ensure valid interpretation and comparability across forms.

Internal consistency is derived by dividing performance on a single assessment into two or more component parts. Performance on those parts is then compared. For example, split-half reliability methods divide the assessment into two parts; often, odd and even items. The coefficient of reliability then is calculated and corrected with the Spearman–Brown prophecy formula. This correction is necessary to account for the unreliability of two shorter tests (i.e., the newly created odd and even tests) by predicting the coefficient for the full-length test (all items). The resulting correct split-half reliability is a robust indicator of internal consistency. A related and often-used procedure is that of Cronbach's alpha. The resulting coefficient represents the average of all possible split-halves or the approximate relationship between performances on all items that make up the test and the composite scores. These types of estimates for internal consistency are used widely, in part, because they are convenient; however, they provide what is often an overestimate of reliability, because they do not tap into many of the extraneous sources of variability that contribute to unreliability (e.g., natural variations in student performance, variations in context, and full accounting of form inequivalence).

Interrater–scorer reliability is substantially similar to that of parallel or alternate form reliability in that similar analyses are conducted across administrators and scorers. This information is especially relevant if the procedures and settings for administrations are more influential over student performances or if the scoring procedures are less objective. Objectively scored tests tend to be less influenced by scorers, especially if they are machine scored. In contrast, scoring with rubrics or expert judgment requires a thorough evaluation of interrater–scorer reliability. Many observational procedures also require a thorough analysis of rater effects (e.g., direct behavior rating, systematic direct observation).

Reliability of difference scores with a battery is notoriously problematic (Watkins, Glutting, & Youngstrom, 2005), as is the *reliability of change scores* (Cronbach, 1960; Cronbach & Furby, 1970). Although difference scores can apply to both (a) intratest profile analyses to identify strengths and weaknesses or (b) change scores as intervention effects, the two methods are divided. The reliability of subtest and difference scores often is poorly analyzed and reported in technical manuals, which tend to highlight the reliability of composite scores. Composite scores almost always are the most reliable scores that emerge from a test because they are based on the highest number of items. Subtest scores almost always are much less reliable, and that unreliability is compounded when profiles are constructed of difference scores. A similar problem exists with change scores. That is, unreliability compounds when two scores are compared. If a test is administered at two points in time and a difference score is computed, the error associated with both administrations is included in the change score. For that reason, the reliabilities of difference and change scores should be calculated—and reported by the developer—before they are used to guide educational decisions. Likewise, consumers should seek reliability information on change scores if a chosen assessment incorporates these values.

The prevalence of triannual screening (fall, winter, spring) and the use of those values to estimate progress and program effects require a little more discussion of change scores. Although there is substantial criticism of change scores in the literature, a full or random sample of change scores will provide an unbiased estimate of true change; therefore, these values can be used on the group level. They also can be used on the individual level to some degree; however, when students are selected systematically based on their risk status (i.e., low achievement on a triannual screener) then the pretest score is not chosen randomly. That score is a biased estimate of the student's pretest performance. It is likely to be a lower estimate of the student's true score than another observation. The students most likely to make more substantial gains from pre- to posttest are those who performed in the low range at pretest. That is, there is typically a negative correlation between pretest and difference scores (i.e., regression to the mean). A validation phase (e.g., retesting, alternate tests) after screening can ameliorate these effects, but it does not eliminate them. Moreover, multiple measurements between pre- and posttesting can contribute to improve the reliability of change scores. Finally, the use of SEM for difference scores can provide useful guidance for interpretation.

Standard Error of Measurement

SEM is an estimate of the error surrounding a student's score. It confers reliability implications at the time that a score is interpreted and used to guide an educational decision. Scores should not be reported or interpreted with a constant *SEM*. As provided by the *Standards*,

> SEM is generally more relevant than the reliability coefficient once a measurement procedure has been adopted and interpretation of scores has become the user's primary concern. . . . Information about the precision of measurement at each of several widely spaced score intervals—that is, conditional standard errors—is usually a valuable supplement to the single statistic for all score levels combined. (AERA et al., 1999, p. 29)

There are a few key ideas therein. First, *SEM* is on the same scale as the test scores. For that reason, *SEM* is difficult to compare across tests. For purposes of test selection and the general evaluation of reliability, reliability coefficients are more comparable and useful; however, these coefficients are much less useful during interpretation because their meaning becomes ambiguous. Second, conditional *SEM* is more meaningful than a single value. Most tests are designed to maximize reliability and minimize *SEM* within a narrow range of abilities. For example, third-grade tests are likely to be most reliable for students who approximate typical third-grade achievement and much less reliable for students below or above that third-grade range. There is likely to be a range of SEMs even within the third-grade range, so that conditional SEMs are useful to estimate the precision of measurement. Any single *SEM* value is likely to be misleading for some portion of examinees, often including the very students for whom screening is most necessary. Third, the estimation of reliability is an intermediary step in estimating *SEM*; therefore, the type of reliability estimate that is used will define how comprehensive *SEM* is to account for the multiple facets that contribute to unreliability. It is not uncommon for test developers to rely on internal consistency to calculate *SEM*, which accounts for the narrowest set of facets.

Classical Notions of Validation

The classical definition of validity *is the degree that a measurement outcome represents what is intended*. Many texts used for introductory measurement and assessment coursework continue to rely on a classical notion of validation, which is composed of criterion-, content-, and construct-related evidence.

The *criterion model* of validation is founded on the correlation between a measurement and a true criterion score. There are two general forms. Concurrent validity applies a criterion value that is obtained at about the same time as the alternate or experimental measure. Predictive validity applies a criterion value that is obtained at a later time; it typically is not available at the time the alternate or experimental measure is collected. This criterion model was especially prominent before 1950, and it is very useful if there is a well-established and acceptable criterion measure that is not inferior to that proposed as the alternate or experimental measure. It is less useful when there is no such measure. For the purpose of screening assessments, there is often a well-established measure, and the purpose of validation is to evaluate how well an inexpensive and highly efficient measure compares to it. For that reason, the criterion model often is useful for validating screening measures. For example, CBM-R is an inexpensive and highly efficient measure of the number of words students can read correctly in 1 minute (WRC); however, there are other well-established measures of general reading ability (e.g., Iowa Test of Basic Skills, state tests in reading). Thus, criterion-related validity evidence often is garnered for CBM-R by correlating WRC with performance on the other measures of reading ability, especially state tests.

The *content model* for validation is founded in the definition and specification of an explicit measurement target. It is a logical argument constructed by test creators that establishes rational grounds for a particular sample of observed performances as a representation of the content. The corresponding skills and behaviors are sequences in a continuum with one or more dimensions, which define the measurement space or matrix. Items are developed for each cell, and the resulting measure is then a valid representation of the content for the domain.

The *construct model* for validation is founded in the theoretical basis for the measure and really is the whole of what was intended by validity from about 1980 until 2000. It is *the degree that a measurement outcome represents what is intended,* which consumes criterion and content validity along with other sources of evidence. Validation in this sense requires a thorough definition of the underlying theory that defines the construct (e.g., What is reading? What is self-efficacy?) and the implications and predictions that might be derived. Analyses evaluate the internal structure of the assessment—how items relate to each other—along with purported and alternative interpretation of test scores, which might include the implications for the use of test scores. The construct model functioned as a unifying principle for validation, which was promoted notably by Messick (1995). His unified theory provided (a) that all possible interpretations of the test score are founded and supported by the evidence for construct and (b) that a particular interpretation of the test is founded in the relevance of the construct to the proposed purpose. Messick's unified theory is sometimes difficult to interpret and apply, making more recent conceptions of argument-based validity more attractive for researchers and consumers alike.

Argument-Based Approach to Validation

Although traditional conceptualizations of reliability and validity provide a necessary introduction to important psychometric concepts, more contemporary notions (e.g., Kane, 2006) expand and combine these concepts into a framework that benefits both test developers and consumers. Here, explicit attention is given to a contemporary perspective on validation as presented by Kane (2006) in *Educational Measurement* and referenced in the *Standards* (AERA et al., 1999). According to the *Standards*, "Validation can be viewed as developing a scientifically sound validity argument to support the intended interpretation of test scores and their relevance to the proposed use" (AERA et al., 1999, p. 9). Kane's approach to validation gets to the heart of screening assessments as they are used in schools. That is, what interpretations of screening data are made in practice? What allows us to put stock in these interpretations? Ultimately, professionals in education must make meaningful decisions regarding students' proficiency in a broad domain by the use of specific test scores. It is the burden of test developers to present a strong argument for the use of a given screening assessment and the responsibility of consumers to evaluate that argument completely and systematically. Kane's interpretive argument is included in addition to previous discussions of reliability and validity, because it both extends and combines traditional discussions of reliability and validity into a framework for evaluating the interpretations intended by those who develop screening assessments. Rather than viewing this section as a compendium of important components related to test creation, readers are encouraged to view it as a coherent narrative for test validation, with many concepts building and relying on each other to provide clarity to a single argument. Readers are encouraged to use Figure 4.2 as a reference throughout the following discussion.

Interpretive Argument: Semantic

Kane (2006) described three types of semantic interpretations. Each confers some description of the examinee based on the resulting test scores. One example is a semantic trait interpretation. A trait is the tendency to behave or perform in a particular manner across a variety of circumstances; however, as discussed, traits are often difficult to observe directly, and their condition must be inferred (refer to the previous discussion of latent traits along with true scores and universe scores). Toward that end, a target domain is defined for which the trait is applied by the examinee and is observable during his or her performance of a task. For example, reading ability might be the latent trait and reading achievement might be the target domain. The test developer, in most cases, can hope to assess only a narrow set of skills or

Hypothesized Empirical Relationships

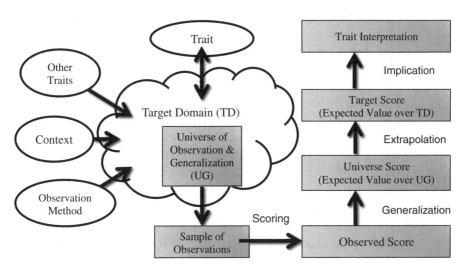

Figure 4.2. Argument-based validity: Measurement procedure and interpretive argument. From *Educational Measurement* (4th ed.; p. 33), by R. L. Brennan (Ed.), 2006, Westport, CT: American Council on Education & Praeger. Copyright 2006 by ABC-CLIO. Adapted with permission.

instances that are defined by the *target domain* (see Figure 4.2). Moreover, many relevant skills are not amenable to standardized testing conditions and others are simply beyond the scope of a measure. This is especially true for instances of screener tests, which are intended to be brief and efficient.

A narrower set of skills or instances from the larger domain come to define the *universe of generalization* (as described in the GT section; see Figure 4.2). For example, in the case of reading, the universe of generalization for CBM-R includes only oral readings of grade-level passages. Student performances on third-grade passages do not generalize to second- or fourth-grade passages (i.e., the universe likely is limited to third-grade passages from particular curriculum or test vendors). In the case of CBM-R, students are directed to read aloud from one or more grade-level passages. That oral reading behavior makes up the *sample of observations* (see Figure 4.2). That sample excludes alternate observation methods that might be used in the reading domain, such as multiple-choice comprehension items. Administration and scoring rules are constructed and applied (see Figure 4.2), such that there are standardized procedures, training, expert judgment, and interrater reliability evidence to support the scoring procedure. The outcome of which is the *observed score* (see Figure 4.2).

The observed score is generalized through inference to indicate performance in the larger universe of generalization (see Figure 4.2). This inference requires support that the sample is stable and representative of the defined universe. This inference is supported with well-developed methods for content sampling along with reliability analysis and GT. Tests with low alternate form reliability or internal consistency have weak evidence for generalization from the test score to the universe score.

The universe score is extrapolated as an indicator of the domain score (see Figure 4.2). The domain is much larger than the universe. To continue with the previous example, CBM-R scores are in units of WRC; however, the reading domain includes any number of alternate item types and behavior samples, some of which are not amenable to assessment (e.g., silent reading comprehension). As such, the validity argument must provide the rationale and evidence to support the use of oral reading rate as a valid indicator of performance in the larger domain. Analytic evidence emerges during development of the assessment, especially during the initial stages when the blueprint, construct, and content are defined. In this sense, construct and content validity both contribute to the analytic evidence. In general, assessments with content, items, and responses that represent broad aspects of the domain provide more convincing evidence for extrapolation from the universe score to the domain score. The argument is more tenuous when the domain is represented narrowly, as is the case for CBM-R, for example. It does not broadly represent the reading domain; however, the domain might be defined more narrowly than broad reading. Instead, it might be defined as automatic decoding and identification of words in context. The analytic evidence relates to face validity. It is necessary but not sufficient as analytic evidence for extrapolation. Empirical evidence for extrapolation includes various measures of content representation and criterion validity.

Finally, the domain score might have an implication for the latent trait (construct or qualitative descriptor; Kane, 2006). Trait evidence requires a supplement to that used for domain evidence. In this case, analytic evidence emerges during test development and generally includes the correspondence between the trait definition and the various tasks, item types, administration, performance, and scoring. It also includes empirical evidence related to definitional and theoretical aspects of the trait. For example, some traits are by definition stable and others are malleable or developmental; thus, the relative stability of test scores (as demonstrated through empirical comparison) can provide evidence to support or refute trait-level interpretations. In general, trait implications are less relevant to the purpose and properties of many academic screening measures; however, they might apply to screeners for developmental disabilities or giftedness.

Interpretative Argument: Decisions

Semantic interpretations and decisions occur in sequence. For example, if CBM-R were used to screen primary students, a teacher would first estimate the student's ability (semantic interpretation) and then make a decision about instruction, services, or eligibility. The prospect of interpretation to make a decision brings to the forefront the criteria to guide those decisions and the accuracy of those decisions. Both the criteria and the eventual accuracy of classification decisions have consequences.

Decisions: Standard Setting

The standards for the interpretation of test scores and classification of students depend on standard setting. Standard setting is part of the test development process. It is necessary to address the question, "How much skill/ability defines passing survey, skill, and subskill assessments?" The process of standard setting inherently is based on human judgment (Hambleton & Pitoniak, 2006), and, generally, there are two broad methods. Normative standards are set so that a prespecified proportion of the population will receive a pass, fail, or intermediate classification. In contrast, criterion standards are based on performance within a particular domain. The classification of an individual is based on absolute—rather than relative—performance standards. All students in a population might receive a pass, fail, or intermediate classification such that performances are not compared across students. Instead, they are compared to the expected amount of knowledge and skills demonstrated during the assessment. Regardless of the method for standard setting, it should be clearly specified in the documentation and it should make sense for the proposed interpretation and decision.

The use of *standards-based assessment* has implications for standard setting. The development and use of the Common Core State Standards (National Governors Association Center for Best Practices Council of Chief State School Officers, 2010a, 2010b) establishes a context that increases the likelihood that absolute criterion-based performance standards will be derived and applied to make classification decisions. Although the application of standards for screening has yet to be fully conceptualized, it is likely that screening assessments will emerge to support mastery measurement of grade-level standards. This approach conflicts with the predominant approach at the time this chapter was written, which is a general outcome norming and benchmarking approach. General outcome measurement surveys performance within a domain generally or applies some generic skill as a robust indicator of broad achievement within a domain. This is the rationale and the standard used to support CBM-R for screening and progress monitoring (Deno, 2003). This approach is consistent with composite scores—and some subtest scores—on assessment batteries of academic skills. As instructional targets are more common and well refined, educators are likely to assert a preference for screeners that are specific to standards. For that, they will expect strength and weakness profiles along with indicators of mastery for specific standards. This approach likely will be useful for instruction, but it will require longer assessments that are less efficient or innovations consistent with computer-adaptive testing.

Decisions: Decision Accuracy

Once the standard-setting methods are selected, the accuracy of classification decisions is evaluated. This process addresses the question, "With what consistency and validity does this test score classify students?" It has become increasingly popular to use receiver operating characteristic analysis along with other, more standard estimates of decision accuracy, which include kappa and phi.

As illustrated in Figure 4.3 there are four possible classification outcomes: true positive (TP; Zone 3), true negative (TN; Zone 2), false positive (FP; Zone 1), and false negative (FN; Zone 4). A TP classification indicates that the predictor (e.g., CBM-R) and criterion (e.g., performance on statewide test) agree that the student is a deficit reader (i.e., accurate classification;

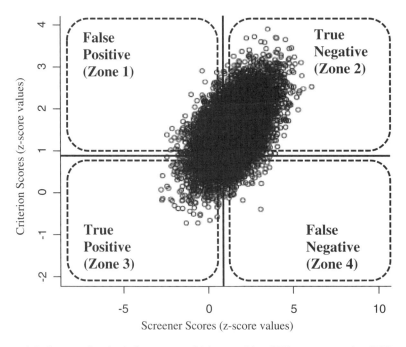

Figure 4.3. Scatterplot depicting areas of false positive (FP), true negative (TN), true positive (TP), and false negative (FN).

Zone 3). TN indicates that the predictor and criterion agree that the student is a proficient reader (i.e., accurate classification; Zone 2). FP indicates disagreement such that the predictor is positive and the criterion is negative (i.e., inaccurate classification; Zone 1). FN indicates disagreement such that the predictor is negative and the criterion is positive (i.e., inaccurate classification; Zone 4). Most professionals in education agree that a FN classification (Zone 4) is the most problematic, as it includes students who are classified as proficient and later are observed to be not proficient. The primary metrics for classification outcomes are sensitivity and specificity. These along with secondary metrics are described in the following list:

- *Sensitivity* (true-positive proportion, TPP): Of the cases with criterion scores below the cutoff point (i.e., criterion = deficient), for what percentage was the screener score below the decision threshold (i.e., screener = deficient)?

$$\frac{TP}{TP + FN}$$

- *Specificity* (true-negative proportion, TNP): Of the cases with true criterion scores above the cutoff point (i.e., criterion = sufficient), for what percentage was the screener score above the decision threshold (i.e., screener = sufficient)?

$$\frac{TN}{FP + TN}$$

- *Positive predictive value* (PPV): Of the cases with screener scores below the decision threshold (i.e., screener = deficient), what percentage have a criterion score also below the cutoff point (i.e., criterion = deficient)?

$$\frac{TP}{TP + FP}$$

- *Negative predictive value* (NPV): Of the cases with screener scores above the decision threshold (i.e., screener = sufficient), what percentage have a criterion score also above the cutoff point (i.e., criterion = sufficient)?

$$\frac{TN}{TN + FN}$$

In addition, phi and kappa coefficients often are used to estimate association, or agreement, between the screener and criterion value. Phi is interpreted as a correlation coefficient for categorical variables. Unlike phi, kappa coefficients are adjusted for chance agreement, which is more desirable. General rules for the interpretation of kappa are as follows: .60 = moderate, .61–.80 = substantial, and .81–1.00 = almost perfect.

It should be apparent from a review of Figure 4.3 that decisions based on the screener are inherently imperfect. The depiction in that particular figure illustrates a correlation of approximately .70 between the predictor and criterion measure. In this example, CBM-R is an imperfect predictor of performance on the state test. Regardless of the measures, there will always be an imperfect relationship. This is true for test–retest (i.e., performance on the same test on two occasions). Tests are inherently unreliable, and all interpretations of scores are tentative. This is especially true for screening assessments, which are designed to be highly efficient and, therefore, often have less reliability and validity than a more comprehensive—albeit inefficient—assessment.

Area Under the Curve

Area under the curve (AUC) is used as a measure of predictive power. It is obtained by calculating the sensitivity and specificity values for all possible cutoff points on the screener by fixing a cutoff point on criterion measure and plotting *sensitivity* (or TPP) against $1 - specificity$ (or TNP). AUC is expected to be .5 if the screener provided little or no information. AUC is expected to be 1 for a perfect diagnostic method to identify the students at risk correctly. Although the criteria that are applied to interpret AUCs are variable, values are considered excellent, good, fair, or poor within ranges of .90–1.0, .85–.89, .75–.84, and .60–.75, respectively. It seems reasonable and generally consistent with the standards outlined by the National Center for Response to Intervention that an AUC of at least .85 is required for routine low-stakes decisions and that an AUC of at least .90 is required for high-stake decisions.

Decision Threshold

A decision threshold is established to maximize the benefits of the decision process relative to its costs (Swets, Dawes, & Monahan, 2000). That threshold is adjusted to establish a neutral, lenient, or strict classification criterion for the predictor. A neutral threshold will balance the proportion of TP and FP, although not all thresholds should be balanced. For example, screening measures for reading often overidentify students (increase the rate of TP as well as FP) to ensure that fewer positive cases are missed. This is a rational choice, because failure to identify TP outweighs the consequences of increased FP.

Thresholds that are more lenient (overidentify) increase sensitivity, thereby increasing the proportion of positive classifications (both TP and

FP). Thresholds that are more strict (underidentify) increase specificity, thereby increasing the proportion of negative classifications (both TN and FN; Swets et al., 2000). The decision threshold is adjusted to obtain the optimal ratio of positive and negative classifications along with that of true and false classifications. For example, Silberglitt and Hintze (2005) systematically modified the CBM-R benchmark scores in third grade to optimize the cut score, which improved classification accuracy.

CURRENT AND FUTURE DIRECTIONS

There is a substantial shift in educational practices that includes the emergence of annual and triannual (fall, winter, spring) screenings. The historical use of the paper-and-pencil multiple-choice tests in the 1980s (e.g., Iowa Test of Basic Skills, Stanford Achievement Test) gave way to more authentic assessments in the 1990s (e.g., portfolio assessments, permanent products). For some, curriculum-based measurement took the place of other, less psychometric, performance-based authentic assessments in the 2000s (AIMSweb, DIBELS, FAST). At the same time, computer-adaptive tests emerged (e.g., MAP, STAR, FAST). Many of these innovations occurred in primary grades and emphasized reading, but there were also innovations for screening in other academic domains, mental health, and social behavior.

Contemporary psychometric theory is dominated by IRT with complementary applications of CTT and GT. School-based assessments soon will be dominated by technology-based applications, which integrate variations of automated administrations, scoring, reporting, and database storage. Although test development and validation remain a complex and nuanced amalgamation of art and science, the capacity to develop and disseminate technology-based assessments will continue to increase with the proliferation of software for test development and the availability of computers—as well as tablet devices—in schools. As the number of instruments for screening increases and the field becomes ever more crowded, decision making will become more difficult for superintendents, principals, and their consultants.

CONCLUSION

Schools have limited resources for meeting the needs of students and must select screening assessments that ultimately will lead to informed and appropriate decisions regarding the allocation of these resources. It is not enough to accept published screening tools at face value and use them for the purpose stated by the test creators. The fact that screening tools exist does not make them technically adequate: Even the strongest screening tool is useless when administered inappropriately or interpreted incorrectly. Those who are tasked with selecting formal screening assessments must recognize this and evaluate potential assessments accordingly. The process is not always simple. This chapter presents an overview of the content consumers should expect test developers to provide and a framework to guide consumers in their efforts to evaluate screening assessments. Readers are encouraged to use the checklist provided in Table 4.1 as a tool for selecting appropriate screening tools. On a fundamental level, professionals in education must have a clear understanding of what they wish to infer from screening assessments and the degree to which these assessments allow for such inferences. A thorough consideration of the available information on the (a) stated purpose, (b) description, (c) technical characteristics, (d) validation, (e) score reporting and interpretations, and (f) supporting references for assessments will promote responsible test selection in educational settings. It is to readers' advantage to recognize that it is the burden of test developers to demonstrate the credibility of screening tools, but it is the burden of professionals in education to evaluate the argument in the context for which the tool will be used.

REFERENCES

American Educational Research Association, American Psychological Association, & National Council on Measurement in Education. (1999). *Standards for educational and psychological testing.* Washington, DC: American Educational Research Association.

Becker, D. F., & Pomplun, M. R. (2006). Technical reporting and documentation. In S. M. Downing & T. M. Haladyna (Eds.), *Handbook of test development* (pp. 711–723). Mahwah, NJ: Erlbaum.

Binet, A., & Simon, T. (1905). Méthodes nouvelles pour le diagnostic du niveau intellectuel des anormaux [New methods for the diagnosis of the intellectual level of the abnormal]. *L'année psychologique, 11,* 191–244.

Binet, A., & Simon, T. (1908). Le développement de l'intelligence chez le enfants [The development of intelligence in children]. *L'année psychologique, 14,* 1–90.

Bransford, J. D., & Stein, B. S. (1984). *The ideal problem solver: A guide for improving thinking, learning, and creativity.* New York, NY: Freeman.

Brennan, R. L. (2003). Generalizability theory. *Journal of Educational Measurement, 40,* 105–107. doi:10.1111/j.1745-3984.2003.tb01098.x

Brennan, R. L. (Ed.). (2006). *Educational measurement* (4th ed.). Westport, CT: American Council on Education & Praeger.

Buckendahl, C. W., & Plake, B. S. (2006). Evaluating tests. In S. M. Downing & T. M. Haladyna (Eds.), *Handbook of test development* (pp. 725–738). Mahwah, NJ: Erlbaum.

Christ, T. J., & Silberglitt, B. (2007). Estimates of the standard error of measurement for curriculum-based measures of oral reading fluency. *School Psychology Review, 36,* 130–146.

Cronbach, L. J. (1960). *Essentials of psychological testing* (2nd ed.). New York, NY: Harper & Row.

Cronbach, L. J., & Furby, L. (1970). How we should measure "change": Or should we? *Psychological Bulletin, 74,* 68–80. doi:10.1037/h0029382

Deno, S. L. (1995). The school psychologist as problem solver. In J. Grimes & A. Thomas (Eds.), *Best practices in school psychology III* (pp. 37–56). Bethesda, MD: National Association of School Psychologists.

Deno, S. L. (2003). Developments in curriculum-based measurement. *Journal of Special Education, 37,* 184–192. doi:10.1177/00224669030370030801

Deno, S. L. (2005). Problem solving assessment. In R. Brown-Chidsey (Ed.), *Assessment for intervention: A problem-solving approach* (pp. 10–40). New York, NY: Guilford Press.

Downing, S. M. (2006). Twelve steps for effective test development. In S. M. Downing & T. M. Haladyna (Eds.), *Handbook of test development* (pp. 3–25). Mahwah, NJ: Erlbaum.

Downing, S. M., & Haladyna, T. M. (Eds.). (2006). *Handbook of test development.* Mahwah, NJ: Erlbaum.

Good, R. H., Simmons, D. C., & Kame'enui, E. J. (2001). The importance and decision-making utility of a continuum of fluency-based indicators of foundational reading skills for third-grade high-stakes outcomes. *Scientific Studies of Reading, 5,* 257–288. doi:10.1207/S1532799XSSR0503_4

Haertel, E. H. (2006). Reliability. In R. L. Brennan (Ed.), *Educational measurement* (4th ed., pp. 65–110). Westport, CT: American Council on Education & Praeger.

Hambleton, R. K., & Pitoniak, M. J. (2006). Setting performance standards. In R. L. Brennan (Ed.), *Educational measurement* (4th ed., pp. 433–470). Westport, CT: American Council on Education & Praeger.

Kane, M. T. (2006). Validation. In R. L. Brennan (Ed.), *Educational measurement* (4th ed., pp. 17–64). Westport, CT: American Council on Education & Praeger.

Linn, R. L. (2006). The standards for educational and psychological testing: Guidance in test development. In S. M. Downing & T. M. Haladyna (Eds.), *Handbook of test development* (pp. 27–38). Mahwah, NJ: Erlbaum.

Lord, F. M. (1953). The relation of test score to the trait underlying the test. *Educational and Psychological Measurement, 13,* 517–549. doi:10.1177/001316445301300401

Lord, F. M., & Novick, M. R. (1968). *Statistical theories of mental test scores.* Reading, MA: Addison-Wesley.

Macmann, G. M., & Barnett, D. W. (1999). Diagnostic decision making in school psychology: Understanding and coping with uncertainty. In C. Reynolds & T. Gutkin (Eds.), *The handbook of school psychology* (pp. 519–543). New York, NY: Wiley.

Messick, S. (1995). Validity of psychological assessment: Validation of inferences from persons' responses and performances as scientific inquiry into score meaning. *American Psychologist, 50,* 741–749. doi:10.1037/0003-066X.50.9.741

National Governors Association Center for Best Practices Council of Chief State School Officers. (2010a). *Common core state standards: English language arts.* Washington, DC: Author.

National Governors Association Center for Best Practices Council of Chief State School Officers. (2010b). *Common core state standards: Mathematics.* Washington, DC: Author.

Silberglitt, B., & Hintze, J. M. (2005). Formative assessment using CBM-R cut scores to track progress toward success on state mandated achievement tests: A comparison of methods. *Journal of Psychoeducational Assessment, 23,* 304–325. doi:10.1177/073428290502300402

Spearman, C. (1904). The proof and measurement of associations between two things. *American Journal of Psychology, 15,* 72–101. doi:10.2307/1412159

Spearman, C. (1907). Demonstration of formulae for true measurement of correlation. *American Journal of Psychology, 18,* 161–169. doi:10.2307/1412408

Spearman, C. (1913). Correlations of sums and differences. *British Journal of Psychology, 5,* 417–426.

Swets, J. A., Dawes, R. M., & Monahan, J. (2000). Psychological science can improve diagnostic decisions. *Psychological Science in the Public Interest, 1,* 1–26. doi:10.1111/1529-1006.001

Watkins, M. W., Glutting, J. J., & Youngstrom, E. A. (2005). Issues in subtest profile analysis. In D. P. Flanagan & P. L. Harrison (Eds.), *Contemporary intellectual assessment: Theories, tests, and issues* (pp. 251–268). New York, NY: Guilford Press.

5

SCREENING AS INNOVATION: IMPLEMENTATION CHALLENGES

SUSAN G. FORMAN, TZIVIA R. JOFEN, AND AUDREY R. LUBIN

As indicated in several chapters in this volume, universal screening in educational settings can be an effective means of identifying students at risk for academic, behavioral, and emotional problems and students in need of academic, behavioral, and mental health interventions. These chapters have described a variety of screening programs that can be useful for these purposes. Unfortunately, the educational literature is replete with reports of sound programs with laudable goals that fail to make the transition from program development and validation to implementation of the program in the natural setting of the school, without the extensive control and support typically provided by researchers during efforts to establish validity and efficacy (Atkins, Frazier, Adil, & Talbott, 2003; Ennett et al., 2003; Gottfredson & Gottfredson, 2007).

Many valid and efficacious new programs have been developed with the promise of improving the academic, behavioral, and emotional functioning of school students, yet these programs are not used or implemented on a

http://dx.doi.org/10.1037/14316-005
Universal Screening in Educational Settings: Evidence-Based Decision Making for Schools, R. J. Kettler, T. A. Glover, C. A. Albers, and K. A. Feeney-Kettler (Editors)
Copyright © 2014 by the American Psychological Association. All rights reserved.

widespread basis in schools. Educational researchers and practitioners are realizing that developing an effective program is only an initial step in improving the functioning of students. Screening instruments and programs can identify students who are at risk for or who manifest problems and can provide information needed to link these students with appropriate interventions and services that have the potential to prevent or ameliorate these problems. Screening instruments and programs, however, will yield positive outcomes for students only if they are implemented and implemented appropriately in school settings.

Implementation is the process of putting new programs into practice. It consists of a set of specific activities designed to incorporate a new program into the routine of an individual, group, or organization. Over the past decade, implementation science and practice have been recognized as areas of major importance.

Development of a screening instrument and program is a first step in improving the academic, behavioral, and emotional functioning of students through early identification. Establishing the use of screening programs in schools is a long-term and complex process. This chapter reviews literature specific to implementation of mental health, behavioral, and academic screening programs in schools; describes what is known about the process of implementation from multidisciplinary literature in this area; discusses implications for effective implementation of screening programs in schools; and suggests future directions for research in this area.

COMPONENTS OF IMPLEMENTATION

Understanding the components of implementation can provide a sound foundation for implementation planning. The components of implementation have been conceptualized in varying ways (Fixsen, Naoom, Blase, Friedman, & Wallace, 2005; Rogers, 2003), although there are commonalities among the ways in which implementation components have been identified. Important components include *an innovation*, which is a practice or program that is perceived as new; *a communication process* between individuals or groups who know about a new practice or program and individuals or groups who do not know about it; and *a social system* in which subsystems (e.g., classrooms in a school) and suprasystems (e.g., in relation to a school, the state, and federal departments of education) influence each other, and within which the implementation process takes place. The individual who is working actively to bring an innovation into a setting, such as a school, may be referred to as a *change agent*. An *implementer* is an individual who will put the new practice or program to use or engage in delivery of the new practice or program to clients. Implementers can be thought of as primary implementers and secondary implementers. *Primary implementers* are individuals who play a direct role in conducting a program, whereas *secondary implementers* are individuals who support the program through their activities. *Stakeholders* are individuals in the implementer's organization or social system who have an interest in the new practice or program. Figure 5.1 depicts how these components may operate and interact when the innovation is a school-based screening program.

Thus, a screening program that has not been used in a particular school before and is therefore new to the individuals in that school can be considered an innovation. The developers of the screening program or other individuals who know about it and want to promote its use, such as school psychologists, will use a communication process to inform school staff about the program. Implementation of the screening program will take place within the social system of the school, in which different parts of the school influence each other; systems outside of the school, such as the state department of education, influence school functioning. Teachers may be primary implementers of some

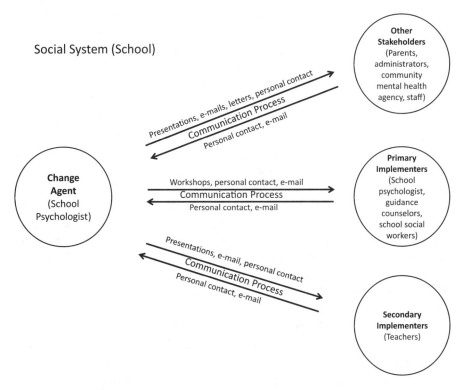

Figure 5.1. Schematic of the components of implementation of a school-based screening program.

screening programs, if they are the ones who administer the screening instruments in their classrooms; and the guidance counselor may be a secondary implementer, if his or her efforts are needed to transfer completed screening forms from classrooms to those who will score and interpret them. For screening programs related to mental health, support services providers are typically the primary implementers. Stakeholders for screening programs may include any school staff member or administrator, parents and students, and staff at other community agencies who may receive referrals as a result of screening.

Implementation Components: School Screening Program Example

For example, in Northeast Urban Middle School, the principal has appointed a task force to examine mental health issues and services at the school after a student attempted suicide. The school psychologist (*change agent*) is a member of the task force and after reading literature in the area has become aware of a validated depression and suicide risk screening program (*innovation*) that she thinks may fit the school's needs and resources. She brings written information and talks about the depression and suicide risk program to the school mental health task force (*communication process*). The task force is impressed with the potential of the program and begins to discuss how to communicate information (*communication process*) about the potential program within the school (*social system*) to the various academic and support services departments in the school (*subsystems*) to get some initial feedback about the potential new program from teachers (*stakeholders*) and support services personnel (*primary and secondary implementers*). The principal, who is a member of the task force, plans to communicate with the school superintendent's office (*suprasystem*) about the program to develop district-level support and asks the task force chairperson, who is a highly regarded social studies teacher, to contact the state department of education (*suprasystem*) to see whether any grant funding for this program may be available.

Participation in this depression and suicide risk screening program is voluntary, requiring parent consent and teen assent. The screening program is introduced to students, screening program consent forms are distributed by guidance counselors (*primary implementers*) during health class (thus, the health education teacher is a *secondary implementer*), and completed forms are returned to the head guidance counselor's office (*primary implementer* and *program coordinator*). Participating eighth-grade students will take a validated screening questionnaire during their health education class period, administered and scored by guidance counselors or school social workers (*primary implementers*). On the basis of their scores, students then will meet individually with a guidance counselor (*primary implementer*) for a debriefing interview or participate in an individual clinical interview with a school psychologist (*primary implementer*) to determine whether the student may be at risk for depression, suicide, or other mental health problems. Parents of students (*stakeholders*) found to be at risk are immediately notified by a school psychologist (*primary implementer*) and provided assistance with obtaining an appointment for a complete evaluation from a community mental health services provider (*stakeholder* and *secondary implementer*).

STAGES OF IMPLEMENTATION

The process of implementation generally is thought of as having stages. The notion of stages of implementation has practical importance because different actions are required during different stages to support implementation progress and success. Understanding the stages of implementation and the actions expected at each stage by change agents and implementers is an important prerequisite for effective implementation. The stages or phases typically are conceptualized in terms of dissemination, in which information about the innovation is dispersed; adoption, in which a decision is made to try the innovation; implementation, in which the innovation is first tried; and sustainability, in which the program is maintained over time (Durlak & DuPre, 2008). Various authors have conceptualized the stages of implementation in different ways. Table 5.1 shows stages of implementation as conceptualized by Fixsen et al. (2005) and Rogers (2003). Fixsen et al. identified six stages, focusing on activities or events related to the innovation or new practice or program. Rogers focused on the potential implementers in his conceptualization of stages, viewing the stages as an *innovation decision process* in which the potential implementer is motivated to reduce uncertainties about the advantages and disadvantages of the innovation. He identified five stages for individuals and groups as well as a five-stage innovation decision process in organizations, pointing out that the process is more complex in organizations because many individuals are involved.

An additional conceptualization of implementation stages, specifically in school settings, can be found in the work of Hall and Hord (1987). They have stated that in the preadoption stage, it is important that potential adopters are aware of the innovation, have information about what it does and how to use it, and understand how it will affect them personally. During early use of an innovation, they have contended, success is more likely if implementers have continuing access to information about what the innovation does as well as to training and support about how to fit the innovation to their daily tasks. Hall and Hord indicated that, later in implementation, success is more likely if adequate feedback is provided about the consequences of implementation and if the implementer has sufficient opportunity and support to adapt the innovation.

TABLE 5.1
Three Conceptualizations of Implementation Stages

Fixsen et al. (2005): Stages of innovation of a new practice or program	Rogers (2003): Innovation decision process—individuals and groups	Rogers (2003): Innovation decision process—organizations
Exploration and adoption Innovation is explored and need and fit are determined; decision to adopt is made; information about the innovation is shared with the organization.	Knowledge Individual or group learns about the innovation.	Agenda setting Organizational problem is defined that creates a perceived need.
Program installation Supports for the innovation, such as funding, staff development and new staff, responsibilities, procedures, technology, and policies, are put into place.	Persuasion Individual or group attitude about the innovation is formed; opinions of peers and others are sought.	Matching An innovation that fits the problem is identified; feasibility of use is determined.
Initial implementation Program begins; implementers deal with fear of change/inertia/difficulty of doing something new.	Decision Adoption or rejection of innovation; small-scale trial or demonstration may be used to guide decision.	Redefining and restructuring Innovation is adapted to fit the organization; the organization's structure may be modified to fit the innovation.
Full operation Innovation carried out proficiently, with organizational support.	Implementation Program put into place; adaptation may occur; implementer addresses concerns and problems.	Clarifying Use of the innovation spreads in the organization; organizational members gain common understanding of it.
Innovation Adaptations are made for better fit.	Confirmation Integrated into routine; support for decision sought; dissatisfaction and replacement may occur.	Routinizing The innovation is incorporated into regular activities.
Sustainability Innovation continues to be implemented; changes in context may have impact.		

Implications of Stage Theories for Successful Implementation of Screening Programs

Although the aforementioned specific stages vary from author to author, practical implications for successful implementation of screening programs in educational settings can be drawn from this work.

Early Stages

In the early stages of attempts at implementing screening programs in schools, an important task for the change agent will include assessment of the match between the screening program and school structure and resources and identification of potential primary and secondary implementers. Thus, for the depression and suicide risk screening program described previously, the school psychologist will want to look into issues such as the cost of the questionnaire forms and the computerized scoring program for the questionnaire and the specific tasks that have to be accomplished in delivery of the screening program (e.g., questionnaire administration, questionnaire scoring, debriefing interviews, clinical interviews, parent notification). Other concerns include how much time each task will take and whether potential implementers, such as guidance counselors, school social workers, and psychologists in the school, will have the time to take on these tasks.

In addition, as peer and social influences will become important as implementation proceeds, mapping social networks and important players in those networks in the target school or school district will be useful. In Northeast Urban Middle School, the school psychologist change agent may begin to map out how information typically is spread in the school (e.g., formal faculty meetings, discussions in the teachers' lounge) and which staff members may be most influential in developing support for the screening program (e.g., the chairperson of the social studies department, who is known to be the most influential person in the school).

As implementation progresses, the change agent may need to manage the process of procuring organizational supports (e.g., additional personnel, professional development programs, data analysis and management systems) that are prerequisites for conducting the program. In addition, information about the importance of screening and how the program works will have to be provided to primary and secondary implementers as well as to other stakeholders through such means as workshops and presentations, newsletters, and e-mail communications. Change agents also will need to communicate with primary implementers to begin to address how the screening program will affect them personally in terms of their work activities and responsibilities. For the depression and suicide risk screening program, the school psychologist change agent may begin to talk with the guidance counselors about how implementing the program may consolidate the focus of their work on mental health activities and their role as a student mental health expert.

Middle Stages

As the implementation process moves forward, the change agent may want to engage primary implementers in visiting a demonstration of the screening program at another site that is already using it or may wish to facilitate a small-scale trial of the program for potential implementers. During the middle stages of implementation, use of technical assistance, or coaching, and performance feedback becomes particularly important in ensuring that those who are implementing the screening program are able to fit implementation of the screening program within their other daily tasks and that they are conducting the program accurately. Performance feedback can keep program fidelity at optimum levels. In the case of the depression and suicide risk screening program, the school psychologist may recommend that a sample of the classroom presentations describing the program and classroom administrations of the questionnaire be observed to assess fidelity and that the head guidance counselor have regular discussions with her staff about how the new screening program may be affecting other areas of the counselors' work.

Later Stages

During the later stages of implementation, provision of information about the results and impact of the screening program to implementers and stakeholders becomes important. This information can enhance motivation to continue to implement and support the screening program. In the case of the depression and suicide risk screening program, group data about number of referrals made to external mental health services providers based on the screening might be provided periodically to stakeholders. During the later stages of implementation, the change agent also should focus on providing guidance about the ways in which the screening program might be adapted to better fit the needs and structure of the school setting in which it has been implemented, while maintaining the integrity of the program. For example, for the depression and suicide risk screening program, the task force might consider whether health education classes are the best settings in which to administer the screening questionnaire and also might consider methods of enhancing the school's relationship with external mental health services providers to facilitate referrals.

STUDIES OF FACTORS AFFECTING IMPLEMENTATION OF SCREENING PROGRAMS IN SCHOOLS

What do we know about factors that have an impact on implementation success with school-based screening programs? Data-based literature that directly addresses implementation of screening programs in educational settings is scarce. Only a handful of studies have focused on the factors that affect implementation of screening programs in schools.

Suicide Screening

Most of the studies on screening programs in schools have targeted suicide prevention programs for investigation and have examined the acceptability of these programs. Acceptability refers to perceptions of whether an intervention is fair, appropriate, and reasonable for a particular problem (Kazdin, 1980) and the extent to which individuals describe themselves as liking an intervention. It is assumed that individuals are more likely to implement interventions that they like.

In a study that examined the attitudes of school psychologists in terms of acceptability, Eckert, Miller, DuPaul, and Riley-Tillman (2003) evaluated three types of suicide prevention programs: schoolwide curriculum-based programs presented to students, in-service presentations to school staff, and students' self-report screening programs. Reynolds's (1991) two-stage screening and assessment procedure was the model for the screening program examined in this study. In this model a classwide or schoolwide self-report screening measure is administered to identify potentially suicidal students, and individual interviews are conducted with those who score above clinically significant levels to obtain a more precise assessment of suicide risk. The description of the screening program provided to study participants indicated that all high school students would receive brief self-report scales to complete to assess whether they were at risk for engaging in suicidal behaviors. The school psychologist then would be responsible for interviewing and determining the magnitude of suicidal risk for students whose scores were above a specific cutoff, and parents of those students would be informed and provided with referral information. School psychologists rated the staff in-service training and curriculum-based programs as significantly more acceptable than the schoolwide screening program, and the schoolwide screening program was rated as more intrusive than the staff in-service training or curriculum-based program. Ratings for the schoolwide screening program were in the unacceptable range, whereas the other approaches were rated as acceptable.

Acceptability of these approaches to suicide prevention also has been examined in studies of secondary school principals (Miller, Eckert, DuPaul,

& White, 1999), public school superintendents (Scherff, Eckert, & Miller, 2005), and older adolescent students in college (Eckert, Miller, Riley-Tillman, & DuPaul, 2006). In all of these studies, schoolwide screening was less acceptable than staff in-service training and curriculum-based programs. The study of school superintendents also found that screening was rated as more intrusive than the other approaches. These findings do not bode well for implementation of screening programs as an approach to suicide prevention, despite a number of researchers contending that the screening approach may be more effective and efficient than other approaches (Reynolds & Mazza, 1994) to the prevention of suicide.

Hypothesized reasons for the low acceptability of screening for suicide prevention include concern that screening will be time consuming, will result in parental consent difficulties, will not be valid because of the unreliability of adolescent self-report (Eckert et al., 2006), will lead to labeling or stigmatizing of students, and will lead to demands for treatment resources that do not exist (Miller et al., 1999). An additional concern often cited is fear that asking about suicidal ideation or behavior during a screening program will create distress and increase suicidal ideation (Eckert et al., 2006). High school students exposed to suicide questions, however, have been found to be no more likely than unexposed students to report suicidal ideation (Gould et al., 2005).

Tolerance for False Cases

False positives are cases in which a screening program identifies an individual as at risk for or as having the problem that is the target of screening, when in fact the individual does not have the problem. False negatives are cases in which a screening program does not identify an individual as having the problem that is the target of screening, when in fact he or she does (see Chapter 4 in this volume). False positives are problematic because individuals may be labeled and stigmatized or may be subject to further testing and intervention that is not warranted, which may have negative side effects. False negatives are problematic because individuals may not receive interventions that they need and that could be helpful in preventing or ameliorating problems.

Because of the perceived potential negative effects of screening and the fact that attitudes toward false positives and false negatives influence stakeholders' willingness to support and implement screening programs, there has been some investigation of the number of false alarms (false positives) that stakeholders find acceptable in screening programs. In a study of a national sample of school psychologist practitioners, Forman, Walkup, Chu, Fagley, and Marsalowicz (2010) found that school psychologists were willing to tolerate up to approximately 19 false-positive screens out of 100 screens for mental health problems. Thus, screening programs that exceed this percentage of false positives may result in opposition from this group of professionals. In an additional analysis, Forman, Fagley, Chu, and Walkup (in press) found that although school psychologists had greater perceptions of stigma for students with mental health problems than for students with health problems, they were more committed to implementing interventions for students with mental health problems than for students with health problems. Thus, although school psychologists may resist screening programs with high percentages of false positives, it appears that perceived stigma that may result from identification during screening is not likely to have a negative impact on school psychologists' willingness to implement interventions. School psychologists' commitment to treatment for mental health problems, despite recognized stigma, points to the value of professional training that frames mental health needs as opportunities for intervention rather than triggers for social exclusion.

Screening Within Response to Intervention

Again, few studies have directly addressed factors related to implementation of academic screening programs. Barriers to implementation of a response-to-intervention (RTI) model were examined as part of a larger study in which school psychologists completed a survey about the identification of reading disabilities (Machek & Nelson, 2010). Although the definition of RTI has varied, most descriptions of RTI include a schoolwide or classroomwide process in which all students receive empirically supported instruction; have frequent assessments of their academic progress; and, if needed, are provided with more intensive instruction and additional assessment, before being considered for special education services. Curriculum-based measurements (Deno, 1985) consisting of brief (1 minute) probes of basic academic skills commonly are used to assess student progress within the RTI model. Study participants perceived their schools to have inadequate financial resources, personnel, and available time to implement the RTI model. Participants in elementary schools expressed more desire to take on roles associated with the use of an RTI model, including engaging in curriculum-based measurement, than did those who worked in junior high or high schools. The desire to perform RTI roles, however, was greater than the actual perceived ability to perform RTI roles. The majority of participants perceived the RTI model to be more likely to result in improvements for students with reading disabilities than the more traditional intelligence quotient–achievement discrepancy model for several reasons, including (a) ruling out poor instruction as a cause for academic difficulty, (b) identifying academic problems early, (c) providing the basis for appropriate intervention, and (d) providing a means for use of formative assessment (for more information on universal screening and RTI, see Chapter 2 of this volume).

Teacher Attitudes and Perspectives: Academic Screening

Kettler, Elliott, and Albers (2008) provided a rare example of the development of a universal screening program in which teacher attitudes about the screening program were evaluated, along with reliability and validity data. In the development of the Brief Academic Competence Evaluation Screening System (BACESS), the developers asked teachers if the time spent using the different phases of the BACESS was reasonable, if it was easy to use, if it was useful for identifying students with problems, and if it was useful in making decisions about developing individual academic plans for students. Results indicated that most teachers thought that all phases of the instrument were necessary and that teachers thought the BACESS was easy to use, useful for identifying students for a prereferral or building intervention team, and useful for developing an individual academic plan for a student. Thus, this study provides a good example of the manner in which screening program developers can develop information about issues related to implementation, such as perceived utility, at the same time they are establishing reliability and validity.

Implications

These studies emphasize the importance of addressing the attitudes of potential implementers toward screening. Information and communication about new programs tend to focus on the content of the program and how to go about administering or conducting it (program process). Equally important in efforts to initiate and support implementation are communications that directly address implementer and stakeholder perceptions and attitudes that may undermine implementation attempts. For example, from the aforementioned research about suicide screening, we can conclude that communications in presentations, workshops, and discussions about adopting and implementing this type of program should include information about the fact that research has shown that students who are screened do not have increased suicidal ideation. Both the suicide screening studies and the RTI study indicate the importance of ensuring that staff resources, resources for interventions that will be needed for students postscreening, and a plan that addresses how implementers will incorporate the new screening program with their daily tasks and work goals will be necessary if implementation is to proceed successfully.

MULTIDISCIPLINARY LITERATURE: FACTORS RELATED TO IMPLEMENTATION SUCCESS

Although research literature on implementation of screening programs in schools is scarce, additional relevant information can be drawn from the broader literature on implementation. Several reviews of the literature on implementation identify a number of factors that affect implementation effectiveness (Durlak & DuPre, 2008; Fixsen et al., 2005; Greenhalgh, Robert, Macfarlane, Bate, & Kyriakidou, 2004; Rogers, 2003; Stith et al., 2006). The literature comes from many disciplines, including psychology, education, anthropology, sociology, public health, medicine, and management, and it examines implementation in a variety of organizational settings, such as mental health and other human service agencies, health care organizations, public health agencies, and schools as well as communities. Durlak and DuPre's (2008) recent review is of special interest, as they reviewed 81 data-based implementation studies (quantitative and qualitative) on factors affecting implementation and also compared their results with three other previous reviews (Fixsen et al., 2005; Greenhalgh et al., 2004; Stith et al., 2006). They identified a factor as important to implementation (a) if the factor was found to be related to implementation in at least 5 of the 81 studies they reviewed and (b) if the findings were consistent in investigations that were more rigorous in methodology. Across this literature on implementation, a number of factors, including innovation and program characteristics, implementer characteristics, and social and organizational factors, as well as training and technical assistance, have been found to influence implementation of new programs in organizational settings, such as schools.

Innovation and Program Characteristics

The literature on innovation and program characteristics provides information on the types of practices and programs that likely will be implemented successfully in a given organizational context. For example, Rogers (2003) indicated that innovations that are perceived as having a greater relative advantage, compatibility, trialability (i.e., innovations that can be tried out before complete implementation), and observability as well as less complexity will be adopted more rapidly than other innovations. Additional attributes of innovations that have been found to influence adoption include riskiness and task relevance (i.e., the perceived relationship between the innovation and the implementer's work tasks; Greenhalgh et al., 2004). The Durlak and DuPre (2008) review found that adaptability (flexibility), compatibility, and the perceived need and benefit of the innovation were consistently related to implementation. Thus, to assess the likelihood that a new

EXHIBIT 5.1
Questions to Guide Implementation: Program Characteristics

1. Do decision makers, implementers, and other stakeholders think that having the screening program would be better than currently existing screening-related activities, or having no screening program, if that is what currently exists?
2. Is the screening program viewed as compatible with school philosophy, mission, needs, and other existing school programs?
3. Is the screening program relatively easy to understand and use?
4. Can the screening program be tried on an experimental or partial basis?
5. Can stakeholders observe a demonstration of the screening program?
6. Does the program include methods of providing feedback to stakeholders about the results or outcomes of screening?
7. Does the school face any perceived risk in using the screening program?
8. Will the screening program help the school accomplish its main goals better and will it help individual implementers accomplish their work goals better?
9. Can the screening program be modified to better fit the context of the school in which it will be implemented?

program will be successfully implemented, the change agent should consider a number of questions related to characteristics of the innovation. Exhibit 5.1 contains a list of questions that should be considered when implementing a new screening program in a school or school district.

Implementer and Stakeholder Characteristics

Attitudes and beliefs about an innovation have been identified as key factors that affect implementation success. Greenhalgh et al. (2004) pointed out that many of the aforementioned innovation characteristics are perceived characteristics and that those perceptions can be shaped and changed through communications between the change agent and stakeholders as well as through communications among stakeholders. Thus, change agents working to establish the use of screening programs in schools should be prepared to work to establish positive perceptions of screening programs in their presentations, workshops, formal and informal discussions, and consultation. Frequently, presentations and workshops about screening programs or other school-based programs focus on how a program works. These communication vehicles, however, also should call attention to the ways in which the screening program meets the desired characteristics described earlier (e.g., how the screening program is compatible with school philosophy, mission, and goals).

Rogers (2003) indicated that most individuals do not form opinions about innovations based on the scientific literature; rather, they depend on the subjective opinions of others, especially their peers. Thus, individuals considering whether to implement a program tend to base their decision on what others like themselves think about the program. This tendency implies that in addition to working with potential implementers of a screening program, the change agent should be prepared to work with a broader array of individuals in the potential implementer's social network because those individuals are likely to influence the implementer's attitudes toward the screening program.

Durlak and DuPre (2008) found that a particular type of stakeholder, called a *program champion*, is important in engaging in successful implementation. A program champion is an individual who puts his or her support behind an innovation. The program champion does not necessarily have formal power in an organization but is trusted and respected and skillful in persuasion and negotiation. To successfully implement screening programs in schools, the change agent should identify the school opinion leaders—those who seem to influence the attitudes and beliefs of others—and work to enlist those individuals as champions for screening.

Self-efficacy is a characteristic of potential implementers that has been found to be related to effective implementation (Durlak & DuPre, 2008). Individuals with high self-efficacy feel confident in their ability to accomplish tasks and are likely to produce sufficient effort on a new task and persist despite setbacks. Teacher beliefs about their teaching efficacy have been found to influence their implementation of new instructional programs (Guskey, 1988). Thus, positive self-efficacy is an important personal characteristic to consider when choosing implementers for a new screening program, and this area should also be addressed in training and technical assistance for new implementers of screening programs.

Organizational and Systems Characteristics

The literature on implementation consistently recognizes the influence that the *work organization* and the *social systems* related to potential implementers have on implementation effectiveness. Significant aspects of organizational functioning related to implementation include adequate budget, staff, technology, and other resources to conduct the new program; the fit of the new program with existing resources, organizational activities and structures, and values and norms; staff buy-in; administrator support and leadership; shared decision making; capacity to monitor the new program and evaluate its impact; and effective communication and feedback mechanisms (Durlak & DuPre, 2008; Greenhalgh et al., 2004; Rogers, 2003). In the literature on innovation implementation in the workplace (Klein & Sorra, 1996), the organization's climate for implementation—defined as staff perceptions of the extent to which use of the innovation is rewarded, supported, and expected—has been seen as a factor having substantial impact on implementation success.

A positive work climate in which staff have positive views of morale, trust, and collegiality; means used to resolve disagreements (Durlak & DuPre, 2008; Fixsen et al., 2005; Greenhalgh et al., 2004; Stith et al., 2006); and organizational openness to trying new approaches and change (Durlak & DuPre, 2008; Greenhalgh et al., 2004) have also been found to affect the implementation process.

There are implications of these organizational and systems characteristics for the implementation of screening programs in schools. First, the fit between a screening program and a school or school district should be examined in terms of goals, resources, and existing ways of working in the school setting. Next, other aspects of school functioning should be considered, including the school climate and the methods used to make decisions. Implementation attempts in schools in which work climates are positive and adoption and implementation decisions are made collaboratively, with input from relevant stakeholders, are more likely to be successful. Administrative support, especially principal support, will be essential, as the principal typically sets school priorities, manages school resources, and can offer incentives tied to screening program implementation. In particular, the actions of a principal in terms of communicating support for the screening program and encouraging the activities of implementers can be instrumental in the success of the program. The change agent will need to establish an ongoing positive relationship with the principal as well as other school leaders.

Other essential ingredients for screening program implementation success cited earlier include the capacity to evaluate the implementation process and screening program outcomes as well as the capacity to provide this information to relevant parties (e.g., parents, support services providers). Primary implementers and the school staff member designated to manage the screening program need to have quick access to feedback on program operation, so that adjustments can be made in program operation when necessary. Primary implementers and other stakeholders (e.g., teachers, guidance counselors) must be provided with information on program outcomes to sustain their motivation to implement the program. The change agent will need to ensure that these organizational capacities exist and, if they do not, will need to work with school leaders or school district-level administrators to develop them.

Suprasystems

The external environment and suprasystems of an organization will affect implementation success. For schools and school districts, state and federal policy have a major impact on functioning (Forman & Selman, 2011), including school funding, school goals, and school staff activities, and must be considered in planning for implementation.

Federal policy in recent years has supported screening for academic problems, particularly reading. For example, the 2001 No Child Left Behind Act included grants that required conducting screening to identify children at risk for reading failure to support development of reading skills ("Early Reading First," 2010). State-level support for academic screening has gained momentum in many states that have mandated the use of RTI as a model for the provision of prevention and intervention services (Harr-Robins, Shambaugh, & Parrish, 2009). Support at the national and state levels for mental health screening, however, has been controversial. The President's New Freedom Commission on Mental Health (2002) recommended routine mental health screening in schools. This recommendation was met with strong opposition from some politicians and citizen groups, with resistance focusing on such fears as overdiagnosis and overmedication of children, excessive government intrusiveness and control of citizen private lives, and violation of family and citizen privacy (Citizens Commission on Human Rights International, 2011). Similar controversy has been present at the state level. For example, although the task force report leading to the Illinois Children's Mental Health Act of 2003 recommended screening in schools for mental health problems (VanLandeghem, 2003), this recommendation was not included in the law (Illinois Department of Healthcare and Family Services, 2011).

National professional and scientific organizations also can have an impact on support for screening in schools and on policy. The American Psychological Association (2011) and the National Institute of Mental Health (2011) have issued statements supportive of mental health screening that have the potential to influence public opinion and state and federal policy and that thereby may increase the probability that school-based mental health screening programs will be implemented. Toward this end, advocacy efforts of professionals, such as school psychologists, related to developing political support for mental health screening will be important.

Training and Technical Assistance

Training and technical assistance have been identified as essential prerequisites to implementation (Durlak & DuPre, 2008; Fixsen et al., 2005; Greenhalgh et al., 2004; Stith et al., 2006). Implementers and stakeholders need information about what the new program is, how it works, why it works, what their role in the program will be, and how to carry out that role. Implementers also need information about how to fit the use of the program with their other daily tasks as well as feedback about the accuracy of their program delivery. Without an adequate level of knowledge, implementers are unlikely to carry out a program with adequate fidelity. Training through workshops and presentations has been viewed as an efficient way to provide a potential implementer with background information and information on program theory and evidence base, program philosophy, program rationale, program components and content, program processes and practices, and acceptable forms of implementation, flexibility, and adaptation. Skills typically are introduced in training, but learning on the job through technical assistance or consultation provides the support necessary for more comprehensive and in-depth understanding of a new program and the skill to deliver it. Participation in training has been associated with higher levels of fidelity (Ransford, Greenberg, Domitrovich, Small, & Jacobson, 2009), and provision of technical assistance and coaching after training also has been linked to better program fidelity (Payne & Eckert, 2010). Literature on good training and professional development practices indicates that training should be multisession, should include written materials, and should include goal setting, modeling, practice, feedback, and follow-up "booster sessions" and technical assistance (Joyce & Showers, 2002). Literature on technical assistance indicates that effective work in this area typically includes modeling and performance feedback (Han & Weiss, 2005; Noell et al., 2005). In addition to improving implementers' skill in program delivery, technical assistance can deal with issues related to motivation, self-efficacy, coping with problems and setbacks, and the implementer's need for emotional support when engaging in new behaviors.

Thus, when the professional development needs of individuals who are potential implementers of screening programs are considered, a primary concern should be the provision of technical assistance that includes monitoring and performance feedback. Many school-based professional development programs continue to utilize the one-session workshop approach, although this has been found to be inadequate to change school staff behavior and support implementation of new programs (Joyce & Showers, 2002).

IMPLEMENTATION ADVICE FROM SCREENING
PROGRAM DEVELOPERS

As indicated, few studies have directly investigated the factors that affect implementation of screening programs in educational settings. Those who have developed, validated, and, as a result, engaged in the implementation of screening programs have offered advice in their publications. In many cases, their advice is consistent with conclusions from the interdisciplinary literature on implementation. These lessons from the field provide some implications for practice specific to implementation of school screening programs, although the lack of empirical studies in this area is a concern.

Screening Program Characteristics

A number of authors have identified critical characteristics to consider when choosing a screening program. The theoretical and empirical support for the screening program and the fit with the target population have been cited as important program characteristics to examine (Glover & Albers, 2007). In addition, the feasibility of administering the program in the target setting, with a focus on time requirements, has been deemed to be important, with time requirements for administration of the screening instrument and the program and time requirements for implementer training specified as issues of significance (Glover & Albers, 2007; Invernizzi, Landrum, Teichman, & Townsend, 2010). In general, Invernizzi et al. (2010) have recommended examining screening programs for their clarity of requirements and for purposes of use. Invernizzi et al. (2010) also discussed the importance of consequential validity in academic screening (e.g., the validity of using data from the screening program to improve instruction) and recommended that teachers be informed of the instructional utility of the program.

Attitudes Toward Screening Programs

As stated, attitudes and beliefs of implementers and stakeholders will affect the likelihood of implementation success, and several authors have discussed how these attitudes and beliefs are likely to provide direction for those attempting to implement screening programs. Weist, Rubin, Moore, Adelsheim, and Wrobel (2007) have indicated that many individuals are opposed to mental health screening in schools because they believe that it is an encroachment of government on families' right to privacy. Carter, Briggs-Gowan, and Davis (2004) pointed to a general reluctance on the part of school personnel to address mental health needs because of issues of stigma and a concomitant reluctance to engage in mental health screening. Other negative attitudes and beliefs about mental health screening seen in this literature include the notions of overdiagnosing and inappropriate labeling for mental health problems as well as subsequent overuse of medication for mental health problems (Levitt, Saka, Romanelli, & Hoagwood, 2007). In addition, some are concerned that screening may lead to identification of too many children and adolescents with mental health problems for existing community mental health services (Dowdy, Ritchey, & Kamphaus, 2010; Levitt et al., 2007). As indicated, for suicide prevention, some fear that screening can lead to an increase in the problem (Joe & Bryant, 2007). Some authors, however, have indicated that attitudes related to mental health stigma have been improving and that this may lead to a more supportive context for mental health screening (Dowdy et al., 2010).

Screening for academic problems has not appeared to face the same resistance as screening for mental health problems. This may be due to federal legislation supporting assessment (Deno et al., 2009). Much of the literature on academic screening indicates that when teachers are aware of the importance and utility of this type of screening, they are likely to endorse and engage in it (Invernizzi et al., 2010).

In recommendations to address attitudes and beliefs, the importance of taking the time to obtain buy-in from multiple stakeholders has been emphasized as crucial to implementation and sustainability. Such buy-in can result from including a broad array of stakeholders in the planning and implementation process, including administrators, school staff, parents, and students, and choosing a screening program or instrument that is aligned with constructs that are of interest to these stakeholders. In addition, the importance of highlighting the utility and benefits of screening has been emphasized as a way of decreasing negative attitudes and beliefs and of increasing buy-in (Glover & Albers, 2007; Invernizzi et al., 2010). The presence and discussion of safeguards to protect confidentiality has been recommended as a strategy that will reassure parents and students about respect for their right to privacy (Weist et al., 2007), and it has been recommended that decisions about whether to participate in and give consent for mental health screening be required from students as well as parents (Levitt et al., 2007).

Organizational and Systems Support for Screening Programs

To ensure appropriate organizational and systems support for a new screening program, Weist et al. (2007) advised that schools go through a self-assessment process to determine their screening needs, goals, and available resources. Involvement of and collaboration with multiple stakeholders, including school staff, teachers, parents, students, and community members, are recommended as a means of ensuring the prerequisites and ongoing supports necessary for an effective screening program (Glover & Albers, 2007). When initiating implementation of a mental health screening program, it has been suggested, training for implementers and stakeholders should address increasing awareness of child and adolescent mental health issues, in addition to addressing the specifics of the screening program.

The ability of the school to address the results of screening is a key organizational support factor; resources must be available to address problems that are identified through screening if the screening program is to be useful. Thus, it has been recommended that the decision to engage in screening, as well as the selection of a screening program and instrument, should be based on consideration of the information needs identified by the school as well as the resources that will be available to address screening results (Glover & Albers, 2007; Levitt et al., 2007). Weist et al. (2007) also suggested that school-based mental health screening and addressing the results of such screening should be a community effort in which communitywide resources are utilized in implementation planning.

EFFECTIVE IMPLEMENTATION OF SCREENING PROGRAMS IN SCHOOLS: SUMMARY AND CONCLUSION

Effective implementation of screening programs is a multistep process that requires analysis of the specific context for screening and development of a plan to address factors that have been found to affect implementation success. A comprehensive implementation plan should include a number of components. These are summarized in checklist form in Exhibit 5.2. These implementation planning activities will help to build a school context conducive to successful screening program implementation.

Implementation Planning: Context Analysis

An analysis of resource and infrastructure requirements of the screening program of interest is essential. This type of analysis includes requirements for time, staffing, equipment, materials, supplies, space, professional development, and financial requirements. In addition, an analysis of the fit of the target school or school district with the characteristics and requirements of the screening program should be conducted. Identification of potential implementers and stakeholders groups, potential sources of opposition to the screening program, and school or school district communication networks is necessary.

Implementation Planning: Defining Implementation Strategies

A comprehensive implementation plan will include specification of strategies for meeting resource requirements and developing implementer, school administrator, and other stakeholder buy-in and support, including strategies for dealing with social influence, based in part on an analysis of school or district communication networks. Strategies for developing one or more screening program champions should be identified. In addition, strategies for the provision of training and technical assistance will be important in providing the knowledge and skill prerequisites for implementation. Building an understanding of the function of screening, the process

EXHIBIT 5.2
Change Agent's Screening Program Implementation Planning Checklist

Resources and Infrastructure Analysis
____Determine what is required for the screening program in terms of time, staffing, equipment, materials, supplies, space, professional development, funds, other
____Determine whether these requirements match the resources of my school or school district
____If not, determine whether it is likely that required resources will be procured
____Identify the potential screening program implementers
____Identify other screening program stakeholders
____Identify potential screening program champions
____Identify potential sources of opposition to the screening program
____Identify how information is communicated through the school or school district

Implementation Strategies
____Determine how needed resources will be procured
____Determine how administrator and school leader support will be developed
____Determine how implementer support will be developed
____Determine how champion support will be developed
____Determine how needed organizational support structures, such as a screening program task force or leadership team, will be developed
____Determine how the school or school district communication channels will be used or developed to build support for the screening program
____Determine how training and technical assistance will be provided

Implementation Evaluation Plan
____Determine how screening program fidelity will be assessed
____Determine how screening program satisfaction will be monitored
____Determine how barriers to implementation will be assessed
____Determine how implementation evaluation information will be communicated to stakeholders
____Determine how screening program student outcomes will be assessed

Sustainability Planning
____Determine how implementation evaluation information will be used to reduce barriers to implementation
____Determine how screening program student outcomes will be communicated to stakeholders
____Determine how staff turnover will be handled
____Determine how ongoing professional development related to the screening program will be provided
____Determine how financial support will be maintained

of the screening program, and the utility of screening relative to positive student outcomes, school goals, and staff work activities and requirements is key. Strategies for developing or changing organizational structures necessary to support the implementation of the screening program, such as a leadership team focused on screening, data management systems, or staff positions responsible for providing feedback about screening to stakeholders, also are needed.

Planning Implementation Evaluation

Implementation evaluation is another significant issue to consider when planning for implementation. Identification of instruments and methods for obtaining information about program fidelity and about the effectiveness of implementation is essential for change agents and program managers for several reasons. Implementation evaluation information can provide rapid feedback to the program manager during initial implementation, so changes in strategies and procedures can be made, if necessary, to enhance program effectiveness. In addition, implementation evaluation can provide important, meaningful feedback to implementers and stakeholders that can lead to improved program fidelity and to program support and success.

Planning for Sustainability

Finally, sustainability issues should be addressed in implementation planning. Doing this involves defining the strategies that will be used to maintain the screening program after the first complete implementation. Issues of particular importance will be how program outcome information will be provided to implementers and stakeholders, how staff turnover will be addressed, how new staff members will be informed about the screening program, and how financial support for the program will be maintained.

Program Developer Roles

Several supporting activities are necessary to facilitate the change agents' development of effective screening program implementation plans. Program developers should include guidelines for implementation in their screening instrument and program manuals. Although implementation plans are always context specific, the screening instrument or program manual can provide the change agent and program manager with important information, in an easily accessible format, about resource and infrastructure requirements and about any research-based implementation information that has been developed specific to the screening instrument or program. A best-case scenario would be to include a protocol for implementation as part of the screening instrument or program manual.

Professional Advocacy Efforts

As indicated, policy can be either a significant support or a barrier to implementation of screening programs in schools. Therefore, professional advocacy efforts will be important in the development of state and federal policies that support school-based screening for academic and mental health problems. Advocacy is especially important for mental health screening programs, for which issues of stigma and false stereotypes as well as perceptions of intrusion on privacy are at play. In addition, efforts are needed to increase awareness of the impact of students' mental health on their academic performance.

Training Program Roles

Graduate educators can be helpful in providing the supports necessary for effective implementation of screening programs. The provision of education and training in graduate programs on implementation and how to bring about change in organizations and organizational staff will be a useful way to address this issue. This training can be accomplished in the context of courses that include information about the process of implementation and principles of implementation science (Forman, 2009).

Future Research Needs

Although research literature on implementation has increased in recent years, there is still little specifically related to implementation of screening programs in schools. Future work in this area should address a number of issues. As illustrated in the work of Kettler et al. (2008), screening program developers should be concerned with developing information about the feasibility of implementation in a variety of school contexts as well as with establishing the reliability and validity of their instruments. We need to know more about what screening programs can be implemented in what types of schools and school districts and with what types of student and teacher populations. Research on implementation strategies and organizational interventions that support effective implementation of screening programs is sorely needed. When barriers to implementation of school-based screening programs are identified, we need to know what strategies and interventions can be used to deal with them. Finally, we need additional knowledge about what constitutes appropriate training and coaching for conducting screening programs and for developing effective screening program implementation plans.

REFERENCES

American Psychological Association. (2011). *APA urges IOM Committee to strengthen depression and violence screening recommendations*. Retrieved from http://www.apa.org/about/gr/issues/women/iom.aspx

Atkins, M. S., Frazier, S. L., Adil, J., & Talbott, E. (2003). School-based mental health services in urban communities. In M. D. Weist, S. W. Evens, & N. A. Lever (Eds.), *Handbook of school mental health: advancing practice and research* (pp. 165–178). New York, NY: Plenum Press.

Carter, A. S., Briggs-Gowan, M. J., & Davis, N. O. (2004). Assessment of young children's social–emotional development and psychopathology: Recent advances and recommendations for practice. *Journal of Child Psychology and Psychiatry, 45,* 109–134. doi:10.1046/j.0021-9630.2003.00316.x

Citizens Commission on Human Rights International. (2011, August 22). Ron Paul reintroduces the Parental Consent Act 2011: Prohibits federal funding for psychiatric "screening" of kids. Retrieved from http://www.cchrint.org/2011/08/22/ron-paul-reintroduces-the-parental-consent-act-2011-prohibits-federal-funding-for-psychiatric-'screening'-of-kids

Deno, S. L. (1985). Curriculum-based measurement: The emerging alternative. *Exceptional Children, 52,* 219–232.

Deno, S. L., Reschly, A. L., Lembke, E. S., Magnusson, D., Callender, S. A., Windram, H., & Stachel, M. (2009). Developing a school-wide progress-monitoring system. *Psychology in the Schools, 46,* 44–55. doi:10.1002/pits.20353

Dowdy, E., Ritchey, K., & Kamphaus, R. W. (2010). School-based screening: A population-based approach to inform and monitor children's mental health needs. *School Mental Health, 2,* 166–176. doi:10.1007/s12310-010-9036-3

Durlak, J. A., & DuPre, E. P. (2008). Implementation matters: A review of research on the influence of implementation on program outcomes and the factors affecting implementation. *American Journal of Community Psychology, 41,* 327–350. doi:10.1007/s10464-008-9165-0

Early reading first. (2010). Retrieved from http:/www.ed.gov/programs/earlyreading/index.html

Eckert, T., Miller, D., DuPaul, G., & Riley-Tillman, T. (2003). Adolescent suicide prevention: School psychologists' acceptability of school-based programs. *School Psychology Review, 32,* 57–76.

Eckert, T. L., Miller, D. N., Riley-Tillman, C. R., & DuPaul, G. J. (2006). Adolescent suicide prevention: Gender differences in students' perceptions of the acceptability and intrusiveness of school-based screening programs. *Journal of School Psychology, 44,* 271–285. doi:10.1016/j.jsp.2006.05.001

Ennett, S. T., Ringwalt, C. L., Thorne, J., Rohrbach, L. A., Vincus, A., Simons-Rudolph, A., & Jones, S. (2003). A comparison of current practice in school-based substance use prevention programs with meta-analysis findings. *Prevention Science, 4,* 1–14. doi:10.1023/A:1021777109369

Fixsen, D. L., Naoom, S. F., Blase, K. A., Friedman, R. M., & Wallace, F. (2005). *Implementation research: A synthesis of the literature.* Tampa: University of South Florida.

Forman, S. G. (2009). Innovation implementation: Developing leadership for evidence-based practice. In S. Rosenfield & V. Berninger (Eds.), *Implementing evidence-based academic interventions in school settings* (pp. 655–676). New York, NY: Oxford University Press.

Forman, S. G., Fagley, N. S., Chu, B. C., & Walkup, J. (in press). Factors influencing school psychologist "willingness to implement" evidence-based interventions. *School Mental Health*.

Forman, S. G., & Selman, J. S. (2011). Systems-based service delivery in school psychology. In M. A. Bray & T. J. Kehle (Eds.), *The Oxford handbook of school psychology* (pp. 628–646). New York, NY: Oxford University Press.

Forman, S. G., Walkup, J., Chu, B. C., Fagley, N. S., & Marsalowicz, A. J. (2010, August). Factors influencing implementation of screening for health problems of youth. In R. J. Kettler (Chair), *Identifying students in need of assistance: Multistage and multimethod screening*. Symposium conducted at the meeting of the American Psychological Conference, San Diego, CA.

Glover, T. A., & Albers, C. A. (2007). Considerations for evaluating universal screening assessments. *Journal of School Psychology, 45*, 117–135. doi:10.1016/j.jsp.2006.05.005

Gottfredson, D. C., & Gottfredson, G. D. (2007). Quality of school-based prevention programs: Results from a national survey. *Journal of Research in Crime and Delinquency, 44*, 3–35. doi:10.1177/002242780203900101

Gould, M. S., Marrocco, F. A., Kleinman, M., Thomas, J. G., Mostkoff, K., Cote, J., & Davies, M. (2005). Evaluating iatrogenic risk of youth suicide screening programs: A randomized controlled trial. *JAMA: Journal of the American Medical Association, 293*, 1635–1643. doi:10.1001/jama.293.13.1635

Greenhalgh, T., Robert, G., Macfarlane, F., Bate, P., & Kyriakidou, O. (2004). Diffusion of innovations in service organizations: Systematic review and recommendations. *Milbank Quarterly, 82*, 581–629. doi:10.1111/j.0887-378X.2004.00325.x

Guskey, T. R. (1988). Teacher efficacy, self-concept, and attitudes toward the implementation of instructional innovation. *Teaching and Teacher Education, 4*, 63–69. doi:10.1016/0742-051X(88)90025-X

Hall, G. E., & Hord, S. M. (1987). *Change in schools: Facilitating the process*. Albany: State University of New York Press.

Han, S. S., & Weiss, B. (2005). Sustainability of teacher implementation of school-based mental health programs. *Journal of Abnormal Child Psychology, 33*, 665–679. doi:10.1007/s10802-005-7646-2

Harr-Robins, J. J., Shambaugh, L. S., & Parrish, T. (2009, August). *The status of state-level response to intervention policies and procedures in the West Region states and five other states* (Report REL 2009-No. 077). Retrieved from http://ies.ed.gov/ncee/edlabs/regions/west/pdf/rel_2009077.pdf

Illinois Department of Healthcare and Family Services. (2011). *Children's Mental Health Public Act 93-0495*. Retrieved from http://www.hfs.illinois.gov/sass/930495.html

Invernizzi, M., Landrum, T., Teichman, A., & Townsend, M. (2010). Increased implementation of emergent literacy screening in pre-kindergarten. *Early Childhood Education Journal, 37*, 437–446. doi:10.1007/s10643-009-0371-7

Joe, S., & Bryant, H. (2007). Evidence-based suicide prevention screening in schools. *Children and Schools, 29,* 219–227. doi:10.1093/cs/29.4.219

Joyce, B., & Showers, B. (2002). *Student achievement through staff development* (3rd ed.). Alexandria, VA: Association for Supervision and Curriculum Development.

Kazdin, A. E. (1980). Acceptability of alternative treatments for deviant child behavior. *Journal of Applied Behavior Analysis, 13,* 259–273. doi:10.1901/jaba.1980.13-259

Kettler, R. J., Elliott, S. N., & Albers, C. A. (2008). Structured teacher ratings to identify students in need of academic assistance: Validation of the brief academic competence evaluation screening system. *Journal of Psychoeducational Assessment, 26,* 260–273. doi:10.1177/0734282907304236

Klein, K. J., & Sorra, J. S. (1996). The challenge of innovation implementation. *Academy of Management Review, 21,* 1055–1080.

Levitt, M. J., Saka, N., Romanelli, L., & Hoagwood, K. (2007). Early identification of mental health problems in schools: The status of instrumentation. *Journal of School Psychology, 45,* 163–191. doi:10.1016/j.jsp.2006.11.005

Machek, G. R., & Nelson, J. M. (2010). School psychologists' perceptions regarding the practice of identifying reading disabilities: Cognitive assessment and response to intervention considerations. *Psychology in the Schools, 47,* 230–245.

Miller, D. N., Eckert, T., DuPaul, G., & White, G. (1999). Adolescent suicide prevention: Acceptability of school-based programs among secondary school principals. *Suicide and Life-Threatening Behavior, 29,* 72–85.

National Institute of Mental Health. (2011, July 6). *Thinking globally to improve mental health: NIH announces international research initiative* [Press release]. Retrieved from http://www.nimh.nih.gov/science-news/2011/thinking-globally-to-improve-mental-health.shtml

Noell, G. H., Witt, J. C., Slider, N. J., Connell, J. E., Gatti, S. L., Williams, K. L., . . . Resetar, J. L. (2005). Treatment implementation following behavioral consultation in schools: A comparison of three follow-up strategies. *School Psychology Review, 34,* 87–106.

Payne, A. A., & Eckert, R. (2010). The relative importance of provider, program, school, and community predictors of the implementation quality of school-based prevention programs. *Prevention Science, 11,* 126–141. doi:10.1007/s11121-009-0157-6

President's New Freedom Commission on Mental Health. (2002) *Executive summary: Goal 4—Early mental health screening, assessment, and referral to services are common practice.* Retrieved from http://govinfo.library.unt.edu/mentalhealthcommission/reports/FinalReport/FullReport.htm

Ransford, C. R., Greenberg, M. T., Domitrovich, C. E., Small, M., & Jacobson, L. (2009). The role of teachers' psychological experiences and perceptions of curriculum supports on the implementation of social and emotional learning curriculum. *School Psychology Review, 38,* 510–532.

Reynolds, W. M. (1991). A school-based procedure for the identification of adolescents at risk for suicidal behaviors. *Family and Community Health, 14*, 64–75.

Reynolds, W. M., & Mazza, J. J. (1994). Suicide and suicidal behaviors in children and adolescents. In W. M. Reynolds & H. Johnston (Eds.), *Handbook of depression in children and adolescents* (pp. 525–580). New York, NY: Plenum Press.

Rogers, E. M. (2003). *Diffusion of innovations.* New York, NY: Free Press.

Scherff, A. R., Eckert, T., & Miller, D. (2005). Youth suicide prevention: A survey of public school superintendents' acceptability of school-based programs. *Suicide and Life-Threatening Behavior, 35*, 154–169. doi:10.1521/suli.35.2.154.62874

Stith, S., Pruitt, I., Dees, J., Fronce, M., Green, N., Som, A., & Linkh, D. (2006). Implementing community-based prevention programming: A review of the literature. *Journal of Primary Prevention, 27*, 599–617. doi:10.1007/s10935-006-0062-8

VanLandeghem, K. (2003, April). *Illinois Children's Mental Health Task Force: Final report.* Retrieved from http://www.isbe.net/spec-ed/pdfs/cmh_priority.pdf

Weist, M. D., Rubin, M., Moore, E., Adelsheim, S., & Wrobel, G. (2007). Mental health screening in schools. *Journal of School Health, 77*, 53–58. doi:10.1111/j.1746-1561.2007.00167.x

III

CONTENT-SPECIFIC SCREENING

6

EARLY CHILDHOOD LITERACY SCREENING

SCOTT R. McCONNELL, TRACY A. BRADFIELD,
AND ALISHA K. WACKERLE-HOLLMAN

Reading (and, more broadly, literacy) is seen as a cultural imperative and essential academic skill for students in the United States and other industrial countries. Since the latter part of the 20th century, we have witnessed rapid expansion in theoretical and empirical analyses of the preschool components of later reading and lifelong literacy (Dickinson & Neuman, 2006; Neuman

This work was supported in part by grant R324C080011, the Center for Response to Intervention in Early Childhood, from the Institute of Education Sciences, U.S. Department of Education, to the University of Kansas; Charles Greenwood and Judith Carta, Principal Investigators. However, the opinions and recommendations presented in this paper are those of the authors alone, and no official endorsement from the Institute of Education Sciences should be inferred.

Drs. McConnell, Bradfield, and Wackerle-Hollman have developed assessment tools and related resources known as Individual Growth and Development Indicators and Get it, Got it, Go! This intellectual property is subject to technology commercialization by the University of Minnesota, and portions have been licensed to Early Learning Labs, Inc. Scott McConnell has equity interest in Early Learning Labs, Inc., a for-profit company. The University of Minnesota also has equity and royalty interests in Early Learning Labs, which, in turn, may benefit McConnell, Bradfield, and Wackerle-Hollman. These relationships have been reviewed and are being managed by the University of Minnesota in accordance with its conflict of interest policies.

http://dx.doi.org/10.1037/14316-006
Universal Screening in Educational Settings: Evidence-Based Decision Making for Schools, R. J. Kettler, T. A. Glover, C. A. Albers, and K. A. Feeney-Kettler (Editors)
Copyright © 2014 by the American Psychological Association. All rights reserved.

& Dickinson, 2001, 2011; Snow, Burns, & Griffin, 1998). As a result of this growing attention to the contributions of early childhood development to later academic and life skills competence, we also have witnessed a rapid expansion in intentional programming to promote early literacy development, particularly among populations considered to be at risk, in communities, states, and nations (W. S. Barnett & Frede, 2011).

Attention to language and literacy development in preschool, and the provision of educational and other services to promote language and early literacy development, can be seen directly as preventative interventions (Good & Kaminski, 1996; Juel, 2006; Scarborough, 2001; Whitehurst & Lonigan, 2001). Research over the past 2 decades has identified developmental skills of preschoolers that are functionally, and importantly, related to later elementary-grade reading success. More recent intervention research is emerging that suggests (a) that identification of deficits in these developmental skills, and early intervention during preschool to address these deficits, will reduce the likelihood of reading delays and disabilities in later grades (National Early Literacy Panel [NELP], 2009) and (b) that this instruction can be rigorous and effective as well as consistent with the nature and tradition of early childhood education (Christie, 2008).

As the earlier chapters in this volume demonstrate, screening practices in educational settings share at least two characteristics with work in other disciplines. First, they are part of broader multitiered systems of support—most typically (but not exclusively) response-to-intervention (RTI) initiatives (Greenwood, Kratochwill, & Clements, 2008). These multitiered systems of support are designed to monitor the development of all children (or other individuals) in a population, to identify those individuals who are (in an educational sense) not making developmental achievements at expected levels, and to provide supplemental or alternative intervention to those individuals in ways that effectively and efficiently promote development *across the population*.

Assessment activities in RTI and other educational multitiered systems of support share many features, including conceptual and methodological underpinnings, with the universal screening and comprehensive assessment and surveillance systems most commonly found in public health and other medical disciplines (Detels, Beaglehole, Lansang, & Gulliford, 2011). These similarities provide strong support and historical foundations for what otherwise might seem to be an emerging set of practices in educational settings.

"Screening" as an isolated activity, however, is only the beginning of a comprehensive approach to tiered intervention in early childhood programs (Greenwood, 2009). Although some confusion exists in terminology used in RTI and other tiered interventions, "screening" in this sense refers to assessment that identifies children who may benefit from more intensive intervention, and ongoing progress monitoring that confirms this intervention placement or prompts a revision in intervention services (Greenwood, 2009; for more information on universal screening and RTI, see Chapter 2, this volume).

This chapter reviews the current status of screening assessment for tiered interventions in early literacy for preschool-age children and highlights emerging and needed research in this area. It first provides an overview of shifts in intervention and assessment in early childhood services broadly and early literacy development specifically, and provides a general introduction to the core elements of early literacy development. Next, it critically reviews current approaches to language and early literacy assessment and screening in early care and education. It then identifies the state of knowledge and practice regarding these approaches and discusses challenges to ongoing development and opportunities for future research in this area.

DOMAINS OF CONCERN

Assessment for language and literacy in early childhood must be directed to areas of child development that are salient for future academic success, and accessible to intervention in preschool. To articulate domains of concern, we must understand both the context of intervention in early childhood and early childhood education, and skill acquisition in language and literacy development.

Intervention in Early Childhood and Early Childhood Education

Historically, formal reading instruction and differentiated educational services associated with achievement in this area were made available only to children age 5 and older who were enrolled in kindergarten and elementary or secondary grades. Since the late 20th century, however, we have seen dramatic increases in the provision of early childhood services—particularly for high-risk youngsters. With the advent of federally funded preschool programs like Head Start (Zigler, Styfco, & Gilman, 1993) and Early Reading First (U.S. Department of Education, 2004), expansion of similar programs (including school readiness, improved child care, and state-funded voluntary or universal prekindergarten programs) at state and local levels (W. S. Barnett, Epstein, Friedman, Sansanelli, & Hustedt, 2009), and the promising results of these efforts, we have seen an evolution of focus in recent years.

Additionally, many sectors of early childhood education have a weak tradition of assessment and intervention, particularly directed at relatively narrow or explicit developmental goals, such as vocabulary and early literacy (Carta, Schwartz, Atwater, & McConnell, 1991; McConnell, 2000; Strain et al., 1992). With growing evidence of the role of preschool development as foundational to later academic competence and related attention to intervention for high-risk children to address early developmental delays and improve long-term outcomes, discernible shifts are under way to increase both assessment and related intervention to address risk and promote competence in early childhood settings (Pianta, Cox, & Snow, 2007; Snow et al., 1998).

Language and Literacy

This growing attention to purposeful assessment and related intervention is perhaps most apparent in programming for language and early literacy development. As we have noted, a growing and compelling body of evidence demonstrates both the predictive and, increasingly, functional importance of early childhood development in later reading and academic performance (Dickinson & Neuman, 2006; Neuman & Dickinson, 2001, 2011; Snow et al., 1998). This knowledge in turn creates a growing emphasis on intervention— intervention that is developmentally appropriate but also effective at helping young children acquire essential developmental skills that support later reading (Christie, 2008).

Oral language development was a "leading indicator" of this growing emphasis. Hart and Risley (1995) demonstrated both significant variations in language development during the first 3 years of life, and consequent relations with elementary reading performance that highlighted the importance of these variations (Walker, Greenwood, Hart, & Carta, 1994). Oral language, including vocabulary and more complex syntactic elements, appears to have a central role in early literacy development (Fernald & Weisleder, 2011; Scarborough, 2001; Vasilyeva & Waterfall, 2011; Vernon-Feagans, Scheffner Hammer, Miccio, & Manlove, 2002). Although robust interventions for promoting language development still prove somewhat elusive (e.g., Dickinson, Freiberg, & Barnes, 2011), it remains a major focus of assessment and intervention in the preschool years (Hancock, Kaiser, & Delaney, 2002).

Phonological awareness and analysis, or children's skills at discriminating and acting on smaller sound components of individuals words, is another important predictor and precursor of later reading proficiency (Goswani, 2001; NELP, 2009; Whitehurst & Lonigan, 2001). Although the specific contributions of phonological awareness intervention when provided to preschool children remain somewhat uncertain (Paris, 2011), best practices in early education currently include an emphasis on assessment and intervention in this developmental area (NELP, 2009; Snow et al., 1998).

Alphabetic knowledge and concepts about print, or children's general and specific knowledge of letter names and sounds and the conventions of written text (e.g., reading from left to right and top to bottom), is a third area of essential preschool development related to later reading proficiency (NELP, 2009; Snow et al., 1998; Whitehurst & Lonigan, 1998). Specific skills, such as letter naming, that appear to be solely statistical predictors (as opposed to developmental prerequisites) and more general, functional skills like letter-sound correspondence, alphabetic knowledge, and concepts about print represent a rich area for assessment and intervention in early childhood literacy (Justice & Piasta, 2011).

Comprehension, or children's skill at understanding and making meaning from narratives and text, remains something of the "third rail" of early childhood literacy assessment and intervention. Theoretical and conceptual analyses have produced various definitions and perspectives, and logically it is easy to argue that "understanding" is an important part of reading (Fernald & Weisleder, 2011; Hays, Wackerle-Hollman, Bradfield, & McConnell, 2010) and that this understanding likely begins developing during preschool. Empirical analyses show preschool-to-elementary relations (Kendeou, van den Broek, White, & Lynch, 2009). Consistent definitions and related empirical analyses, however, continue to elude both early childhood researchers and their elementary reading research colleagues; as a result, this domain of early literacy development likely will remain important while continued empirical and theoretical refinement improve assessment and intervention focus in coming years.

CURRENT APPROACHES TO EARLY CHILDHOOD LANGUAGE AND LITERACY SCREENING

While we continue to see growth in both our knowledge of early literacy development and the factors that promote (or inhibit) it, and we see expansion in federal and local efforts to promote development in this important domain, this work is still rather new. Unlike assessment in educational and clinical settings with older children, foundations for and wide-scale examples of assessment with young children are just now emerging (Greenwood, Carta, & McConnell, 2011; Snow & Oh, 2011).

In *Early Childhood Assessment: Why, What and How*, a report of the National Academy of Sciences Committee on Developmental Assessment and Outcomes for Young Children, Snow and Van Hemel (2008) argued that those who purport to assess the skills of young children need to explicitly address three main questions: (a) *Why* is the assessment needed? (b) *What* aspect of a young child's functioning should be assessed? and (c) *How* will assessment be conducted to yield actionable information that minimizes burden on children and the systems that serve them?

For screening in early childhood literacy, the "why?" question is easy to answer: Within an early childhood RTI model focused on the domain of language and early literacy, the purpose of screening is to identify individual children who require more intensive levels of intervention to make expected developmental gains and who, once identified, will receive levels of instruction sufficient to support their development.

Similarly, the answer to "what aspects of a child's functioning will be assessed?" is fairly straightforward. Within the four domains of early literacy development described earlier, research makes clear that a child's vocabulary at school entry is a powerful predictor of later literacy and reading outcomes (Dickinson & Tabors, 2001; Poe, Burchinal, & Roberts, 2004; Roth, Speece, & Cooper, 2002; Snow, Porche, Tabors, & Harris, 2007). Furthermore, key findings from the NELP specify that alphabet knowledge and phonological awareness skills have medium to large predictive relationships with later literacy outcomes (NELP, 2009), and comprehension appears to carry unique variance in long-term child outcomes (Kendeou et al., 2009).

The final, and perhaps most complex, question to answer, then, is "how?" In early childhood settings, teachers do not have the luxury of spending large amounts of individual time with students. Teachers need efficient methods for accurately determining which children appear to be making sufficient progress given the current level of instruction and which children require more intensive instruction and intervention (Gersten et al., 2008; McConnell, 2010; McConnell & Missall, 2008). To do this, measures must be brief, but still maintain a high level of reliability (coefficient $\alpha \geq .70$; Gersten et al., 2008). More importantly, screening measures of language and early literacy skill for a preschool RTI model must demonstrate high degrees of construct validity with identified domains of early literacy development, and they must show concurrent and predictive relations to measures of language, early literacy, and later reading skill (McConnell & Missall, 2008; Missall & McConnell, 2010; VanDerHeyden, 2010).

In addition to logistical efficiency, reliability, and relevant construct validity, early literacy screening measures must demonstrate capacity to accurately classify students who are candidates for supplemental or alternative intervention that, in turn, contributes to later reading proficiency. As with other approaches, early literacy screening measures should demonstrate adequate levels of *sensitivity* (or accuracy in identifying those children who indeed will benefit from supplemental or alternative intervention) and *specificity* (or accuracy in identifying those children who will achieve adequately without supplemental or additional intervention; Jenkins et al., 2007).

The field is still developing consensus on specific standards for sensitivity and specificity—a system's accuracy at both identifying individuals who are good candidates for additional or different intervention (sensitivity) and ruling out a need for additional or different intervention for those who are not good candidates (specificity)—in early literacy screening measures. Jenkins and colleagues (Jenkins, 2003; Jenkins et al., 2007) have argued that the optimal level of sensitivity for a screening measure should be .90 or above. This degree of precision is not always attainable, however, particularly given that high levels of sensitivity often result in a corresponding decrease in specificity. To balance this trade-off between sensitivity and specificity, it has been argued that the most appropriate way to assess a measure's classification accuracy is to choose a desired sensitivity level and then evaluate the acceptability of the corresponding specificity. Using this approach, Catts et al. (2009) suggested that given an acceptable level of sensitivity (typically .70 or higher), a specificity of 50% or greater would be deemed acceptable in most educational RTI models, given that Tier 2 is designed to further identify those who truly do and do not require more intensive levels of intervention (for more information on interpreting the magnitude of sensitivity, specificity, and related indices, see Chapter 1, this volume).

Taken together, then, current standards for early literacy screening to support instructional decision making within an early childhood RTI model would favor measures that (a) sample performance in four key domains (oral language, alphabet knowledge–concepts about print, phonological awareness, and comprehension), (b) are brief and easy to collect across all children in an enrolled program, (c) maintain high degrees of reliability (generally, ≥ .7 as suggested by Gersten et al., 2008) within measures and across raters or assessors, (d) maintain similarly high validity relations with relevant measures of assessed constructs and future performance, and (e) maintain high levels (≥ .9) of sensitivity. These four broad standards serve as the basis for our review of available early literacy screening measures.

CRITICAL REVIEW OF EXISTING MEASURES

Given the relatively brief history of formal attention to early childhood literacy intervention and screening, it is not surprising that few well-developed and broadly used measures yet exist. Although research teams across the United States have described work on several sets of measures in early stages of empirical evaluation and applied use (e.g., Buysse & Peisner-Feinberg, 2010; Coleman, Buysse, & Neitzel, 2006; Phillips, Lonigan, & Wyatt, 2009; Wilson & Lonigan, 2010), we identified three measures that are sufficiently developed to support instructional decision making within an early childhood RTI framework to support early language and literacy instruction, which are reviewed here: Get Ready to Read! Revised (GRTR-R; Lonigan & Wilson, 2008), CIRCLE–Phonological Awareness, Language, and Literacy

System+ (C-PALLS+; Children's Learning Institute, 2011), and Individual Growth and Development Indicators, Version 2.0 (IGDIs 2.0; Greenwood et al., 2011). For each measure, we describe the current state of research and development; administration procedures; scales and scores provided; and summaries of reliability, validity, sensitivity and specificity.

Get Ready to Read! Revised

GRTR-R (Lonigan & Wilson, 2008) is an early literacy screening measure composed of 20 multiple-choice items related to print knowledge and phonological awareness. The measure is appropriate for use with children who are between the ages of 3 and 6 years (Lonigan & Wilson, 2008).

State of Research and Development

Items used in GRTR-R were selected based on a longitudinal study that tested emergent literacy skills of 4-year-old Head Start students and followed students through Grade 2. Pools of items that discriminated between successful and unsuccessful readers were selected. From these items, those that correlated highly with the Developing Skills Checklist (DSC, CTB Early Childhood System, 1990), had high internal consistency, and difficulty levels near .50 were included in the final GRTR-R item set. GRTR-R has been administered to a nationally representative sample of preschool children to allow national norms to be developed.

Administration Procedures

GRTR-R uses a two-sided easel as the stimulus material, presenting images representing the four response choices to the child, with the administrator directing the child to point to an answer. The examiner's side of the easel contains the administration prompt and the label for the four response choices, with the correct answer highlighted (Lonigan & Wilson, 2008). The assessment also can be administered through the use of an online screening mechanism (http://www.getreadytoread.org), in which the stimulus images are presented electronically and the administrator reads the standardized test prompts aloud to the child.

Scales and Scores

GRTR-R reports four types of scores, including *raw scores* based on the total number of items answered correctly; *step scores* that report four score ranges based on correct responses with regard to print knowledge and letter-sound associations; *percentile ranks* at 3-month intervals, which also form the basis for the "performance level" categories (below average, average, and above average); and *standard scores* with a mean of 100 and standard deviation of 15.

Reliability

GRTR-R test developers report only internal consistency estimates for this scale. Overall internal consistency (coefficient α) is high (.88), ranging from .77 to .84 across separate age groups (Lonigan & Wilson, 2008).

Concurrent and Predictive Validity

The technical report for the GRTR-R (Lonigan & Wilson, 2008) reports concurrent validity information for GRTR-R with the Test of Preschool Early Literacy (TOPEL; Lonigan, Wagner, Torgesen, & Rashotte, 2007). On the basis of a sample of 201 children 3 and 4 years old, GRTR-R developers reported significant correlations with TOPEL Print Knowledge ($r = .76, p < .001$), TOPEL Phonological Awareness ($r = .39, p < .001$), TOPEL Definitional Vocabulary ($r = .44, p < .001$), and TOPEL Overall Early Literacy Index ($r = .72, p < .001$).

With regard to the predictive validity of the GRTR-R, Phillips, Lonigan, and Wyatt (2009) found that the GRTR-R was predictive of blending, elision (omission of one or more sounds in a word), rhyming, letter knowledge, and word identification, as measured by tasks included in an early research version of the phonological awareness subtest on the TOPEL (Lonigan et al., 2007). Predictive relation was moderate ($r = .25–.40$; median $r = .32$) at 20, 28, and 35 months after initial assessment. Although these correlations do provide a degree of validity-related evidence for the GRTR-R, the criterion measures used in this study were from a research version of an early literacy assessment. Additional investigations will need to be completed to examine the predictive relation of the GRTR-R with a well-accepted criterion of the intended domain. Furthermore, the criterion measures on which the existing predictive validity evidence is based (blending, elision, and rhyming) are seen more accurately as indicators or necessary conditions for early literacy, rather than for early literacy itself. As such, future investigation should examine the predictive relation between the GRTR-R and more formal assessments of later reading ability.

Sensitivity and Specificity

GRTR-R reports sensitivity and specificity values in relation to the overall Early Literacy Index and three subtests of the Test of Preschool Early Literacy. Sensitivity coefficients for GRTR-R range from .90 to .95. Specificity ranges from .15 to .69 (Wilson & Lonigan, 2010).

CIRCLE—Phonological Awareness, Language, and Literacy System+

C-PALLS+ is one portion of a more comprehensive early education screening tool. This tool, developed originally for research by Dr. Susan Landry and colleagues at the Children's Learning Institute, is now available commercially. Until 2008, the system was called C-PALLS and was designed as a progress-monitoring system for evaluating early language and literacy skills of children in preschool settings.

State of Research and Development

The language and literacy portions of C-PALLS+ seem to be based conceptually and practically on earlier versions of Individual Growth and Development Indicators (Early Childhood Research Institute on Measuring Growth and Development, 1998). In 2008, a Math Screener was added to C-PALLS, and the name was changed to C-PALLS+ to reflect this addition. The mCLASS:CIRCLE system is the electronic counterpoint of C-PALLS+ and, as such, it allows for electronic data entry on a personal digital assistant, instant tracking and tabulating of child scores on progress-monitoring measures, and grouping children into ability levels, and it provides teachers with suggested activities to address a child's area of weakness. C-PALLS+ is validated for use with children from 3.5 years of age through kindergarten entry (Children's Learning Institute, 2011).

Administration Procedures

The C-PALLS+ is composed of several subtests. A thorough description of the administration procedures for each subtest follows.

Rapid Letter Naming. This subtest assesses the number of letters a child is able to name in 60 seconds. Testing progresses to the next item when one of the following occurs: (a) the child makes a correct response, (b) the child makes an incorrect response, or (c) 3 seconds elapse without a response. Stimuli include all of the letters of the English alphabet. Letters are presented individually in uppercase. The order of presentation of letters was determined randomly, but it is the same for all children.

Rapid Vocabulary Naming. This subtest assesses the number of pictures a child is able to label in 60 seconds. Pictures illustrate words selected from a review of national lists of appropriate vocabulary words and preschool curricula on Texas's state-adopted list. Words were selected based on the frequency that they showed up on vocabulary lists within published curricula. Other factors that determined word selection were age appropriateness and whether the objects, actions, or concepts could be illustrated by black-and-white line drawings. Content experts determined acceptable answers for the Rapid Vocabulary Naming test.

Phonological Awareness. The phonological awareness screener contains seven tasks comprising 43 items. Tasks include (a) listening (discriminating between like-sounding words), (b) rhyme recognition (Do these words rhyme? /frog/ /dog/), (c) rhyme production (What word rhymes with fan?), (d) alliteration (Do these words start with the same sound? /silly/ /sun/), (e) sentence segmentation (Move a block for each different word you hear in "My books are new"), (f) syllabication (How many parts do you hear in /cow/ /boy/?), and (g) blending of onset and rime (Repeat these parts and then say the word I am making: /m/ /om/). A single phonological awareness score is totaled across the seven tasks.

Scales and Scores

For each of the C-PALLS+ subtests, the raw score is reported and interpreted in relation to a cut point for each of the three subtest areas. The cut score distinguishes between children "making acceptable progress" and those who "need more assistance or support." Review of the technical manual that supports use of the C-PALLS+ does not specify the process by which these cut scores were established. For the phonological awareness subtest (which includes seven smaller subtests), the overall raw score (sum of correct items across all seven subtests) is used to determine whether a child is struggling within the area of phonological awareness.

Reliability

Across all age groups, the raw and standardized coefficient α of .93 was obtained. Information on internal consistency within subscales or particular ages was not made available to the authors of this chapter during the review process. Without this information, it is difficult to fully assess the acceptability of the reliability estimates for this measure.

Sensitivity and Specificity

The C-PALLS+ authors have not provided, to date, information on sensitivity and specificity of the scale for differentiated instruction, nor were we able to find any published reports that do so. Rather, C-PALLS+ was developed to mark progress for individual children in preschool classrooms.

Concurrent and Predictive Validity

To establish evidence for the concurrent validity of the C-PALLS+, each subtest was correlated with well-recognized criterion measures of early literacy. The correlation between the Rapid Vocabulary Naming subtest and the Expressive One Word Picture Vocabulary Test (Gardner, 1990), a standardized measure of expressive vocabulary, was examined and found to be .59

in the fall and .45 in the spring. The correlation between the Rapid Letter Naming subtest and the Preschool Comprehensive Test of Phonological Processing and Print Awareness (Lonigan et al., 2002) Print Awareness subscale also was examined and found to be .76 in the fall and .79 in the spring. In addition, the correlation between the Phonological Awareness subtest and the DSC also were examined and found to be .39 in the fall and .37 in the spring. No evidence to support the predictive validity of the C-PALLS+ was reported in the technical manual.

Individual Growth and Development Indicators, Version 2.0

IGDIs (Early Childhood Research Institute on Measuring Growth and Development, 1998) originally were developed to provide developmental assessment across all domains for children from birth to third grade. The original work on IGDIs led to the development of a variety of measures for infants and toddlers (Carta, Greenwood, Walker, & Buzhardt, 2010) and served as the foundation for the suite of measures that came to be called Dynamic Indicators of Basic Early Literacy Skills (Good, Gruba, & Kaminski, 2002). This work also led to a group of measures used broadly to assess the effects of early reading first and other programs for preschool children (McConnell & Missall, 2008).

State of Research and Development

The original IGDIs for preschool children have been extensively redesigned, developed, and evaluated since 2009. IGDIs 2.0 are measures of early literacy development that have been designed under the auspices of the Center for Response to Intervention in Early Childhood (CRtIEC; http://www.crtiec.org) to support the identification of students requiring additional levels of intervention in the key early literacy domains of oral language, phonological awareness, alphabet knowledge, and comprehension. Most significantly, item response theory (and, specifically, Rasch modeling) has been used to construct sets of IGDIs 2.0 items that closely align with the instructional decisions that need to be made (Rodriguez, 2010).

As part of a larger model of RTI in early childhood programs, IGDIs 2.0 were developed to inform decisions about whether children are demonstrating adequate levels of performance given the general level of instruction (Tier 1), or whether their performance indicates a need for more intense levels of instruction (Tier 2 or Tier 3). IGDIs 2.0 have been designed specifically at this point for use with children who are attending preschool in the year before kindergarten.

Administration Procedures

The IGDIs 2.0 are composed of several separate scales. A thorough description of the administration procedures for each scale follows.

Picture Naming 2.0. Picture Naming 2.0 assesses oral language development. It is an individually administered 15-item test that takes less than a minute to be completed by a child. Each item contains a photographic image of a common object, and the child is asked to label the depicted image.

Rhyming 2.0. Rhyming 2.0 is a measure of phonological awareness development. Rhyming 2.0 is a 15-item individually administered test that takes about a minute to be completed by a child. For Rhyming 2.0, each item presents a single image for the target word and two images representing response choices. During administration, the administrator provides a standardized prompt in which she labels all three images and then asks the child to identify the pair that rhymes. For example, given a card that depicts a target image of a toy and response choices of "boy" and "mask," the prompt would be "Toy, boy, mask. Which two rhyme? Is it /toy, boy/ or /toy, mask/?"

First Sounds. First Sounds is also a measure of phonological awareness development. First Sounds is a 15-item individually administered test that takes about a minute to be completed by a child. Each First Sounds item presents two images that differ in the onset of their dominant label. To deliver First Sounds, the administrator provides the child with a standardized prompt in which she labels each image and then asks which one starts with a target phoneme. For example, given the target sound /d/ and the images "tree" and "duck," the administrator would say, "Tree, duck. Which one starts with /d/?" The correct response choice is identified in bold lettering on the back of the item for ease of scoring.

Sound Identification. Sound Identification is a measure of alphabet knowledge. It is an individually administered 15-item test that takes less than a minute to be completed by a child. Each item depicts three upper- or lowercase letters printed in Zaner-Bloser font, aligned horizontally and centered on the card. The letters are the response choices for the item. The child is asked to identify the letter that corresponds with a phoneme presented by the administrator. For example, "Which letter makes the /s/ sound?"

Which One Doesn't Belong? Which One Doesn't Belong? (WODB) is a measure of early comprehension. WODB captures the domain of early comprehension in that it examines the degree to which children understand categorical relations between objects. It is an individually administered 15-item test that takes about a minute to be completed by a child. Each item depicts three images that represent response choices. The child is asked to point to, or verbally identify, the picture that does not fit categorically with the other two response choices. For example, given a card that depicts an image of a cat, a key, and a dog, the administrator would provide the prompt "Cat, key, dog. Which one doesn't belong?" and expect the child to identify the key.

Scales and Scores

The IGDIs 2.0 consist of three seasonal Identification sets, corresponding to typical screening time points (fall, winter, and spring). Scoring is developed separately for each set for each measure.

For each IGDI measure at each season, users are provided with a cut score that indicates whether a child is demonstrating an adequate level of progress given Tier 1 instruction (above the cut) or whether a child likely requires additional Tier 2 or Tier 3 levels of early literacy instruction and intervention (below the cut). Cut scores are Rasch scale θ values, calculated through a series of analyses, including Contrasting Groups Designs and Receiver Operating Characteristic (ROC) curve analysis (Rodriguez, 2010). These θ values are converted to "card counts," or the number of correct items needed to exceed the Tier 1 cut score, for each seasonal measure.

Reliability

A large-scale data collection effort in 25 classrooms with a total sample of 275 children yielded coefficient αs from .93 to .97 across the five IGDIs 2.0 measures. When examining each measure on an item-by-item basis, item-total correlations were found to range from about .3 to .8 with a majority of items demonstrating an item-total correlation around .5 for each of the measures.

Concurrent and Predictive Validity

IGDIs 2.0 demonstrate moderate to strong evidence of concurrent criterion validity as documented by correlations with several standardized measures of early literacy skills. Specifically, the IGDIs 2.0 Sound Identification reports a significant correlation with the TOPEL Print Knowledge subtest ($n = 58$; $r = .76$, $p < .01$). IGDIs 2.0 Rhyming reports a significant correlation with TOPEL Phonological Awareness subtest ($n = 57$; $r = .45$, $p < .01$). IGDIs First Sounds reports a significant correlation with TOPEL Phonological Awareness subtest ($n = 57$; $r = .52$, $p < .01$). IGDIs 2.0 Picture Naming reports a significant correlation with the Peabody Picture Vocabulary Test–4th Edition (PPVT-4; Dunn & Dunn, 2007; $n = 58$; $r = .66$, $p < .01$). Finally, IGDIs 2.0 WODB reports significant correlations with the Clinical Evaluation of Language Fundamentals–Preschool, 2nd Edition (CELF Preschool-2; Wiig, Secord, & Semel, 2004) Core Language subtests (word structure, sentence structure, and expressive vocabulary). Correlations with the CELF Preschool-2 yielded word structure .67, sentence structure .68, and expressive vocabulary .71 ($n = 54$). Evidence to support the predictive validity of the IGDIs 2.0 is yet to be documented.

Sensitivity and Specificity

Evidence of sensitivity and specificity was obtained during a study conducted during the 2011–2012 academic year, in which approximately 452 children from several states, including Minnesota, Ohio, Kansas, and Oregon, were tested with the IGDIs 2.0 measure battery. In addition to the IGDIs 2.0 data, teachers were asked to complete a survey in which they rated each child's typical level of performance for each domain as Tier 1 (has little or no difficulty in the domain), Tier 2 (has moderate difficulty in the domain), or Tier 3 (has significant difficulty in the domain). Teacher ratings have been used in this research because of their central role in other standard-setting activities in high-stakes assessment and based on an assumption by IGDI developers that teachers' judgments were an easy-to-collect proxy for other, perhaps more rigorous, standards (e.g., long-term predictive validity of later reading performance).

Using these teacher ratings of children's level of performance as the criterion, a ROC curve analysis was conducted to identify cut scores that maximized the product of sensitivity and specificity, with a minimum level of sensitivity set at .70. This ROC curve analysis was then verified for accuracy through logistic regression and an analysis of the effect of the selected cut score on the distributions of scores was conducted. The classification accuracy of the cut scores has been further documented through post hoc analysis with performance on criterion tests of the same construct (Greenwood et al., 2013). Although some might argue that teacher ratings are not an objective criterion, the standard-setting process used to establish IGDIs 2.0 cut scores is consistent with the *Standards for Educational and Psychological Testing* (American Educational and Psychological Research Association, American Psychological Association, & National Council on Measurement in Education, 1999) and mirrors procedures used for No Child Left Behind (NCLB, 2001) assessments (Cizek & Bunch, 2007).

Table 6.1 summarizes the observed sensitivity and specificity for each IGDIs 2.0 scale. As can be observed, in setting optimal sensitivity at .70, an adequate level of specificity was achieved across all measures (.50 or higher, as supported by Catts et al., 2009). Although these levels of classification accuracy are "good enough" for freestanding measures, the observed levels of imprecision in both sensitivity and specificity would have undesirable consequences in practice (i.e., perhaps as many as 30% of children who would

TABLE 6.1
IGDIs 2.0 Sensitivity and Specificity Values

Measure	Sensitivity	Specificity
Sound identification	.71	.57
First sounds	.73	.57
Picture naming	.73	.63
Rhyming	.75	.69
Which one doesn't belong?	.77	.57

Note. IGDIs = Individual Growth and Development Indicators.

benefit from supplemental intervention not receiving it, and some fraction of children who do not need that supplemental support receiving it nonetheless). For this reason, a larger decision-making framework is being developed that solicits additional information to support and increase the accuracy of instructional decision making.

SUMMARY OF MEASURES

This section reviews three widely used early language and literacy measures and evaluates them against essential criteria for use within an early childhood RTI model to support language and early literacy development. Table 6.2 summarizes these review criteria.

Predictive evidence has been reported only for GRTR-R. The predictive validity evidence reported for the GRTR-R, however, is fairly limited in that the outcome measure used in this analysis was a research version of a preliteracy measurement tool. No evidence exists, to date, on the predictive relation between the GRTR-R and more formal literacy measures. The IGDIs 2.0 also require further published research that examines the strength of their predictive relations with later, more formal literacy measures, to fully evaluate this set of measures against the essential criteria.

Across the other evaluation standards, it appears that both GRTR-R and IGDIs 2.0 demonstrate adequate technical adequacy to be used for making universal screening decisions regarding early language and literacy development. GRTR-R has higher levels of sensitivity when used alone. IGDIs 2.0, however, more comprehensively cover the four essential domains of early literacy development, as the GRTR-R does not include items that sample the constructs of oral language development or comprehension. The C-PALLS+ requires additional published research to fully document its technical adequacy before it can be evaluated against the essential early language and literacy screening criteria.

TABLE 6.2
Summary of Measures Against Review Criteria

Criteria	GRTR-R	C-PALLS+	IGDIs 2.0
Age	3–6 years	3.5 years to kinder-garten entry	4-year-olds (year before kindergarten)
Domains assessed	Print and book knowledge, phonological awareness	Alphabet knowl-edge, oral language, phonological awareness	Oral language, pho-nological aware-ness, alphabet knowledge, comprehension
Task formats	20-item test format (online) that includes the following tasks: concepts of print and book knowledge (8), letter recognition (2), letter–sound correspondence (3), alliteration (2), rhyming (1), blending (3), elision (1)	Subtests: rapid letter naming, rapid vocabulary naming, listen-ing, rhyme rec-ognition, rhyme production, allit-eration, sentence segmentation, syllabication, blending	Subtests: sound-identification, picture naming, rhyming, first sounds (identifi-cation), WODB (categorization)
Format	Easel stimulus or online	Stimuli presented and recorded on a personal digital assistant	Flash card stimuli; paper-and-pencil recording
Reliability	α = .88 (.77–.84)	α = .93	α = .93–.97
Concurrent validity	TOPEL PK (r = .76, p < .001), TOPEL PA (r = .39, p < .001), TOPEL DV (r = .44, p < .001), TOPEL Overall Early Literacy Index (r = .72, p < .001).	Rapid Vocabulary Naming and EOWPVT = .45–.59. Rapid Letter Naming and Pre-CTOPPP = .76–.79. Phonological Awareness subtest and DSC = .37–.39.	Sound-ID and TOPEL PK = .76. Rhyming and TOPEL PA = .45. First Sounds and TOPEL PA = .52. Picture Naming and PPVT-4 = .66. WODB and CELF Preschool-2 = .67–.71.
Predictive validity	.32 (.25–.40) at 20, 28, and 35 months after ini-tial assessment	None reported	None reported
Sensitivity, specificity	Sensitivity: .90–.95 Specificity: .15–.69	None reported	Sensitivity: .71–.77 Specificity: .57–.69

Note. CELF = Clinical Evaluation of Language Fundamentals; C-PALLS+ = CIRCLE–Phonological Awareness, Language, and Literacy System+; EOWPVT = Expressive One Word Picture Vocabulary Test; GRTR-R = Get Ready to Read! Revised; IGDIs 2.0 = Individual Growth and Development Indicators, version 2.0; Pre-CTOPPP = Preschool Comprehensive Test of Phonological Processing and Print Awareness; PPVT-4 = Peabody Picture Vocabulary Test–4th edition; TOPEL DV = Test of Preschool Early Literacy Definitional Vocabulary; TOPEL PA = Test of Preschool Early Literacy Phonological Awareness; TOPEL PK = Test of Preschool Early Literacy Print Knowledge; WODB = Which One Doesn't Belong.

EXAMINING THE CURRENT STATE OF THE FIELD

Although only a brief history of assessment for tiered interventions in early childhood exists, important lessons are emerging. As we examine the current state of the field, we might consider the broad context affecting practice, program improvements that will affect these practices, research and theoretical foundations for this work, and future directions for professional development and research.

Setting the Context for Practice

Like other authors in this volume, we assume that screening for tiered interventions is affected directly by the context and features of the environment in which the screening is conducted. This is particularly true in language and literacy development, in which we assume that differences in observed performance within and across children are largely a function of differences in *opportunity* for interaction and learning (D. W. Barnett et al., 1997; Greenwood, Carta, Kamps, & Arreaga-Mayer, 1990). As such, we cannot examine the utility and results of early literacy screening in early childhood programs without also considering factors that are likely to affect performance. At least three factors—the extent and quality of Tier 1 services, the qualifications and skills of early childhood teachers, and the overall strength and alignment of developmental experiences and curriculum—will affect both how well different screeners "work" and the types of results they produce.

Extent and Quality of Tier 1, or Generic, Experiences

The breadth and variety of diverse practices and resources available in early childhood education has resulted in inconsistent and heterogeneous experiences for 3- to 5-year-old children. In the year before kindergarten, children may spend a significant proportion of their time in structured or unstructured family, friend, and neighbor care; community center-based preschool and day care; licensed Head Start and Title One–supported public education programs; or private tuition-based preschool programs. This diverse collection of settings has provided challenges in defining and assessing *typical* and appropriate preschool-age skill sets, compared with those skill sets that warrant intervention. Existing research literature calls attention to the notion that although expectations can be provided for early childhood performance standards, we are remiss to assume that all early childhood experiences are created equal (Early et al., 2007).

Teacher Qualifications and Skills

At the same time, teacher preparation also varies within and across programs, ranging from less than a high school diploma to advanced higher education degrees (Burchinal, Cryer, Clifford, & Howes, 2002). Research has demonstrated that degree level alone does not predict student success or quality of a classroom; however, level and frequency of professional development, longevity, and teaching with a child-centered approach significantly correlate with measures of classroom quality (Pianta et al., 2005). These findings suggest that level of commitment, preparation, and professional development contribute to the diversity of skills among early childhood staff.

Curriculum Quality and Alignment

Similarly, curricular content and academic standards also contribute to the varied quality of early childhood programming. Although leading organizations, such as the Division of Early Childhood (DEC) and the National Association for Education of Young Children (NAEYC), promote early learning standards, it is improbable that all programs currently serving young children recognize or implement these expectations; as a result, we expect tremendous variation in the extent to which programs implement instructional practices that promote language and literacy development. Without universal application of common early childhood standards, program curricula remain copious and eclectic. This diversity in curricular content leads to significant challenges in assessing student performance because of the breadth of standards provided to guide instructional opportunities.

Program Improvements That Will Affect Screening

To respond to these challenges, a series of improvements are warranted. First, improvement in the implementation of quality Tier 1 curricula and related instructional practices is paramount. Having effective Tier 1 curricula is a necessary condition for promoting development across all children and for screening children as candidates for more intensive intervention (Fuchs & Deshler, 2007).

Evidence-based curricula and sound research-based strategies are available (e.g., Literacy Express; Farver, Lonigan, & Eppe, 2009), but few program exemplars exist. This lack of effective Tier 1 programs in practice may be partly due to the evolving status of early childhood RTI models from leading agencies, such as Recognition and Response (Buysse & Peisner-Feinberg, 2010) and CRtIEC (Greenwood et al., 2008), as these models continue to be refined and shared.

Within those programs that utilize research-based models of RTI, preliminary findings suggest that significant proportions of students are identified within screening as candidates for Tier 2 or Tier 3 intervention. For example, data from various sources suggest that 40% to 57% of children in different classrooms may be candidates for Tier 2 intervention (Koutsoftas, Harmon, & Gray, 2009; Nylander, 2012; Wackerle-Hollman, Carta, & Kaminski, 2012). These findings significantly exceed the initial proportion estimates for Tier 2 and Tier 3 candidates represented as 15% and 5%, respectively (Mellard, McKnight, & Jordan, 2010). As such, the discrepancy between the resources available to reach students in need of Tier 2 or Tier 3 services and the amount of children in need of those services is concerning. This discrepancy may suggest that early childhood programs serve a disproportionate amount of children needing more intensive intervention, that Tier 1 curricula in early childhood programs are not implemented in ways that meaningfully affect student performance, or that programmatic early literacy content standards are not aligned with the early literacy content represented within the screening tools used. Furthermore, preschool classrooms that emphasize social development and reduce focus on any academic skill, such as early literacy, may be less likely to value screening results of the measures described here, simply because their content focus does not align with the academic early literacy standards recognized by early childhood leadership programs, such as NAEYC, NELP, and DEC, that are presented in this chapter.

Second, as programs increase their effectiveness in implementing curricula and research-based strategies, an expanded catalog of resources—including the addition of new screening measures, evidence-based curricula, and intervention strategies for corresponding tier levels—will contribute significantly to the practical application of early childhood RTI. Furthermore, improvements in the reliability and fidelity of implementation of assessment tools used for identification of tier-level candidates and progress monitoring will result in increased accuracy and sensitivity to intervention.

The third, and potentially most compelling, improvement is the need for universally accessible preschool. By focusing resources on localized access points, RTI implementation might be adopted more broadly and with increasing success (Ackerman, Barnett, Hawkinson, Brown, & McGonigle, 2007). Research suggests that universal programs are likely to be more effective at identifying and reaching all children, including Tier 2 and Tier 3 candidates (W. S. Barnett, Brown, & Shore, 2004).

Indeed, without universal early childhood programs, identifying candidates for more intensive intervention becomes tedious, if not impossible. When children attend programs that represent the heterogeneity previously mentioned, it is difficult to employ an assessment system that screens *all* children. We simply cannot access all children during the preschool years when there is no central system of education and care. Furthermore, if we cannot access those children, we also cannot screen to identify which children are in need of more intensive intervention or adequately supply those interventions.

These considerations for improvements to the field of early childhood aid in addressing challenges related to content, policy, and access, but they do not recognize the paradigm shift that has occurred reflecting practitioner motivation and obligation, potentially affecting the implementation of screening and tiered intervention. That is, as the field of early childhood moves toward improved evidence-based practices, we also have shifted toward obligating ourselves to employ those practices to actually change developmental outcomes for children during the preschool years (e.g., validated screening, evidence-based intervention). Early childhood special education has embraced this obligation for many years, particularly since the creation of federal mandates for services to young children with disabilities in the latter half of the 20th century. If a child is in need of special education service as determined by qualifying evaluation criteria, teachers supply these services, confirming such support is *essential* for a child's academic success. Increasingly, general education practitioners have begun to assume that same responsibility, albeit without federal mandates and evaluation criteria. This intervention imperative suggests that teachers can be empowered to provide highly adaptive and engaging instruction and intervention, advancing toward success within an RTI model.

Research and Theoretical Foundations

To continue to sharpen the utility and power of early literacy universal screening, an expanded research base validating the relation between preschool early literacy skills and later reading success is needed. Current research demonstrates skills acquired during the preschool years contribute to the acquisition of reading in elementary school and thus are related to proficiency in primary and later grades (Juel, 2006; Missall et al., 2007; NELP, 2009; Snow et al., 1998). Furthermore, conceptual and empirical analyses indicate that scientifically based, high-quality early literacy programs can ameliorate risk and improve reading acquisition later in the child's life (NELP, 2009; Whitehurst et al., 1999).

As the research base continues to improve, programmatic efforts also are shifting toward emphasizing academic objectives, such as the skills representative of language and literacy development. This change represents a recent interest in academic outcomes at the early childhood level mirroring the focus on accountability present in the primary grades, and this has been supported by local and national initiatives to provide indicators of student success during early childhood as well as robust measures for screening and progress monitoring (e.g., Individuals With Disabilities Education Improvement Act, 2004; NCLB, 2001; Yell & Drasgow, 2007).

Professional Development

Given the challenges documented in implementing early childhood RTI and the suggested avenues for remedy, teachers and other early educators and early childhood professionals (e.g., school psychologists) must be prepared to deliver the proposed supports, including screening measures, at the ready (Buysse, Winton, & Rous, 2009). To prepare early educators and early childhood professionals to best utilize an early childhood RTI model, professional development within three domains is warranted: support for improved Tier 1 services; support for data-based decision making, including the use of evidence-based assessment practices (e.g., screening and progress monitoring); and support for intervention selection.

To appropriately evaluate student performance, early educators and professionals must be skilled in data-based decision making. High-quality data-based decision making includes rigorous and critical evaluation of evidence-based interventions and assessments, such as progress-monitoring and screening practices, as well as of individual student data (Justice & Pullen, 2003). Emerging research on intervention practices and supporting resources (including assessment, fidelity of implementation, and training) is shaping the foundation for practical application within early childhood RTI. Providing early educators and professionals with the information to evaluate empirically proven practices will allow for improved data-based decision making both at the intervention selection level and the student performance level (Justice & Pullen, 2003). In addition, resources to support data-based decision making can be mined from such databases as the What Works Clearinghouse (http://ies.ed.gov/ncee/wwc) and current models of early childhood RTI such as Recognition and Response (http://www.recognitionandresponse.org) and CRtIEC (http://www.crtiec.org) to provide conceptual and theoretical perspectives on assessment and intervention. Furthermore, K–12 technical assistance centers that offer generic evaluation templates of instruction may also support data-based decision making in an early childhood RTI model (e.g., Florida's Center for Reading Research).

Finally, practitioners must be able to evaluate formative progress during intervention delivery to determine whether services are allocated appropriately. Consistent and robust review of student data can provide practitioners with meaningful information to inform instructional practices. Currently, few robust assessment tools are designed specifically for progress monitoring within an early childhood RTI model, but emerging practices such as IGDIs 2.0, mCLASS:CIRCLE, and curriculum-specific mastery monitoring tools will aid in improving assessment practices and support expanded use of evidence-based assessment and screening practices.

Future Directions for Research

Although in its earliest stages, research on universal early literacy screening is growing in scope and sophistication. As research progresses and the pool of screening measures expands, experts may benefit from considering a common metric or criterion standard to validate screening tools. Across the tools reviewed within this chapter, different approaches and different standardized measures are used to demonstrate evidence of validity. These different standards provide robust evidence within any one application, but they are difficult to compare across screening measures because of differences in metrics (e.g., standardized criterion assessments with the addition of teacher ratings vs. standardized criterion assessments alone) and differences within criterion standards (e.g., TOPEL, PPVT-4, CELFPreschool-2). Without an accepted set of criteria to evaluate validity evidence across measures, it is difficult for those who interact with these tools at a practical level to compare and contrast different measures. Future research might benefit from designing a best practice approach to early literacy screening validation, such that specific standardized criterion measures and a metric for comparison might be recognized as gold standard criteria, leading to clear and easily interpretable information across screening measures.

At the same time, research supporting the relation between early childhood language and literacy skills with later reading success, and other early childhood skills, such as early numeracy and social and emotional development, is expanding (NELP, 2009). Refined measures for screening and identification are setting a strong precedent for practical and evidence-based resources. Evidence also is needed, however, to demonstrate and strengthen the relation between preschool and primary grade performance. Robust indicators of performance and predictive models established through longitudinal studies sorely are needed to support early childhood RTI and the effectiveness of identification measures.

Additional research also is needed to support policy *and* practice to promote universally available preschool programming both by pursuing changes in procedural laws as well as by developing models to accommodate the current lack of universal access. Additional research examining the relation between universal preschool programming availability and assessment for identification may provide powerful data on the current state of need for prevention and intervention in early childhood.

Similarly, empirical evidence to define the relation between differentiation of intervention services through evidence-based teaching strategies (e.g., differentiated instruction) and outcomes for preschool students also is needed. Investigations supporting the nature of intervention allocation, intensity, duration, and strategies will provide critical evidence to aid in defining standards for effective implementation of early childhood RTI.

REFERENCES

Ackerman, D., Barnett, S., Hawkinson, L., Brown, K., & McGonigle, E. (2007). *Providing preschool education for all 4-year olds: Lessons from six state journeys* (Preschool Policy Brief, Issue No. 18). Rutgers, NJ: National Institute for Early Education Research.

American Educational and Psychological Research Association, American Psychological Association, & National Council on Measurement in Education. (1999). *Standards for educational and psychological testing.* Washington, DC: Author.

Barnett, D. W., Lentz, F. E., Bauer, A. M., Macmann, G., Stollar, S., & Ehrhardt, K. E. (1997). Ecological foundations of early intervention: Planned activities and strategic sampling. *Journal of Special Education, 30,* 471–490. doi:10.1177/002246699703000407

Barnett, W. S., Brown, K., & Shore, R. (2004). *The universal vs. targeted debate: Should the United States have preschool for all?* Rutgers, NJ: National Institute for Early Education Research.

Barnett, W. S., Epstein, D. J., Friedman, A. J., Sansanelli, R., & Hustedt, J. T. (2009). *The state of preschool 2009.* Rutgers, NJ: National Institute for Early Education Research.

Barnett, W. S., & Frede, E. C. (2011). Preschool education's effects on language and literacy. In S. B. Neuman & D. K. Dickinson (Eds.), *Handbook of early literacy research* (Vol. 3, pp. 435–450). New York, NY: Guilford Press.

Burchinal, M., Cryer, D., Clifford, R., & Howes, C. (2002). Caregiver training and classroom quality in child care centers. *Applied Developmental Science, 6,* 2–11. doi:10.1207/S1532480XADS0601_01

Buysse, V., & Peisner-Feinberg, E. (2010). Recognition and response: Response to intervention for PreK. *Young Exceptional Children, 13,* 2–13. doi:10.1177/1096250610373586

Buysse, V., Winton, P., & Rous, B. (2009). Reaching consensus on a definition of Professional Development for the early childhood field. *Topics in Early Childhood Special Education, 28,* 235–243. doi:10.1177/0271121408328173

Carta, J. J., Greenwood, C. R., Walker, D., & Buzhardt, J. (2010). *Using IGDIs: Monitoring progress and improving intervention for infants and young children*. Baltimore, MD: Brookes.

Carta, J. J., Schwartz, I. S., Atwater, J. B., & McConnell, S. R. (1991). Developmentally appropriate practice: Appraising its usefulness for young children with disabilities. *Topics in Early Childhood Special Education, 11*, 1–20. doi:10.1177/027112149101100104

Catts, H. W., Petscher, Y., Schatschneider, C., Sittner Bridges, M., & Mendoza, K. (2009). Floor effects associated with universal screening and their impact on the early identification of reading disabilities. *Journal of Learning Disabilities, 42*, 163–176.

Children's Learning Institute. (2011). *C-PALLS+: The Circle Phonological Awareness Language and Literacy System+ technical report*. Unpublished manuscript, University of Texas Health Science Center at Houston, Houston, TX.

Christie, J. (2008). The scientifically based reading research approach to early literacy instruction. In L. M. Justice & C. Vukelich (Eds.), *Achieving excellence in preschool literacy instruction* (pp. 25–40). New York, NY: Guilford Press.

Cizek, G. J., & Bunch, M. B. (Eds.). (2007). *Standard setting: A guide to establishing and evaluating performance standards on tests*. Thousand Oaks, CA: Sage.

Coleman, M. R., Buysse, V., & Neitzel, J. (2006). *Recognition and response: An early intervening system for young children at-risk for learning disabilities*. Chapel Hill: Frank Porter Graham Child Development Institute, University of North Carolina at Chapel Hill. Retrieved from http://www.recognitionandresponse.org/images/downloads/2006fpgsynthesis_recognitionandresponse.pdf

CTB Early Childhood System. (1990). *Developing skills checklist*. Monterey, CA: McGraw-Hill.

Detels, R., Beaglehole, R., Lansang, M. A., & Gulliford, M. (Eds.). (2011). *Oxford textbook of public health* (5th ed.). New York, NY: Oxford University Press.

Dickinson, D. K., Freiberg, J. B., & Barnes, E. M. (2011). Why are so few interventions really effective? A call for fine-grained research methodology. In S. B. Neuman & D. K. Dickinson (Eds.), *Handbook of early literacy research* (Vol. 3, pp. 337–357). New York, NY: Guilford Press.

Dickinson, D. K., & Neuman, S. B. (Eds.). (2006). *Handbook of early literacy research* (Vol. 2). New York, NY: Guilford Press.

Dickinson, D. K., & Tabors, P. O. (Eds.). (2001). *Beginning literacy with language*. Baltimore, MD: Brookes.

Dunn, L. M., & Dunn, L. M. (2007). *Peabody Picture Vocabulary Test—Fourth Edition (PPVT-IV)*. New York, NY: Pearson.

Early Childhood Research Institute on Measuring Growth and Development. (1998). *Research and development of individual growth and development indicators for children between birth and age eight* (Technical Report No. 4). Minneapolis: University of Minnesota.

Early, D. M., Maxwell, K. L., Burchinal, M., Alva, S., Bender, R. H., Bryant, D., . . . Zill, N. (2007). Teachers' education, classroom quality, and young children's academic skills: Results from seven studies of preschool programs. *Child Development, 78*, 558–580. doi:10.1111/j.1467-8624.2007.01014.x

Farver, J. A. M., Lonigan, C. J., & Eppe, S. (2009). Effective early literacy skill development for young Spanish-speaking English language learners: An experimental study of two methods. *Child Development, 80*, 703–719. doi:10.1111/j.1467-8624.2009.01292.x

Fernald, A., & Weisleder, A. (2011). Early language experience is vital to developing fluency in understanding. In S. B. Neuman & D. K. Dickinson (Eds.), *Handbook of early literacy research* (Vol. 3, pp. 3–19). New York, NY: Guilford Press.

Fuchs, D., & Deshler, D. (2007). What we need to know about responsiveness to intervention (and shouldn't be afraid to ask). *Learning Disabilities Research and Practice, 22*, 129–136. doi:10.1111/j.1540-5826.2007.00237.x

Gardner, M. (1990). *Expressive One-Word Picture Vocabulary Test* (rev. ed.). Novato, CA: Academic Therapy.

Gersten, R., Compton, D., Connor, C. M., Dimino, J., Santoro, L., Linan-Thompson, S. S., & Tilly, W. D. (2008). *Assisting students struggling with reading: Response to Intervention and multi-tier intervention for reading in the primary grades. A practice guide* (NCEE 2009-4045). Washington, DC: National Center for Education Evaluation and Regional Assistance, Institute of Education Sciences, U.S. Department of Education. Retrieved from http://www.crtiec.org/RTI/documents/rti_reading_pg_021809.pdf

Good, R. H., Gruba, J., & Kaminski, R. A. (2002). Best practices in using dynamic indicators of basic early literacy skills (DIBELS) in an outcomes-driven model. In A. Thomas & J. Grimes (Eds.), *Best practices in school psychology* (4th ed., Vol. 1, pp. 699–720). Washington, DC: National Association of School Psychologists.

Good, R. H., & Kaminski, R. A. (1996). Assessment for instructional decisions: Toward a proactive/prevention model of decision-making for early literacy skills. *School Psychology Quarterly, 11*, 326–336. doi:10.1037/h0088938

Goswani, U. (2001). Early phonological development and the acquisition of literacy. In S. B. Neuman & D. K. Dickinson (Eds.), *Handbook of early literacy research* (Vol. 1, pp. 111–125). New York, NY: Guilford Press.

Greenwood, C. R. (2009). Introduction. In M. R. Coleman, F. P. Roth, & T. West (Eds.), *Roadmap to Pre-K RTI: Applying response to intervention in preschool settings* (pp. 5–6). New York, NY: National Center for Learning Disabilities.

Greenwood, C. R., Carta, J. J., Atwater, J., Goldstein, H., Kaminski, R., & McConnell, S. R. (2013). Is a response to intervention (RTI) approach to preschool language and early literacy instruction needed? *Topics in Early Childhood Special Education, 33*, 48–64. doi:10.1177/0271121412455438

Greenwood, C. R., Carta, J. J., Kamps, D., & Arreaga-Mayer, C. (1990). Ecobehavioral analysis of classroom instruction. In S. R. Schroeder (Ed.), *Ecobehavioral analysis and developmental disabilities* (pp. 33–63). New York, NY: Springer-Verlag. doi:10.1007/978-1-4612-3336-7_2

Greenwood, C. R., Carta, J. J., & McConnell, S. R. (2011). Advances in measurement for universal screening and individual progress monitoring of young children. *Journal of Early Intervention, 33,* 254–267. doi:10.1177/1053815111428467

Greenwood, C. R., Kratochwill, T. R., & Clements, M. (Eds.). (2008). *Schoolwide prevention models: Lessons learned in elementary schools.* Baltimore, MD: Guilford Press.

Hancock, T. B., Kaiser, A. P., & Delaney, E. M. (2002). Teaching parents of high-risk preschoolers strategies to support language and positive behavior. *Topics in Early Childhood Special Education, 22,* 191–212. doi:10.1177/027112140202200402

Hart, B., & Risley, T. (1995). *Meaningful differences in the everyday experiences of young American children.* Baltimore, MD: Brookes.

Hays, A., Wackerle-Hollman, A., Bradfield, T. A., & McConnell, S. R. (2010, February). *What is the meaning of comprehension for preschools? Pioneering progress monitoring tools in a disputed domain.* Paper presented at the 7th Biennial Conference on Research Innovations in Early Intervention (CRIEI), San Diego, CA.

Individuals With Disabilities Education Improvement Act (2004), 20 U.S.C. § 1400 *et seq.*

Jenkins, J. R. (2003, December). *Candidate measures for screening at-risk students.* Paper presented at the Conference on Response to Intervention as Learning Disabilities Identification, sponsored by the National Research Center on Learning Disabilities, Kansas City, MO.

Jenkins, J. R., Hudson, R. F., & Johnson, E. S. (2007). Screening for at-risk readers in a response to intervention framework. *School Psychology Review, 36,* 582–600.

Juel, C. (2006). The impact of early school experiences on initial reading. In D. K. Dickinson & S. B. Neuman (Eds.), *Handbook of early literacy research* (Vol. 2, pp. 410–426). New York, NY: Guilford Press. doi:10.1177/02711214 030230030101

Justice, L. M., & Piasta, S. (2011). Developing children's print knowledge through adult-child storybook reading interactions: Print referencing as an instructional practice. In S. B. Neuman & D. K. Dickinson (Eds.), *Handbook of early literacy research* (Vol. 3, pp. 200–213). New York, NY: Guilford Press.

Justice, L. M., & Pullen, P. C. (2003). Promising interventions for promoting emergent literacy skills. *Topics in Early Childhood Special Education, 23,* 99–113.

Kendeou, P., van den Broek, P., White, M. J., & Lynch, J. S. (2009). Predicting reading comprehension in early elementary school: The independent contributions of oral language and decoding skills. *Journal of Educational Psychology, 101,* 765–778. doi:10.1037/a0015956

Koutsoftas, A. D., Harmon, M., & Gray, S. (2009). The effects of Tier 2 intervention for a phonemic awareness in a response-to-intervention model in low-income preschool classrooms. *Language, Speech, and Hearing Services in Schools, 40,* 116–130. doi:10.1044/0161-1461(2008/07-0101)

Lonigan, C., Wagner, R., Torgesen, J., & Rashotte, C. (2007). *The test of preschool early literacy (TOPEL)*. Austin, TX: Pro-ed.

Lonigan, C., & Wilson, S. (2008). *Report on the Revised Get Ready to Read! Screening Tool: Psychometrics and normative information*. Retrieved from http://www.getreadytoread.org/images/content/downloads/GRTR_screening_tool/grtrnormingreportfinal-july-2008.pdf

McConnell, S. R. (2000). Assessment in early intervention and early childhood special education: Building on the past to project into our future. *Topics in Early Childhood Special Education, 20*, 43–48. doi:10.1177/027112140002000108

McConnell, S. R. (2010, October). *Using teachers' judgments of individual student performance to set initial benchmarks for identification assessment in early childhood RTI*. Paper presented at the Annual Summit on Response to Intervention in Early Childhood, Kansas City, KS.

McConnell, S. R., & Missall, K. N. (2008). Best practices in monitoring progress for preschool children. In A. Thomas & J. Grimes (Eds.), *Best practices in school psychology* (5th ed., pp. 561–573). Washington, DC: National Association of School Psychologists.

Mellard, D., McKnight, M., & Jordan, J. (2010). RTI Tier structures and instructional intensity. *Learning Disabilities Research and Practice, 25*, 217–225. doi:10.1111/j.1540-5826.2010.00319.x

Missall, K. N., & McConnell, S. R. (2010). Early literacy and language IGDIs for preschool-aged children. In J. J. Carta & C. R. Greenwood (Eds.), *Individual growth and development indicators: Tools for monitoring progress and measuring growth in very young children* (pp. 181–201). Baltimore, MD: Brookes.

Missall, K. N., Reschly, A., Betts, J., McConnell, S. R., Heistad, D., Pickart, M., . . . Marston, D. (2007). Examination of the predictive validity of preschool early literacy skills. *School Psychology Review, 36*, 433–452.

National Early Literacy Panel. (2009). *Developing early literacy: Report of the National Early Literacy Panel: A scientific synthesis of early literacy development and implications for intervention*. Jessup, MD: National Institute for Literacy.

Neuman, S. B., & Dickinson, D. K. (Eds.). (2001). *Handbook of early literacy research* (Vol. 1). New York, NY: Guilford Press.

Neuman, S. B., & Dickinson, D. K. (Eds.). (2011). *Handbook of early literacy research* (Vol. 3). New York, NY: Guilford Press.

No Child Left Behind Act (2001), 20 U.S.C. 70 § 6301 *et seq.* (2002).

Nylander, D. (2012, October). *Implementing an innovating Tier 2 intervention that improved vocabulary and comprehension skills for preschoolers*. Paper presented at the Annual Summit on Response to Intervention in Early Childhood, Santa Ana Pueblo, MN.

Paris, S. G. (2011). Developmental differences in early reading skills. In S. B. Neuman & D. K. Dickinson (Eds.), *Handbook of early literacy research* (Vol. 3, pp. 228–241). New York, NY: Guilford Press.

Phillips, B. M., Lonigan, C. J., & Wyatt, M. A. (2009). Predictive validity of the Get Ready to Read! Screener: Concurrent and long-term relations with reading-related skills. *Journal of Learning Disabilities, 42,* 133–147. doi:10.1177/0022219408326209

Pianta, R., Howes, C., Burchinal, M., Bryant, D., Clifford, R., Early, D., & Barbarin, O. (2005). Features of pre-kindergarten programs, classrooms, and teachers: Do they predict observed classroom quality and child-teacher interactions? *Applied Developmental Science, 9,* 144–159. doi:10.1207/s1532480xads0903_2

Pianta, R. C., Cox, M. J., & Snow, K. L. (Eds.). (2007). *School readiness and the transition to kindergarten in the era of accountability.* Baltimore, MD: Brookes.

Poe, M. D., Burchinal, M., & Roberts, J. (2004). Early Language and the development of children's reading skills. *Journal of School Psychology, 42,* 315–332. doi:10.1016/j.jsp.2004.06.001

Rodriguez, M. C. (2010). *Building a validity framework for second-generation IGDIs.* Minneapolis: University of Minnesota.

Roth, F. P., Speece, D. L., & Cooper, D. H. (2002). A longitudinal analysis of the connection between oral language and early reading. *Journal of Educational Research, 95,* 259–272. doi:10.1080/00220670209596600

Scarborough, H. S. (2001). Connecting early language and literacy to later reading (dis)abilities: Evidence, theory and practice. In S. B. Neuman & D. K. Dickinson (Eds.), *Handbook of early literacy research* (Vol. 1, pp. 97–110). New York, NY: Guilford Press.

Snow, C. E., Burns, M. S., & Griffin, P. (Eds.). (1998). *Preventing reading difficulties in young children.* Washington, DC: National Academy Press.

Snow, C. E., & Oh, S. S. (2011). Assessment in early literacy research. In S. B. Neuman & D. K. Dickinson (Eds.), *Handbook of early literacy research* (Vol. 3, pp. 375–395). New York, NY: Guilford Press.

Snow, C. E., Porche, M., Tabors, P., & Harris, S. (2007). *Is literacy enough? Pathways to academic success for adolescents.* Baltimore, MD: Brookes.

Snow, C. E., & Van Hemel, S. B. (Eds.). (2008). *Early childhood assessment: Why, what, and how.* Washington, DC: National Academies Press.

Strain, P. S., McConnell, S. R., Carta, J. J., Fowler, S. A., Neisworth, J. T., & Wolery, M. (1992). Behaviorism in early intervention. *Topics in Early Childhood Special Education, 12,* 121–141. doi:10.1177/027112149201200111

U.S. Department of Education. (2004). *A synopsis of the 2004 Early Reading First project grantees* (CFDA #84.359B). Washington, DC: Author.

VanDerHeyden, A. M. (2010). Technical adequacy of Response to Intervention decisions. *Exceptional Children, 77,* 335–350.

Vasilyeva, M., & Waterfall, H. (2011). Variability in language development: Relation to socioeconomic status and environmental input. In S. B. Neuman & D. K. Dickinson (Eds.), *Handbook of early literacy research* (Vol. 3, pp. 36–48). New York, NY: Guilford Press.

Vernon-Feagans, L., Scheffner Hammer, C., Miccio, A., & Manlove, E. (2002). Early language and literacy skills in low-income African American and Hispanic children. In S. B. Neuman & D. K. Dickinson (Eds.), *Handbook of early literacy research* (Vol. 1, pp. 192–210). New York, NY: Guilford Press.

Wackerle-Hollman, A., Carta, J., & Kaminski, R. (2012, February). *Examining the challenges of RTI for young children in need of special education services.* Presentation at the Conference for Research Innovations in Early Intervention, San Diego, CA.

Walker, D., Greenwood, C. R., Hart, B., & Carta, J. J. (1994). Prediction of school outcome based on early language production and socioeconomic factors. *Child Development, 65*, 606–621. doi:10.2307/1131404

Whitehurst, G. J., & Lonigan, C. J. (1998). Child development and emergent literacy. *Child Development, 69*, 848–872.

Whitehurst, G. J., & Lonigan, C. (2001). Emergent literacy: Development from pre-readers to readers. In S. B. Neuman & D. K. Dickinson (Eds.), *Handbook of early literacy research* (Vol. 1, pp. 11–29). New York, NY: Guilford Press.

Whitehurst, G. J., Zevenbergen, A. A., Crone, D. A., Schultz, M. D., Velting, O. N., & Fischel, J. E. (1999). Outcomes of an emergent literacy intervention from Head Start through second grade. *Journal of Educational Psychology, 91*, 261–272. doi:10.1037/0022-0663.91.2.261

Wiig, E. H., Secord, W. A., & Semel, E. (2004). *Clinical evaluation of language fundamentals–Preschool* (2nd ed.). San Antonio, TX: Harcourt Assessment.

Wilson, S. B., & Lonigan, C. J. (2010). Identifying preschool children at risk of later reading difficulties: Evaluation of two emergent literacy screening tools. *Journal of Learning Disabilities, 43*, 62–76. doi:10.1177/0022219409345007

Yell, M. L., & Drasgow, E. (2007). Assessment for eligibility under IDEIA and the 2006 regulations. *Assessment for Effective Intervention, 32*, 202–213.

Zigler, E., Styfco, S. J., & Gilman, E. (1993). The national Head Start Program for disadvantaged preschoolers. In E. Zigler & S. J. Styfco (Eds.), *Head Start and beyond: A national plan for extended childhood intervention* (pp. 1–41). New Haven, CT: Yale University Press.

7

SCREENING FOR EARLY READING SKILLS: USING DATA TO GUIDE RESOURCES AND INSTRUCTION

MATTHEW K. BURNS, KATHERINE HAEGELE,
AND SHAWNA PETERSEN-BROWN

This book, and several previous publications, has argued convincingly the need for universal screening to systematically identify students at risk for difficulties (Deno, 2003). Universal screening emerged from prevention science, in which the goal is to identify key risk and protective factors related to a problem, measure the factors, and deliver services based on assessment results (Coie et al., 1993). The process for implementing a prevention approach within an educational setting starts with school personnel identifying screening measures that assess areas for preventive intervention that predict future academic outcomes (Jenkins, Hudson, & Johnson, 2007) and that are aligned with the curriculum and instruction delivered within the school system (Ikeda, Neesen, & Witt, 2008).

Although identifying students who are at risk for failure is an important step in the prevention process, the data also should be useful in making service delivery decisions for individuals and groups of students. One of the

http://dx.doi.org/10.1037/14316-007
Universal Screening in Educational Settings: Evidence-Based Decision Making for Schools, R. J. Kettler,
T. A. Glover, C. A. Albers, and K. A. Feeney-Kettler (Editors)
Copyright © 2014 by the American Psychological Association. All rights reserved.

basic tenets of prevention science is to target those at highest risk (Coie et al., 1993), and many schools are implementing a prevention approach by employing a tiered service delivery model that focuses increasing resources on the more severe problems (Lembke, McMaster, & Stecker, 2010). Thus, screening is a critical feature of prevention models implemented in schools, including multitiered systems of supports (MTSS) or response-to-intervention (RTI) models (Jenkins et al., 2007), but schools often use these data to address only one aspect of prevention (i.e., identifying students at risk for failure).

An MTSS includes varying levels of service intensity that are delivered to students based on need (Tilly, 2008). The needs of students are determined through a set of decisions, each based on the systematic use of assessment data. The first tier of instruction is designed to address the needs of approximately 80% of students within a system (Batsche et al., 2005). At this tier, classwide problems can be identified, and decisions about curricula and instruction are made. Moreover, school personnel use screening data within Tier 1 to decide which students may require supplemental instruction. The second tier of instruction is supplemental and is designed to meet the needs of approximately 15% of students who are not responding adequately to the first tier of instruction (Batsche et al., 2005). At this tier, school personnel make decisions about identifying areas for preventive intervention for small groups of students. The third tier of instruction is individualized and intensive, and it is designed to meet the needs of approximately 5% of students who have not responded adequately to the first or second tiers of instruction (Batsche et al., 2005).

Screening data collected within a tiered model can be used to answer two major questions about instruction that align with the decisions made within the first two tiers of an MTSS (Burns & Gibbons, 2012). The first question asks, "Is there a classwide problem?" A classwide problem occurs when a large percentage of students experiences a difficulty and suggests that the difficulty is specific to the system in which they operate (i.e., class, school, or district) rather than the individual students. Second, school personnel ask, "What is the category of the problem?" After screening measures are used to identify students who may need additional support, school personnel examine the data further to determine areas for preventive intervention.

A third question that drives the MTSS process, and is important to prevention efforts, asks, "What is the causal variable of the problem?" This third question cannot be answered using screening data, however, and an in-depth problem analysis with additional data is needed. Thus, screening data are useful at the first tier of instruction for identifying classwide problems as well as identifying which students may require supplemental instruction. Moreover, screening data may be helpful in determining which interventions would be appropriate for Tier 2.

This chapter discusses how to use screening data within the first two tiers of an MTSS to identify who needs additional support and to make hypotheses about what service to provide. Throughout this chapter, a hypothetical school (Burgelesen Elementary) will be used to describe how screening procedures can be implemented in schools. Burgelesen Elementary is an elementary school in the Upper Midwest serving 400 students in Grades K–5, 52% of which were eligible to receive a free or reduced price lunch, and 58% of the third- and fourth-grade students received passing scores on the state reading accountability test. The district adopted an MTSS that utilizes assessment data in response to the relatively low percentage of students who demonstrated proficient reading skills. Burgelesen Elementary assembled a task force to oversee the implementation of this model. This chapter will follow the team's journey to identifying, implementing, and interpreting screening procedures for reading.

IDENTIFYING UNIVERSAL SCREENING TOOLS

Identifying measures is the first step in implementing universal screening for reading. Their primary considerations in selecting screening measures are (a) psychometric adequacy, (b) the ability to accurately identify students who are at risk for reading difficulties, and (c) alignment with the school's curriculum and instructional practices. We will elaborate on these three points in the following sections.

Psychometric Adequacy

Of course, psychometric considerations (i.e., reliability and validity) are of primary importance when selecting measures that accurately identify students who are at risk for reading difficulties. Reliability coefficients for screening assessments should be .80 or higher (Salvia, Ysseldyke, & Bolt, 2013) because screening decisions are relatively low stakes, but the lower the reliability coefficient, the more likely school personnel are to have error in their decisions. Validity often is established based on relations to other variables (e.g., correlations with other measures), which is assessed by comparing the rank order of two sets of scores. There are no established criteria to interpret correlations between two measures, but correlational coefficients of .40–.50 and higher suggest that the assessment of interest probably measures the target construct, as long as the criterion measure has well-established psychometric properties (for more information, see Chapter 4 in this volume).

Accurate Identification of Students at Risk

Although reliability and validity are important, there are other factors to consider. For example, if every student scored high on a screener but failed the criterion measure, and the rank order remained the same on both assessments (e.g., the same student scored the highest on both measures, the second highest, the third highest, etc.), then the correlation would be strong, but the resulting data would not be particularly useful because they would not identify any students who would need remediation to pass the second measure. In other words, all of the students needed intervention because none passed the criterion measure, but the screener failed to identify a single student.

How well a screening measure predicts whether a student will pass or fail a criterion measure (i.e., the state accountability test) is called diagnostic accuracy. When data from a screening measure incorrectly predict that a student will pass the state test, it is referred to as a false negative because the term is borrowed from medical research and refers to a negative medical exam in which no condition was identified when one actually existed. When there is a false negative, students may not receive an intervention when one was needed, which makes it quite important to avoid false negatives.

Most practitioners can compute diagnostic accuracy by counting (A) the number of students who passed the screener and passed the state test (true negative), (B) the number of students who passed the screener and failed the state test (false negative), (C) the number of students who failed the screener but passed the state test (false positive), and (D) the number of students who failed the screener and failed the state test (true positive). To compute the negative predictive value (NPV), simply divide the number of students who passed the screener and passed the state test (A) by the total number who passed the screener (A + B). The positive predictive value (PPV) is computed by dividing the number of students who failed the screener and failed the state test (D) by the total number who failed the screener (C + D). Total diagnostic accuracy (or hit rate) is then the total true positive and true negative (A + D) divided by the total number of students. Although there are no accepted standards for diagnostic accuracy, the higher the percentage the better and 70–80% is likely acceptable for a reading screener. A diagnostic accuracy of 50% is equal to chance and suggests a high likelihood of erroneous decisions.

Some measures commonly used by schools to screen students' reading skills do not have sufficient psychometric properties or diagnostic accuracy to be used in such a manner. For example, informal reading inventories (IRIs) frequently are used as screening measures in schools (Paris, 2002; Paris, Paris, & Carpenter, 2002), despite questionable or absent reliability data (Spector, 2005). Data from IRIs correlate with other measures of reading at acceptable levels (between $r = .62$ and $r = .69$; Fountas & Pinnell, 2007), but an independent estimate of diagnostic accuracy equaled 54% (Parker et al., in press). Thus, if school personnel are interested in identifying students who may be at risk for reading failure, using an IRI may be about as accurate as flipping a coin and may require 20–30 minutes for each student to complete.

Align to Curriculum and Instructional Practice

In addition to psychometric considerations, screening measures also should align with curriculum and instructional approaches. Although it would be difficult to develop screening measures for each individual curriculum, the major instructional targets identified by the National Reading Panel (NRP; National Institute of Child Health and Human Development [NICHD], 2000) could provide guidance for measures that would align with quality core instruction. It goes beyond the scope of this chapter to adequately describe the instructional targets identified by the NRP, so we will state succinctly that quality core reading instruction should address phonemic awareness, phonics, fluency, vocabulary, and comprehension, as should the screening measures.

The National Research Council has suggested that instruction should emphasize certain aspects of reading at developmentally appropriate times (Snow, Burns, & Griffin, 1998). For example, reading instruction in kindergarten and first grade should focus on phonemic awareness and phonics, in second grade the focus is on explicit phonics and reading fluency, in third grade reading fluency and reading comprehension are emphasized, and vocabulary and comprehension become prominent instructional goals in fourth grade and beyond (Snow et al., 1998). Therefore, screening assessments should align with the instructional goals and should assess phonemic awareness in kindergarten, phonemic awareness and alphabetic principle in first grade, alphabetic principle and fluency in second grade, fluency in third grade, and fluency and comprehension in fourth grade (for more information on early childhood literacy screening, see Chapter 6 of this volume).

Specific Measures

Curriculum-based measures (CBMs; Deno, 1985) often are selected for screening because they are efficient (most are administered in 1 minute), have well-established sound psychometric properties (L. S. Fuchs & Fuchs, 1986; Marston, 1989), are predictive of later reading skills (McGlinchey & Hixson, 2004; Stage & Jacobsen, 2001), and align with classroom instruction in most cases (Powell-Smith & Bradley-Klug, 2001). CBMs correlate highly with performance on statewide achievement tests ($r = .69$; Yeo, 2010) and estimates of diagnostic accuracy are high. The diagnostic accuracy data, however, usually have been derived from concurrent measures of reading and not long-term indicators of reading skills. Thus, additional research is needed to determine the long-term diagnostic accuracy of the measures described in the following example.

All of the measures selected by Burgelesen Elementary are considered CBMs. A variety of CBM packages provide free assessment materials, including Dynamic Indicators of Basic Early Literacy Skills (DIBELS; Good & Kaminski, 2002; https://dibels.uoregon.edu), AIMSweb (2010; http://www.aimsweb.com), Easy CBM (Alonzo, Tindal, Ulmer, & Glasgow, 2006; http://www.easycbm.com), and Computer-Based Assessment System for Reading (Kroll, Krall, & Christ, 2006; http://www.faip.umn.edu). A thorough review of various screening measures can be found at the National Center on Response to Intervention (NCRTI) website (http://rti4success.org/screeningTools). Basic psychometric information for these tools, as provided by the NCRTI, and for other group-administered screening measures for reading with students in third grade and below are included in Table 7.1.

Initial Sound Fluency

Initial sound fluency (ISF) is a measure of phonological awareness that assesses a child's ability to recognize and produce the initial sound in an orally presented word (Good, Kaminski, Simmons, & Kame'enui, 2001). During an ISF administration, an examiner presents four pictures to the child, names each picture, and then asks the child to identify the picture that begins with the sound produced orally by the examiner (Hintze, Ryan, & Stoner, 2003). The child also is asked to orally produce the beginning sound for an orally presented word that matches one of the given pictures. The examiner calculates the amount of time taken to identify or produce the correct sound and converts the score into the number of initial sounds correct in a minute. The ISF measure takes about 3 minutes to administer (Kaminski & Good, 1996).

Reliability for ISF has been consistently around .80. Alternate form reliability is between .72 and .86 (Good, Simmons, & Kame'enui, 2001; Hintze et al., 2003). ISF has established concurrent validity. ISF is related to a concurrently administered reading task, with a correlation of .36 (Good, Simmons, & Kame'enui, 2001). ISF also has established predictive validity. ISF administered in kindergarten is predictive of performance on a reading task in first grade, with a correlation of .45 (Good, Simmons, & Kame'enui, 2001). Diagnostic accuracy for ISF ranges from acceptable to very good. Previous research found correct classifications (considering both true positive and true negative) of 74–91% (Johnson, Jenkins, Petscher, & Catts, 2009) and 69–78% (Hintze et al., 2003).

TABLE 7.1
Psychometric Data for Screening Measures of Discrete Early Reading Skills

Measure	Alternate form reliability	Test–retest reliability	Concurrent validity	Predictive validity	Diagnostic accuracy (%)
Gates-MacGinitie Reading	Not reported	.85–.96	.79–.92	Not reported	86
Group Reading Assessment and Diagnostic Evaluation	.81–.94	.77–.96	.69–.90	.76–.86	91
Initial sound fluency	.72–.86	Not reported	.36	.45	69–91
Iowa Test of Basic Skills	Not reported	Not reported	.69–.82	Not reported	71–86
Istation's Indicators of Progress	Not reported	.84–.93	.59–.89	.70–.90	94–97
Letter naming fluency	.80–.93	.90	.63–.77	.44–.71	70–80
Letter–sound fluency	.82	.83	.58–.68	.62–.71	77–78
Nonsense word fluency	.94	.94	.65–.91	.57–.71	76–90
Maze	.69–.91	Not reported	.64–.68	.56–.77	61–79
Measures of Academic Progress for Reading	Not reported	.65–.86	.58–.83	.63–.82	82–89
Observation Survey of Early Literacy Achievement	Not reported	Not reported	Not reported	.72–.83	80
Oral reading fluency	.89–.96	.94–.98	.67–.92	.62–.92	66–87
Phoneme segmentation fluency	.84–.88	.85	.43–.65	.42–.62	60–90
Phonological Awareness Literacy Screening–Early Literacy	Not reported	.78–.95	Not reported	.29–.78	93
Scholastic Phonics Inventory	.94–.98	Not reported	.66–.70	.43–.78	87
STAR Early Literacy	Not reported	.86–.91	.54–.88	.58–.79	73
STAR Reading	Not reported	.80–.90	.71–.87	.68–.86	76–81

Note. Information provided by the National Center on Response to Intervention.

Phoneme Segmentation Fluency

Phoneme segmentation fluency (PSF) is another measure that is based on phonemic awareness and most commonly is employed beginning in the winter of kindergarten through the spring of first grade. PSF assesses a child's ability to segment three- and four-syllable words into individual phonemes (Hintze et al., 2003). Words are presented orally to the student for 1 minute and the child is instructed to repeat the word orally in segmented syllables. The number of correct phonemes per minute represents the child's score. The materials used during PSF include the examiner probe (an 8.5 × 11 sheet of white paper with two columns of 12 words and their corresponding phoneme segments) and a stopwatch.

Reliability for PSF has been consistently above .80. Alternate form reliability has been estimated between .84 and .88 (Elliott, Lee, & Tollefson, 2001; Kaminski & Good, 1996), test–retest reliability has been estimated at .85 (Elliott et al., 2001), and interrater reliability has been estimated at .87 (Elliott et al., 2001).

PSF has established predictive validity. PSF administered in kindergarten is predictive of performance on reading tasks in first and second grade, with correlations ranging from .42 to .62 (Burke, Hagan-Burke, Kwok, & Parker, 2009; Good, Simmons, & Kame'enui, 2001). PSF also has established concurrent validity. PSF is related to concurrently administered reading tasks, with correlations between .43 and .65 (Good, Simmons, & Kame'enui, 2001; Kaminski & Good, 1996). A few studies have examined the diagnostic accuracy of PSF, and the estimates ranged from approximately 60% (Hintze et al., 2003) to higher estimates of 73–90% (Johnson et al., 2009).

Letter Naming Fluency

Letter naming fluency (LNF) often is employed in kindergarten and beginning first grade as an early reading screening tool. Although it does not explicitly address one of the five instructional areas of reading identified by the NRP (NICHD, 2000), it consistently has been shown to predict later reading achievement. The materials used during LNF include an 8.5 × 11 sheet of white paper with 11 rows of 10 upper- and lowercase letters. The student has 1 minute to name as many letters as possible (Good & Kaminski, 2002).

Reliability for LNF has been consistently above .80. Alternate form reliability is between .80 and .93 (Elliott et al., 2001; Good, Simmons, & Kame'enui, 2001). Test–retest reliability has been estimated at .90 (Elliott et al., 2001), and interrater reliability previously was shown to be .94 (Elliott et al., 2001).

LNF administered in kindergarten is predictive of performance on reading tasks in first grade, with correlations ranging from .44 to .71 (Good,

Simmons, & Kame'enui, 2001; Speece, Mills, Ritchey, & Hillman, 2003). LNF administered in kindergarten is predictive of performance on reading tasks in second grade, with correlations ranging from .51 to .62 (Burke et al., 2009). LNF also has established concurrent validity. LNF is related to concurrently administered reading-related tasks, with correlations between .63 and .77 (Elliott et al., 2001; Good, Simmons, & Kame'enui, 2001; Speece et al., 2003). Research regarding diagnostic accuracy of LNF also suggests acceptable utility. LNF scores correctly predicted who would and would not score well on a concurrent measure of early reading skills 70–80% of the time (Hintze et al., 2003).

Letter–Sound Fluency

Letter–sound fluency (LSF) is a basic measure of beginning phonics skills (letter–sound correspondence) that generally is used during kindergarten and first grade. Letters are again printed in lowercase on a page with 10 letters per row and 11 rows per page, and the students are prompted to provide the sounds for as many letters as possible in 1 minute (AIMSweb, 2010).

The reliability of the data obtained from LSF measure is acceptable. An estimate of alternate form reliability equaled .82, while test–retest reliability was .83, and interrater reliability was estimated at .82 (Elliott et al., 2001). LSF has been shown to predict later reading achievement, and it also is related to concurrently administered reading measures. LSF during kindergarten is related to oral reading in second grade with a correlation between .62 and .71 (Stage, Sheppard, Davidson, & Browning, 2001). Additionally, LSF during kindergarten is related to concurrently administered standardized reading assessments, with a correlation between .58 and .68. Diagnostic accuracy was evaluated with first- and second-grade students and correctly identified 76.8–77.5% of the students who later would demonstrate significant reading difficulties (Speece & Case, 2001).

Nonsense Word Fluency

Nonsense word fluency (NWF) generally is used later in the kindergarten year through first grade, and it measures a student's ability to read nonsense words by sounding them out as an indicator of phonetic skills. During NWF, the student reads nonsense words from an 8.5 × 11 paper. All words follow consonant–vowel–consonant and consonant–vowel patterns, and the student can read either each sound in each word or each word. The score is the number of correct letter sounds given in 1 minute.

Reliability of NWF has been studied on multiple occasions and consistently demonstrated sufficient reliability for screening (i.e., coefficients above .80). Test–retest reliability has been estimated at .94 (Harn, Stoolmiller, &

Chard, 2008), and alternate form reliability also has been estimated as .94 (Speece et al., 2003).

NWF has been shown to predict performance on later reading tasks. First-grade NWF data correlated performance on standardized reading assessments in second grade at .57–.71 (Fien et al., 2008; Speece et al., 2003). Additionally, predictive validity ranges from .61 to .67 with NWF performance in first grade are used to predict performance on reading fluency in second grade (Fien et al., 2008). NWF performance also is related to performance on concurrently administered reading tasks. Concurrent validity ranges from .65 to .91 when performance on NWF is correlated with standardized assessments of reading. Additionally, the correlation between NWF and concurrently administered reading fluency is .76 (Fien et al., 2008). There are only limited diagnostic accuracy data for NWF, but the estimates were quite high, ranging from 76% to 90% (Johnson et al., 2009) in one study and from 69% to 84% in another (Powell-Smith, Hudson, Dedrick, & Castillo, 2008).

Oral Reading Fluency

Oral reading fluency (ORF) generally is administered beginning in the winter of first grade as an overall indicator of reading skills. It also directly assesses one of the NRP (NICHD, 2000) reading instructional areas. During ORF, students are asked to read from a grade-level passage for 1 minute. Hesitations of longer than 3 seconds, omissions, and substitutions are counted as errors. The final score is the number of words read correctly over the number of errors. Three 1-minute administrations are generally given for screening assessments, and the median number of words read correctly per minute (WCPM) is recorded as the ORF score (Good et al., 2011).

Of all of the CBMs, ORF is by far the most researched. Reliability of ORF has been consistently above .80. Test–retest reliability has been estimated between .94 and .98 (Baker et al., 2008). Alternate form reliability has been estimated between .89 and .96 (Roberts, Good, & Corcoran, 2005).

ORF has well-established predictive validity. ORF administered at the beginning of first grade is predictive of performance on ORF at the end of first grade with correlations ranging from .85 to .92 (Harn et al., 2008). Moreover, ORF administered at the beginning of first grade is predictive of NWF performance at the end of first grade with correlations between .62 and .69 (Harn et al., 2008). Finally, ORF measures given in the fall or winter of first–third grade are predictive of performance on a standardized achievement test given in the spring of first–third grade with correlations ranging from .58 to .79 (Baker et al., 2008). ORF also has established concurrent validity with standardized achievement tests with correlations ranging from .67 to .82

(Baker et al., 2008) and other reading-related tasks with correlations between .77 and .92 (Burke & Hagan-Burke, 2007).

Diagnostic accuracy for ORF data has been well researched and often used long-term relationships to state-mandated accountability test scores. Estimates with state-administered tests resulted in diagnostic accuracy between 66% and 76% (McGlinchey & Hixson, 2004; Stage & Jacobsen, 2001), which increased to 80% when using a national test (Parker et al., in press) and to 79–87% when considering long-term reading growth (Speece & Case, 2001).

Maze

We suggest that school personnel include a direct measure of reading comprehension in their screening system for students in the fourth grade and higher. Previous research found that ORF predicted state test scores quite well until about sixth grade, at which time measures of comprehension worked at least as well if not better (Silberglitt, Burns, Madyun, & Lail, 2006). Thus, comprehension is likely the best screener for students in middle and high school, but including comprehension data for earlier grades may assist in identifying intervention targets.

Maze often is considered a measure of comprehension. During a Maze administration, a student receives a leveled passage in which every seventh word is replaced by three possible word choices, one of which is the correct word and the other two are distractor words of approximately the same length as the correct word. The student has 3 minutes to read the passage silently and select as many correct words as possible. Unlike most other CBM measures, Maze can be administered individually or in a group. DIBELS recently released a Maze measure called Daze that is available for third- through sixth-grade students, and AIMSweb's Maze measures are available for first- through eighth-grade students. DIBELS and AIMSweb Maze measures are scored differently: Within DIBELS, the adjusted score is equal to the number of correct selections minus the number of errors divided by 2, and within AIMSweb, the score is equal to the number of correct selections.

The validity and reliability of Maze measures recently was evaluated in the DIBELS Next technical manual (Good et al., 2011). Alternate form reliability ranged from .75 to .83 for third- through fifth-grade Daze administrations. An earlier study of another set of Maze passages estimated alternate form reliability as .81, with a range of .69–.91 (Shin, Deno, & Espin, 2000). Interrater reliability was .98–.99 for third- through sixth-grade Daze passages.

The predictive validity of Daze when a fall administration was used to predict a spring administration of a standardized, norm-referenced achievement test in reading was .56–.67 for third- through sixth-grade students. When a fall Daze administration was used to predict a spring DIBELS composite, the predictive validity was .69–.77. Concurrent validity estimates ranged from .64 to .68 when compared with a concurrently administered standardized norm-referenced reading assessment for third- through sixth-grade students. Diagnostic accuracy for one version of Maze reported by the NCRTI ranged from 61% to 79%, which was rated as partially convincing evidence for classification accuracy.

Group-Administered Comprehension Assessments

There are several well-constructed group-administered measures of reading comprehension, such as the Measures of Academic Progress for Reading (MAP-R; Northwest Evaluation Association, 2003), STAR Reading (Renaissance Learning, 2003), the Iowa Test of Basic Skills (Hieronymus, Lindquist, & Hoover, 1979), and the Gates-MacGinitie Reading Test (MacGinitie, MacGinitie, Maria, & Dreyer, 2000). Because there are so many potential screeners for comprehension, we cannot go into detail about each one. These four tools, however, were rated highly by the NCRTI, information from which is included in Table 7.1.

COLLECTING SCREENING DATA

Benchmark reading assessments typically are conducted three times per year in the fall, winter, and spring and serve several important functions (Burns & Gibbons, 2012). First, benchmark assessments serve as a screening tool that examines the skill level of every student. Next, benchmark data establish schoolwide norms that can be used for goal setting. Finally, benchmark data can be used to evaluate the effectiveness of the school's curricula. In the sections that follow, we discuss procedures for screening and describe the procedures at Burgelesen Elementary.

Screening Procedures

Before conducting benchmark assessments, several decisions must be made, including what measures will be used, who will conduct the assessments, how and when the assessors will be trained, and what specific procedures will be used for the assessments. It is also important that districts identify an assessment window for collecting their benchmark data, which will allow schools to make comparisons across years.

Depending on the grade being benchmarked and the skill that the assessors would like to target, assessments can be conducted using any number of measures. For example, ORF data are collected with three 1-minute administrations, and the median score is recorded as the student's result. After the data have been collected, scores should be entered into a spreadsheet or database (e.g., Microsoft Excel or an online database such as AIMSweb). Finally, the data should be reviewed and used to assist in the decision-making process.

Screening at Burgelesen Elementary

As part of their district initiative to adopt an MTSS, the task force at Burgelesen Elementary convened to discuss their approach for screening using benchmark assessments. They began by determining which measures they would use for screening (see the previous section for a reminder). Then, they decided to conduct benchmark assessments three times per year; fall benchmarking occurred during the last 2 weeks of September, winter benchmarking occurred during the last 2 weeks of January, and spring benchmarking occurred during the last 2 weeks of May.

The next step for the team at Burgelesen was to determine who would be involved in conducting the benchmark assessments. The school psychologist, who was a member of the MTSS task force, volunteered to be the head of the benchmarking team. She was able to assemble a group that consisted of paraprofessionals, special education teachers, and volunteers from the local parent–teacher association. After the team was identified, the school psychologist conducted a 90-minute training session that included information on administration and scoring of the measure, recording student scores, and data privacy. The training also included a brief practice session that featured feedback on administering and scoring the measures. All participants correctly implemented the assessment procedures with 100% fidelity before completing the training session.

After the team had been trained, the school psychologist worked to gather the necessary materials, including student and assessor probes, pencils, stopwatches, and clipboards. She also reserved the school's multipurpose room for 3 days and had each classroom teacher sign up for a 15-minute time slot. On the first day of benchmarking, the team set up several stations so that when a class entered, several students could be assessed at once. This helped ensure an efficient assessment session. After the benchmark data were collected, the scores were entered into Microsoft Excel. From there, the team examined the data on a classwide and individual level and used those data to make the decisions about classwide problems, and to determine who requires supplemental support and what intervention is most appropriate for a given group of students.

IDENTIFYING CLASSWIDE PROBLEMS

Upon collecting screening data within a tiered model, the first question that can be answered is "Is there a classwide problem?" This question is of primary importance because researchers have found consistently that the first step in identifying individual students with difficulties is to rule out the effect of a potential system problem (VanDerHeyden & Burns, 2005; VanDerHeyden, Witt, & Naquin, 2003). In other words, the first task in an MTSS is to determine whether the problems are specific to individual students or to the system in which they are functioning. We use the classroom as the unit of analysis, rather than grade level, school, or district, because interventions based on the data will be delivered at the classroom level.

Procedures

Consider what would happen if 18 of 25 students in one class were identified as requiring a Tier 2 intervention. Would it be possible to conduct small-group interventions with 18 of 25 students? It is likely that the entire classroom would benefit from additional support and doing so would improve decisions regarding who needs Tier 2 interventions.

Recall that a classwide problem occurs when a large percentage of students experiences a difficulty and suggests that the area for preventive intervention exists at the level of the system in which they operate (i.e., class, school, or district) rather than the individual students. Recall that the first tier of instruction is designed to address the needs of approximately 80% of students within a system (Batsche et al., 2005). If less than 80% of students are meeting a criterion, it can be assumed that a classroom problem exists, and the core instruction and curriculum should be reevaluated and strengthened (Ikeda et al., 2008)

Another approach with a strong research base for determining whether there is a classwide problem involves comparing the class median for the benchmark scores to a criterion, such as national norms, instructional-level criteria, or empirically derived criteria. Burns and Gibbons (2012) suggested using the 25th percentile as the criterion because it represents the lowest end of the average range. In other words, a classroom problem likely exists if a classroom's benchmark median falls below the 25th percentile on a national norm. It is important to use the class median, rather than the average, because the average for a data set of 30 students or less can be substantially affected by outlying data. For example, all it would take is for two third graders reading five WCPM to render the average ORF score useless.

Instructional-level criteria also can be used to determine whether a classwide problem exists. For example, Deno and Mirkin (1977) suggested a criterion of 40–60 WCPM (for Grades 1 and 2) and 70–100 WCPM (Grades 3–6). If the class median is above that instructional standard, those who perform below the standard receive a Tier 2 intervention. If the class median is below the instructional standard, however, a classwide intervention is performed before identifying individual children for further assessment (VanDerHeyden, Witt, & Gilbertson, 2007).

Regardless of the approach used to help identify whether a classwide problem exists, the steps that follow are the same. If a classwide problem is deemed to exist, a classwide intervention should be implemented. Although several interventions have been researched, it is beyond the scope of this chapter to discuss them individually. Generally speaking, classwide interventions take place for approximately 15 minutes each day over the course of a few weeks (VanDerHeyden & Burns, 2005). They often include such strategies as modeling, guided instruction, and peer tutoring. When the class median exceeds the criterion, a classwide problem can be factored out, and individual students can be targeted for intervention (Burns & Gibbons, 2012).

Classwide Problems at Burgelesen Elementary

The grade-level teams at Burgelesen Elementary were trained to examine the screening data, and the school psychologist attended the meeting at which they examined the data to guide the process. The grade-level teams' first step in examining the fall benchmark data was to determine whether any classwide problems existed. To do this, they determined a median benchmark score for each classroom and compared it with national norms, and median scores below the 25th percentile indicated that a classroom problem existed. Unfortunately, there were many classwide problems at Burgelesen. In fact, there were classwide problems in almost every classroom, with the exception of third grade. For example, the median ORF for one fourth-grade classroom was 78 WCPM, which fell below the score (81 WCPM) that represented the 25th percentile according to AIMSweb national norms (AIMSweb, 2010).

The presence of a classwide problem in this fourth-grade classroom suggested that an intervention was needed. The fourth-grade team decided on an empirically based classroom intervention that utilized peer tutoring and focused on reading fluency and comprehension (D. Fuchs, Fuchs, Mathes, & Simmons, 1997) and agreed to assess ORF with every student each week until the median score exceeded the 25th percentile on the national norm. The intervention took place for 15 minutes each day. The classroom median for the ORF data was above the 25th percentile after only 3 weeks, at which time the intervention was removed. The grade-level team decided to continue to screen each student in the class on a monthly basis to carefully monitor this classroom to ensure that the classwide problem was remediated effectively.

IDENTIFYING STUDENTS REQUIRING SUPPLEMENTAL SERVICES

Procedures

After identifying or ruling out a classwide problem, students requiring supplemental (or Tier 2) services are identified. Two potential methods for identifying students requiring Tier 2 services include identifying all students below a criterion-referenced cutoff and identifying students based on normative data.

Identifying Students Based on a Criterion-Referenced Cutoff

Students may be identified for supplemental intervention based on performance below a criterion that is associated with poor future performance. For instance, DIBELS provides benchmarks that are related to scoring at or above the 40th percentile on a standardized, norm-referenced assessment of reading achievement at the end of the school year (Good et al., 2011). Of course, criterion-referenced cutoffs are useful only to the extent that the screening instruments used have criterion-related validity and diagnostic accuracy, as discussed previously.

Identifying Students Based on a Norm-Referenced Cutoff

Students also may be identified based on national, local, or classroom norms. For instance, AIMSweb provides norms based on a nationwide sample of students (AIMSweb, 2010), and those students who score below a specified percentile (e.g., 25th) are identified for supplemental services. Alternatively, school districts also may create their own local norms, which have the advantage of being more relevant to the local population in some instances (Deno, 2003). One additional alternative is selecting the lowest performing students in the school (e.g., the bottom 20%) for supplemental intervention (Burns & Gibbons, 2012), which can be considered a school-based normative approach. One disadvantage of using local norms is that it does not provide a reference point for students' scores relative to proficiency expectations outside the school. For example, if students as a whole perform poorly on the assessment, then even those in the 90th percentile may perform below national expectations.

Additional Considerations

Identifying students for Tier 2 interventions is not as easy as drawing a line below a certain cut score, and grade-level teams have to consider other factors as well. First, if the student is diagnosed with a special education disability, has an Individualized Educational Program (IEP) that includes a reading goal, and receives reading instruction from special education, then it may not be appropriate to provide a supplemental intervention as well. Students should receive whatever service will most likely ensure learning while providing a free and appropriate public education in the least restrictive environment. Thus, it may be possible that the grade-level team decides that the Tier 2 intervention will be sufficient to address the student's needs, which would require a new IEP, but most often teams will determine that the specialized instruction would be more beneficial and that the student would not be part of the school's Tier 2 intervention.

Second, as stated earlier, ORF has quite high diagnostic accuracy, but no screening system can be free of error. Thus, grade-level teams should discuss students who scored just above and below the criterion to determine whether any students were misidentified. Teams should err on the side of caution when it comes to identifying students and would rather overidentify than underidentify. In other words, it would be much worse to miss a student who actually needed an intervention to be successful than it would be to provide an intervention to a student who did not actually need it. Thus, teams should look at students whose screening data fell above the cut score and should examine other types of data besides ORF. For example, if the ORF score was above the cut score, but the MAP-R score was low (e.g., below the 25th percentile), then the team might consider providing an intervention for that student.

Many schools administer multiple screening measures, including CBM and a group-administered measure of comprehension (e.g., MAP-R). Together, these two sources of data provide a solid picture of a student's reading skills, but the accuracy with which students read also can provide useful information. Previous research consistently has supported the instructional utility of examining accuracy of reading skills, which was defined as the percentage of items successfully completed (Burns, 2007; Hosp & Ardoin, 2008; Treptow, Burns, & McComas, 2007). Accuracy for ORF is determined by the percentage of words read correctly, which results in data that are sufficiently reliable for instructional decision making (i.e., at or above .80; Burns et al., 2000). The percentage of words read correctly is compared with the research-based criterion of 93% or higher (Gickling & Armstrong, 1978; Treptow et al., 2007). Thus, students who read less than 93% of the words correctly are likely struggling to decode the text and likely would benefit from reading instruction (Burns & Parker, in press). Other reading skills that do not involve reading connected text (e.g., NWF, LSF) should be completed with 90% accuracy (Burns, 2004).

Identifying Students at Burgelesen

We will use the third-grade data to demonstrate how to identify students as needing a Tier 2 intervention. The data shown in Table 7.2 are the ORF score for every student, the percentage of words read correctly from the ORF reading probe, and the percentile rank for the MAP test of reading. As can be seen in Table 7.2, there are 49 third graders at Burgelesen Elementary among two classrooms with two different teachers. The class median for Teacher A's students was 86.0 WCPM, and 84.5 WCPM for Teacher B. Both class medians were above the 25th percentile of 54.0 WCPM for fall of third grade, and no classwide problems were identified.

The next step after addressing classwide problems is to determine which students need supplemental services. The task force at Burgelesen decided to use the 25th percentile for the fall for third grade, which equaled a score of 54 WCPM (AIMSweb, 2010). Thus, any third-grade student who scored at or less than 54 WCPM would have received a Tier 2 intervention. As shown in Table 7.2, 11 third-grade students scored at or below the 25th percentile. However, Student 22, who read 16 WCPM, already was identified as learning disabled in reading and received reading instruction from special education. Thus, the grade-level team decided to not provide a Tier 2 intervention for that student. There were 49 total students in the third grade. Ideally, 20% of the students would receive a Tier 2 intervention, which would be approximately 10 students in third grade. The grade-level team considered providing supplemental support for Student 40, who scored below the normative criterion, but his accuracy (above 93%) and MAP-R data suggested that a supplemental intervention was not needed at that time. Thus, the 10 students in Table 7.2 whose records are bolded received Tier 2 interventions.

IDENTIFYING INTERVENTION TARGETS

Once students are identified as needing supplemental interventions, teams then can turn their attention to creating small groups and identifying areas for preventive intervention. In the sections that follow, we discuss procedures for identifying intervention targets with screening data.

TABLE 7.2
Fall Screening Data for Third Grade at Burgelesen Elementary

Student	Teacher	Grade	WCPM	Accuracy (%)	MAP-R percentile
22	**A**	**3**	**16**	**69.6**	**2**
48	**A**	**3**	**22**	**88.0**	**12**
26	**B**	**3**	**22**	**73.3**	**10**
3	**A**	**3**	**35**	**75.6**	**22**
27	**B**	**3**	**39**	**88.6**	**19**
6	**A**	**3**	**40**	**83.3**	**10**
33	**A**	**3**	**40**	**95.2**	**18**
28	**B**	**3**	**47**	**100**	**24**
4	**A**	**3**	**51**	**98.1**	**21**
29	**B**	**3**	**51**	**96.2**	**22**
30	**B**	**3**	**54**	**98.2**	**35**
40	B	3	59	93.5	45
32	B	3	66	96.8	29
1	A	3	67	98.7	44
5	B	3	68	96.3	56
23	A	3	70	95.1	58
34	B	3	78	95.1	68
24	A	3	79	97.5	55
7	A	3	80	96.4	46
8	A	3	80	96.4	85
35	B	3	80	97.6	58
9	A	3	81	95.3	66
36	B	3	81	96.4	75
2	B	3	84	84.0	43
47	B	3	85	97.6	55
25	A	3	86	93.2	57
46	B	3	88	93.2	78
10	A	3	90	94.7	72
49	B	3	90	95.7	64
11	A	3	91	95.8	77
12	A	3	93	100	90
39	B	3	93	96.9	82
13	A	3	95	96.0	56
38	B	3	95	97.9	44
37	B	3	97	99.0	59
31	B	3	103	99.0	92
41	B	3	104	98.1	89
14	A	3	117	97.5	88
42	B	3	118	99.2	78
15	A	3	119	96.0	85
16	A	3	133	100	93
17	A	3	134	97.1	98
18	A	3	139	99.3	97
43	B	3	139	99.3	90
19	A	3	141	100	79
44	B	3	141	98.6	95
20	A	3	145	100	97
21	A	3	146	99.2	98
45	B	3	168	100	94

Note. Records in bold indicate students who received Tier 2 intervention. MAP-R Percentile = percentile rank on the Measures of Academic Progress for Reading; WCPM = words read correctly per minute from oral reading fluency assessments.

Procedures

Given their supplemental nature, Tier 2 interventions generally target the same skills that are targeted in Tier 1 instruction and also should be aligned with the benchmarking measures used for that grade. Additionally, Tier 2 interventions should target critical basic reading skills, such as those identified by the NRP (NICHD, 2000), phonemic awareness, phonics, reading fluency, comprehension, and vocabulary.

Tier 2 interventions usually are implemented in small groups, and methods for grouping students are an important consideration. Research syntheses indicate that homogeneous groupings for reading (Slavin, 1987) and instruction that are geared toward specific areas of intervention increased student learning (Connor, Morrison, Fishman, Schatschneider, & Underwood, 2007). The NRP areas of reading instruction provide a useful heuristic to guide intervention targeting (Burns, Christ, Boice, & Szadokierski, 2010). Reading theorists have suggested that students progress from phonemic awareness to alphabetic principles and decoding, to reading fluently, to comprehending what they read (Adams, 1990; Chall, 1983), and research has supported this progression among struggling readers (Berninger, Abbott, Vermeulen, & Fulton, 2006; Snow et al., 1998). CBMs can directly assess the NRP (NICHD, 2000) areas because PSF is a measure of phonemic awareness, NWF of decoding, and ORF of reading fluency. Alternatively, the percentage of words read correctly within ORF that fell below 93% also could suggest a potential difficulty with decoding. Maze is linked closely to comprehension and may provide an indicator, but group-administered measures of comprehension such as MAP-R or Star Reading may more directly assess comprehension. Thus, grade-level teams could examine measures of the NRP areas to home in their intervention efforts and should provide interventions in the areas that the screening data suggest for preventive intervention. If a student scores low in more than one area, then the intervention would target the more foundational skill (Burns et al., 2010). For example, if a student scored low in comprehension and fluency, then the intervention would start with fluency, but a student who also scored low in decoding likely would receive a phonics intervention.

Identifying Intervention Targets at Burgelesen

The grade-level teams at Burgelesen Elementary identified 10 third graders who needed supplemental intervention. After identifying who needed intervention, the team then identified intervention targets. They started by listing the students from highest to lowest ORF scores, as shown in Table 7.2. All 10 students scored below the 25th percentile for ORF, and all but 1 (Student 30) scored below the 25th percentile on the MAP-R. Thus, all but one student demonstrated difficulties with both comprehension and fluency. However, Students 48, 26, 3, 27, and 6 also read less than 93% of the words correctly (range of 73.3% to 88.6%), which suggested that they also struggled with the code-based aspects of reading. Those five students were grouped together and received a decoding intervention. Certainly, grade-level teams could validate the hypothesis that the students who read less than 93% of the words correctly also struggle with decoding skills by administering measures of decoding, such as NWF, or other nonsense word measures, such as the Word Attack subtest of the Woodcock–Johnson Test of Achievement (3rd ed.; Mather & Woodcock, 2001). It is a reasonable and empirically justified approach, however, to implement a decoding intervention without collecting additional data.

Students 33, 28, 4, 29, and 30 all scored below the 25th percentile for ORF, but they read more than 93% of the words correctly. Thus, those students were grouped together to receive a fluency intervention. Of course, student progress was monitored on a weekly basis, and comprehension interventions began when each student's ORF score met or exceeded the benchmark target, but the interventions began with the more fundamental skill.

TYING IT ALL TOGETHER

The procedures and examples discussed in this chapter require training, dedication, commitment of resources, and time, but they are not difficult to implement. Most schools are already collecting screening data, but they are not using them to their fullest potential. In our opinion, schools generally do an excellent job of collecting data, but they are often much less proficient at consuming the data. The first step has to be identifying classwide problems and providing systems interventions. Remediating classwide problems could be the single most efficient, effective, and underutilized application of screening data. Moreover, most schools use screening data to determine who requires an intervention, but many do not examine the data more deeply to determine what intervention would be most appropriate.

Burgelesen Elementary

Burgelesen began their journey approximately 2 years ago and was a failing school. Just over half of their students demonstrated proficient reading skills in third and fourth grade. Recognizing the need for change, school personnel abandoned many of their current practices and selected psychometrically sound measures that accurately identified students who were at risk for reading difficulties and that aligned with the school's curriculum and instructional practices. They then used those tools to collect screening data and trained their grade-level teams to consume the data, with support from the school psychologist. These relatively straightforward reforms led to dramatic increases in student learning. Two short years ago, there were multiple classwide problems and a large percentage of students who scored below the 25th percentile on various reading measures. This past year, 83% of the students scored within the proficient range on the state accountability test, and no classwide problems were identified in the building. In fact, only two students in the entire school scored below the 25th percentile on the national norm for any of the screening measures that they used.

Directions for Future Research

There is considerably more research regarding screening reading skills in the past 10 years than in any previous decade, and the example provided in this chapter presents reason for optimism. However, additional research is needed. For example, additional research is needed to determine the long-term diagnostic accuracy of measures described in this chapter. Many screening tools have shown sufficient reliability for screening decisions, but reliable data are just the minimum criterion. Researchers are more consistently examining diagnostic accuracy, but many studies addressed only concurrent or short-term predictions.

In addition to diagnostic accuracy, stronger evidence for construct validity may be needed for decisions made from various screening tools. For example, Maze is purported to be a measure of reading comprehension, but it is unclear whether the data actually assess comprehension skills or just overall reading proficiency (January & Ardoin, 2012). If the data are used to screen overall reading proficiency of older students, then they are probably adequate (Silberglitt et al., 2006). If the data are used to identify a specific skill deficit as proposed in this chapter, however, then practitioners need to know how well the measure assesses the specific skill for which it is purported to test. Moreover, the conceptual framework discussed to identify areas for preventive intervention is based on considerable research, but the model in its entirety requires additional empirical scrutiny.

Conclusion

Burgelesen's experience shows that although the word *data* contains four letters, it does not have to be a four-letter word, if school teams know how to unlock their potential. Stiggins (2005) famously suggested that we should shift from assessment of student learning to assessment *for* student learning, and using data to identify potential interventions for groups of students could be a school's first step on that path. Clearly, additional research is needed, but practitioners could use well-established decision-making frameworks to improve the educational outcomes of the students they serve.

REFERENCES

Adams, M. J. (1990). *Beginning to read: Thinking and learning about print*. Cambridge, MA: Harvard University Press.

AIMSweb. (2010). *AIMSweb assessment and data management for RTI*. Bloomington, MN: NCS Pearson. Retrieved from http://www.aimsweb.com

Alonzo, J., Tindal, G., Ulmer, K., & Glasgow, A. (2006). *Easy-CBM online progress monitoring assessment system*. Eugene, OR: Center for Educational Assessment Accountability. Retrieved from http://easycbm.com

Baker, S. K., Smolkowski, K., Katz, R., Fien, H., Seeley, J. R., Kame'enui, E. J., & Beck, C. T. (2008). Reading fluency as a predictor of reading proficiency in low-performing, high-poverty schools. *School Psychology Review, 37,* 18–37.

Batsche, G., Elliott, J., Graden, J. L., Grimes, J., Kovaleski, J. F., Prasse, D., . . . Tilly, W. D., III. (2005). *Response to intervention: Policy considerations and implementation*. Alexandria, VA: National Association of State Board of Directors of Special Education.

Berninger, V. W., Abbott, R. D., Vermeulen, K., & Fulton, C. M. (2006). Paths to reading comprehension in at-risk second-grade readers. *Journal of Learning Disabilities, 39,* 334–351. doi:10.1177/00222194060390040701

Burke, M. D., & Hagan-Burke, S. (2007). Concurrent criterion-related validity of early literacy indicators for middle of first grade. *Assessment for Effective Intervention, 32,* 66–77. doi:10.1177/15345084070320020401

Burke, M. D., Hagan-Burke, S., Kwok, O., & Parker, R. (2009). Predictive validity of early literacy indicators from the middle of kindergarten to second grade. *Journal of Special Education, 42,* 209–226. doi:10.1177/0022466907313347

Burns, M. K. (2004). Empirical analysis of drill ratio research: Refining the instructional level for drill tasks. *Remedial and Special Education, 25,* 167–173. doi:10.1177/07419325040250030401

Burns, M. K. (2007). Reading at the instructional level with children identified as learning disabled: Potential implications for response to intervention. *School Psychology Quarterly, 22,* 297–313. doi:10.1037/1045-3830.22.3.297

Burns, M. K., Christ, T. J., Boice, C. H., & Szadokierski, I. (2010). Special education in an RTI model: Addressing unique learning needs. In T. A. Glover & S. Vaughn (Eds.), *The promise of response to intervention: Evaluating current science and practice* (pp. 267–285). New York, NY: Guilford Press.

Burns, M. K., & Gibbons, K. A. (2012). *Implementing response-to-intervention in elementary and secondary schools: Procedures to assure scientific-based practices*. New York, NY: Routledge.

Burns, M. K., & Parker, D. C. (in press). Using the instructional level as a criterion to determine student phase of learning for reading fluency: Evidence for the learning hierarchy. *Reading and Writing Quarterly.*

Burns, M. K., Tucker, J. A., Frame, J., Foley, S., & Hauser, A. (2000). Interscorer, alternate-form, internal consistency, and test–retest reliability of Gickling's model of curriculum-based assessment for reading. *Journal of Psychoeducational Assessment, 18,* 353–360. doi:10.1177/073428290001800405

Chall, J. S. (1983). *Stages of reading development.* New York, NY: McGraw Hill.

Coie, J. D., Watt, N. F., West, S. G., Hawkins, J. D., Asarnow, J. R., Markman, H. J., . . . Long, B. (1993). The science of prevention: A conceptual framework and some directions for a national research program. *American Psychologist, 48,* 1013–1022. doi:10.1037/0003-066X.48.10.1013

Connor, C. M., Morrison, F. J., Fishman, B. J., Schatschneider, C., & Underwood, P. (2007). Algorithm-guided individualized reading instruction. *Science, 315,* 464–465. doi:10.1126/science.1134513

Deno, S. L. (1985). Curriculum-based measurement: The emerging alternative. *Exceptional Children, 52,* 219–232.

Deno, S. L. (2003). Developments in curriculum-based measurement. *Journal of Special Education, 37,* 184–192. doi:10.1177/00224669030370030801

Deno, S. L., & Mirkin, P. K. (1977). *Data-based program modification: A manual.* Reston, VA: Council for Exceptional Children.

Elliott, J., Lee, S. W., & Tollefson, N. (2001). A reliability and validity study of the Dynamic Indicators of Basic Early Literacy Skills–Modified. *School Psychology Review, 30,* 33–49.

Fien, H., Baker, S. K., Smolkowski, K., Mercier Smith, J. L., Kame'enui, E. J., & Beck, C. T. (2008). Nonsense word fluency to predict reading proficiency in kindergarten through second grade for English learners and native English Speakers. *School Psychology Review, 37,* 391–408.

Fountas, I., & Pinnell, G. S. (2007). *Benchmark assessment system.* Portsmouth, NH: Heinemann.

Fuchs, D., Fuchs, L. S., Mathes, P. G., & Simmons, D. C. (1997). Peer-assisted learning strategies: Making classrooms more responsive to diversity. *American Educational Research Journal, 34,* 174–206. doi:10.3102/00028312034001174

Fuchs, L. S., & Fuchs, D. (1986). Effects of systematic formative evaluation: A meta-analysis. *Exceptional Children, 53,* 199–208.

Gickling, E. E., & Armstrong, D. L. (1978). Levels of instruction difficulty as related to on-task behavior, task completion, and comprehension. *Journal of Learning Disabilities, 11,* 559–566. doi:10.1177/002221947801100905

Good, R. H., & Kaminski, R. A. (Eds.). (2002). *Dynamic Indicators of Basic Early Literacy Skills* (6th ed.). Eugene, OR: Institute for the Development of Educational Achievement.

Good, R. H., Kaminski, R. A., Dewey, E. N., Wallin, J., Powell-Smith, K. A., & Latimer, R. J. (2011). *DIBELS Next Technical Manual* [Draft]. Eugene, OR: Dynamic Measurement Group.

Good, R. H., III, Kaminski, R. A., Simmons, D., & Kame'enui, E. J. (2001). *Using Dynamic Indicators of Basic Early Literacy Skills (DIBELS) in an outcomes-driven model: Steps to reading outcomes*. Eugene, OR: University of Oregon.

Good, R. H., III, Simmons, D. C., & Kame'enui, E. J. (2001). The importance and decision-making utility of a continuum of fluency-based indicators of foundational reading skills for third-grade high-stakes outcomes. *Scientific Studies of Reading, 5*, 257–288. doi:10.1207/S1532799XSSR0503_4

Harn, B. A., Stoolmiller, M., & Chard, D. J. (2008). Measuring the dimensions of alphabetic principle on the reading development of first graders. *Journal of Learning Disabilities, 41*, 143–157. doi:10.1177/0022219407313585

Hieronymus, A. N., Lindquist, E. F., & Hoover, H. D. (1979). *Iowa Test of Basic Skills*. Iowa City: University of Iowa.

Hintze, J. M., Ryan, A. L., & Stoner, G. (2003). Concurrent validity and diagnostic accuracy of the Dynamic Indicators of Basic Early Literacy Skills and the Comprehensive Test of Phonological Processing. *School Psychology Review, 32*, 541–556.

Hosp, J. L., & Ardoin, S. P. (2008). Assessment for instructional planning. *Assessment for Effective Intervention, 33*, 69–77. doi:10.1177/1534508407311428

Ikeda, M. J., Neesen, E., & Witt, J. C. (2008). Best practices in universal screening. In A. Thomas & J. Grimes (Eds.), *Best practices in school psychology V* (pp. 103–115). Bethesda, MD: NASP Publications.

January, S. A., & Ardoin, S. P. (2012). The impact of context and word type on students' Maze task accuracy. *School Psychology Review, 41*, 262–271.

Jenkins, J. R., Hudson, R. F., & Johnson, E. S. (2007). Screening for at-risk readers in a response to intervention framework. *School Psychology Review, 36*, 582–600.

Johnson, E. S., Jenkins, J. R., Petscher, Y., & Catts, H. W. (2009). Can we improve the accuracy of screening instruments? *Learning Disabilities Research and Practice, 24*, 174–185. doi:10.1111/j.1540-5826.2009.00291.x

Kaminski, R., & Good, R. (1996). Toward a technology for assessing basic early literacy skills. *School Psychology Review, 25*, 215–227.

Kroll, A., Krall, L., & Christ, T. J. (2006). *Computer Based Assessment System for Reading (CBAS-R) 1.0: Hierarchy and item development for fluency and decoding* (Tech. Rep. No. 1d). Minneapolis: University of Minnesota, Department of Educational Psychology.

Lembke, E. S., McMaster, K. L., & Stecker, P. M. (2010). The prevention science of reading research within a response-to-intervention model. *Psychology in the Schools, 47*, 22–35.

MacGinitie, W. H., MacGinitie, R. K., Maria, K., & Dreyer, L. G. (2000). *Gates-MacGinitie Reading Test* (4th ed.). Itasca, IL: Riverside.

Marston, D. B. (1989). Curriculum-based measurement: What is it and why do it? In M. R. Shinn (Ed.), *Curriculum-based measurement: Assessing special children* (pp. 137–172). Washington, DC: National Association of School Psychologists.

Mather, N., & Woodcock, R. W. (2001). *Woodcock–Johnson III: Tests of achievement. Examiner's manual, standard and extended batteries*. Itasca, IL: Riverside.

McGlinchey, M. T., & Hixson, M. D. (2004). Using curriculum-based measurement to predict performance on state assessments in reading. *School Psychology Review, 33,* 193–203.

National Institute of Child Health and Human Development. (2000). *Report of the National Reading Panel. Teaching children to read: An evidence-based assessment of the scientific research literature on reading and its implications for reading instruction: Reports of the subgroups* (NIH Publication No. 00-4754). Washington, DC: Government Printing Office.

Northwest Evaluation Association. (2003). *Technical manual for use with Measures of Academic Progress and Achievement Level Tests*. Portland, OR: Author.

Paris, S. G. (2002). Measuring children's reading development using leveled texts. *Reading Teacher, 56,* 168–170.

Paris, S. G., Paris, A. H., & Carpenter, R. D. (2002). *Effective practices for assessing young readers* (CIERA Report No. 3-013). Ann Arbor, MI: Center for the Improvement of Early Reading Achievement.

Parker, D. C., Zaslofsky, A. F., Burns, M. K., Kanive, R., Hodgson, J., Scholin, S. E., & Klingbeil, D. A. (in press). A brief report of the diagnostic accuracy of oral reading fluency and reading inventory levels for reading failure risk among second- and third-grade students. *Reading and Writing Quarterly*.

Powell-Smith, K. A., & Bradley-Klug, K. L. (2001). Another look at the "C" in CBM: Does it really matter if curriculum-based measurement reading probes are curriculum-based? *Psychology in the Schools, 38,* 299–312. doi:10.1002/pits.1020

Powell-Smith, K. A., Hudson, R. F., Dedrick, R., & Castillo, J. M. (2008). *Examining the use of DIBELS nonsense word fluency with first and second grade students in Reading First schools*. Unpublished manuscript.

Renaissance Learning. (2003). *STAR Reading*. Wisconsin Rapids, WI: Author.

Roberts, G., Good, R., & Corcoran, S. (2005). Story retell: A fluency-based indicator of reading comprehension. *School Psychology Quarterly, 20,* 304–317. doi:10.1521/scpq.2005.20.3.304

Salvia, J., Ysseldyke, J. E., & Bolt, S. (2013). *Assessment in special and inclusive education* (12th ed.). Belmont, CA: Wadsworth Cengage Learning.

Shin, J., Deno, S. L., & Espin, C. A. (2000). Technical adequacy of the Maze task for curriculum-based measurement of reading growth. *Journal of Special Education, 34,* 164–172. doi:10.1177/002246690003400305

Silberglitt, B., Burns, M. K., Madyun, N. H., & Lail, K. E. (2006). Relationship of reading fluency assessment data with state accountability test scores: A longitudinal comparison of grade levels. *Psychology in the Schools, 43,* 527–535. doi:10.1002/pits.20175

Slavin, R. E. (1987). Ability grouping and student achievement in elementary schools: A best-evidence synthesis. *Review of Educational Research, 57,* 293–336. doi:10.3102/00346543057003293

Snow, C. E., Burns, M. S., & Griffin, P. (1998). *Preventing reading difficulties in young children.* Washington, DC: National Academies Press.

Spector, J. E. (2005). How reliable are informal reading inventories? *Psychology in the Schools, 42,* 593–603. doi:10.1002/pits.20104

Speece, D. L., & Case, L. P. (2001). Classification in context: An alternative approach to identifying early reading disability. *Journal of Educational Psychology, 93,* 735–749. doi:10.1037/0022-0663.93.4.735

Speece, D. L., Mills, C., Ritchey, K. D., & Hillman, E. (2003). Initial evidence that letter fluency tasks are valid indicators of early literacy skills. *Journal of Special Education, 36,* 223–233. doi:10.1177/002246690303600403

Stage, S. A., & Jacobsen, M. D. (2001). Predicting student success on a state-mandated performance-based assessment using oral reading fluency. *School Psychology Review, 30,* 407–419.

Stage, S. A., Sheppard, J., Davidson, M. M., & Browning, M. M. (2001). Prediction of first-graders' growth in oral reading fluency using kindergarten letter fluency. *Journal of School Psychology, 39,* 225–237. doi:10.1016/S0022-4405(01)00065-6

Stiggins, R. (2005). From formative assessment to assessment for learning: A path to success in standards-based schools. *Phi Delta Kappan, 87,* 324–328.

Tilly, W. D. (2008). The evolution of school psychology to science-based practice: Problem solving and the three-tiered model. In A. Thomas & J. Grimes (Eds.), *Best practices in school psychology V* (pp. 17–36). Bethesda, MD: NASP Publications.

Treptow, M. A., Burns, M. K., & McComas, J. J. (2007). Reading at the frustration, instructional, and independent levels: The effects on students' reading comprehension and time on task. *School Psychology Review, 36,* 159–166.

VanDerHeyden, A. M., & Burns, M. K. (2005). Using curriculum-based assessment and curriculum-based measurement to guide elementary mathematics instruction: Effect on individual and group accountability scores. *Assessment for Effective Intervention, 30,* 15–31.

VanDerHeyden, A. M., Witt, J. C., & Gilbertson, D. A. (2007). Multi-year evaluation of the effects of a response to intervention (RTI) model on identification of children for special education. *Journal of School Psychology, 45,* 225–256. doi:10.1016/j.jsp.2006.11.004

VanDerHeyden, A. M., Witt, J. C., & Naquin, G. (2003). Development and validation of a process for screening referrals to special education. *School Psychology Review, 32,* 204–227.

Yeo, S. (2010). Predicting performance on statewide achievement tests using curriculum-based measurement in reading: A multilevel analysis. *Remedial and Special Education, 31,* 412–422. doi:10.1177/0741932508327463

8

MATHEMATICS SCREENING MEASURES FOR THE PRIMARY GRADES

BEN CLARKE, KELLY HAYMOND, AND RUSSELL GERSTEN

Amid the flurry of day-to-day practice in schools, educators are increasingly aware and informed of the critical importance of science, technology, engineering, and mathematics (STEM) disciplines and their importance in preparing students for the workforce of the next few decades. Whether by presidents in their State of the Union addresses (Bush & The White House, Office of the Press Secretary, 2006; Obama & The White House, Office of the Press Secretary, 2011), national organization (National Council of Teachers of Mathematics [NCTM], 2006), or federal reports (Augustine, 2005; National Mathematics Advisory Panel [NMAP], 2008), it seems the idea that "all young Americans must learn to think mathematically, and they must think mathematically to learn" (Kilpatrick, Swafford, & Findell, 2001, p. 16) has taken firm root in the public consciousness.

In many ways, interest in mathematics mirrors the increased attention paid to reading instruction that occurred in the 1980s and 1990s with public

http://dx.doi.org/10.1037/14316-008
Universal Screening in Educational Settings: Evidence-Based Decision Making for Schools, R. J. Kettler, T. A. Glover, C. A. Albers, and K. A. Feeney-Kettler (Editors)
Copyright © 2014 by the American Psychological Association. All rights reserved.

interest, ideas, research, new materials, and increasingly sophisticated professional development emerging at a greater rate than ever before. In part, interest in mathematics also may stem from schools' current experience in providing reading instruction using strategies aimed at reducing *future* reading difficulties, usually under the umbrella of response to intervention (RTI). Because many schools now embrace a more systematic approach to reading incorporating these elements, a logical argument can be made stipulating that if this approach has worked in reading, then it can and should be applied to efforts in mathematics. This includes the idea of screening students to identify those not on track or likely to struggle in acquiring critical mathematical knowledge. Yet, if we are to encourage and advocate to schools that the time invested in mathematics screening is an efficient and effective use of their time, what information do they need and what questions must be answered? This chapter presents what we consider to be critical information and provides answers to relevant questions schools may have about early mathematics screening.

WHY USE EARLY MATHEMATICS SCREENERS?

Longitudinal research strongly suggests that students who perform poorly at the end of kindergarten and first grade are likely to continue to struggle in mathematics through the later elementary grades (Bodovski & Farkas, 2007; Duncan et al., 2007; Hanich & Jordan, 2001; Morgan, Farkas, & Wu, 2009) and in all likelihood for the remainder of their school careers (Siegler et al., 2012). Using a nationally representative sample of students from the Early Childhood Longitudinal Study–Kindergarten, Morgan et al. (2009) found that students who remained in the lowest 10th percentile at both the beginning and end of kindergarten (often considered an indicator of a learning disability in mathematics [MLD]) had a 70% chance of remaining in the lowest 10th percentile 5 years later. They also tended to score, on average, 2 standard deviation units below students who did not demonstrate MLD in kindergarten. Duncan et al. (2007) documented that the relationship between early and later math proficiency was stronger than the relationship found between beginning and later reading achievement across the same range of time. Duncan et al. analyzed results from six studies and concluded that "rudimentary mathematics skills appear to matter the most, with an average standardized coefficient of .33. The association of reading skill with later achievement was less than half as large (.13)" (2007, p. 1437). Because of the relationship between early and later mathematics understanding, a logical and convincing argument can be made that students in the early elementary grades require immediate attention and assistance to halt a long-term trajectory of low mathematics performance. Although to a lesser extent than in reading, a growing number of intervention programs now target mathematics with evidence of effectiveness (Gersten et al., 2009). To provide support to students who may need preventive service in mathematics, however, the first step for schools is the use of valid tools to engage in routine screening of students to determine their level of need.

The use of screening instruments dovetails with current trends in schools to use multitier or RTI service delivery models. Although RTI originally was conceived as a mechanism by which to identify students with specific learning disabilities (Individuals With Disabilities Education Improvement Act, 2004), implementation in schools often is centered on providing research-based instruction and support to all students across the continuum of student need (Burns & VanDerHeyden, 2006; L. S. Fuchs, Fuchs, & Zumeta, 2008). The most common RTI models consist of three tiers of progressively more intensive instruction (D. Fuchs, Fuchs, & Vaughn, 2008). Tier 1 instruction is provided in the general education setting to all students typically through the use of a core curriculum. Tier 2 instruction is provided to students who either fail to respond to classroom instruction or are identified as at risk on a screening measure. Tier 2 instruction can range widely but often is marked by the use of small groups of three to five students receiving intensive instruction ranging from 20 to 40 minutes, three to five times per week. Last, Tier 3 instruction is provided to students who fail to respond to Tier 2 interventions and typically includes the use of one-on-one tutoring coupled with a range of instructional interventions and more systematic assessment of student progress (Clarke, Gersten, & Newman-Gonchar, 2010). RTI also places a strong emphasis on the prevention of academic problems (Gersten et al., 2009), thus requiring the use of screening instruments to identify students at risk.

CURRENT APPROACHES

Currently, there are two general approaches to early mathematics screening: (a) the use of single-proficiency measures and (b) the use of multiple-proficiency measures. Single-proficiency measures evolved from research in developmental and cognitive psychology that focused on the development of number sense and number competencies. According to the National Research Council, "Number sense refers to interconnected knowledge of numbers and operations," whereas number competencies "is a more balanced term meaning both knowledge and skills that can be taught and learned" (Cross, Woods, & Schweingruber, 2009, p. 95). Number competency measures focus on the most commonly assessed aspects of number proficiency: magnitude comparison, strategic counting, and retrieval of basic number combinations (often called basic arithmetic facts). Other measures also focus on number identification and rote counting, but this chapter focuses on measures that are critical for later mathematics. Number identification and rote counting measures are different in that they serve as more of a readiness indicator, similar to letter identification measures for reading. The single-proficiency measures tend to be quite efficient and brief, often taking only 1 or 2 minutes. They are used to quickly identify students whose mathematics achievement is considered at risk in one or more critical areas related to the development of number sense and number proficiency. In contrast, multiple-proficiency measures include multiple, but related, number competencies. They address a wide array of whole-number concepts and procedures, such as counting and skip counting, addition and subtraction, magnitude comparisons, simple arithmetic word problems, and estimation.

Single-Proficiency Measures

Table 8.1[1] provides specific information on single-proficiency measures used to assess each of the number sense constructs, including the study citation, a brief description of the screening measures, number of participants, grades at which screening assessment were administered,[2] outcome measures, and the correlation between screeners and outcomes. The table is organized by the constructs assessed in each measure and provides a comprehensive summary of the still-developing literature base on early number sense screening measures.

Examining the predictive validities (see Table 8.1) allows us to assess how well the screeners predict student performance in mathematics at the end of the school year or in some cases across multiple years. All coefficients, except for the magnitude comparison measure used by Baglici, Codding, and Tryon (2010), were statistically significant. Excluding the nonsignificant correlation of .02, the set of validity coefficients ranges from .31 to .79 with a median of .53.

Magnitude Comparison

Magnitude comparison is the ability to compare magnitudes and to weigh relative differences in magnitude effectively. For example, magnitude

---

[1] Tables are reprinted from Gersten et al. (2012). In the summer of 2010, we conducted ERIC and PsycINFO searches of the literature to examine the current literature base on screening measures in mathematics administered to students in kindergarten and first grade. We describe this full evidence base further in Gersten et al.

[2] Our review focused on screening measures in mathematics for students in the primary grades. Thus, grades were limited to kindergarten and first grade only.

TABLE 8.1
Predictive Validity of Screening Measures for the Primary Grades

Study	Screening measure	Grade	N^a	Outcome measure	Predictive validity[b] (r)
	Magnitude comparison				
Baglici et al. (2010)	Test of Early Numeracy	K	61	Timed Mathematics Computation	.02 (ns)
Chard et al. (2005)	Name the larger of two items: number sets 0 to 20	K	436	Number Knowledge Test	.50
		1st	483		.53
Clarke et al. (2008)	Name larger of two items: number sets 0 to 10	K	254	Stanford Early School Achievement Test	.62
Clarke, Gersten, et al. (2011)[c]	Name the larger of two items: number sets 0 to 20 for K and 0 to 99 for 1st	K	323	TerraNova	.57
		1st	348		.56
Clarke & Shinn (2004)	Name larger of two items: number sets 0 to 20	1st	52	Woodcock–Johnson Applied Problems	.79
				Timed Computation	.70
Lembke & Foegen (2009)	Name larger of two items: number sets 0 to 10 and 0 to 20 (i.e., 13:8)	K	44	Test of Early Mathematics Achievement–3	.35
		1st	28		.43
Seethaler & Fuchs (2010)	Name the larger of two items: number sets 0 to 10	K	196	Early Math Diagnostic Assessment: Math Reasoning	.53
				Numerical Operations	.75
				Key Math–Revised: Numeration	.34
				Estimation	.65
	Strategic counting				
Baglici et al. (2010)	Name the missing number in a string of numbers between 0 and 20	K	61	Timed Mathematics Computation	.47
Clarke et al. (2008)	Name the missing numeral from a string of numerals between 0 and 10	K	254	Stanford Early School Achievement Test	.64
Clarke, Gersten, et al. (2011)	Name the missing number in a sequence of numbers between 0 and 20 for K and 0 and 99 for 1st	K	323	TerraNova	.61
		1st	348		.56

(continues)

TABLE 8.1
Predictive Validity of Screening Measures for the Primary Grades   (Continued)

Study	Screening measure	Grade	N^a	Outcome measure	Predictive validity[b] (r)
	Strategic counting				
Geary et al. (2009)	Number Sets Test: child determines as quickly and accurately as possible if pairs or trios of object sets, Arabic numerals, or a combination of these matched a target number (5 and 9)	K	228	Wechsler Individual Achievement Test–II Numerical Operations subtest	.58
Lembke & Foegen (2009)	Name missing numbers in a pattern: counting by ones to 20, fives to 50, and by tens to 100 (i.e., 6 _ 8 9); exact same items for K and 1st	K 1st	44 28	Test of Early Mathematics Achievement–3	.37 .68
Methe et al. (2008)	Students "count on" four numbers from a given number between 1 and 20 (e.g., experimenter says 8 and student 9, 10, 11)	K	64	Test of Early Mathematics Achievement–3	.46
	Fact retrieval				
Pedrotty Bryant et al. (2008)	TEMI: addition/subtraction (sums or minuends range from 0 to 18)	1st	126	Stanford Achievement Test–10	.55
Clarke, Gersten, et al. (2011)	ASPENS: Basic Facts: students are presented 40 problems that can be composed and decomposed in base-10 system	1st	329	TerraNova	.58

Note. All coefficients $p < .05$ unless noted otherwise. K = kindergarten; TEMI = Texas Early Mathematics Inventory; ASPENS = Assessing Student Proficiency in Early Number Sense. From "Universal Screening in Mathematics for the Primary Grades: Beginnings of a Research Base," by R. Gersten, B. Clarke, N. C. Jordan, R. Newman-Gonchar, K. Haymond, and C. Wilkins, 2012. *Exceptional Children, 78,* pp. 426–428. Copyright 2012 by the Council for Exceptional Children. Reprinted with permission.
[a]All study samples were from a single district except for the Lembke and Foegen (2009) study, which sampled three districts in two states, and the Clarke, Gersten, et al. (2011) study, which sampled four districts in two states. [b]All predictive validity measured by screeners administered in the fall and mathematics outcomes administered in the spring of that same year except Locuniak and Jordan (2008), which correlated the fall of kindergarten screening measure with criterion measures administered in the winter of first grade. Although Seethaler and Fuchs (2010) reported two predictive validity coefficients, only those calculated for screeners administered in the fall of kindergarten were used in this table. [c]Clarke, Gersten, et al. (2011) coefficients are based on a sample collected over 2 years.

comparison can be as simple as the ability to identify that the number 5 is greater than the number 2. Those with more sophisticated sense of magnitude comparison know that 5 is a bit bigger than 2, but 9 is a lot bigger than 2, and eventually students know that the difference between 5 and 2 is 3 and between 9 and 2 is 7 and know that 7 is a greater difference. This skill is important, as research indicates that the ability to compare numerical magnitudes is related to later mathematics achievement (Gersten, Jordan, & Flojo, 2005; Okamoto & Case, 1996). It is not surprising, then, that magnitude comparison was the most frequently used of all the single-proficiency assessments (Chard et al., 2005; Clarke, Baker, Smolkowski, & Chard, 2008; Clarke, Gersten, Dimino, & Rolfhus, 2011; Clarke & Shinn, 2004; Lembke & Foegen, 2009; Seethaler & Fuchs, 2010).

Typically, a student is shown a sheet of paper containing a series of individual boxes containing two randomly selected numbers (see Figure 8.1) and is asked to choose the greater of two numbers. All the measures included in Table 8.1 were timed; however, they differed in terms of number sets. Several measures used number sets ranging from 0 to 10 for kindergarten students (Clarke et al., 2008; Lembke & Foegen, 2009; Seethaler & Fuchs, 2010). Other measures included numbers ranging from 0 to 20 for kindergarten students (Clarke, Gersten, et al., 2011), first-grade students (Clarke & Shinn, 2004; Lembke & Foegen, 2009), or both kindergarten and first-grade students (Chard et al., 2005). The study with the lowest predictive validity (Baglici et al., 2010) used a timed mathematics computation outcome. It may have been, however, that the use of a computation measure would have been too difficult for kindergarten students, resulting in floor effects and lower correlations.

Strategic Counting

Strategic counting provides an index of student understanding of counting principles and the ability to use counting skills to solve math problems. Typically, strategic counting measures require the student to name the

Kindergarten

3	0	12	4	16	10	12	17

Grade 1

38	16	43	57	4	12	37	48

Figure 8.1. Sample items from the magnitude comparison subtest.

missing number in a sequence of numbers or count on from a given number. Variations of identifying the missing number from a sequence include the Lembke and Foegen (2009) measure, which requires students to count by ones to 20, fives to 50, and tens to 100, and the Geary, Bailey, and Hoard (2009) measure, which requires students to determine as quickly and accurately as possible whether pairs or trios of object sets, Arabic numerals, or a combination of these match a target number. The lowest predictive validity (see Table 8.1) resulted from a skip-counting measure in kindergarten. This measure asked students to skip count by either fives or tens. In all likelihood, the reason for the low coefficient of .37 was that the skill is too difficult for many kindergarten students. Note that the identical measure is fine as a screening measure for first graders ($r = .68$). This finding helps to illustrate an important consideration in designing early screeners in that there is a need for screening measures to differentiate items for varying grade levels.

Fact Retrieval

The ability to fluently recall basic math facts is necessary for students to attain higher order math skills (NMAP, 2008). Indeed, fluency and automaticity with basic math facts is so critical to student success that if not acquired, the development of higher order mathematics skills—such as multiple-digit addition and subtraction, long division, and fractions—may be impaired severely (Geary, 2004; Goldman, Pellegrino, & Mertz, 1988; Jordan, Hanich, & Kaplan, 2003). The fact retrieval measures in Table 8.1 included addition and subtraction with sums and minuend ranging from 0 to 18 (Pedrotty Bryant et al., 2008), and problems that can be composed and decomposed in the base-10 system (Clarke, Gersten, et al. 2011). The ability to automatically recall facts actually entails a good number of critical advances in the understanding of mathematics. These include, for example, an understanding of place value and routine use of the commutative property of addition. For these reasons, and their consistent correlation with an overall proficiency with numbers, some basic facts component issues should be a part of an assessment battery for students beginning at the middle or end of first grade. Because struggles in this area often are related to automatic recall, measures in this vein should be timed to assess ability to both solve the problem and to do so in a fluent manner.

Multiple Number Proficiency Measures

An examination of the current literature on early math screeners indicates that measures encompassing multiple aspects of number competence, such as the number knowledge test (NKT; Okamoto & Case, 1996) and number sense brief (Jordan, Glutting, & Ramineni, 2008), tend to demonstrate somewhat stronger predictive validity than single-proficiency measures. The somewhat stronger predictive validity coefficients, in part, are due to the broader range of competencies these measures encompass in contrast to single-proficiency measures.

The predictive validity of measures such as these is impressive because most of these studies look at long-term prediction, anywhere from 12 months to almost 3 years, and typically predictive validity values decrease for longer time intervals. Table 8.2 includes a description of multiple number proficiency test studies and their reported predictive validity.

One of the earliest attempts to assess students' procedural and conceptual knowledge related to whole numbers is the NKT, developed by Okamoto and Case (1996). The NKT includes a number of the critical proficiencies, including the ability to make magnitude comparisons, count, and use basic arithmetic operations in multiple formats including word problems that are read to the student. It is an individually administered measure that takes about 10–15 minutes and consists of four levels of increasing difficulty. For example, at the second level, children compare single-digit numbers and identify the bigger number, while the same problem type is presented at the third level but with double-digit numbers.

Baker et al. (2002) examined the ability of the NKT administered at the end of kindergarten to predict mathematics achievement on the SAT-9 (Stanford Achievement Test, 9th ed.) at the end of first grade. The predictive validity coefficient of the NKT was .73 for total mathematics. Interestingly, this lengthier multiple-proficiency measure tends to demonstrate slightly higher predictive validity than many of the briefer single-proficiency measures.

Jordan et al. (2008) developed a screening battery based on the same theoretical and empirical underpinnings of the research by Locuniak and Jordan (2008), but it is much more brief and efficient, with an administration time of approximately 15 minutes. Test–retest reliability ranged from .61 to .86 and predictive validity was .63 from kindergarten administration to student mathematics achievement, measured by the Woodcock–Johnson III, in third grade (Woodcock, McGrew, & Mather, 2001).

Seethaler and Fuchs (2010) assessed both a single-proficiency measure, magnitude comparison (Chard et al., 2005), and a multiple-proficiency measure, the number sense (created by the authors). Correlations for the magnitude comparison measure and the number sense collected in kindergarten with conceptual and procedural outcomes measured at the end of first grade ranged from .34 to .75 and .40 to .74, respectively. Comparisons of the single- and multiple-proficiency screeners and conceptual versus procedural outcomes indicated that single- and multiple-proficiency screeners produced good and similar classification accuracy at the fall and spring screening

TABLE 8.2
Multiple Number Proficiency Tests

Study	Screening measure[a]	Grade screen	n	Outcome measure	Grade outcome	Predictive validity[b] (r)
Baker et al. (2002)[c]	Number Knowledge Test: takes about 10–15 minutes	End of K	64	Stanford Achievement Test–9	1st	.73
Clarke, Nese, et al. (2011)	easyCBM: 45 items standardized computer-administered measure with items aligned to the National Council of Teachers in Mathematics Focal Point standards in mathematics	1st	145	TerraNova 3	1st	.58
Jordan et al. (2008)	Number Sense Brief: 33 items assessing counting, one-to-one correspondence, number recognition, nonverbal addition and subtraction	K	204	Woodcock–Johnson III (Written Calculations and Problem-Solving Subtest)	3rd	.63
Seethaler & Fuchs (2010)	Computation Fluency: 5-minute timed assessment with 25 items of counting, addition and subtraction	K	196	Early Math Diagnostic Assessment: Math Reasoning Numerical Operations Key Math–Revised: Numeration Estimation		.57 .62 .44 .68
	Number Sense: 30 items	K	196	Early Math Diagnostic Assessment: Math Reasoning Numerical Operations Key Math–Revised: Numeration Estimation	K	.56 .62 .40 .74

Note. All coefficients $p < .05$. K = kindergarten. From "Universal Screening in Mathematics for the Primary Grades: Beginnings of a Research Base," by R. Gersten, B. Clarke, N. C. Jordan, R. Newman-Gonchar, K. Haymond, and C. Wilkins, 2012, *Exceptional Children, 78*, p. 429. Copyright 2012 by the Council for Exceptional Children. Reprinted with permission. [a]The Number Sense Brief, the Number Knowledge Test, and the easyCBM measures were all untimed assessments. [b]Although the Seethaler and Fuchs (2010) study calculated two predictive validity coefficients, only the fall and spring of kindergarten were used in this table. [c]Baker et al. (2002) reported predictive validity from spring of kindergarten to winter of first grade. Although this time frame does not fall within the criteria we set, we have included the study because, like the other studies, it measures predictive validity over 1 year.

occasions on the conceptual outcome. Seethaler and Fuchs also found that both the single- and multiple-proficiency screeners classified future conceptual MLD status with greater accuracy than future procedural MLD status.

Curriculum Sampling or Sampling From State Standards

Curriculum sampling or sampling from state standards to ensure inclusion of multiple components of mathematics proficiency typically consists of two general types of measures: (a) a computation measure that covers major topics in the standards relating to computation and (b) a concepts and applications subtest that assesses all other topics, including word problems, measurement, money and time, and geometry. The logic behind this approach is explicated in detail by L. S. Fuchs et al. (2008). L. S. Fuchs et al. believed that mathematics disabilities and difficulties sometimes involve only concepts and applications or only computation and thus have chosen this framework. It also is a framework commonly used in norm-referenced achievement tests, and thus it is familiar to teachers and administrators. Measures are timed and vary from 2 to 5 minutes, depending on the student's grade level. Typically, these measures demonstrate acceptable test–retest, interrater, and alternate form reliability above .80. The concurrent and predictive validity of these measures are between .50 and .60 (Foegen, Jiban, & Deno, 2007). An example of this approach is the Monitoring Basic Skills Progress system (L. S. Fuchs, Hamlett, & Fuchs, 1999).

Many of these measures initially were developed based on state standards from the 1980s and 1990s. Because standards at both the state and national level have been modified over time, the content of some of these measures likely requires updating. The idea of creating measures based on a set of mathematics standards, however, does have implications for creating measures based on more contemporary state standards, and possibly based on the Common Core State Standards (CCSS). For example, a set of measures, easyCBM (Clarke, Nese, et al., 2011), were developed based on the 2006 NCTM Focal Points.

INSTRUCTIONAL IMPLICATIONS AND FUTURE CONSIDERATIONS

At its most fundamental level, the process of screening is to make one decision—that is, whether a child needs additional services in mathematics. Yet the technical characteristics often reported to support the use of particular screening instruments, describing the strength of a relationship between a screener and a later mathematics outcome through correlation coefficients, provide information that, though useful, does not answer the primary question of interest: How accurately does a screener classify students as needing services? The idea of classification accuracy is one way to help educators weigh the balance between the potential harm incurred by failing to identify a student who required additional assistance and the chance of wasting limited resources on a student who in fact did not require intervention. It can be calculated to determine the degree to which a screener correctly classifies children who require additional assistance in mathematics.

A screener or screening battery can make two types of mistakes: false positives and false negatives. The first type of classification mistake is to falsely identify students as needing help, when in fact they do not require additional instruction or assistance. A child who scores below the cutoff score of a measure, yet would have done fine without any intervention, is an example of a false positive. To assess this risk, we report on the screener's *specificity*. The second classification mistake, false negatives, involves missing students who truly need help. To assess this risk, we report on the screener's *sensitivity*.

As this approach is relatively new to the field, measures are just beginning to report sensitivity and specificity data. An alternative tool for evaluating the utility of a diagnostic measure is the receiver operating characteristic (ROC) curve (see Table 8.3 for a summary of studies utilizing ROC analyses). According to Jordan, Glutting, Ramineni, and Watkins (2010),

> by systematically using all possible cut scores of a test and plotting the true-positive rate (i.e., sensitivity) against the false-positive rate (i.e., 1-specificity) for each cut score, diagnostic validity can be displayed for the full range of the test's scores. (p. 184)

In essence, the ROC curve provides a graphic representation of sensitivity versus 1-specificity and illustrates the inverse relationship between sensitivity and specificity. Thus, in the selection of a cut score, a trade-off needs to be made between maximizing sensitivity and specificity. Ideally, the user would select the cut point by considering the relative importance of sensitivity and specificity in a particular situation. For example, a false positive might be of great concern to a school with limited resources for providing interventions and of less concern to a school undergoing a radical school improvement effort to raise overall achievement. Thus, in the first case, it may be more important to obtain high specificity, even if this leads to a lower level of sensitivity.

One statistic often reported for ROC curve analyses is the area under the curve (AUC; see Table 8.3). AUC provides an easy-to-understand index of the accuracy of the screener. In general, the greater the AUC, the better the performance in terms of sensitivity and specificity across the range of possible cut scores. Conventionally, values less than .70 are considered poor, .70–.79 are fair, .80–.89 are good, and .90–1 are excellent (Cicchetti, 2001).

TABLE 8.3
Diagnostic Utility Statistics and Receiver Operating Characteristics

Study	Screening measure	Grade screened	n	Outcome measure	MLD or at risk	Grade of outcome	Sensitivity	Specificity	Area under the curve	Duration of prediction
Clarke, Nese, et al. (2011)[a]	easyCBM: standardized computer-administered measure with 45 items aligned to the National Council of Teachers in Mathematics Focal Point standards in mathematics	1st	145	<25th percentile on the TerraNova 3 <40th percentile on the TerraNova 3	At risk Traditional At risk Liberal	End of 1st grade	.83 .73	.74 .73	.83 .78	1 year
L. S. Fuchs et al. (2007)	Number Identification/Counting (L. S. Fuchs & Hamlett, 2005)	1st	170	<10th percentile on the WRAT 3–Arithmetic <10th percentile on Story Problems	MLD Calculation MLD Word Problems	End of 2nd grade	.69 .70	.79 .75	.85 .81	2 years
Geary et al. (2009)[b]	Number Sets Test: child determines as quickly and accurately as possible if pairs or trios of object sets, Arabic numerals, or a combination of these matched a target number (5 and 9)	K	228	<15th percentile on both the 2nd and 3rd grade Wechsler Individual Achievement Test–II Numerical Operations subtest	MLD	End of 3rd grade	.66	.88	—	4 years

(continues)

TABLE 8.3
Diagnostic Utility Statistics and Receiver Operating Characteristics (*Continued*)

Study	Screening measure	Grade screened	n	Outcome measure	MLD or at risk	Grade of outcome	Sensitivity	Specificity	Area under the curve	Duration of prediction
Jordan et al. (2010)	Number Sense Brief: 33 items assessing counting, one-to-one correspondence, number recognition, nonverbal addition and subtraction	K	204	Not meeting standards on the Delaware Student Testing in Mathematics (mix of concepts, procedures, and problem solving)	Low Achieving	End of 3rd grade	.73	.85	.80	4 years
Seethaler & Fuchs (2010)	Quantity Discrimination Computation Fluency[c] Number Sense	K K K	196 196 196	<16th percentile on the EDMA Math Reasoning[c] <16th percentile on the EDMA Numerical Operations subtest[d]	MLD Conceptual MLD Procedural	End of 1st grade	.90 .87 .90 .89 .91 .88	.66 .57 .64 .32 .35 .32	.86 .80 .84 .69 .67 .69	2 years

Note. WRAT = Wide Range Achievement Test; MLD = learning disability in mathematics; K = kindergarten; EDMA = Early Math Diagnostic Assessment. From "Universal Screening in Mathematics for the Primary Grades: Beginnings of a Research Base," by R. Gersten, B. Clarke, N. C. Jordan, R. Newman-Gonchar, K. Haymond, and C. Wilkins, 2012, *Exceptional Children, 78*, pp. 430–431. Copyright 2012 by the Council for Exceptional Children. Reprinted with permission.
[a]Cut score following criteria proposed by Silberglitt and Hintze (2005). [b]True negatives = 109; false negatives = 22; true positives = 23; false positives = 4. [c]For MD–Conceptual: true negatives = 103 on QD, 89 on CF, and 100 on Number Sense; false negatives = 4 on QD, 5 on CF, and 4 on Number Sense; true positives = 36 on QD, 35 on CF, and 36 on Number Sense; false positives = 53 on QD, 67 on CF, and 56 on Number Sense. d For MD–Procedural: true negatives = 44 on QD, 49 on CF, and 44 on Number Sense; false negatives = 6 on QD, 5 on CF, and 7 on Number Sense; true positives = 53 on QD, 54 on CF, and 52 on Number Sense; false positives = 93 on QD, 88 on CF, and 93 on Number Sense.

Because a number of early mathematics screening measures are embedded within systems that generate reports classifying students into categories (e.g., at risk, not at risk), the decision about where to set cut scores (and thus rates of false positives and negatives) is removed from schools and districts. The issue is much more complex, however, and often reflects trade-offs and priorities based on the values of the individuals who have created the measures and corresponding reporting systems. Take, for example, two current methods for determining cut scores proposed by prominent researchers (Johnson, Jenkins, Petscher, & Catts, 2009; Seethaler & Fuchs, 2010; Silberglitt & Hintze, 2005) with extensive experience designing screening systems. Silberglitt and Hintze (2005) outlined their procedure as follows:

> (a) Determine the cut score(s) that yield at least 0.7 for sensitivity and specificity; (b) if possible, increase sensitivity from this point, continuing upward while still maintaining a specificity of 0.7, stopping if sensitivity exceeds 0.8; (c) if sensitivity exceeds 0.8 and specificity can still be increased, continue to maximize specificity (while maintaining sensitivity of 0.8); and (d) if both sensitivity and specificity exceed 0.8, repeat steps 2 and 3, using 0.9 as the next cutoff. (p. 316)

Their model places an equal value on sensitivity and specificity by first ensuring that both sensitivity and specificity meet a minimum criteria and then increasing sensitivity, thus placing an emphasis on making sure that the number of true positives who are identified as at risk is maximized. In contrast, consider a second model in which the first step is to hold sensitivity, regardless of specificity, to a minimum of .90 (Johnson et al., 2009; Seethaler & Fuchs, 2010), which immediately places a premium on ensuring that true positives are identified as at risk.

Clarke, Nese, et al. (2011) used an existing data set to replicate both models with easyCBM (screener) and TerraNova (outcome criterion) data to provide an example of how the two procedures would generate different cut scores and thus have differing implications for how schools would allocate resources. Using winter easyCBM data and risk status defined as below the 25th percentile on the TerraNova 3 in the spring, the Silberglitt and Hintze (2005) procedure produced a cut score of 30. In contrast, the cut score produced by the Johnson et al. (2009) method was 34. The higher cut score produced by the Johnson method reflects the emphasis on increased sensitivity by placing a premium on identifying true at-risk students and casting a wider net (i.e., more students are identified as needing services with a higher cut score). Because a wider net is cast (i.e., a higher cut score), however, a larger number of students who do not need services (i.e., false positives) are identified as needing services. Specifically, a cut score of 30 identifies and theoretically would result in schools providing services to

41 students. Of those 41 students, 18 would truly be at risk and 23 would not be at risk (false positives). Five students who needed services (false negatives) would not receive services. Using a cut score of 34, schools would provide services to 70 students, of whom 22 would be truly at risk and 48 would not be at risk (false positives). Only one student who needed services (false negative) would not receive services.

Although it is easy to argue that schools should identify all students who need services, the reality is much more complex. In this example, to reduce the number of students needing services missed in the data process (false negatives) from five (using a cut score of 30) to one (using a cut score of 34) would mean that an additional 29 students were identified of which only four needed services. If schools were to provide services, such as a small-group intervention, to an additional 29 students, already thin resources would be stretched further. Although this example is specific to the data generated for a study of the easyCBM system, the concepts are illustrative of the real-world trade-offs districts and schools face.

We recommend that when evaluating potential screening instruments or systems, schools and districts pay close attention to the methods by which cut scores were determined. In addition, we see the need for future reporting systems to provide detailed technical reports on their measures that report key metrics at different cut points. Such information would be valuable in allowing schools that wish to consider a different cut point than the default provided by the system to evaluate rates of false positives and false negatives and how those numbers would affect the provision of services in their particular setting.

A recent article by VanDerHeyden (2011) provided an in-depth look at additional limitations of sensitivity and specificity. She demonstrated how the sensitivity and specificity of a screening measure are comparable only when the outcome measures, cut scores, and sample characteristics are the same. As "sensitivity and specificity estimates cannot be applied to samples that differ from the one on which they were derived" (VanDerHeyden, 2011, p. 339), it is easy to see how such statistics can be prone to misuse. She failed to note, however, that the same criticism applies to other indices used to assess the value of a screener, such as predictive validity.

Instead, VanDerHeyden (2011) has suggested the *likelihood ratio* as an alternative and superior method to assess the utility of a measure. There are two versions of a likelihood ratio: a positive likelihood ratio and a negative likelihood ratio. A positive likelihood ratio characterizes the probability of an academic problem given a positive test finding, whereas a negative likelihood ratio provides the probability of no academic problem given a negative test finding. Mathematically, the positive likelihood ratio is calculated as sensitivity divided by 1 minus specificity. Conversely, the negative likelihood ratio is calculated as 1 minus sensitivity divided by specificity.

A likelihood ratio of greater than 1 indicates that the test result is associated with the academic problem. A likelihood ratio of 1 means the pretest and posttest probabilities are equivalent, indicating that the test offers no predictive or diagnostic value. A likelihood ratio less than 1 indicates that the result is associated with the absence of an academic problem. The main advantage of likelihood ratios is that they can be used to compute posttest odds or probability of a condition. According to VanDerHeyden (2011),

> The primary benefit of likelihood ratios is that they can be used to compute posttest odds or probability of a condition given a positive test finding (using a positive likelihood ratio) or negative test finding (using a negative likelihood ratio). (p. 345)

For example, take a test with a cut score of 35, a sensitivity of .87, and a specificity of .34.[3] The positive likelihood ratio for this test is 1.31, while the posttest probability of a positive diagnosis is 12%. This tells us that 12% of the students scoring less than 35 have an academic problem. What is important about this example is that the known prevalence in this particular population is 10%. This tells us that 10% of the sample has an academic problem; however, the likelihood ratio allows us to specifically determine that 12% of students scoring less than 35 have the academic problem. Thus, the likelihood ratio increased the odds of detecting an academic problem over that of prevalence or clinical suspicion alone. Thus, VanDerHeyden provided another statistical approach for districts to use in assessing how well a screening system works for a given school.

FUTURE DIRECTIONS IN MATHEMATICS SCORING

In 2010 the National Governors Association released the CCSS (CCSS Initiative, 2010; see http://www.corestandards.org/Math) detailing instructional focus areas in mathematics by grade level. Across all these efforts, the focus was on teaching less content but with greater intensity and focus with a particular emphasis on whole-number understanding in the early primary grades (Gersten et al., 2009).

We believe similar changes will and need to occur in measures used to screen students. We expect assessment systems linked to critical content, whether defined by NCTM, NMAP, or CCSS, to be part of the next wave of screening work. This movement would be an extension of the curriculum

---

[3] These values were provided in VanDerHeyden (2011, Table 4, p. 345).

sampling measures discussed earlier in this chapter. In part, this is driven by the need to link assessment and instruction. Because they are tied to critical content, results from these assessments may be more valuable in identifying areas in which students have particular strengths or weaknesses that may require additional instructional assistance. One such system that recently was developed using this approach is the easyCBM system (Nese et al., 2010), which because it is aligned with the NCTM Focal Points, breaks down student performance into understanding in three critical areas for each grade level. Thus, if students are particularly weak in one area, they can have their progress monitored in that area at the same time they receive a more targeted intervention based on their screening data. This approach coincides with the calls for intervention programs to target particular areas of critical performance (Gersten et al., 2009; Milgram & Wu, 2005) and coincides with a spate of recent research on mathematics programs centered on developing in-depth understanding of critical mathematics content, which in the early mathematics grades would be focused on whole-number understanding (Pedrotty Bryant et al., 2008; Clarke, Smolkowski, et al., 2011; L. S. Fuchs et al., 2005).

Because of the movement toward a focus on critical content, schools may be better served by screening measures developed to assess performance on key instructional content. In contrast to screening in beginning reading in which measures are linked to a development progression (e.g., phonological awareness to alphabetic principle to connected text reading), a screening progression based on a development of mathematics understanding has not yet been developed. Thus, most single-skill measures are considered in isolation, and although the technical characteristics of single-skill measures may be equal to or exceed the technical characteristics of measures designed to assess a broader understanding of mathematics, they might not be as useful in determining instructional targets (Clarke et al., 2008; Seethaler & Fuchs, 2010). We consider this issue to be one worthy of substantial inquiry.

A second, and we would argue often overlooked, feature of screening systems is the manner in which they provide information that allows schools or districts to make instructional decisions about groups of students. Although our discussion around screening measures often is based on how it affects an individual (e.g., Do they need services?), schools often make decisions based on groups of students. For example, consider a scenario in which a school, through its screening instrument, identifies a large portion of their students as needing services (e.g., 60%). In this case, it makes little sense to think about how to effectively serve individual students, but rather the focus is rightly on serving groups or large numbers of students. Schools may focus on how to provide better core instruction (Clarke, Smolkowski, et al.,

2011) or to provide a standard protocol intervention to students rather than an individually designed intervention (D. Fuchs, Fuchs, & Compton, 2004). The ability to track the impact of these group instructional changes over time is critical and requires examining whether or not a screening system provides reports that detail group changes over time (e.g., decreasing the percent of students at risk over time). Although these types of features are not as easily reported or researched as traditional metrics of screening instruments, we feel strongly that they have equal, if not greater, weight in transforming the instructional practices engaged in by schools.

In addition to considering the impact of varying cut scores on risk designations, the content focus of measures and the quality of reporting features, we believe a number of other variables in early mathematics screening are worthy of future exploration and serious discussion. One of the most critical areas is examining the use of time versus untimed assessments. In part, the use of timed assessments is born from a long line of research in curriculum-based measures (Deno, 1985) that placed a premium on collecting data in the most efficient manner possible. Doing so was critical at the time if schools were going to screen large numbers of students and then monitor their progress on a regular (e.g., weekly) basis. The advent of measures administered via the computer or other technology platform, however, fundamentally changes the discussion around efficiency. If a teacher can administer a 45-minute screener to all her students using the school's computer lab, that may be more efficient than individually administering a set of 1-minute measures to a class of 25 students. Despite promise in computer-based screening, we urge caution, as schools and researchers will have to consider how this may affect the link between screening and progress monitoring (i.e., the use of the same measure for both purposes) that often is a hallmark of current screening systems. Because computer-based screeners may be broader and more time-intensive than measures currently used in screening, they may not be as viable for repeated use in progress monitoring. Research exploring the use of the same measure for both purposes, or a system that uses different instruments, or adaptations of the same instrument, for screening and progress monitoring, thus capitalizing on the characteristics of each assessment for its specific intended purpose, is both warranted and needed.

The current state of screening in early mathematics is changing rapidly. We believe that schools currently have an array of defensible and suitable instruments from which to select and implement early mathematics screening systems. We also expect, however, that significant advances will occur in the future that will enable schools to make better instructional decisions for students and to positively affect the mathematics achievement of all students.

REFERENCES

Augustine, N. R. (2005). Rising above the gathering storm: Energizing and employing America for a brighter economic future. Retrieved from http://www.commerce.senate.gov/pdf/augustine-031506.pdf

Baglici, S. P., Codding, R., & Tryon, G. (2010). Extending the research on the tests of early numeracy: Longitudinal analyses over two school years. *Assessment for Effective Intervention, 35,* 89–102. doi:10.1177/1534508409346053

Baker, S., Gersten, R., Flojo, J., Katz, R., Chard, D., & Clarke, B. (2002). *Preventing mathematics difficulties in young children: Focus on effective screening of early number sense delays* (Tech. Rep. No. 0305). Eugene, OR: Pacific Institutes for Research.

Bodovski, K., & Farkas, G. (2007). Do instructional practices contribute to inequality in achievement? The case of mathematics instruction in kindergarten. *Journal of Early Childhood Research, 5,* 301–322. doi:10.1177/1476718X07080476

Burns, M., & VanDerHeyden, A. (2006). Using response to intervention to assess learning disabilities: Introduction to the special series. *Assessment for Effective Intervention, 32,* 3–5. doi:10.1177/15345084060320010201

Bush, G. W., & The White House, Office of the Press Secretary. (2006). *Remarks by the president in State of Union address.* Retrieved from http://georgewbush-whitehouse.archives.gov/stateoftheunion/2006

Chard, D. J., Clarke, B., Baker, S., Otterstedt, J., Braun, D., & Katz, R. (2005). Using measures of number sense to screen for difficulties in mathematics: Preliminary findings. *Assessment for Effective Intervention, 30,* 3–14. doi:10.1177/073724770503000202

Cicchetti, D. V. (2001). The precision of reliability and validity estimates revisited: Distinguishing between clinical and statistical significance of sample size requirements. *Journal of Clinical and Experimental Neuropsychology, 23,* 695–700. doi:10.1076/jcen.23.5.695.1249

Clarke, B., Baker, S., Smolkowski, K., & Chard, D. J. (2008). An analysis of early numeracy curriculum-based measurement: Examining the role of growth in student outcomes. *Remedial and Special Education, 29,* 46–57. doi:10.1177/0741932507309694

Clarke, B., Gersten, R., Dimino, J., & Rolfhus, E. (2011). Assessing Student Proficiency in Early Number Sense (ASPENS) [Measurement instrument]. Frederick, CO: Sopris.

Clarke, B., Gersten, R., & Newman-Gonchar, R. (2010). RTI in mathematics: Beginnings of a knowledge base. In T. A. Glover & S. Vaughn (Eds.), *The promise of response to intervention: Evaluating current science and practice* (pp. 187–203). New York, NY: Guilford Press.

Clarke, B., Nese, J. F. T., Alonzo, J., Smith, J. M., Tindal, G., Kame'enui, E., & Baker, S. (2011). Classification accuracy of easyCBM first grade mathematics measures: Findings and implications for the field. *Assessment for Effective Intervention, 36,* 243–255. doi:10.1177/1534508411414153

Clarke, B., & Shinn, M. (2004). A preliminary investigation into the identification and development of early mathematics curriculum-based measurement. *School Psychology Review, 33*, 234–248.

Clarke, B., Smolkowski, K., Baker, S. K., Fien, H., Doabler, C. T., & Chard, D. J. (2011). The impact of a comprehensive Tier 1 core kindergarten program on the achievement of students at-risk in mathematics. *Elementary School Journal, 111*, 561–584. doi:10.1086/659033

Common Core State Standards Initiative. (2010). *Common Core State Standards for Mathematics.* Retrieved from http://www.corestandards.org/assets/CCSSI_Math%20Standards.pdf

Cross, C. T., Woods, T. A., & Schweingruber, H. (Eds.). (2009). *Mathematics learning in early childhood: Paths toward excellence and equity.* Washington, DC: National Academies Press.

Deno, S. L. (1985). Curriculum-based measurement: The emerging alternative. *Exceptional Children, 52*, 219–232.

Duncan, G. J., Dowsett, C. J., Claessens, A., Magnuson, K., Huston, A. C., Klebanov, P., . . . Japel, C. (2007). School readiness and later achievement. *Developmental Psychology, 43*, 1428–1446. doi:10.1037/0012-1649.43.6.1428

Foegen, A., Jiban, C., & Deno, S. (2007). Progress monitoring measures in mathematics: A review of the literature. *Journal of Special Education, 41*, 121–139. doi:10.1177/00224669070410020101

Fuchs, D., Fuchs, L. S., & Compton, D. L. (2004). Identifying reading disability by responsiveness-to-instruction: Specifying measures and criteria. *Learning Disability Quarterly, 27*, 216–227. doi:10.2307/1593674

Fuchs, D., Fuchs, L. S., & Vaughn, S. (Eds.). (2008). *Response to intervention.* Newark, DE: International Reading Association.

Fuchs, L. S., Compton, D. L., Fuchs, D., Paulsen, K., Bryant, B., & Hamlett, C. (2005). The prevention, identification, and cognitive determinants of math difficulty. *Journal of Educational Psychology, 97*, 493–513. doi:10.1037/0022-0663.97.3.493

Fuchs, L. S., Fuchs, D., Compton, D. L., Bryant, J. D., Hamlett, C., & Seethaler, P. M. (2007). Mathematics screening and progress monitoring at first grade: Implications for responsiveness to intervention. *Exceptional Children, 73*, 311–330.

Fuchs, L. S., Fuchs, D., & Zumeta, R. O. (2008). Response to intervention: A strategy for the prevention and identification of learning disabilities. In E. L. Grigorenko (Ed.), *Educating individuals with disabilities: IDEIA 2004 and beyond* (pp. 115–135). New York, NY: Springer.

Fuchs, L. S., & Hamlett, C. L. (2005). Number identification/counting [Unpublished instrument]. Nashville, TN: Vanderbilt University.

Fuchs, L. S., Hamlett, C. L., & Fuchs, D. (1999). *Monitoring Basic Skills Progress: Basic math concepts and applications* (2nd ed.). Austin, TX: Pro-Ed.

Geary, D. C. (2004). Mathematics and learning disabilities. *Journal of Learning Disabilities, 37*, 4–15. doi:10.1177/00222194040370010201

Geary, D. C., Bailey, D. H., & Hoard, M. K. (2009). Predicting mathematical achievement and mathematical learning disability with a simple screening tool: The Number Sets Test. *Journal of Psychoeducational Assessment, 27*, 265–279. doi:10.1177/0734282908330592

Gersten, R., Beckmann, S., Clarke, B., Foegen, A., Marsh, L., Star, J. R., & Witzel, B. (2009). *Assisting students struggling with Mathematics: Response to intervention (RtI) for elementary and middle schools* (NCEE 2009-4060). Washington, DC: National Center for Education Evaluation and Regional Assistance, Institute of Education Sciences, U.S. Department of Education. Retrieved from http://ies.ed.gov/ncee/wwc/publications/practiceguides

Gersten, R., Clarke, B., Jordan, N. C., Newman-Gonchar, R., Haymond, K., & Wilkins, C. (2012). Universal screening in mathematics for the primary grades: Beginnings of a research base. *Exceptional Children, 78*, 423–445.

Gersten, R., Jordan, N. C., & Flojo, J. (2005). Early identification and interventions for students with mathematics difficulties. *Journal of Learning Disabilities, 38*, 293–304. doi:10.1177/00222194050380040301

Goldman, S. R., Pellegrino, J. W., & Mertz, D. L. (1988). Extended practice of basic addition facts: Strategy changes in learning disabled students. *Cognition and Instruction, 5*, 223–265. doi:10.1207/s1532690xci0503_2

Hanich, L., & Jordan, N. (2001). Performance across different areas of mathematical cognition in children with learning disabilities. *Journal of Educational Psychology, 93*, 615–626. doi:10.1037/0022-0663.93.3.615

Individuals With Disabilities Education Improvement Act, 20 U.S.C. § 1400 *et seq.* (2004).

Johnson, E., Jenkins, J., Petscher, Y., & Catts, H. (2009). How can we improve the accuracy of screening instruments? *Learning Disabilities Research and Practice, 24*, 174–185. doi:10.1111/j.1540-5826.2009.00291.x

Jordan, N. C., Glutting, J., & Ramineni, C. (2008). A number sense assessment tool for identifying children at risk for mathematical difficulties. In A. Dowker (Ed.), *Mathematical difficulties: Psychology and intervention* (pp. 45–58). San Diego, CA: Academic Press. doi:10.1016/B978-012373629-1.50005-8

Jordan, N. C., Glutting, J., Ramineni, C., & Watkins, M. W. (2010). Validating a number sense screening tool for use in kindergarten and first grade: Prediction of mathematics proficiency in third grade. *School Psychology Review, 39*, 181–195.

Jordan, N. C., Hanich, L. B., & Kaplan, D. (2003). A longitudinal study of mathematical competencies in children with specific mathematics difficulties versus children with comorbid mathematics and reading difficulties. *Child Development, 74*, 834–850. doi:10.1111/1467-8624.00571

Kilpatrick, J., Swafford, J., & Findell, B. (Eds.). (2001). *Adding it up: Helping children learn mathematics.* Washington, DC: National Academies Press.

Lembke, E. S., & Foegen, A. (2009). Identifying early numeracy indicators for kindergarten and Grade 1 students. *Learning Disabilities Research and Practice, 24*, 12–20. doi:10.1111/j.1540-5826.2008.01273.x

Locuniak, M. N., & Jordan, N. C. (2008). Using kindergarten number sense to predict calculation fluency in second grade. *Journal of Learning Disabilities, 41*, 451–459. doi:10.1177/0022219408321126

Methe, S. A., Hintze, J. M., & Floyd, R. G. (2008). Validation and decision accuracy of early numeracy skill indicators. *School Psychology Review, 37*, 359–373.

Milgram, R. J., & Wu, H. (2005). *Intervention program.* Retrieved from http://math.berkeley.edu/~wu/

Morgan, P. L., Farkas, G., & Wu, Q. (2009). Five-year growth trajectories of kindergarten children with learning difficulties in mathematics. *Journal of Learning Disabilities, 42*, 306–321. doi:10.1177/0022219408331037

National Council of Teachers of Mathematics. (2006). *Curriculum Focal Points for prekindergarten through Grade 8 mathematics: A quest for coherence.* Reston, VA: Author.

National Mathematics Advisory Panel. (2008). *Foundations for success: The final report of the National Mathematics Advisory Panel.* Washington, DC: U.S. Department of Education. Retrieved from http://www.ed.gov/MathPanel

Nese, J., Lai, C. F., Anderson, D., Jamgochian, E. M., Kamata, A., & Sáez, L., . . . Tindal, G. (2010). *Technical adequacy of the easyCBM mathematics measures: Grades 3–8, 2009–2010 version* (Tech. Rep. No. 1007). Eugene, OR: Behavioral Research and Teaching, University of Oregon. Retrieved from http://www.brtprojects.org/publications/technical-reports

Obama, B., & The White House, Office of the Press Secretary. (2011). *Remarks by the president in State of Union address.* Retrieved from http://www.whitehouse.gov/the-press-office/2011/01/25/remarks-president-state-union-address

Okamoto, Y., & Case, R. (1996). Exploring the microstructure of children's central conceptual structures in the domain of number. *Monographs of the Society for Research in Child Development, 61*, 27–58. doi:10.1111/j.1540-5834.1996.tb00536.x

Pedrotty Bryant, D., Bryant, B. R., Gersten, R., Scammacca, N., & Chavez, M. (2008). Mathematics intervention for first and second grade students with mathematics difficulties: The effects of Tier 2 intervention delivered as booster lessons. *Remedial and Special Education, 29*, 20–32. doi:10.1177/0741932507309712

Seethaler, P. M., & Fuchs, L. S. (2010). The predictive utility of kindergarten screening for math difficulty. *Exceptional Children, 77*, 37–60.

Siegler, R. S., Duncan, G. J., Davis-Kean, P. E., Duckworth, K., Claessens, A., Engel, M., . . . Chen, M. (2012). Early predictors of high school mathematics achievement. *Psychological Science, 23*, 691–697. doi:10.1177/0956797612440101

Silberglitt, B., & Hintze, J. M. (2005). Formative assessment using CBM-R cut scores to track progress toward success on state-mandated achievement tests: A comparison of methods. *Journal of Psychoeducational Assessment, 23*, 304–325. doi:10.1177/073428290502300402

VanDerHeyden, A. M. (2011). Technical adequacy of response to intervention decisions. *Exceptional Children, 77*, 335–350.

Woodcock, R. W., McGrew, K. S., & Mather, N. (2001). *Woodcock–Johnson III Tests of Achievement standard test book.* Itasca, IL: Riverside.

9

BROADBAND SCREENING OF ACADEMIC AND SOCIAL BEHAVIOR

JAMES C. DiPERNA, CATHERINE G. BAILEY,
AND CHRISTOPHER ANTHONY

During the past 2 decades, researchers, practitioners, and policy makers have argued that the "wait-to-fail" model of service delivery present in many school systems has resulted in increasing numbers of children receiving special education services, skill deficits that were more difficult to treat, and fewer resources available to serve students with the most significant needs. In response to these challenges, federal education laws, such as the No Child Left Behind Act (2002) and the Individuals With Disabilities Education Improvement Act (2004), promoted implementation of evidence-based practices to identify students as they begin to experience academic difficulty, resulting in early skill remediation.

As a result of these changes, models began to emerge that reflected a public health orientation to the provision of assessment and intervention services in schools (Doll & Cummings, 2008). Core features of these models include recognition of different levels of student risk or impairment,

http://dx.doi.org/10.1037/14316-009
Universal Screening in Educational Settings: Evidence-Based Decision Making for Schools, R. J. Kettler,
T. A. Glover, C. A. Albers, and K. A. Feeney-Kettler (Editors)
Copyright © 2014 by the American Psychological Association. All rights reserved.

complementary levels (or types) of intervention services intended to address the needs of individuals with different levels of risk, monitoring implementation to ensure intervention fidelity, and continuous assessment to evaluate students' outcomes in response to services received (Glover & DiPerna, 2007). Building on this conceptual framework, models of service delivery have been developed, disseminated, and implemented to address both academic (e.g., response to intervention [RTI]; Martinez, & Nellis, 2008) and behavioral (e.g., schoolwide positive behavior support; Horner et al., 2009) outcomes in schools (Lane, Oakes, & Menzies, 2010).

Regardless of the target skill or behavior domain, screening plays an essential role in the implementation of such multitiered models of service delivery. The concept of screening emerged from the field of medicine, with the primary goal of identifying presence of disease in its earliest, or preclinical, form (Morabia & Zhang, 2004). The rationale for implementing a screening program was that by identifying presence of a disease or disorder early in its clinical course, the likelihood for successful treatment outcomes dramatically increases. Similarly, the primary goal for universal screening within a school context is to identify students who are at risk for, or have a high probability of, experiencing significant difficulty as they advance through their academic career (see Chapter 1 in this volume). As evidenced by the content of state education standards, the primary goal for schooling is to promote students' mastery of academic skills and content in multiple domains (reading, writing, mathematics, science, social studies, etc.). As such, universal screening to prevent academic skill difficulty is of critical importance in school settings.

Deno and colleagues (e.g., Deno, 1985; Deno & Mirkin, 1977; Espin & Deno, 1993) began developing brief curriculum-based measures or "probes" to accurately and efficiently monitor students' development of fundamental academic skills (reading, mathematics, and writing). Although primarily developed for progress-monitoring purposes, the efficiency of these measures, along with their intended goal of informing early intervention service provision when a learner begins to experience difficulty, led others (e.g., Good & Kaminski, 2002) to develop related measures that were focused on specific subskills (e.g., phonemic awareness). In addition, these researchers began to develop data-based frameworks that could be used to inform screening for early academic skill problems in reading, mathematics, and writing.

Although academic outcomes represent the primary goal of schooling, a number of studies have suggested that other domains, such as students' social and emotional functioning, are related to their educational success. Wentzel (1993) and Malecki and Elliott (2002), for example, observed moderate relationships between students' prosocial behavior and their academic outcomes. Caprara, Barbaranelli, Pastorelli, Bandura, and Zimbardo (2000) concluded that students' third-grade prosocial behaviors were stronger predictors of academic outcomes 5 years later than their third-grade academic skills. In a seminal meta-analysis, Durlak, Weissberg, Dymnicki, Taylor, and Schellinger (2011) found that implementation of social–emotional learning programs in school settings yielded positive effects on students' academic outcomes.

In addition to these studies, most educators, administrators, and policy makers acknowledge the importance of students' social–emotional functioning for both interpersonal and academic success. According to the Collaborative for Academic, Social, and Emotional Learning, all 50 states include at least some benchmarks related to students' social–emotional functioning in their current K–12 education standards, and several are developing comprehensive independent standards in social–emotional learning (see http://casel.org/policy-advocacy/sel-in-your-state). At the preschool level, 96% of states have created specific, individual standards for young children's social–emotional development. Legislation also has been proposed at the federal level to promote implementation of evidence-based social–emotional learning programs in the schools (Academic, Social, and Emotional Learning Act of 2011).

In sum, evidence from a variety of sources suggests that both academic and social–emotional outcomes are valued and important for success in school settings. Although several screening systems and measures have been developed to identify students who are academically at risk in specific skill areas (e.g., Dynamic Indicators of Basic Early Literacy Skills, AIMSweb), screening systems for student behavior have tended to focus on behavior disorders (Lane et al., 2010). For example, the Systematic Screening for Behavior Disorders (SSBD; Walker & Severson, 1992) is intended to identify students who are at risk for internalizing (e.g., depression, anxiety) or externalizing (e.g., conduct, oppositional defiant) behavior disorders. The SSBD uses a multistep process featuring teacher reports and direct observation to identify students who are most at risk for behavior disorders and could benefit from early intervention. Similarly, the Behavioral Assessment for Children, Second Edition–Behavioral and Emotional Screening System (BASC-2 BESS; Kamphaus & Reynolds, 2007) uses a multi-informant, multistep process to identify students at risk for a variety of behavior disorders.

Despite the strengths of these behavior-screening systems to identify students with behavior disorders, they do not focus on students' prosocial behavior. In addition, neither the behavior screening systems nor the aforementioned academic measures concurrently screen for potential problems or deficits in other key domains of student functioning. During the past decade, systems have begun to emerge that reflect such a "broadband" approach to academic screening and simultaneously consider academic, prosocial, and related classroom behaviors during the screening process. In the remainder of this chapter, we discuss conceptual and practical considerations in the development of such systems, briefly review one example of a published system (including current evidence to support its use), and then turn to future considerations and directions for development of broadband academic screening systems.

CONCEPTUAL AND PRACTICAL CONSIDERATIONS

Several conceptual and practical issues should be considered when using broadband academic screening systems. First, a conceptual framework must be identified to specify the skill and behavior domains to be assessed. In addition, it is important to evaluate possible measures based on alignment with the conceptual framework, method of assessment, and feasibility of use. Finally, psychometric evidence must be evaluated relative to the target skills and population for screening. Each of these considerations is reviewed briefly in the sections that follow.

Framework for Screening of Academic and Social Behavior

Development of a broadband academic screening (and ultimately a service delivery) system requires a framework to help guide the identification and prioritization of key domains of student functioning within an academic context. As noted previously, a number of studies (e.g., Caprara et al., 2000; Durlak et al., 2011; Wentzel, 1993) have suggested a relationship between students' social or emotional functioning and their academic achievement; however, fewer studies have examined a comprehensive model detailing the key skills, attitudes, and behaviors of learners that contribute to academic success. The first author, along with several colleagues (e.g., DiPerna & Elliott, 1999; DiPerna, Volpe, & Elliott, 2005), proposed and subsequently studied a student-centered model of academic competence intended to provide insight regarding specific pathways between student behaviors and their academic outcomes.

DiPerna and Elliott (1999) conducted a review of empirical literature to identify which factors were associated with positive academic outcomes for students. On the basis of this review, they identified models that reflected both student skills (e.g., Carroll, 1963) and environmental factors (e.g., Walberg, 1981). Results of studies included in this review (e.g., Cool & Keith, 1991) suggested that student variables demonstrated the strongest relationships with their academic outcomes. Specifically, DiPerna and Elliott (2000) identified four skill domains that consistently demonstrated significant positive relationships with students' academic success: social skills, motivation, engagement, and study skills. Given these positive relationships, DiPerna and Elliott (2000) hypothesized that these skills, attitudes, and behaviors helped facilitate learning in classroom environments and ultimately characterized these domains as "academic enablers."

Although many studies documented relationships between individual academic enablers, such as social skills, and academic achievement, few considered how these variables related to one another within the context of academic learning. As such, DiPerna, Volpe, and Elliott (2002) developed a model delineating individual pathways to describe the relationships among these academic enablers (see Figure 9.1). This model identified academic motivation (persistence, approach, goal-directed behavior) as playing a central, but indirect, role in the facilitation of academic learning. The influence of motivation was mediated through students' study skills (e.g., organization, homework) and engagement (participatory behaviors in the classroom), which were hypothesized to have direct pathways to academic outcomes. The model also hypothesized that students' prior academic achievement and social skills directly influenced their motivation, thus indirectly contributing to academic achievement. The pathway from social skills to motivation reflects the hypothesis that children who are socially skilled tend to have positive experiences in social environments such as the classroom. These positive experiences, in turn, are reinforcing and result in increased effort to be successful in school.

Since proposing this model of academic competence, DiPerna and colleagues have engaged in a program of research to examine the validity of the academic enabler constructs and hypothesized relationships among them. DiPerna et al. (2002, 2005) tested the model in the areas of reading and mathematics, respectively, with students in the elementary grades. Results of both

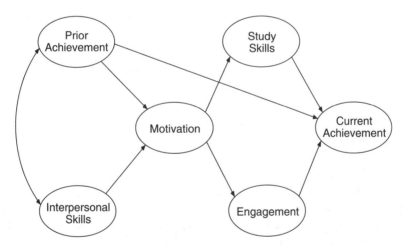

Figure 9.1. Model of the relationships between social behavior, motivation, engagement, study skills, and academic outcomes. From "A Model of Academic Enablers and Elementary Reading/Language Arts Achievement," by J. C. DiPerna, R. J. Volpe, & S. N. Elliott, 2002, *School Psychology Review, 31,* p. 301. Copyright 2002 by the National Association of School Psychologists. Reprinted with permission.

studies indicated that the model demonstrated reasonable fit with the data. Volpe et al. (2006) extended this work to examine the fit of the model for students with attention-deficit/hyperactivity disorder (ADHD). As hypothesized, they found the model to have similar fit for students with and without ADHD; however, the presence of the disorder substantially (and negatively) influenced the core of the model (motivation, engagement, and study skills). DiPerna, Lei, and Reid (2007) tested a predictive model of longitudinal growth in mathematics skills during the primary grades and found that both social skills and motivation or engagement positively related to mathematics achievement over time, although these constructs shared variance when considered as simultaneous predictors of growth, suggesting there may be underlying processes (e.g., self-control, regulation) contributing to these skill domains.

Although just one example, such a model of student functioning can serve as a conceptual framework to inform the development of broadband screening systems focused on academic and social functioning in school settings. Later in the chapter, we review a published screening system (Social Skills Improvement System–Performance Screening Guides [SSIS-PSG]; Gresham & Elliott, 2008b) that reflects aspects of this academic competence model.

Broadband and Narrowband Assessment

After specifying a conceptual framework to guide the identification of the key domains of functioning that will be targeted within a screening system, practitioners must select (or develop) a screen that is closely aligned with that framework. Depending on the goals for screening and number of skill domains to be considered, the screening system may reflect either a broadband or narrowband approach to assessment. In his discussion of behavioral disorders, Achenbach (1984) distinguished between general "broadband" syndromes measured by brief behavioral checklists and specific "narrowband" syndromes measured by differentiated behavioral checklists. Extending this distinction to screening, a system based on the conceptual model outlined in the previous section of this chapter would reflect a broadband approach because it assesses multiple broad skill or behavior domains (e.g., academic and social functioning).

Such an approach can maximize limited resources in school settings and can be augmented by the use of focused, narrowband measures with students who are identified for further assessment as a result of the initial screen. If, however, the goal of a screening system is to focus on a specific domain of functioning (e.g., early literacy), a narrowband approach to assessment would be justified, even at the initial phase of screening. Narrowband measures provide a more in-depth assessment and potentially greater insight regarding a specific target skill or content area. In addition, such assessments often are utilized in later stages of a screening or service delivery system to guide intervention development and evaluate progress. Table 9.1 provides a brief comparison of broadband and narrowband approaches within the context of screening.

Methodological Considerations for Broadband Screening

Both direct and indirect assessment methods often are utilized within the school environment to identify potential academic and behavioral areas

TABLE 9.1
Comparison of Broadband and Narrowband Approaches to Assessment

	Broadband	Narrowband
Purpose	Assess multiple domains functioning simultaneously	Assess a specific area of functioning (e.g., early reading skills, attention-related difficulties)
Strengths	Provide a broad picture of overall student functioning Efficient method for universal screening across multiple skill domains	Provide more intensive assessment in a specific target skill or content area Can be used to complement broadband screening to provide more in-depth information to inform intervention
Considerations	Provide less specificity regarding target skills/ behaviors Require follow-up assessment to inform intervention development	Focus on only one specific content area (e.g., early literacy skills) Can be time and labor intensive to implement multiple assessment systems
Recommended uses	Appropriate for screening across multiple domains of functioning simultaneously Evaluation of intervention effectiveness/ generalization	Appropriate for screening when primary goal is focused on specific domain of functioning During latter phases of multitiered service delivery system to inform intervention development and evaluation
Examples	Systematic Screening for Behavior Disorders (Walker & Severson, 1990) Social Skills Improvement System–Performance Screening Guide (Elliott & Gresham, 2007b)	Dynamic Indicators of Basic Early Literacy Skills (Good & Kaminski, 2002) Reynolds Adolescent Depression Scale–Short Form (Reynolds, 2002)

for early intervention. In the academic domain, direct approaches may include evaluations of student work, such as written products, demonstrations, performances, and examinations. In the behavioral domain, direct approaches often involve observation of behavior under authentic (e.g., classroom) or analogue conditions (e.g., functional behavior assessment; O'Neill et al., 1997). Although direct assessment approaches may provide valuable insight regarding academic and behavioral functioning, such methods can require significant resources (e.g., time, personnel) when used within a universal screening context. In addition, when assessing multiple skill domains within a broadband system, direct assessment of target skills and behaviors is less feasible and limits the utility of this method for this purpose.

In contrast to direct approaches, indirect screening methods occur in a different time and place from the measured phenomena (Floyd, Phaneuf, & Wilczynski, 2005). Examples of common indirect assessments include teacher, parent, and self-rating scales (Cone, 1978). Such methods can require less time than their direct counterparts and easily incorporate multiple skill domains (e.g., academics and behavior). In addition, relatively minimal training, expertise, and resources are required for use of indirect assessment methods (Floyd et al., 2005). Given the goals of a broadband academic screening system and limited resources now available in schools, indirect methods, such as teacher, student, or parent ratings, may serve as a more viable alternative for implementing such systems in a universal context. As such, we briefly summarize the evidence for these types of judgments in the assessment of students' academic skills and social behavior. (Readers interested in direct assessment screening for specific academic skills are encouraged to review Chapters 6, 7, and 8 in this volume; for more information about behavioral screening, see Chapter 10.)

Teacher Judgments

When screening students' academic and social functioning, teacher ratings may be utilized as an integral component for predicting students at risk for later difficulties. Although standardized assessments reflect performance at a single point in time, teacher judgments are able to incorporate student performance across a predetermined time period (Kettler, Elliott, Davies, & Griffin 2011). In a review of teacher judgment studies, Hoge and Coladarci (1989) found a median correlation of .66 between a variety of teacher judgments (e.g., ratings of ability, ranking of ability within class, prediction of test items correct) and standardized achievement scores. Demaray and Elliott (1998) also reported a correlation of .70 between indirect teacher prediction and students' performance. Similarly, Flynn and Rahbar (1998) found that teachers correctly identified 80% of students achieving in the bottom third of their class.

Teacher judgments of student social behavior have been shown to be similarly accurate. Ollendick, Oswald, and Francis (1989) asked teachers to assign students into one of three behavioral groups (aggressiveness, withdrawal, and popularity) on the basis of observed classroom behaviors. Students within each of the three groups exhibited significant differences across a variety of behavioral measures, such as sociometrics (i.e., a systematic method to determine students' social status among their peers), self-report, and direct observations. Further, teacher ratings on the Social Skills Rating Scale–Teacher (SSRS-T) form have been shown to exhibit reliable differences in social skills between control and treatment groups receiving a primary prevention program for social skills development (Salzman & D'Andrea, 2001). Finally, Malecki and Elliott (2002) found that teachers' SSRS-T ratings of social skills exhibited a moderate positive correlation (.40–.54) with student performance on the Iowa Test of Basic Skills (Hoover, Dunbar, & Frisbie, 2001).

Although there is good evidence to support the use of teacher judgments, there are several potential limitations to consider as well. Teachers' academic and behavioral judgments are often more accurate when assessing older students (Kenny & Chekaluk, 1993) or when specific information on the method of comparison is provided in advance (Demaray & Elliott, 1998). Teachers also may be more likely to consistently overestimate or underreport student behaviors and academic skills on the basis of subjective factors (Chafouleas, Riley-Tillman, & Sassu, 2007). In addition, teachers may miss key behaviors because of the time and attention-related constraints resulting from having a large classroom of students. Maintaining attention to all behaviors within a classroom can be challenging, which particularly may result in underreporting internalizing behaviors (e.g., low self-esteem, depression, anxiety). Finally, reactivity effects may be introduced as teachers serve dual roles as a rater and classroom manager.

Parent Judgments

Although often more challenging to attain in the school environment, parent judgments can provide valuable insight into student functioning at home. Accuracy of parent judgments has been demonstrated across a variety of domains. In the case of children with developmental difficulties, information from standardized parent report measures has been shown to significantly increase overall psychoeducational evaluation accuracy (Glascoe & Dworkin, 1995). Further, some research suggests that standardized parental ratings may identify disabilities with similar levels of accuracy to developmental–behavioral screening assessments (e.g., Glascoe, 1997; Thompson & Thompson, 1991; Young, Davis, Schoen, & Parker, 1998). Parent rating scales are similarly important to the identification of certain childhood disorders, such as ADHD (Barkley, 1997; Zelko, 1991).

In terms of academic performance, evidence on the accuracy of parent judgment is limited. Parental reports of various cognitive and academic skills (e.g., memory, language, cognitive) have been linked significantly linked to children's psychometric assessment scores (Dewey, Crawford, Creighton, & Sauve, 2000). Finally, parents often are able to identify child strengths and weaknesses (e.g., insightfulness, perseverance) that are not measured by direct psychoeducational assessments (Dewey et al., 2000). As with teacher ratings, an important consideration is that parent ratings may be biased by beliefs about their child. In addition, parent and teacher ratings often exhibit low levels of agreement, potentially because of situational differences in student behavior (Achenbach, McConaughy, & Howell, 1987).

Student Judgments

Students themselves can serve as another reliable source for indirect assessment. Evidence suggests that children across various levels of intelligence and ages may be capable of providing accurate self-reports regarding use of external strategies (Bray, Huffman, & Fletcher, 1999; Ericsson & Simon, 1980, 1993). Gathering self-report data from the child serves not only as an additional source of information but also as a method of gathering the child's perceptions and behaviors (Achenbach, 1995; Loeber, Green, & Lahey, 1990). Furthermore, children are able to report on behaviors across environments, including school, home, and extracurricular activities. Students' self-reports of social behavior have been shown to exhibit moderate positive correlations with teacher ratings of the same behavior domains (DiPerna & Volpe, 2005). Children's self-report assessments have exhibited accuracy across a variety of behavior domains, including coping skills (Causey & Dubow, 1992), depression (Birelson, 1981; Kovacs, 1981), and overall functioning (Achenbach, 1991).

Ultimately, indirect measures such as teacher, parent, or student reports can serve as an integral component of a universal broadband academic and behavioral screening system, given that such assessments are administered easily across settings and typically are inexpensive (Beitchman & Corradini, 1988). Regardless of informant, use of additional data is necessary to confirm results of screening outcomes and all higher stakes decisions, such as diagnosis (Ridley, Li, & Hill, 1998).

Evaluating the Technical Adequacy of Screening Measures

Although intended to be efficient and yield preliminary decisions about risk, scores from screening measures must have sufficient psychometric evidence to justify their use. Before selecting and using any screener, it is important to consider multiple sources of evidence regarding the accuracy and utility of the scores produced by the measure. The way in which screening measures are used is also pertinent to how they should be evaluated for technical adequacy. As discussed earlier in this chapter, the intent of school-based screening is to identify children at risk before the problems become intractable. Typically, scores from screening measures are used to make decisions about the need for additional assessment or initial intervention. Thus, the reliability of scores and accuracy of decisions based on screening data are crucial when considering the technical adequacy of screening measures.

Reliability

Many screening measures are constructed on the foundation of classical test theory, which posits that scores produced by a measure (observed scores) are composed of a true score and measurement error. Theoretically, the true score is the precise numerical value that accurately represents the construct being measured. This score is free from error and consistent across time, rater, and item of the measure. Error in measurement results from a host of systematic or random factors that do not relate to the construct being measured. In the classical framework, the reliability of a score indicates how well an observed score represents a true score (Suen, 2008). Reliability coefficients can be generated through several methods, including internal consistency, test–retest reliability, and interrater reliability. These methods address different aspects of score reliability and should be used in conjunction to determine the adequacy of screening measures.

Internal consistency estimates the amount of error resulting from differences across test items. As such, metrics of internal consistency (e.g., Cronbach's α; Cronbach, 1951) indicate the extent to which items on a measure cohere and perform consistently. Another index of reliability, test–retest, examines the stability or consistency of scores and is estimated by correlating scores from the same measure derived from two or more time points. A third method of estimating reliability, interrater, addresses the error resulting from different raters or scorers of a measure. It is estimated by correlating the scores of different raters or scorers. When evaluating the reliability of scores from a screening measure, no single indicator is sufficient. Instead, multiple forms of reliability should be used in conjunction with one another (Suen, 2008; for more information on the theoretical foundations of reliability in universal screening, see Chapter 4 in this volume).

Validity

Another important aspect to consider when determining the adequacy of screening measures is the validity of the scores (Suen, 2008). In screening and other forms of testing, educational professionals are interested in a score insofar as it represents an underlying construct. Validity refers to the extent to which a score on a measure represents the construct of interest. The most definitive guidelines for the understanding and evaluating of validity evidence are found in the *Standards for Educational and Psychological Testing* (American Educational Research Association, American Psychological Association, & National Council on Measurement in Education, 1999), which identified five sources of validity evidence: (a) evidence based on test content, (b) evidence based on response processes, (c) evidence based on internal structure, (d) evidence based on relations to other variables, and (e) evidence based on consequences.

Although all of these forms of evidence are important to consider, relationships to other variables, and specifically the predictive validity between screening scores and a criterion (e.g., need for intervention or further assessment), are of primary importance in the context of screening decisions. Conditional probability analysis is a prominent method used to assess the predictive validity of screening measures (Kettler & Feeney-Kettler, 2011). When a dichotomous cut score is used in a screening context and a decision about further service provision is made on the basis of this cut score, four outcomes are possible: correct identification of a student who is at risk and in need of additional assessment or intervention (true positive), correct identification of a student who is not at risk and requires no additional assessment or intervention (true negative), incorrect identification of a student as at risk who is not at risk (false positive), and incorrect identification of a student as not at risk who is at risk and in need of additional assessment or intervention (false negative).

From these different types of outcomes, several indices can be generated. The sensitivity value of a measure is the ratio of the true positives to the total number of children who should have been identified (true positives plus false negatives). It represents the likelihood that a measure will identify correctly those in need of further preventive intervention. The specificity value of a measure refers to the ratio of true negatives to the total number of children who should not have been identified (true negatives plus false positives). It represents the likelihood that a measure will identify correctly those who do not require further preventive intervention. The positive predictive value (PPV) of a measure refers to the ratio of true positives to total identified positives, which represents the extent to which the measure is accurate when it leads to positive classification. The negative predictive value (NPV) of a measure refers to the ratio of true negatives to total identified negatives and represents the extent to which a measure is accurate when it leads to negative classification (Kettler & Feeney-Kettler, 2011). Finally, the accuracy (or hit rate) of a measure refers to the ratio of true positives and true negatives to total number of participants identified. This metric is a general measure of the predictive accuracy of the instrument (Fawcett, 2006), but it often is difficult to interpret because of inaccurate inflation (Glover & Albers, 2007; Gredler, 2000).

Evaluation of assessments using conditional probability indices is influenced greatly by the circumstances surrounding the use of the measure. In general, PPV and sensitivity are especially important to consider when evaluating screening measures. In the context of screening within an RTI framework, a false positive results in a child receiving unnecessary intervention or assessment services. The cost of this mistake is generally less than the cost of a false negative, which results in a child who needs early intervention or further assessment not receiving these services. A low sensitivity value indicates that a measure is underidentifying children at risk, whereas a low PPV indicates that a measure is overidentifying risk. In the initial phases and tiers of an RTI model of service delivery, practitioners may prioritize sensitivity over precision (specificity, PPV, and NPV) to minimize false negatives. In the latter phases of an RTI system, however, as assessment results are used to inform higher stakes decisions and the intensity of intervention (and costs of implementation) increases, the other indices (especially PPV) become more important to minimize false positives, resulting in overprovision of costly and intensive services (Glover & Albers, 2007; for more information on universal screening and RTI, see Chapter 2 in this volume).

Given the variety of assessment contexts, a number of standards have been proposed for determining the adequacy of conditional probability indices. Cicchetti, Volkmar, Klin, and Showalter (1995) recommended the following sensitivity and specificity ranges: .90–1 (excellent), .80–.90 (good), .70–.79 (fair); under .70 (poor). Kettler and Feeney-Kettler (2011) proposed that across indices, values exceeding .80 are high, values of .60–.80 are moderate and potentially acceptable, values of .40–.60 are low and potentially problematic, and values lower than .40 are not acceptable. In summarizing standards offered by several researchers (e.g., Carter, Briggs-Gowan, & Davis, 2004; Gredler, 2000), Glover and Albers (2007) suggested that measures with sensitivity, specificity, or PPV lower than .75–.80 were of questionable appropriateness. Thus, although there are some differences regarding the lower bound threshold for minimally acceptable evidence across these standards, acceptable-to-excellent evidence consistently exceeds .80. In addition, it is critical to consider the primary purposes of the assessment and implications of decisions (particularly inaccurate decisions) when evaluating conditional probability indices for a screening measure.

One common and effective way to assess the classification accuracy of a measure is through receiver operating characteristic (ROC) curve analysis (Fawcett, 2006). This technique is a graphical method by which practitioners and researchers can assess the costs and benefits of various classification cutoffs. ROC curves involve plotting several cutoff values on a graph in which the true positive rate is plotted on the y-axis and the false positive rate is plotted on the x-axis. By examining the shape of the curve produced by this analysis, educational professionals can make decisions about which cut scores are most appropriate, taking into account considerations about what the risks and benefits of each type of error are in the context of the screener being used (Fawcett, 2006).

Availability of Comprehensive Assessment and Intervention Services

A final consideration that is of critical importance to the development of any effective screening program is the presence of infrastructure to support what happens after the initial screen. Morabia and Zhang (2004) identified three assumptions on which the concept of screening is predicated. The first assumption is the availability of a screening test that yields scores with sufficient reliability and validity evidence to justify their use for screening decisions. The second is that diagnostic assessments (i.e., comprehensive measures that yield definitive decisions regarding presence or absence of a disorder) are available to confirm the "true" cases among those that are identified through screening. The third and final assumption is that treatments are made available in a timely fashion to those identified through the act of screening.

The majority of this chapter and volume are focused on considerations related to the first assumption—development, validation, and implementation of measures to conduct school-based screening in a variety of domains. Although these measures and activities represent a critical first step to implementation of an effective screening program, Morabia and Zhang's (2004) latter two assumptions are equally important to ensure that the limited resources available within schools are being used as effectively as possible when allocated for the purpose of screening. Fortunately, comprehensive diagnostic assessment has been a primary focus of school psychology since the inception of the field, and many such assessments are available in the academic, cognitive, and behavioral domains of student functioning. Nonetheless, models and methods continue to evolve for even the most widely studied disorders (e.g., movement toward an RTI model for learning disability identification), so prospective screeners and screening programs will require monitoring and refinement as these changes occur.

Perhaps an even greater challenge for achieving effective screening programs in school settings is the last of Morabia and Zhang's (2004) assumptions—availability and timely provision of treatment. Although specialized services and programs have been provided within schools for nearly 4 decades, services such as special education are intended for students with identified disabilities rather than students who are identified as at risk through a screening process. As noted at the beginning of this chapter, changes in federal and state laws during the past decade have created opportunity for districts to implement multitiered models of service delivery to provide intervention services as problems begin to emerge rather than waiting for them to achieve the severity of a disabling condition. Although such opportunities have become available, a number of barriers exist regarding the implementation of such models (Glover & DiPerna, 2007) and the provision of timely, evidence-based interventions for students identified through screening efforts in school settings.

In sum, development of a comprehensive screening program requires a number of conceptual and practical considerations, including identification of the domains of functioning to be screened, determination of the best methods for assessing these domains, documentation of evidence to justify the use of scores from the screen, and implementation of infrastructure to provide treatment to those identified through screening. The following section provides an overview of a published screening system that considers multiple domains of student functioning consistent with the aforementioned model of academic competence.

EXAMPLE OF BROADBAND SCREENING FOR ACADEMIC AND SOCIAL BEHAVIOR

One prime example of a broadband social and academic screening measure is the SSIS-PSG (Elliott & Gresham, 2007b). The SSIS-PSG is the universal phase of assessment within the SSIS (Elliott & Gresham, 2007a) and is intended to identify children who are experiencing difficulty within the classroom. The theoretical framework underlying the SSIS is consistent with the conceptual model presented earlier in this chapter and focuses on three domains of classroom functioning: social skills, problem behaviors, and academic competence. Social skills are behaviors that lead to positive interactions and minimize negative interactions in social settings. The social skill domains on the SSIS include communication, cooperation, assertion, responsibility, engagement, and self-control (Gresham & Elliott, 2008a). The SSIS also focuses on problem behaviors, which are behaviors that interfere with academic and social success. These include externalizing behaviors, bullying, hyperactivity–inattention, internalizing behaviors, and autism spectrum behaviors. Finally, because academic difficulties often are related to the presence of problem behaviors or social skills deficits, the SSIS also focuses on academic competence (reading and math performance, motivation, parental support, and general cognitive function; Gresham & Elliott, 2008a).

The SSIS-PSG consists of teacher ratings of students in four key skill areas (prosocial behavior, motivation to learn, reading, and mathematics) using five performance levels[1] to identify students who may be at risk. Each level is described in detail in booklets provided to teachers rating each student. Ratings of 1 indicate that students likely need further support through interventions. Ratings of 2 or 3 indicate that the student possibly needs further support. Finally, ratings of 4 to 5 indicate that the student does not need further assessment or intervention in that particular domain. These ratings are recorded for each child in the classroom, and further assessment is conducted as necessary to determine the student's level of need and to inform intervention (Gresham & Elliott, 2008a).

Initial psychometric evidence for the SSIS-PSG was gathered through the Social Skills Improvement System–Rating Scale (SSIS-RS) standardization process (Gresham & Elliott, 2008a). Participants were drawn from the standardization sample for the SSIS-RS. In all, 138 teachers (30 preschool teachers, 76 elementary teachers, and 32 high school teachers) from across the country completed the SSIS-PSG in addition to the SSIS-RS. On the basis of these data, SSIS-PSG scores demonstrated test–retest reliability coefficients (intraclass correlations) ranging from .53 to .62 for the preschool form, from .68 to .74 for the elementary form, and from .56 to .73 for the secondary form. These values would be classified as moderate to substantial according to criteria proposed by Landis and Koch (1977). SSIS-PSG scores also demonstrated adequate interrater reliability (intraclass correlations) for the preschool (.53–.62) and elementary (.55–.68) levels. Coefficients for secondary students ranged from low (.37) to adequate (.60).

Subsamples of the SSIS-RS standardization sample also were used to test the concurrent validity of the scores produced by the SSIS-PSG. These subsamples consisted of 22 children at the preschool level and 63 students at the elementary and secondary levels. On the basis of these data, ratings from the SSIS-PSG were related moderately to scores from the SSIS-RS, which are more comprehensive measures of social skills, problem behaviors, and academic competence (Gresham & Elliott, 2008b). Specifically, the Social Skills subscale of the SSIS-RS was correlated positively with all domains of the SSIS-PSG, with correlation coefficients ranging from .63 to .81 (adjusted r) for preschool students and from .34 to .70 for elementary and secondary students. In addition, the Academic Competence subscale of the SSIS-RS was correlated positively with all domains of the SSIS-PSG, with correlation coefficients ranging from .40 to .67 for elementary and secondary students. All domains of the

---

[1] In the SSIS-PSG, preschool students are evaluated on four performance levels as opposed to the five performance levels on which elementary and secondary students are scored. In the preschool form, a score of 1 indicates a high level of concern, a score of 2 indicates a moderate level of concern, and a score of 3 or 4 indicates that a student is at or above the expected level of functioning (Gresham & Elliott, 2008a).

SSIS-PSG were correlated moderately negatively with the Problem Behaviors subscale of the SSIS-RS, with correlation coefficients ranging from .33 to .69 for preschoolers and from .23 to .55 for elementary and secondary students.

Kilgus, Chafouleas, Riley-Tillman, and Welsh (2012) also correlated the SSIS-PSG motivation to learn and prosocial behavior domains with the Direct Behavior Rating–Single Item Scales (DBR-SIS; Chafouleas, 2011) of Disruptive Behavior (DB), Academic Engagement (AE), and Compliance (CO) and with scores from the BASC-2 BESS (Kamphaus & Reynolds, 2007). On the basis of data collected from 120 second-grade students, the SSIS-PSG motivation to learn domain was correlated negatively with the DBR-SIS DB domain (.61) and the BASC-2 BESS (.82) and positively correlated with the DBR-SIS AE domain (.77) and the DBR-SIS CO domain (.66). Likewise, the SSIS-PSG prosocial behavior domain was correlated negatively with the DBR-SIS DB domain (.54) and the BASC-2 BESS (.71) and positively correlated with the DBR-SIS AE domain (.67) and the DBR-SIS CO domain (.52).

In an international study (Kettler et al., 2012), 20 third- and fifth-grade teachers completed the SSIS-PSG and the SSIS-RS for their students (N = 360). Although the data were collected in Australia, the results mirrored those of the standardization study (Gresham & Elliott, 2008a), with correlations ranging from .44 to .74 between the Social Skills subscale of the SSIS-RS and the domains of the SSIS-PSG and from .49 to .66 between the Problem Behaviors subscale of the SSIS-RS and the domains of the SSIS-PSG. The Academic Competence subscale of the SSIS-RS also was correlated positively with all domains of the SSIS-PSG with coefficients ranging from .59 to .82.

Kettler et al. (2012) also conducted conditional probability analyses on the SSIS-PSG using minimum standard scores of the Australian national achievement test as criterion of risk. In this study, the SSIS-PSG was found to have a sensitivity value of .95, a specificity value of .45, a PPV of .20, an NPV of .99, and an overall accuracy rate (hit rate) of .51. Kilgus et al. (2012) also completed a conditional probability analysis between the SSIS-PSG prosocial behavior and motivation to learn domains and risk status according to the BASC-2 BESS (Kamphaus & Reynolds, 2007). ROC curve analyses indicated that an optimal cutoff score of 3 for the SSIS-PSG prosocial behavior domain resulted in a sensitivity value of .83, a specificity value of .76, a PPV of .47, an NPV of .95, and an accuracy rate of .79. Furthermore, ROC curve analysis indicated that an optimal cutoff score of 3 for the SSIS-PSG motivation to learn domain resulted in a sensitivity value of .91, a specificity value of .79, a PPV of .51, an NPV of .97, and an accuracy rate of .82. Combining these two domains resulted in a sensitivity value of .78, a specificity value of .85, a PPV of .56, an NPV of .94, and an accuracy rate of .84.

According to the criteria of Cicchetti et al. (1995), the SSIS-PSG evidences a pattern of fair to excellent sensitivity (ranging from .78 to .95), excellent NPV (ranging from .94 to .99), low to good specificity (ranging from .45 to .85), and poor PPV (ranging from .20 to .56). According to conditional probability index values recommended by Glover and Albers (2007), the SSIS-PSG showed adequate sensitivity and NPV, with somewhat questionable specificity and questionable PPV. In addition, according to the Kettler and Feeney-Kettler (2011) criteria, the SSIS-PSG evidences a pattern of moderate to high sensitivity, high NPV, low to high specificity, and very low to low PPV. Although somewhat more lenient than the other sets of criteria, the Kettler and Feeney-Kettler criteria lead to similar conclusions about the predictive validity of the SSIS-PSG. Overall, all sets of criteria indicate that the SSIS-PSG shows acceptable sensitivity and NPV, mostly acceptable specificity, and questionable PPV.

Glover and Albers (2007) suggested that the primary purpose of screening elevates the importance of sensitivity and PPV because a screener must accurately identify those at risk without identifying a large number of false positives and thus wasting resources. The high sensitivity and low PPV of the SSIS-PSG indicate that, although the instrument correctly identifies most students who truly are at risk, it may overidentify a fair number of children who do not need additional early intervention or assessment. Thus, the pattern of findings supports the use of the SSIS-PSG as an early screening measure within a multistage screening and intervention process, provided positive classification according to the SSIS-PSG proximally results in relatively low-intensity follow-up services (e.g., further assessment). Additional studies are necessary to examine the decision-making accuracy of the SSIS-PSG and to determine optimal cut scores for screening decisions.

Finally, two other considerations especially important to evaluating the validity of screening measures are social acceptability and intervention utility. Social acceptability refers to the perceived usability and feasibility of interventions or assessments in educational settings (Schwartz & Baer, 1991). Similarly, intervention utility refers to the extent to which scores on a measure inform and lead to interventions (Elliott, Gresham, Frank, & Beddow, 2008). The results of an acceptability study of the SSIS-PSG (Gresham & Elliott, 2008a) indicated that a majority of teachers reported that the SSIS-PSG was clearly written, easy to use, well organized, and efficient. In addition, the SSIS-PSG is an integral part of the SSIS, which includes additional comprehensive assessments (SSIS-RS) and intervention protocols (SSIS Intervention Guide) for students who are identified as at risk through the screening process. Although some evidence supports its use, further validation of the SSIS-PSG is warranted. Currently, a limited number of studies examine the technical adequacy of the SSIS-PSG, and only two have been completed beyond the standardization process. As such, future studies should further examine reliability, validity, and accuracy of screening decisions based on scores from the SSIS-PSG across a variety of districts and classrooms.

FUTURE DIRECTIONS

As screening measures and multitiered service delivery systems become more commonplace in school settings, there are a number of directions for future research and development efforts to ensure that broadband screening in the academic and social domains is as effective, efficient, and informative as possible. From a conceptual perspective, two important considerations include (a) further specification and evolution of student competence models and (b) development of screening and diagnostic measures that reflect such models. Earlier in this chapter, we briefly described one model of students' functioning (academic competence) that integrates students' academic enablers (social skills, motivation, study skills, and engagement) with their academic skills. We also suggested that such a framework could be useful for guiding the development of a screening system and presented the SSIS-PSG as an example of such a measure. Nonetheless, this academic competence model represents only one model for linking academic outcomes and student behavior, and it considers a subset of student skills identified through theory and empirical study. As such, elaboration of this model and the development of alternative models featuring additional constructs (e.g., self-regulatory behaviors, executive function) may lead to the development of more comprehensive and accurate screening measures.

In addition to refining conceptual models, several practical issues must be studied further to inform implementation of broadband screening systems in school settings. For example, timing of the screen within the academic year may need to be adjusted depending on the methods used for screening, skill domains targeted by the screen, and age range of the target students. In the academic domain, many students experience a "summer slide" during which their skills regress as a result of not being enrolled in school (Cooper, Nye, Charlton, Lindsay, & Greathouse, 1996). In addition, teachers establish their classroom routines and behavioral expectations during the first month of the academic year. During this period, they also become familiar with their students' academic skills, motivation, and social behavior in the classroom setting. Thus, screening for academics and academically related behavior—particularly if using indirect assessment methods, such as teacher judgments—may be more likely to yield inaccurate decisions regarding who is at risk and in need of further diagnostic assessment or intervention.

Another practical consideration from both an efficiency and accuracy perspective is that the skills assessed within the initial screen may need to be adjusted for different ages or developmental levels. As an example, although classroom participation and independent studying behavior tend to be valued by teachers throughout the K–12 education system (DiPerna & Elliott, 2000), some evidence suggests that classroom participation demonstrates stronger relationships with academic outcomes in the earlier grades, whereas studying behaviors demonstrate stronger relationships with achievement as students advance through the education system (DiPerna et al., 2002, 2005). Similarly, as students progress through the education system, expectations for their academic skill proficiency advance as well. Recognizing such developmental differences and adjusting screening measures accordingly will ensure that the most salient skills and skill domains are being assessed during a specific developmental period.

A third set of practical considerations reflects the resources necessary to implement a broadband screening system focusing on multiple domains of student skills and behaviors. Such resources include time, personnel, and follow-up services for individuals identified through the screening process. The current combination of dwindling resources and increased emphasis on accountability has caused time to be at a premium for students and faculty alike. Screening systems—especially those focused on multiple domains of functioning—must be developed to maximize decision-making accuracy while minimizing the time required of these key stakeholders to complete the screening process. In addition, screening systems require a person or team to be responsible for coordination of the screening process, collection and analysis of screening data, and execution of decisions resulting from screening. Although few teachers have sufficient training (or time) to serve in such a role, psychologists in school settings typically have expertise in assessment and can serve effectively in this capacity. Many psychologists' training, however, often places greater emphasis on individual diagnostic assessment rather than screening, and additional training may be necessary to ensure that psychologists can successfully coordinate the implementation of such systems.

As noted earlier in this chapter, effective screening cannot occur in a vacuum. Instead, additional resources must be in place to address the needs of those identified through the screening process. Specifically, diagnostic assessments and evidence-based interventions should be available to confirm the presence of risk and provide timely interventions to address specific skill areas of concern. As a result of RTI, many schools have begun to implement academic interventions (particularly in the area of reading) for students identified as being at risk for future difficulty. Similarly, frameworks such as Schoolwide Positive Behavior Support (Horner et al., 2009) and systems such as the SSIS (Elliott & Gresham, 2007a) have led to the implementation of interventions to reduce problem behavior and promote prosocial outcomes in schools. Although these are promising first steps toward development of a system to facilitate early intervention in school settings, they focus primarily on academics or behavior rather than offer a coordinated system addressing multiple domains. In addition, assessment and intervention protocols still are lagging in other core academic skill areas (mathematics, writing, study) and enabling behaviors (e.g., studying, engagement).

Finally, as evidenced by the other chapters in this volume, multiple domains of student functioning are considered to be important within the school setting, and a critical issue confronting school personnel is how to realistically implement screening systems (and related intervention services) in each of these target areas. For the benefits of screening systems and early intervention to be realized, models and methods must be developed to facilitate the implementation of screening systems in a coordinated and complementary fashion.

REFERENCES

Academic, Social, and Emotional Learning Act of 2011, H.R. 2437, 112th Cong. (2011). Retrieved from http://www.govtrack.us/congress/bills/112/hr2437

Achenbach, T. M. (1984). Psychopathology of childhood. *Annual Review of Psychology, 35*, 227–256. doi:10.1146/annurev.ps.35.020184.001303

Achenbach, T. M. (1991). *Integrative guide for the 1991 CBCL/4–18, YSR, and TRF profiles*. Burlington: University of Vermont, Department of Psychiatry.

Achenbach, T. M. (1995). Empirically based assessment and taxonomy: Applications to clinical research. *Psychological Assessment, 7*, 261–274. doi:10.1037/1040-3590.7.3.261

Achenbach, T. M., McConaughy, S. H., & Howell, C. T. (1987). Child/adolescent behavioral and emotional problems: Implications of cross-informant correlations for situational specificity. *Psychological Bulletin, 101*, 213–232. doi:10.1037/0033-2909.101.2.213

American Educational Research Association, American Psychological Association, & National Council on Measurement in Education. (1999). *Standards for educational and psychological testing*. Washington, DC: Author.

Barkley, R. A. (1997). *Defiant children: A clinician's manual for assessment and parent training* (2nd ed.). New York, NY: Guilford Press.

Beitchman, J. H., & Corradini, A. (1988). Self-report measures for use with children: A review and commentary. *Journal of Clinical Psychology, 44*, 477–490. doi:10.1002/1097-4679(198807)44:4477::AID-JCLP22704404023.0.CO;2-K

Birelson, P. (1981). The validity of depressive disorder in childhood and the development of a self-rating scale: A research report. *Journal of Child Psychology and Psychiatry, 22*, 73–88. doi:10.1111/j.1469-7610.1981.tb00533.x

Bray, N. W., Huffman, L. F., & Fletcher, K. L. (1999). Developmental and intellectual differences in self-report and strategy use. *Developmental Psychology, 35,* 1223–1236. doi:10.1037/0012-1649.35.5.1223

Caprara, G. V., Barbaranelli, C., Pastorelli, C., Bandura, A., & Zimbardo, P. G. (2000). Prosocial foundations of children's academic achievement. *Psychological Science, 11,* 302–306. doi:10.1111/1467-9280.00260

Carroll, J. B. (1963). A model of school learning. *Teachers College Record, 64,* 723–733.

Carter, A. S., Briggs-Gowan, M., & Davis, N. O. (2004). Assessment of young children's social emotional development and psychopathology: Recent advances and recommendations for practice. *Journal of Child Psychology and Psychiatry, 45,* 109–134. doi:10.1046/j.0021-9630.2003.00316.x

Causey, D. L., & Dubow, E. F. (1992). Development of a self-report coping measure for elementary school children. *Journal of Clinical Child Psychology, 21,* 47–59. doi:10.1207/s15374424jccp2101_8

Chafouleas, S. M. (2011). Direct behavior rating: A review of the issues and research in its development. *Education and Treatment of Children, 34,* 575–591. doi:10.1353/etc.2011.0034

Chafouleas, S. M., Riley-Tillman, T. C., & Sassu, K. A. (2007). Daily behavior report cards: An investigation of the consistency of on-task data across raters and methods. *Journal of Positive Behavior Interventions, 9,* 30–37. doi:10.1177/10983007070090010401

Cicchetti, D. V., Volkmar, F., Klin, A., & Showalter, D. (1995). Diagnosing autism using ICD-10 criteria: A comparison of neural networks and standard multivariate procedures. *Child Neuropsychology, 1,* 26–37. doi:10.1080/09297049508401340

Cone, J. D. (1978). The behavioral assessment grid (BAG): A conceptual framework and a taxonomy. *Behavior Therapy, 9,* 882–888. doi:10.1016/S0005-7894(78)80020-3

Cool, V. A., & Keith, T. Z. (1991). Testing a model of school learning: Direct and indirect effects on academic achievement. *Contemporary Educational Psychology, 16,* 28–44. doi:10.1016/0361-476X(91)90004-5

Cooper, H., Nye, B., Charlton, K., Lindsay, J., & Greathouse, S. (1996). The effects of summer vacation on achievement test scores: A narrative and meta-analytic review. *Review of Educational Research, 66,* 227–268. doi:10.3102/00346543066003227

Cronbach, L. (1951). Coefficient alpha and the internal structure of tests. *Psychometrika, 16,* 297–334. doi:10.1007/BF02310555

Demaray, M. K., & Elliott, S. N. (1998). Teachers' judgments of students' academic functioning: A comparison of actual and predicted performances. *School Psychology Quarterly, 13,* 8–24. doi:10.1037/h0088969

Deno, S. L. (1985). Curriculum-based measurement: The emerging alternative. *Exceptional Children, 52,* 219–232.

Deno, S. L., & Mirkin, P. K. (1977). *Data-based program modification: A manual.* Reston, VA: Council for Exceptional Children.

Dewey, D., Crawford, S. G., Creighton, D. E., & Sauve, R. S. (2000). Parents' ratings of everyday cognitive abilities in very low birth weight children. *Journal of Developmental and Behavioral Pediatrics, 21*, 37–43. doi:10.1097/00004703-200002000-00006

DiPerna, J. C., & Elliott, S. N. (1999). Development and validation of the Academic Competence Evaluation Scales. *Journal of Psychoeducational Assessment, 17*, 207–225. doi:10.1177/073428299901700302

DiPerna, J. C., & Elliott, S. N. (2000). *Academic competence evaluation scales (K–12 edition)*. San Antonio, TX: Psychological Corporation.

DiPerna, J. C., Lei, P., & Reid, E. L. (2007). Kindergarten predictors of mathematical growth in the primary grades: An investigation using the Early Childhood Longitudinal Study–Kindergarten cohort. *Journal of Educational Psychology, 99*, 369–379. doi:10.1037/0022-0663.99.2.369

DiPerna, J. C., & Volpe, R. J. (2005). Self-report on the Social Skills Rating System: Analysis of reliability and validity for an elementary sample. *Psychology in the Schools, 42*, 345–354. doi:10.1002/pits.20095

DiPerna, J. C., Volpe, R. J., & Elliott, S. N. (2002). A model of academic enablers and elementary reading/language arts achievement. *School Psychology Review, 31*, 298–312.

DiPerna, J. C., Volpe, R. J., & Elliott, S. N. (2005). A model of academic enablers and mathematics achievement in the elementary grades. *Journal of School Psychology, 43*, 379–392. doi:10.1016/j.jsp.2005.09.002

Doll, B., & Cummings, J. A. (2008). *Transforming school mental health services: Population-based approaches to promoting the competency and wellness of children*. Thousand Oaks, CA: Corwin Press.

Durlak, J. A., Weissberg, R. P., Dymnicki, A. B., Taylor, R. D., & Schellinger, K. B. (2011). The impact of enhancing students' social and emotional learning: A meta-analysis of school-based universal interventions. *Child Development, 82*, 405–432. doi:10.1111/j.1467-8624.2010.01564.x

Elliott, S. N., & Gresham, F. M. (2007a). *Social Skills Improvement System: Classwide intervention program guide*. Bloomington, MN: Pearson Assessments.

Elliott, S. N., & Gresham, F. M. (2007b). *Social Skills Improvement System: Performance screening guides*. Bloomington, MN: Pearson Assessments.

Elliott, S. N., Gresham, F. M., Frank, J. L., & Beddow, P. A. (2008). Intervention validity of social behavior rating scales. *Assessment for Effective Intervention, 34*, 15–24. doi:10.1177/1534508408314111

Ericsson, K. A., & Simon, H. A. (1980). Verbal reports as data. *Psychological Review, 87*, 215–251. doi:10.1037/0033-295X.87.3.215

Ericsson, K. A., & Simon, H. A. (1993). *Protocol analysis: Verbal reports as data* (rev. ed.). Cambridge, MA: MIT Press.

Espin, C. A., & Deno, S. L. (1993). Performance in reading from content area text as an indicator of achievement. *Remedial and Special Education, 14*, 47–59. doi:10.1177/074193259301400610

Fawcett, T. (2006). An introduction to ROC analysis. *Pattern Recognition Letters*, *27*, 861–874. doi:10.1016/j.patrec.2005.10.010

Floyd, R. G., Phaneuf, R. L., & Wilczynski, S. M. (2005). Measurement properties of indirect assessment methods for functional behavioral assessment: A review of research. *School Psychology Review*, *34*, 58–73.

Flynn, J. M., & Rahbar, M. H. (1998). Improving teacher prediction of children at risk for reading failure. *Psychology in the Schools*, *35*, 163–172. doi:10.1002/(SICI)1520-6807(199804)35:2163::AID-PITS83.0.CO;2-Q

Glascoe, F. P. (1997). Parents' concerns about children's development: Prescreening techniques or screening test? *Pediatrics*, *99*, 522–528. doi:10.1542/peds.99.4.522

Glascoe, F. P., & Dworkin, P. H. (1995). The role of parents in the detection of developmental and behavioral problems. *Pediatrics*, *95*, 829–836.

Glover, T. A., & Albers, C. A. (2007). Considerations for evaluating universal screening assessments. *Journal of School Psychology*, *45*, 117–135. doi:10.1016/j.jsp.2006.05.005

Glover, T. A., & DiPerna, J. C. (2007). Service delivery for response to intervention: Core components and directions for future research. *School Psychology Review*, *36*, 526–540.

Good, R. H., & Kaminski, R. A. (2002). *Dynamic Indicators of Basic Early Literacy Skills* (6th ed.). Eugene, OR: Institute for the Development of Educational Achievement. Retrieved from http://dibels.uoregon.edu

Gredler, G. R. (2000). Early childhood screening for developmental and educational problems. In B. A. Bracken (Ed.), *The psychoeducational assessment of preschool children* (3rd ed., pp. 399–411). Needham Heights, MA: Allyn & Bacon.

Gresham, F. M., & Elliott, S. N. (2008a). *Social Skills Improvement System: Rating scales manual*. Minneapolis, MN: Pearson.

Gresham, F. M., & Elliott, S. N. (2008b). *Social Skills Improvement System: Teacher rating scales*. Bloomington, MN: Pearson.

Hoge, R. D., & Coladarci, T. (1989). Teacher-based judgments of academic achievement: A review of literature. *Review of Educational Research*, *59*, 297–313. doi:10.3102/00346543059003297

Hoover, H. D., Dunbar, S. B., & Frisbie, D. A. (2001). *Iowa Test of Basic Skills*. Itasca, IL: Riverside.

Horner, R. H., Sugai, G., Smolkowski, K., Eber, L., Nakasato, J., Todd, A. W., & Esperanza, J. (2009). A randomized, wait-list controlled effectiveness trial assessing school-wide positive behavior support in elementary schools. *Journal of Positive Behavior Interventions*, *11*, 133–144. doi:10.1177/1098300709332067

Individuals With Disabilities Education Improvement Act, 20 U.S.C. § 1400 *et seq.* (2004).

Kamphaus, R. W., & Reynolds, C. R. (2007). *BASC-2 Behavioral and Emotional Screening System*. Minneapolis, MN: Pearson.

Kenny, D. T., & Chekaluk, E. (1993). Early reading performance: A comparison of teacher-based and test-based assessments. *Journal of Learning Disabilities, 26,* 227–236. doi:10.1177/002221949302600403

Kettler, R. J., Elliott, S. N., Davies, M., & Griffin, P. (2012). Testing a multi-stage screening system: Predicting performance on Australia's national achievement test using teachers' ratings of academic and social behaviors. *School Psychology International, 33,* 93–111. doi:10.1177/0143034311403036

Kettler, R. J., & Feeney-Kettler, K. A. (2011). Screening systems and decision making at the preschool level: Application of a comprehensive validity framework. *Psychology in the Schools, 48,* 430–441. doi:10.1002/pits.20565

Kilgus, S. P., Chafouleas, S. M., Riley-Tillman, T. C., & Welsh, M. E. (2012). Direct behavior rating scales as screeners: A preliminary investigation of diagnostic accuracy in elementary school. *School Psychology Quarterly, 27,* 41–50. doi:10.1037/a0027150

Kovacs, M. (1981). Rating scales to assess depression in school-age children. *Acta Paedopsychiatrica, 46,* 305–315.

Landis, J. R., & Koch, G. (1977). The measurement of observer agreement for categorical data. *Biometrics, 33,* 159–174. doi:10.2307/2529310

Lane, K. L., Oakes, W., & Menzies, H. (2010). Systematic screenings to prevent the development of learning and behavior problems: Considerations for practitioners, researchers, and policy makers. *Journal of Disability Policy Studies, 21,* 160–172. doi:10.1177/1044207310379123

Loeber, R., Green, S. M., & Lahey, B. B. (1990). Mental health professionals' perception of the utility of children, mothers, and teachers as informants on child psychopathology. *Journal of Clinical Child Psychology, 19,* 136–143. doi:10.1207/s15374424jccp1902_5

Malecki, C. K., & Elliott, S. N. (2002). Children's social behaviors as predictors of academic achievement: A longitudinal analysis. *School Psychology Quarterly, 17,* 1–23. doi:10.1521/scpq.17.1.1.19902

Martinez, R. S., & Nellis, L. M. (2008). Response to intervention: A school-wide approach for promoting academic wellness for all students. In B. Doll & J. Cummings (Eds.), *Transforming school mental health services: Population-based approaches to promoting the competency and wellness of children* (pp. 143–164). Thousand Oaks, CA: Corwin Press.

Morabia, A., & Zhang, F. F. (2004). History of medical screening: From concepts to action. *Postgraduate Medical Journal, 80,* 463–469. doi:10.1136/pgmj.2003.018226

No Child Left Behind Act of 2001, 20 U.S.C. 70 § 6301 *et seq.* (2002).

Ollendick, T. H., Oswald, P. D., & Francis, G. (1989). Validity of teacher nominations in identifying aggressive, withdrawn, and popular children. *Journal of Clinical Child Psychology, 18,* 221–229. doi:10.1207/s15374424jccp1803_4

O'Neill, R. E., Horner, R. H., Ablin, R. W., Sprague, J. R., Storey, K., & Newton, J. S. (1997). *Functional assessment and program development for problem behaviors: A practical handbook*. New York, NY: Brooks/Cole.

Reynolds, W. R. (2002). *Reynolds Adolescent Depression Scale–Short Form* (2nd ed.). Lutz, FL: Psychological Assessment Resources.

Ridley, C. R., Li, L. C., & Hill, C. L. (1998). Multicultural assessment: Reexamination, reconceptualization, and practical application. *Counseling Psychologist, 26*, 827–910. doi:10.1177/0011000098266001

Salzman, M., & D'Andrea, M. (2001). Assessing the impact of a prejudice prevention project. *Journal of Counseling and Development, 79*, 341–346. doi:10.1002/j.1556-6676.2001.tb01979.x

Schwartz, I. S., & Baer, D. M. (1991). Social validity assessments: Is current practice state of the art? *Journal of Applied Behavior Analysis, 24*, 189–204. doi:10.1901/jaba.1991.24-189

Suen, H. K. (2008). Measurement. In N. Salkind (Ed.), *Encyclopedia of educational psychology* (pp. 641–647). Thousand Oaks, CA: Sage.

Thompson, M. D., & Thompson, G. (1991). Early identification of hearing loss: Listen to parents. *Clinical Pediatrics, 30*, 77–80. doi:10.1177/000992289103000202

Volpe, R. J., DuPaul, G. J., DiPerna, J. C., Jitendra, A. K., Lutz, J. G., Tresco, K., & Vile-Junod, R. (2006). Attention-deficit/hyperactivity disorder and scholastic achievement: A model of mediation via academic enablers. *School Psychology Review, 35*, 47–61.

Walberg, H. J. (1981). A psychological theory of educational productivity. In F. H. Farley & N. Gordon (Eds.), *Psychology and education* (pp. 81–110). Chicago, IL: National Society for the Study of Education.

Walker, H. M., & Severson, H. H. (1990). *Systematic Screening for Behavior Disorders (SSBD)*. Longmont, CO: Sopris West.

Walker, H. M., & Severson, H. H. (1992). *Systematic Screening for Behavior Disorders: Technical manual*. Longmont, CO: Sopris West.

Wentzel, K. R. (1993). Does being good make the grade? Social behavior and academic competence in middle school. *Journal of Educational Psychology, 85*, 357–364. doi:10.1037/0022-0663.85.2.357

Young, K. T., Davis, K., Schoen, C., & Parker, S. (1998). Listening to parents: A national survey of parents with young children. *Archives of Pediatrics and Adolescent Medicine, 152*, 255–262.

Zelko, F. A. (1991). Comparison of parent-completed behavior rating scales: Differentiating boys with ADD from psychiatric and normal controls. *Journal of Developmental and Behavioral Pediatrics, 12*, 31–37. doi:10.1097/00004703-199102000-00007

10

BEHAVIORAL AND MENTAL HEALTH SCREENING

RANDY W. KAMPHAUS, CECIL R. REYNOLDS, AND BRIDGET V. DEVER

The 20th century was about treating disease. The 21st century is about prevention.

—William Castell,
former chief executive officer,
GE Healthcare

The need for childhood screening for behavioral and emotional risk in schools has been documented for decades (Reynolds, 1979), and, in fact, measures to use for screening have been developed and their reliability and validity assessed for just as long (Cowen et al., 1973). B. F. Skinner said that it takes about 50 years for an innovation to take hold; thus, it is due time for screening to become popular.

Universal screening for behavioral and emotional risk serves the overarching goal of prevention. Other reasons for its newfound popularity include (a) documented poor outcomes for children classified as cases of emotional disturbance by U.S. schools, (b) the emphasis on early intervention that undergirds response-to-intervention (RTI) paradigms, and (c) the availability of measures with better evidence of reliability and validity that are, perhaps more importantly, more practical for widespread use.

http://dx.doi.org/10.1037/14316-010
Universal Screening in Educational Settings: Evidence-Based Decision Making for Schools, R. J. Kettler,
T. A. Glover, C. A. Albers, and K. A. Feeney-Kettler (Editors)
Copyright © 2014 by the American Psychological Association. All rights reserved.

There is convincing evidence that academic outcomes are relatively poor for children with severe emotional and behavioral problems, as classified for special education purposes in U.S. public schools. In one study, for example, 75% of students with significant emotional and behavioral problems were achieving below expected grade levels in reading, and 97% were below expected levels in mathematics (Bradley, Doolittle, & Bartolotta, 2008). In addition, children with emotional and behavioral problems have higher rates of suspensions, expulsions (Wagner, Kutash, Duchnowski, & Epstein, 2005), and absenteeism (Lane, Carter, Pierson, & Glaeser, 2006). In the United States, the majority of students identified as having significant emotional or behavioral problems drop out of school, and of those who remain in school, only about 42% graduate with a diploma (Bradley et al., 2008; U.S. Public Health Service, 2000). Other research findings reveal that only 20% of students participating in special education for emotional and behavioral disorders pursue any type of postsecondary education (Wagner et al., 2005). On the other hand, strong evidence is showing that early intervention can mitigate behavioral and emotional problems of childhood and improve academic outcomes (Atkins, Frazier, Adil, & Talbott, 2003; Catalano, Haggerty, Osterle, Fleming, & Hawkins, 2004; McIntosh, Flannery, Sugai, Braun, & Cochrane, 2008).

The implementation of RTI service delivery models in U.S. schools is premised on knowing the general prevalence of academic and behavioral problems to find those children who need Tier 1 or Tier 2 prevention and secondary prevention services. To date, however, the universal screening and detection aspects of RTI have been implemented haphazardly in the case of child behavioral or emotional problems. Whereas screening for academic, speech, and hearing problems in schools is universal and measures are supported by some evidence of reliability and validity, continued dependence on teacher referral as the de facto screening assessment for behavioral and emotional problems has not worked well. For example, children with the most significant risk for developing severe behavioral and emotional problems often never are identified for services by schools (Kamphaus, DiStefano, Dowdy, Eklund, & Dunn, 2010). In fact, children with more than mere risk, those with diagnosable psychopathology, often are not identified, thus making the probability of identification and services even lower for children with subclinical or subsyndromal problems that have not yet developed into full-fledged disorders (Jamieson & Romer, 2005).

Large-scale epidemiological studies have revealed that approximately 20% of children in the United States have a diagnosable disorder (Costello, Mustillo, Erkanli, Keeler, & Angold, 2003), but only 15% to 30% of these children receive any type of mental health service (Ringel & Sturm, 2001; U.S. Public Health Service, 2000). The fact that children with significant problems may never be identified is exemplified by a self-report screening study of 229 students from middle and high schools in Washington, D.C. Although few of these students were referred for special education or related services, an alarming 45% reported making a previous suicide attempt and having some current symptoms of depression or anxiety (Brown & Grumet, 2009). These internalizing problems of anxiety and depression are even more difficult for schools to detect in the absence of a universal screening program. In fact, teachers routinely underidentify such children, as their difficulties tend to be less overt (Kauffman, 1999; Lloyd, Kauffman, Landrum, & Roe, 1991).

AVAILABLE SCREENING METHODS

Screening measures and methods have proliferated in the past decade or so, offering school districts many more options for universal screening. Some studies in the past have used omnibus rating scales, such as the Child Behavior Checklist (Achenbach & Rescorla, 2001), as screening measures. New measures that were designed specifically for universal screening programs in schools have a fraction of the items of omnibus behavior rating scales, typically 30 or fewer items, and include forms that can be completed by parents, teachers, or children in 5–10 minutes. The Strengths and Difficulties Questionnaire (SDQ; R. Goodman, 1997, 1999, 2001) is one example of a newer measure designed specifically for universal screening of schoolchildren for behavioral and emotional problems. The SDQ is a brief, 25-item behavioral screening test for youths ages 11–17 years old (http://www.sdqinfo.com). Teacher, parent, and student self-report forms are available. Respondents rate items on a 3-point scale, ranging from 0 (*not at all*) to 2 (*very much or all the time*). The SDQ contains five scales, each consisting of five items: Emotional Symptoms, Conduct Problems, Hyperactivity/Inattention, Peer Relationship Problems, and Prosocial Behavior. The Behavior Assessment System of Children—Second Edition (BASC-2) Behavioral and Emotional Screening System (BESS; Kamphaus & Reynolds, 2007) is another dedicated screening measure that has been used widely in the United States in recent years. The BESS consists of brief screening measures (30 items or less) that can be completed by teachers, parents, or students to identify behavioral and emotional risk in youth ranging from preschool through high school (Kamphaus & Reynolds, 2007).

A third option, which is more limited in scope and age as well as grade ranges, is the Student Risk Screening Scale (SRSS; Drummond, 1994). The SRSS is a seven-item teacher rating scale designed to detect "antisocial behavior" among children in kindergarten through 12th grade. Elementary school teachers can complete forms for all of the students in their classroom in about 15 minutes. The content coverage of behavioral and emotional risk symptoms in the SRSS is more limited, making it better at identifying externalizing problems than internalizing problems (Lane et al., 2009). Internalizing items have been added at the elementary school level in a recent investigation by Lane et al. (2012). Brief screening measures, such as the BESS, SRSS, and SDQ, are creating new opportunities for universal screening. They are specifically designed for this purpose and are practical in terms of time demands on school personnel and students, where personnel time is the most significant financial cost associated with universal screening (Dobrez et al., 2001).

We now turn to the specifics of implementing a universal screening program in U.S. schools. Guided by available research and our own experiences conducting screening in California and Georgia, we discuss and provide guidance regarding definition of the construct of interest, selection of informants and measures, and use of the results as part of a comprehensive approach to early intervention and prevention, among other practical topics. We conclude by identifying those issues for which more research is needed to guide practice.

DEFINING BEHAVIORAL AND EMOTIONAL RISK

For the purposes of screening, we have adopted that National Academies definition of behavioral and emotional risk (BER), which defines the construct as early symptoms of disorders that eventually may result in special education placement or mental health treatment (O'Connell, Boat, & Warner, 2009). The National Academies report gives the following BER definition:

> For prevention, one of the goals of screening should be to identify communities, groups, or individuals exposed to risks or experiencing *early symptoms* that increase the potential that they will have negative emotional or behavioral outcomes and take action prior to there being a diagnosable disorder. (O'Connell et al., 2009, p. 223)

Adoption of this definition provides a content blueprint for creation of BER measures, in that they should include early marker symptoms of a mental health disorder and should cover those preliminary symptoms associated with a variety of child disorders so they have broad predictive validity for poor schooling or mental health outcomes. Thus, the content of screening measures could be drawn from popular omnibus rating scales, such as the BASC-2 (Reynolds & Kamphaus, 2004) and Achenbach System of Empirically Based Assessment (ASEBA; Achenbach & Rescorla, 2001), to obtain wide content coverage. On the other hand, suicidal ideation, for example, would not be a good choice for a screening measure, because this symptom is a key symptom of a problem that has progressed to the stage of being a depression disorder. Items assessing unhappiness would be a better choice if one is interested in assessing BER.

Methods and Measurement Issues

Choosing which screening instrument to utilize will affect subsequent decisions. When a screening instrument for potential adoption and use is evaluated, the measure should be evaluated on the basis of its norm samples and derived scores, reliability, and validity evidence to support score inferences. Many mental health screeners are available (Glover & Albers, 2007); however, many of these have not enjoyed widespread use for school-based screening. As screening researchers and test authors, we often get requests from school districts in the United States (and to a lesser extent internationally) for technical assistance with screener selection and use.

The inquiries we receive suggest that, at the time of this writing, universal screening is nascent but growing rapidly. Only a few screeners and screening systems, including the Systematic Screening for Behavior Disorders (SSBD; U.S. Department of Education, 1995), BESS, and SDQ, are being used on a broad scale. It is, however, too early to sense which of these screeners or others will become standard selections by schools. Because universal screening in schools is in its infancy, currently available screeners that are practical for school use generally lack evidence in support of the ability to predict future untoward outcomes, such as special education referral or placement, academic achievement, school incompletion (i.e., dropout), or onset of a mental health disorder. This predictive validity question, after all, is the score inference of greatest importance for a screening measure; therefore, future research on screening measures should incorporate evaluations of predictive validity evidence.

Given the need to discuss several aspects of screening for BER in this chapter, we refer the interested reader to Glover and Albers (2007); Severson, Walker, Hope-Doolittle, Kratochwill, and Gresham (2007); Feeney-Kettler et al. (2010); and other sources for focused reviews of screening measures. We limit ourselves here to discussing a few strengths and weaknesses of the emerging popular measures, with special attention given to the issue of evidence of long-term predictive validity. In reality, we highlight the lack of available evidence to support the predictive validity score inference.

Systematic Screening for Behavior Disorders

Considerable cross-sectional, criterion-related validity research is available for the SSBD. The multiple-gate SSBD method is designed primarily for children in kindergarten through sixth grade. It does not include a student self-report measure. Longitudinal evidence of predictive validity of scores still is needed (see Table 10.1).

TABLE 10.1
Comparison of Four Brief Screening Systems

Test	Informants/age	Constructs	Reliability	Validity
BESS	Teachers for ages 3–5; parents for ages 3–5 and grades K–12; students for grades 3–12	25 items for teachers; 30 items for parents; 30 items for students	Internal consistency (.96 for teachers, .94 for parents, and .92 for students); test–retest stability (.80–.91); interrater reliability (.71–.83)	Concurrent validity (Eklund et al., 2009); convergent validity with Achenbach system, Conner's rating scales, etc.; predictive validity for teachers and students, not available for parent
SDQ	Teachers and parents for ages 3–17; students for ages 11–17	25-item behavioral screening test with five dimensions	Internal consistency (>.70); test–retest stability (>.60; R. Goodman, 2001; Lane et al., 2007)	Concurrent and discriminative validity (R. Goodman, 2001)
SRSS	Teachers for grades K–12	Seven-item teacher rating scale	Internal consistency (.70–.86); test–retest stability (.22–.71); interrater reliability (.19–50; Lane et al., 2008)	Convergent validity (.47) with SDQ (Lane et al., 2008); discriminant validity; concurrent validity (Lane et al., 2008); short-term predictive validity
SSBD	Teachers for grades K–8	Three-stage, multiple-gating mass screening system; externalizing and internalizing dimensions	Internal consistency; test–retest stability (Lane et al., 2008)	Concurrent validity (low to moderate; Lane et al., 2008); convergent validity with SAED; not available for predictive validity

Note. BESS = Behavioral and Emotional Screening System; SDQ = Strengths and Difficulties Questionnaire; SRSS = Student Risk Screening Scale; SSBD = Systematic Screening for Behavior Disorders; SAED = Scale for Assessing Emotional Disturbance. We gratefully acknowledge the work of Dr. Jihye Kim for creating Table 10.1. Printed with permission.

Student Risk Screening Scale

Considerably more research is available for the SRSS (Drummond, 1994). Lane and colleagues (Lane, Kalberg, Parks, & Carter, 2008; Lane et al., 2009; Lane, Parks, Kalberg, & Carter, 2007) have studied the use of the SRSS at the middle and high school levels and compared it with that of the SDQ and SSBD. In one study, Lane et al. (2009) used the SRSS and compared it with the SSBD at the kindergarten through third-grade levels in seven elementary schools. The ethnicity of students in these schools was fairly homogeneous at 95% White. SRSS scores were used as the predictor variable, and SSBD risk classification was used as the outcome variable in a cross-sectional design. The SRSS performed fairly well at identifying external-izing problems of children in the same manner as the SSBD, but it fared poorly for children with internalizing problems. Thus, Lane et al. (2009) concluded,

> When searching for students with internalizing behavior patterns, the SRSS was less useful than it was for detecting students with external-izing behaviors. The accuracy (92.84%) was still greatest when contrast-ing the low- and high-risk groups according to the SRSS compared to other contrasts (e.g., low vs. moderate risk or low vs. combined risk). Yet although the tool had strong specificity (a 4.91% false-positive rate), the SRSS lacked sensitivity, with a false-negative rate of 55.56%. (p. 102)

Some short-term predictive validity evidence for office discipline reports and student grade point average (GPA) showed that SRSS-defined BER groups could be differentiated according to these outcome variables, although the results were less convincing for the academic variable of GPA. As for many screeners, long-term predictive validity studies that span several years of development, such as 4 years or more, are lacking for the SRSS.

Strengths and Difficulties Questionnaire

The SDQ has been the beneficiary of a sustained cross-national research program. Foundational internal consistency estimates for total and subscale scores produced by the SDQ have been below the standard of practice in some studies, with internal consistency estimates as low as .63 and generally not much higher than .83 (A. Goodman & Scott, 1999; Hysing, Eigen, Gillberg, Lie, & Lundervold, 2007). Ruchkin, Jones, Vermeiren, and Schwab-Stone (2008) found subscale internal consistency estimates to be frequently below .60 for an urban sample. They concluded that the reliability of score infer-ences was insufficient and the issue should be investigated further, perhaps ultimately resulting in test modifications.

Extensive cross-cultural studies of the internal factor structure of the SDQ have produced mixed results (Van Roy, Veenstra, & Clench-Aas, 2008). One study concluded that the SDQ factor structure was so problematic that the SDQ should be used with caution and in conjunction with other scales (Mellor & Stokes, 2007). In particular, factor analyses conducted on large U.S. samples have yielded poor fit for a five-factor model in favor of a three-factor model consisting of externalization problems, internalization problems, and positive construal (Dickey & Blumberg, 2004; Percy, McCrystal, & Higgins, 2008; Ruchkin et al., 2008). Similar support for a three-factor model was found in Flemish (Van Leeuwen, Meerschaert, Bosmans, De Medts, & Braet, 2006), Norwegian (Rønning, Handegaard, Sourander, & Morch, 2004), and Russian (Ruchkin, Koposov, & Schwab-Stone, 2007) samples.

With regard to predictive validity, a study of 7,912 students by Goodman and Goodman (2009) yielded evidence of statistically significant predictive validity of psychiatric diagnosis for scores yielded by all three SDQ informants (self, teacher, and parent) over a 3-year period. In an earlier study of 1,615 students followed over a 2-year period, 10.1% of males and 12.9% of females reported significant psychological distress on the self-report SDQ, with higher rates of adolescents reporting at least some symptoms of depression (Clark et al., 2007). Overall, the SDQ is an example of a modern screening instrument: It is far more practical in terms of the costs of professional time and limited interference with instructional time, which are two major impediments to universal screening in the United States, particularly in large urban school districts (Kamphaus et al., 2010).

Behavior and Emotional Screening System

The BESS (Kamphaus & Reynolds, 2007) manual includes considerable evidence to support score inferences, including high reliabilities with median internal consistency coefficients for the teacher, parent, and student forms of .96, .94, and .92, respectively. The cut score of $T = 60$ has been supported in an independent study by DiStefano and Morgan (2011), several factor structure studies have noted that the BESS measures the major dimensions of child BER (Dever, Mays, Kamphaus, & Dowdy, 2012; Dowdy, Chin, Twyford, & Dever, 2011; Dowdy, Dever, DiStefano, & Chin, 2011), and measurement invariance was supported by a study of children with limited English proficiency in a study by Dowdy, Dever, et al. (2011). Only one 4-year longitudinal study of the predictive validity of the BESS forms for academic outcomes is available (Kamphaus & Reynolds, 2007). The important finding from this study is that only the teacher and student scores were significantly predictive of GPA 4 years later. Parent form scores were not predictive. This study lends some validity support to the use of the student form, which often is considered suspect a priori according to inquiries that we receive from the field.

Implementation of Universal Screening

There are many considerations in implementation of a screening program at school, in addition to the measurement adequacy of the screening tests used. This section covers measurement considerations, but, equally important, it illuminates some of the often not discussed practical issues of implementation. Glover and Albers (2007), for example, recommended that screening instruments be evaluated in terms of their (a) cost, (b) feasibility of administration, (c) acceptability to multiple stakeholders, (d) infrastructure for collecting and interpreting screening data, (e) appropriateness of use for entire targeted population, and (f) utility of the information obtained to provide improved treatment decisions. The special needs of the school milieu must be taken into account as well.

Cut Scores

Although some error in classification of BER is unavoidable, decisions should be made in a way that is least likely to be harmful (Ikeda, Neesen, & Witt, 2008). Four possible outcomes can result from using a screener to classify individuals according to a criterion (e.g., at risk or not at risk; diagnosed or not diagnosed): true positives, false positives, true negatives, and false negatives. The goal of all screening programs is to maximize the number of true positives and negatives and minimize the number of false positives and negatives. When the number of false negatives is reduced as a result of changes in cut score selection, the number of false positives is conversely increased, necessitating a prioritization of which outcome is more tolerable. In screening, a higher number of false positives often is tolerated in favor of more false negatives. This preference is due to the fact that a child classified as a false negative would be excluded from eventual discovery. Conversely, under a multigating screening approach, children identified as false positives simply would undergo additional assessment to determine which children were identified but do not, in fact, have BER.

Screening instruments typically report their screening accuracy and decisions regarding setting cut scores in terms of sensitivity and specificity. Sensitivity refers to the proportion of individuals with the disorder who are identified correctly by the instrument as having the disorder; in other words, the number of true positives divided by the number of people who have the disorder. Specificity refers to the proportion of individuals without the disorder who are identified correctly as not having the disorder, or the number of true negatives divided by the number of persons who do not have the disorder. Additionally, the positive predictive value (PPV) of a screener often is reported. It is calculated as the proportion of students correctly identified as at risk (true positives) out of all students identified as at risk on the screener. When the PPV is low, a large number of false positives are present. This is tolerated and expected in most screening scenarios (Levitt, Saka, Romanelli, & Hoagwood, 2007), given that when the PPV is optimized, false positives are minimized at the risk of missing true cases. The negative predictive value (NPV) of the instrument is the proportion of students correctly identified as not at risk (true negatives) out of all of the students identified as not at risk on the screener. A large number of false negatives result when the NPV is low, which is an untenable situation for universal screening at school.

PPV and NPV are best interpreted in light of information on the base rate of the outcome of interest, as the base rate significantly will affect the PPV and NPV of a screener (Meehl & Rosen, 1955). As Hill, Lochman, Coie, Greenberg, and the Conduct Problems Prevention Research Group (2004) explained, the accuracy rate of a measure will be affected significantly when reported without reference to PPV, NPV, and base rates. For example, "a test with sensitivity of .80 and specificity of .95 has a PPV of about 74% if the base rate is 15%, but the PPV is reduced to 46% if the base rate is 5%" (Hill et al., 2004, p. 810). Prior research suggests that for emotional and behavioral problems in general, an annual base rate would be around 20% (Campaign for Mental Health Reform, 2005; Friedman, Katz-Leavy, Manderscheid, & Sondheimer, 1996; Hill et al., 2004), and this base rate will be lower for a single disorder.

DiStefano and Morgan (2011) used item response theory (IRT) methods to examine cut scores for the BESS by assessing their accuracy when set at about the 84th percentile rank or $T \approx 60$, and the 98th percentile rank, or $T \approx 70$. They tried to balance sensitivity and specificity, as we recommended in the previous section, and found that these two cut scores were reasonable compromises for general use in identifying either BER or extreme BER, which may, in fact, not be BER but be a case of disorder per se. There may remain, however, a need to adjust cut scores based on local needs, cultural, linguistic, personnel, or other special circumstances. Generally speaking, however, it is somewhat reassuring to know that the simply normative sample-based percentile ranks are still employable for the identification of BER.

Selecting Informants

Considerable research regarding choice of informants for behavioral and emotional screening measures remains conflicting in the sense that all raters show evidence of validity under some conditions (VanDeventer & Kamphaus, in press). In addition, there is no evidence to support combining raters to make a classification decision. Although this is an oft-advised practice (Jensen et al., 1999; Power et al., 1998; Verhulst, Dekker, & van der Ende, 1997), the advantage, or incremental validity, of combining ratings from multiple raters is not clearly supported according to reviews by Johnston and Murray (2003) and McFall (2005). Support for this conclusion may be found in studies (Biederman, Keenan, & Faraone, 1990; Lochman & the Conduct Problems Prevention Research Group, 1995) that have demonstrated that adding another informant added little variance to the identification process beyond that provided by the first informant. Jones, Dodge, Foster, and Nix (2002) concluded, similarly, that the effect of combining parent and teacher ratings was equal to or minimally better than that of the teacher-only rating.

Although correspondence is poor among parent, teacher, and self-report ratings, ample evidence exists to support the contention that each has potential utility for the identification of behavioral and emotional risk in children, depending on the context of use and outcome variables of interest. Research by Mattison, Carlson, Cantwell, and Asarnow (2007) supports earlier findings, which show that teachers rate externalizing and internalizing problems as well as or better than parents do. Similarly, Grills and Ollendick (2003) produced conflicting results, but some evidence supports the use of child and adolescent self-report measures of externalizing and internalizing symptomatology. More research is needed, however, as in one study, incarcerated male adolescents failed to identify their own risk (Vreugdenhil, van den Brink, Ferdinand, Wouters, & Doreleijers, 2006). We suggest, as have others (Levitt et al., 2007), that adolescents may be in the best position to report on their own BER as it relates to important future academic outcomes and personal adjustment. A more recent study found children to self-report more symptoms of psychopathology than reported by their parents (Vierhaus & Lohaus, 2008), and the 4-year longitudinal study in the BESS manual found the student ratings to be as predictive of later GPA as the teacher ratings.

In most cases, the practicalities of school-based screening will determine the selection of an informant. This is why it is reassuring to know the predictive validity research suggesting that teachers and students similarly are effective, with parents being less effective for predicting academic outcomes at school. Essentially, the practicalities of availability of informants and validity evidence suggest the following informants:

- teachers and parents at preschool and daycare settings;
- parents in pediatrician offices and other health care settings;
- teachers in elementary school and, perhaps middle school; and
- students in middle, high school, and colleges or universities.

We have learned these practicalities as a result of our experiences in applied settings, primarily thanks to the work of carrying out our screener development research grant in the Los Angeles Unified School District

(LAUSD), the nation's second largest. We found teachers willing and able to complete screeners at the kindergarten through the fifth-grade levels, but parents were difficult to capture. We had to give up collecting parent data after the first year of the grant. We found that many middle school teachers were not confident of their knowledge of the behavior and emotions of their students. Students, on the other hand, tolerated the screeners well, and, with appropriate staffing, we found that we could screen an entire middle school in less than 1 hour per academic year by collecting data simultaneously in all homerooms. A protocol for completing group screening in schools, developed by Dr. Bridget Dever, is given in Exhibit 10.1. The use of this script allows all school personnel to assist with the screening process, thus creating less than 1 hour of impact on instructional time per academic year.

Multiple Gates

Screening ideally should be implemented through a multiple-gating approach. This approach is consistent with the multitiered approach to service delivery advocated by prevention scientists (Weisz, Sandler, Durlak, & Anton, 2005) in that it narrows down the population and provides more intensive assessment only to those identified with BER. In a multiple-gating approach, the first gate generally entails all children being screened, which provides for a universal screening (universal assessment). Then, those children who are identified based on universal assessment pass into a second gate in which an additional assessment is provided (selected assessment). The selected assessment strategy often utilizes a more comprehensive, thorough tool (such as a full omnibus behavior rating scale) or an additional screener utilizing a different rater or informant. Finally, the children who continue to be identified as having significant BER through the selected assessment strategy are evaluated with a more comprehensive, individualized assessment as a third gate assessment (indicated assessment). This indicated, comprehensive assessment would be more aligned with a full diagnostic assessment and could result in a diagnosis or eligibility for services being offered. The multiple-gating approach allows progressively more precise, specific, and intensive assessments to be provided to students with increased levels of risk. This type of procedure has been shown to increase identification and diagnostic accuracy and to reduce costs resulting from inefficient identification (Hill et al., 2004; Lochman & the Conduct Problems Prevention Research Group, 1995; Walker & Severson, 1990).

One example of a multiple-gating screening procedure is the SSBD (Walker & Severson, 1992). The SSBD utilizes a three-stage process including teacher training and rankings (i.e., nomination), teacher ratings of child behavior, and classroom observations. The first stage consists of teachers rank ordering all of the students in their classroom on both externalizing

EXHIBIT 10.1
BESS Universal Screening Administration Protocol

Hi! My name is _____. I'm with a group that is trying to develop programs to help you learn better and feel better about your experiences in school. You will be asked to answer several questions about how you feel and how you have felt over the last few weeks. Please be honest in your responses as we will use this information to find ways to support students like you in this school and other schools. Unless we think you need specific support at this time, we will not share your answers with your teachers or parents. We are truly interested in your opinion so we can know more about students like you. This is *not a* test, and there are no right or wrong answers.

When you get the survey, don't start working. Please wait for me. We are all going to go through the instructions together. Some of you might have questions about some of the things that are asked, and I want everyone to hear the answers.

<Pass out packets now.>

Make sure you are using a #2 pencil. If you need a pencil, please raise your hand.

<Pass out pencils as needed.>

On the front of the survey, please print your first and last name in the area marked student's name. Please write one letter in each box beginning with the first box. Bubble in the same letters below.

<Walk around to be sure that every student writes his/her name. Without a name, we can't use their information.>

Please complete the boxes marked Date of Birth and Today's date. Make sure you write and bubble your information. Please also bubble in your grade and sex.

Please turn the booklet over to the back. Write and bubble your student ID number in the area labeled "Field A".

<Walk around to be sure that every student is on the back page now. They should be working on Field A only.>

Please open the booklet and follow along while I read the instructions:

<Read instructions from inside of BESS form aloud.>

If you want to change an answer that you've already marked, please erase it completely and fill in your new choice. If you do not understand one of the statements, please raise your hand and I'll come around to answer your question.

When you have finished, close your booklet and I will collect it. After I collect your completed survey, please work quietly at your desk until everyone else finishes. Please begin.

<When students are finished and all forms and pencils are collected.>

Thank you again for helping us. We really appreciate your honesty.

and internalizing behavior dimensions. Although all students are supposed to be considered, only the top 10 students in each dimension (externalizing and internalizing) are nominated and ranked in terms of the severity of their symptoms. Out of the 10 students nominated, the top three students in each category proceed through the first gate into the second gate assessment. The second gate assessment requires teachers to complete two rating scales: the Critical Events Index to discern whether the student has engaged in various significantly disruptive activities, such as being physically cruel to animals; and the Combined Frequency Index to gather information about adaptive and maladaptive behaviors. Students who exceed normative cut points on these two instruments proceed to stage three. The third gate assessment involves systematically observing the students in naturalistic school environments, including assessing for academic engaged time in the classroom and positive social interactions while on the playground. The results from this stage-three assessment are used to determine the next level of assessment or intervention that is appropriate, such as a referral for special education testing.

The BESS also has been used as part of a multiple-gate screening process. Following the administration of the BESS, children and youths who are identified as at risk then proceed to the second gate in which the BASC-2 (Reynolds & Kamphaus, 2004) is given. The BASC-2 has the advantage of having a comprehensive software interpretative system that links the three highest subscale scores on the BASC-2 directly to evidence-based interventions drawn from the *BASC-2 Intervention Guide* (BASC-2 IG; Vannest, Reynolds, & Kamphaus, 2008). This system helps school district personnel ensure that screening leads children with needs to appropriate interventions and, in the case of the BASC-2 IG, interventions supported by considerable empirical research (Glover & Albers, 2007).

The number of stages a screening process requires and the amount of personnel time required at each stage highlight the practical limitations of multiple-gating approaches. Practitioners should consider the time and resources that are available before implementing a screening system. It is still unknown whether multiple screening gates are, in fact, superior to single-stage screenings, and the optimal number of gates to be utilized is undecided. Multiple factors in addition to diagnostic accuracy should be considered, including the feasibility and cost-effectiveness of multiple-gate screening procedures. In fact, Lane et al. (2009) found the seven-item SRSS (Drummond, 1994) to perform comparatively to the three-stage SSBD for the identification of externalizing problems. Therefore, brevity may not denote inferiority. A study investigating a two-stage screening process using the BESS and the BASC-2, however, demonstrated that adding a comprehensive behavior rating scale as a second gate significantly improved identification accuracy over a single-gate procedure (VanDeventer & Kamphaus, in press). Furthermore, these questions require further research because many screening studies have estimated the effect of using multiple gates rather than actually implementing real-world multiple-gate screening procedure (VanDeventer & Kamphaus, in press; for a thorough discussion of multiple gating, universal screening, and related issues, see Chapter 3 in this volume).

Timing

A practitioner interested in screening should consider when the screener should be administered. For instance, in the context of screening in schools, a common time point may be as one enters a new school, such as before entrance to kindergarten, or as one transitions to middle school or high school. Vander Stoep et al. (2005), for example, targeted students during the transition from elementary to middle school in the Developmental Pathways Screening Program, suggesting that this was a critical transitional stage. Preschool screeners allow practitioners to identify problems early in their developmental trajectories (DiStefano & Kamphaus, 2007; Kamphaus & Reynolds, 2007). Time points involving transitions may be chosen for practicality reasons, as other paperwork or screeners commonly are administered at these times. Additionally, schools can get a sense of the potential problems that the new student body may have at an early stage, so early interventions can be planned accordingly. Research also shows that children may be particularly vulnerable to emotional or behavioral problems when they move to a new school (Csorba et al., 2001; Vander Stoep et al., 2005), which gives sufficient reason to screen for problems at this time.

BER Surveillance

Universal screening not only is useful for assessing BER in individual children but also may be used to assess the BER of groups, such as classrooms, schools, school district regions, or entire school districts, and to compare geographic regions and nations. Surveillance often has been used to track the spread of diseases, but the term is not used as often in the school screening literature, although the concept is equally applicable.

Citing the National Academies report, the goals of universal screening for BER are delineated as follows:

> The goals and design of these initiatives should be targeted to relatively narrow and specific purposes, for example, (1) improving school success for struggling students, (2) preventing bullying and student harassment, (3) improving teacher and peer relationships, (4) increasing school safety and security, or (5) learning to regulate and control behavior. (O'Connell et al., 2009, p. 230)

All five of these goals could be informed by universal screening for BER. Kamphaus, Dever, Raines, DiStefano, and Dowdy (2011) conducted a study of BER in the interest of meeting goal 4 in the previous quote: increasing school safety and security. They reviewed the literature on school screening and found that surveillance is being conducted in schools by the Centers for Disease Control and Prevention and some state departments of education or mental health. The measures used for this purpose assess a variety of risk behaviors (e.g., using tobacco and alcohol) but not BER. This conclusion was supported by a study by Dowdy, Furlong, and Sharkey (2013), who conducted a study of the California Healthy Kids Survey (CHKS). They found that supplementing the CHKS with a self-report measure of subsyndromal BER, the student BESS in this case, significantly increased the prediction of cigarette, marijuana, and alcohol use; binge drinking; physical fighting; threatening or injury by a weapon; skipping school; and serious consideration of suicide.

Brown and Grumet (2009) provided an example of a school-based surveillance study. They conducted clinical interviews to survey suicide risk in 13 middle and high schools in the Washington, D.C., area. Their study documented 45% of adolescents screened positive for "previous suicide attempt or ideation, symptoms of depression or anxiety, and/or other emotional problems" (Brown & Grumet, 2009, p. 111). Findings such as these may be used to guide prevention practices, including the deployment of mental health personnel in this case.

Permissions

Screening occurs in U.S. schools routinely and without controversy. Speech, hearing, health, and academic screening are just some examples. Academic achievement screening occurs most frequently, allowing schools to make numerous decisions about how to help a child achieve. The process of obtaining parental consent and student assent for screening remains controversial and conflicting, particularly with regard to screening for mental health disorders. Informed consent may be either active or passive (Eaton, Lowry, Brener, Grunbaum, & Kann, 2004) and commonly is decided by the respective school district and how they interpret the Protection of Pupil Rights Amendment (PPRA; Chartier et al., 2008). The PPRA "seeks to ensure that schools and contractors obtain written parental consent before minor students are required to participate in any U.S. Department of Education funded survey, analysis, or evaluation that reveals information concerning" (Chartier et al., 2008, p. 157) a variety of sensitive behaviors, such as political affiliation and sexual behavior and attitudes. One area included is "mental and psychological problems potentially embarrassing to the student and his/her family" (U.S. Department of Education, 2006). These guidelines can be interpreted in various ways; therefore, it is important to evaluate the differences between active and passive consent for mental health screening. Active consent requires that the written consent form be returned with a signature from a parent approving the screening. Passive consent requires that parents be provided with an explanation of the screening program in writing, with the option of declining to have their child participate by selecting this option and returning the passive consent form to their child's school. If the consent form is not returned, the parent is assumed to have given consent. Each of these methods has benefits and drawbacks.

The explicit parental consent received through active consent provides solid assurance of parent approval. Although this method appears legally sound, the sometimes lengthy and complicated process of distributing and collecting signed consent forms can introduce an element of bias in the sample. This bias may undermine the effectiveness of a universal screening approach whereby all individuals have equal opportunity for follow-up and resulting interventions. Active consent processes yield varying return rates from 34% to 67% (Eaton et al., 2004; Esbensen et al., 1996). The decreased sample size can be disadvantageous, as students who would benefit from the screener or services associated with it may miss out because of the active consent process. It is important that parents are informed of and have control over what their children are subjected to, but consent forms frequently are not returned and the children might be adversely affected. Chartier et al. (2008) found that after switching the school-based depression screening process from passive consent to active consent, participation decreased from 85% to 66%. The decrease in participation was not equivalent across subgroups of students, and the percentage of students positively screened for depression was reduced significantly. This illustrates how more stringent consent procedures potentially can reduce the effectiveness of the screener, in which at-risk populations may be less likely to be identified and served.

Terminology is important, however, and the legal literature on screening for BER is virtually nonexistent. In contrast, most of the consent literature cited here is accessed by using search terms associated with screening for the presence of a mental health disorder. The construct of BER differs somewhat in that when BER is present, most children identified will not have a mental health disorder requiring diagnosis, treatment, or psychotropic medication. It has been our experience to date that most school districts do not require active parental consent for universal screening, but they have required active parental consent for second gate assessment or individualized interventions for children for whom BER is identified. This consent and assent pattern could be emerging as the de facto standard (for a thorough discussion of implementation issues and universal screening as innovation, see Chapter 5 of this volume).

Mental Health Screening

The research on mental health screening is far larger than that on BER screening. In some ways, the differences between mental health and BER screening are more conceptual than functional or methodological. The basic principles of mental health screening, laid out by the World Health Organization in the 1960s (Wilson & Jungner, 1968), still hold today. The goal of mental health screening differs from that of BER screening. Whereas BER screening is concerned with the identification of behavioral and emotional problems that place a child at risk for developing a mental health disorder, mental health screening is aimed at the "early detection of disease" (O'Connell et al., 2009). Thus, communities and governments sponsor screening days and initiatives aimed at finding individuals with undetected disorders, including, in the United States, national depression, alcohol abuse and dependency, suicide, and eating disorders screening days (http://www. mentalhealthscreening.org/events/national-depression-screening-day.aspx).

Some of the functional and methodological differences characteristic of mental health screening include (a) a historical focus on adult populations with more recent attention to adolescent screening; (b) use of primary care, military, workplace, and emergency room settings to conduct screening; (c) employment of single-disorder assessment methods and measures where only one construct or disorder is the focus of the screen, such as depression; (d) a focus on detecting disorders that are documented as producing the poorest individual outcomes, for example, screening for alcohol abuse versus reading disability; (e) use of active patient or parental consent; and (f) inclusion of a near-in-time direct link to treatment where, for example, further assessment and treatment for the disorder may occur at the time of a positive screen in an emergency room setting.

These differing characteristics of mental health screening to some extent overlap with procedures, practices, and methods of BER screening. Much about mental health screening, however, can be used to inform BER screening in schools. The interested reader is referred to the five-decade history of this work as summarized by O'Connell et al. (2009).

CONCLUSION

It should be reassuring to children and their parents to know that BER screening increasingly is available for improving child well-being. Both a recognition of the need for the practice and the tools to do so are now in place. Conversely, a standard of practice is not yet in place. It takes considerable time and consensus to develop standards of practice regarding preferred settings, informants, consent and assent, and other issues discussed in this chapter and elsewhere. Some of the standards will be decided by research on BER screening and others by deliberation, compromise, and practicality. Nevertheless, it is about time that the leading work of the 1970s by Cowen et al. (1973), Reynolds (1979), and others be realized.

Evidence of long-term predictive validity of BER measures still is lacking, especially as screening practices lead to interventions designed to mitigate onset of disorders. We hope that this scientific gap can be closed relatively soon, so the practice of screening does not get too far in front of the science.

REFERENCES

Achenbach, T. M., & Rescorla, L. A. (2001). *Manual for the ASEBA School-Age Forms and Profiles*. Burlington: University of Vermont, Research Center for Children, Youth, and Families.

Atkins, M. S., Frazier, S. L., Adil, J. A., & Talbott, E. (2003). School-based mental health services in urban communities. In M. D. Weist, S. W. Evans, & N. A. Lever (Eds.), *Handbook of school mental health: Advancing practice and research* (pp. 165–178). New York, NY: Kluwer Academic/Plenum.

Biederman, J., Keenan, K., & Faraone, S. V. (1990). Parent-based diagnosis of attention deficit disorder predicts a diagnosis based on teacher report. *Journal of the American Academy of Child & Adolescent Psychiatry, 29,* 698–701. doi:10.1097/00004583-199009000-00004

Bradley, R., Doolittle, J., & Bartolotta, R. (2008). Building on the data and adding to the discussion: The experiences and outcomes of students with emotional disturbance. *Journal of Behavioral Education, 17,* 4–23. doi:10.1007/s10864-007-9058-6

Brown, M. M., & Grumet, J. G. (2009). School-based suicide prevention with African American youth in an urban setting. *Professional Psychology: Research and Practice, 40,* 111–117. doi:10.1037/a0012866

Campaign for Mental Health Reform. (2005). *A public health crisis: Children and adolescents with mental disorders* [Congressional briefing]. Retrieved from http://www.mhreform.org/kids

Catalano, R. F., Haggerty, K. P., Osterle, S., Fleming, C. B., & Hawkins, J. D. (2004). The importance of bonding to school for healthy development: Findings from the Social Development Research Group. *Journal of School Health, 74,* 252–261. doi:10.1111/j.1746-1561.2004.tb08281.x

Chartier, M., Vander Stoep, A., McCauley, E., Herting, J. R., Tracy, M., & Lymp, J. (2008). Passive versus active parental permission: Implications for the ability of school-based depression screening to reach youth at risk. *Journal of School Health, 78,* 157–164. doi:10.1111/j.1746-1561.2007.00278.x

Clark, C., Haines, M. M., Head, J., Klineberg, E., Arephin, M., Vilner, R., . . . Stansfeld, S. A. (2007). Psychological symptoms and physical health and health behaviours in adolescents: A prospective 2-year study in East London. *Addiction, 102,* 126–135. doi:10.1111/j.1360-0443.2006.01621.x

Costello, E. J., Mustillo, S., Erkanli, A., Keeler, G., & Angold, A. (2003). Prevalence and development of psychiatric disorders in childhood and adolescence. *Archives of General Psychiatry, 60,* 837–844. doi:10.1001/archpsyc.60.8.837

Cowen, E. L., Dorr, D., Clarfield, S. P., Kreling, B., McWilliams, S. A., Pokracki, F., . . . Wilson, A. B. (1973). The AML: A quick-screening device for early identification of school maladaption. *American Journal of Community Psychology, 1,* 12–35. doi:10.1007/BF00881243

Csorba, J., Rozsa, S., Vetro, A., Gadoros, J., Makra, J., Somogyi, E., . . . Kapornay, K. (2001). Family- and school-related stresses in depressed Hungarian children. *European Psychiatry, 16,* 18–26. doi:10.1016/S0924-9338(00)00531-9

Dever, B. V., Mays, K. L., Kamphaus, R. W., & Dowdy, E. (2012). The factor structure of the BASC-2 Behavioral and Emotional Screening System Teacher Form, Child/Adolescent. *Journal of Psychoeducational Assessment, 30,* 488–495. doi:10.1177/0734282912438869

Dickey, W. C., & Blumberg, S. J. (2004). Revisiting the factor structure of the Strengths and Difficulties Questionnaire: United States, 2001. *Journal of the American Academy of Child & Adolescent Psychiatry, 43,* 1159–1167. doi:10.1097/01.chi.0000132808.36708.a9

DiStefano, C., & Morgan, G. (2011). Examining classification criteria: A comparison of three cut score methods. *Psychological Assessment, 23,* 354–363. doi:10.1037/a0021745

DiStefano, C. A., & Kamphaus, R. W. (2007). Development and validation of a behavioral screening for preschool-age children. *Journal of Emotional and Behavioral Disorders, 15,* 93–102. doi:10.1177/10634266070150020401

Dobrez, D., Sasso, A. L., Holl, J., Shalowitz, M., Leon, S., & Budetti, P. (2001). Examining the cost of developmental and behavioral screening of preschool children in generic pediatric practice. *Pediatrics, 108,* 913–922. doi:10.1542/peds.108.4.913

Dowdy, E., Chin, J. K., Twyford, J. M., & Dever, B. V. (2011). A factor analytic investigation of the BASC-2 Behavioral and Emotional Screening System Parent Form: Psychometric properties, practical implications, and future directions. *Journal of School Psychology, 49,* 265–280. doi:10.1016/j.jsp.2011.03.005

Dowdy, E., Dever, B. V., DiStefano, C., & Chin, J. K. (2011). Screening for emotional and behavioral risk among students with limited English proficiency. *School Psychology Quarterly, 26,* 14–26. doi:10.1037/a0022072

Dowdy, E., Furlong, M. J., & Sharkey, J.D. (2013). Using surveillance of mental health to increase understanding of youth involvement in high risk behaviors: A value added analysis. *Journal of Emotional and Behavioral Disorders, 21,* 33–44. doi:10.1177/1063426611416817

Dowdy, E., Twyford, J. M., Chin, J. K., DiStefano, C. A., Kamphaus, R. W., & Mays, K. L. (2011). Factor structure of the BASC-2 Behavioral and Emotional Screening System Student Form. *Psychological Assessment, 23*, 379–387. doi:10.1037/a0021843

Drummond, T. (1994). *The Student Risk Screening Scale (SRSS)*. Grants Pass, OR: Josephine County Mental Health Program.

Eaton, D. K., Lowry, R., Brener, N. D., Grunbaum, J. A., & Kann, L. (2004). Passive versus active parental permission in school-based survey research: Does the type of permission affect prevalence estimates of risk behaviors? *Evaluation Review, 28*, 564–577. doi:10.1177/0193841X04265651

Eklund, K., Renshaw, T. L., Dowdy, E., Jimerson, S. R., Hart, S. R., Jones, C. N., & Earhart, J. (2009). Early identification of behavioral and emotional problems in youth: Universal screening versus teacher-referral identification. *California School Psychologist, 14*, 89–95.

Esbensen, F. A., Deschenes, E. P., Vogel, R. E., West, J., Arboit, K., & Harris, L. (1996). Active parental consent in school-based research: An examination of ethical and methodological issues. *Evaluation Review, 20*, 737–753. doi:10.1177/0193841X9602000605

Feeney-Kettler, K. A., Kratochwill, T. R., Kaiser, A. P., Henneter, M. L., & Kettler, R. J. (2010). Screening young children. *Assessment for Effective Intervention, 35*, 218–230. doi:10.1177/1534508410380557

Friedman, R. M., Katz-Leavy, J., Manderscheid, R. W., & Sondheimer, D. (1996). Prevalence of serious emotional disturbance in children and adolescents. In R. W. Manderscheid & M. A. Sonnenschein (Eds.), *Mental health, United States, 1996* (pp. 71–88). Rockville, MD: Center for Mental Health Services. doi:10.1037/e375732004-006

Glover, T., & Albers, C. (2007). Considerations for evaluating universal screening assessments. *Journal of School Psychology, 45*, 117–135. doi:10.1016/j.jsp.2006.05.005

Goodman, A., & Goodman, R. (2009). Strengths and Difficulties Questionnaire as a dimensional measure of child mental health. *Journal of the American Academy of Child & Adolescent Psychiatry, 48*, 400–403. doi:10.1097/CHI.0b013e3181985068

Goodman, R. (1997). The Strengths and Difficulties Questionnaire: A research note. *Journal of Child Psychology and Psychiatry, 38*, 581–586. doi:10.1111/j.1469-7610.1997.tb01545.x

Goodman, R. (1999). The extended version of the Strengths and Difficulties Questionnaire as a guide to child psychiatric cases and consequent burden. *Journal of Child Psychology and Psychiatry, 40*, 791–799. doi:10.1111/1469-7610.00494

Goodman, R. (2001). Psychometric properties of the Strengths and Difficulties Questionnaire. *Journal of the American Academy of Child & Adolescent Psychiatry, 40*, 1337–1345. doi:10.1097/00004583-200111000-00015

Goodman, R., & Scott, S. (1999). Comparing the Strengths and Difficulties Questionnaire and the Child Behavior Checklist: Is small beautiful? *Journal of Abnormal Child Psychology, 27*, 17–24. doi:10.1023/A:1022658222914

Grills, A. E., & Ollendick, T. H. (2003). Multiple informant agreement and the Anxiety Disorders Interview Schedule for parents and children. *Journal of the American Academy of Child & Adolescent Psychiatry, 42*, 30–40. doi:10.1097/00004583-200301000-00008

Hill, L. G., Lochman, J. E., Coie, J. D., Greenberg, M. T., & the Conduct Problems Prevention Research Group. (2004). Effectiveness of early screening for externalizing problems: Issues of screening accuracy and utility. *Journal of Consulting and Clinical Psychology, 72*, 809–820. doi:10.1037/0022-006X.72.5.809

Hysing, M., Eigen, I., Gillberg, C., Lie, S. A., & Lundervold, A. J. (2007). Chronic physical illness and mental health in children: Results from a large-scale population study. *Journal of Child Psychology and Psychiatry, 48*, 785–792. doi:10.1111/j.1469-7610.2007.01755.x

Ikeda, M. J., Neesen, E., & Witt, J. C. (2008). Best practices in universal screening. In A. Thomas & J. Grimes (Eds.), *Best practices in school psychology V* (pp. 721–734). Bethesda, MD: National Association of School Psychologists.

Jamieson, K., & Romer, D. (2005). A call to action on adolescent mental health. In D. L. Evans, E. B. Foa, R. E. Gur, H. Hendin, C. P. O'Brien, M. E. P. Seligman, & B. T. Walsh (Eds.), *Treating and preventing adolescent mental health disorders: What we know and what we don't know: A research agenda for improving the mental health of our youth* (pp. 617–623). New York, NY: Oxford University Press.

Jensen, P. S., Rubio-Stipec, M., Canino, G., Bird, H. R., Dulcan, M. K., Schwab-Stone, M. E., & Lahey, B. B. (1999). Parent and child contributions to diagnosis of mental disorder: Are both informants always necessary? *Journal of the American Academy of Child & Adolescent Psychiatry, 38*, 1569–1579. doi:10.1097/00004583-199912000-00019

Johnston, C., & Murray, C. (2003). Incremental validity in the psychological assessment of children and adolescents. *Psychological Assessment, 15*, 496–507. doi:10.1037/1040-3590.15.4.496

Jones, D., Dodge, K. A., Foster, E. M., & Nix, R. (2002). Early identification of children at risk for costly mental health service use. *Prevention Science, 3*, 247–256. doi:10.1023/A:1020896607298

Kamphaus, R. W., Dever, B. V., Raines, T. C., DiStefano, C., & Dowdy, E. (2011, August). *Implementation of an adolescent behavioral and emotional risk surveillance protocol in schools*. Poster session presented at the annual convention of the American Psychological Association, Washington, DC.

Kamphaus, R. W., DiStefano, C., Dowdy, E., Eklund, K., & Dunn, A. R. (2010). Determining the presence of a problem: Comparing two approaches for detecting youth behavioral risk. *School Psychology Review, 39*, 395–407. Retrieved from http://www.nasponline.org/publications/spr/39-3/spr393kamphaus.pdf

Kamphaus, R. W., & Reynolds, C. R. (2007). *BASC-2 Behavioral and Emotional Screening System*. Minneapolis, MN: Pearson Assessment.

Kauffman, J. M. (1999). How we prevent the prevention of emotional and behavioral disorders. *Exceptional Children, 65*, 448–468.

Lane, K. L., Carter, E. W., Pierson, M. R., & Glaeser, B. C. (2006). Academic, social, and behavioral characteristics of high school students with emotional disturbances or learning disabilities. *Journal of Emotional and Behavioral Disorders, 14,* 108–117. doi:10.1177/10634266060140020101

Lane, K. L., Kalberg, J. R., Parks, R. J., & Carter, E. W. (2008). Student Risk Screening Scale: Initial evidence for score reliability and validity at the high school level. *Journal of Emotional and Behavioral Disorders, 16,* 178–190. doi:10.1177/1063426608314218

Lane, K. L., Little, M. A., Casey, A. M., Lambert, W., Wehby, J., & Weisenbach, J. L. (2009). A comparison of systematic screening tools for emotional and behavior disorders. *Journal of Emotional and Behavioral Disorders, 17,* 93–105. doi:10.1177/1063426608326203

Lane, K. L., Oakes, W. P., Harris, P. J., Menzies, H. M., Cox, M. L., & Lambert, W. (2012). Initial evidence for the reliability and validity of the Student Risk Screening Scale for internalizing and externalizing behaviors at the elementary level. *Behavioral Disorders, 37,* 99–122.

Lane, K. L., Parks, R. J., Kalberg, J. R., & Carter, E. W. (2007). Systematic screening at the middle school level: Score reliability and validity of the Student Risk Screening Scale. *Journal of Emotional and Behavioral Disorders, 15,* 209–222. doi:10.1177/10634266070150040301

Levitt, J. M., Saka, N., Romanelli, L. H., & Hoagwood, K. (2007). Early identification of mental health problems in schools: The status of instrumentation. *Journal of School Psychology, 45,* 163–191. doi:10.1016/j.jsp.2006.11.005

Lloyd, J. W., Kauffman, J. M., Landrum, T. J., & Roe, D. L. (1991). Why do teachers refer pupils for special education? An analysis of referral records. *Exceptionality, 2,* 115–126. doi:10.1080/09362839109524774

Lochman, J. E., & the Conduct Problems Prevention Research Group. (1995). Screening of child behavior problems for prevention programs at school entry. *Journal of Consulting and Clinical Psychology, 63,* 549–559. doi:10.1037/0022-006X.63.4.549

Mattison, R. E., Carlson, G. A., Cantwell, D. P., & Asarnow, J. R. (2007). Teacher and parent ratings of children with depressive disorders. *Journal of Emotional and Behavioral Disorders, 15,* 184–192. doi:10.1177/10634266070150030501

McFall, R. M. (2005). Theory and utility: Key themes in evidence-based assessment: Comment on the special section. *Psychological Assessment, 17,* 312–323. doi:10.1037/1040-3590.17.3.312

McIntosh, K., Flannery, K., Sugai, G., Braun, D., & Cochrane, K. (2008). Relationships between academics and problem behavior in the transition from middle school to high school. *Journal of Positive Behavior Interventions, 10,* 243–255. doi:10.1177/1098300708318961

Meehl, P. E., & Rosen, A. (1955). Antecedent probability and the efficiency of psychometric signs, patterns, or cutting scores. *Psychological Bulletin, 52,* 194–216. doi:10.1037/h0048070

Mellor, D., & Stokes, M. (2007). The factor structure of the Strengths and Difficulties Questionnaire. *European Journal of Psychological Assessment, 23*, 105–112. doi:10.1027/1015-5759.23.2.105

O'Connell, M. E., Boat, T., & Warner, K. E. (Eds.). (2009). *Preventing mental, emotional, and behavioral disorders among young people: Progress and possibilities.* Washington, DC: National Academy Press.

Percy, A., McCrystal, P., & Higgins, K. (2008). Confirmatory factor analysis of the adolescent self-report Strengths and Difficulties Questionnaire. *European Journal of Psychological Assessment, 24*, 43–48. doi:10.1027/1015-5759.24.1.43

Power, T. J., Andrews, T. J., Eiraldi, R. B., Doherty, B. J., Ikeda, M. J., DuPaul, G. J., & Landau, S. (1998). Evaluating attention deficit hyperactivity disorder using multiple informants: The incremental utility of combining teacher with parent reports. *Psychological Assessment, 10*, 250–260. doi:10.1037/1040-3590.10.3.250

Reynolds, C. R. (1979). Should we screen preschoolers? *Contemporary Educational Psychology, 4*, 175–181. doi:10.1016/0361-476X(79)90073-0

Reynolds, C. R., & Kamphaus, R. W. (2004). *Behavior Assessment System for Children–Second Edition (BASC-2).* Bloomington, MN: Pearson.

Ringel, J. S., & Sturm, R. (2001). National estimates of mental health utilization and expenditure for children in 1998. *Journal of Behavioral Health Services and Research, 28*, 319–333. doi:10.1007/BF02287247

Rønning, J. A., Handegaard, B. H., Sourander, A., & Morch, W. T. (2004). The Strengths and Difficulties Self-Report Questionnaire as a screening instrument in Norwegian community samples. *European Child and Adolescent Psychiatry, 13*, 73–82. doi:10.1007/s00787-004-0356-4

Ruchkin, V., Jones, S., Vermeiren, R., & Schwab-Stone, M. (2008). The Strengths and Difficulties Questionnaire: The self-report version in American urban and suburban youth. *Psychological Assessment, 20*, 175–182. doi:10.1037/1040-3590.20.2.175

Ruchkin, V., Koposov, R., & Schwab-Stone, M. (2007). The Strength and Difficulties Questionnaire: Scale validation with Russian adolescents. *Journal of Clinical Psychology, 63*, 861–869. doi:10.1002/jclp.20401

Severson, H. H., Walker, H. M., Hope-Doolittle, J., Kratochwill, T. R., & Gresham, F. M. (2007). Proactive, early screening to detect behaviorally at-risk students: Issues, approaches, emerging innovations, and professional practices. *Journal of School Psychology, 45*, 193–223. doi:10.1016/j.jsp.2006.11.003

U.S. Department of Education. (1995). *Educational programs that work.* Retrieved from www.ed.gov/pubs/EPTW/eptw12/eptw12h.html

U.S. Department of Education. (2006). *IDEA regulations: Early intervention services.* Retrieved from http://idea.ed.gov

U.S. Public Health Service. (2000). *Report of the Surgeon General's Conference on Children's Mental Health: A national action agenda.* Washington, DC: Department of Health and Human Services. Retrieved from http://www.surgeon general.gov/topics/cmh/childreport.htm

Vander Stoep, A., McCauley, E., Thompson, K. A., Herting, J. R., Kuo, E. S., Stewart, D. G., . . . Kushner, S. (2005). Universal emotional health screening at the middle school transition. *Journal of Emotional and Behavioral Disorders, 13*, 213–223. doi:10.1177/10634266050130040301

VanDeventer, M. C., & Kamphaus, R. W. (in press). *Universal emotional and behavioral screening for children and adolescents: Prospects and pitfalls.* New York, NY: Springer.

Van Leeuwen, K., Meerschaert, T., Bosmans, G., De Medts, L., & Braet, C. (2006). The Strengths and Difficulties Questionnaire in a community sample of young children in Flanders. *European Journal of Psychological Assessment, 22*, 189–197. doi:10.1027/1015-5759.22.3.189

Vannest, K. M., Reynolds, C. R., & Kamphaus, R. W. (2008). *Behavior Assessment System for Children–Second Edition (BASC-2): Intervention guide (BASC-2 IG).* Bloomington, MN: Pearson.

Van Roy, B., Veenstra, M., & Clench-Aas, J. (2008). Construct validity of the five-factor Strengths and Difficulties Questionnaire (SDQ) in pre-, early, and late adolescence. *Journal of Child Psychology and Psychiatry, 49*, 1304–1312. doi:10.1111/j.1469-7610.2008.01942.x

Verhulst, F. C., Dekker, M. C., & van der Ende, J. (1997). Parent, teacher, and self-reports as predictors of signs of disturbance in adolescents: Whose information carries the most weight? *Acta Psychiatrica Scandinavica, 96*, 75–81. doi:10.1111/j.1600-0447.1997.tb09909.x

Vierhaus, M., & Lohaus, A. (2008). Children and parents as informants of emotional and behavioural problems predicting female and male adolescent risk behaviour: A longitudinal cross-informant study. *Journal of Youth and Adolescence, 37*, 211–224. doi:10.1007/s10964-007-9193-3

Vreugdenhil, C., van den Brink, W., Ferdinand, R., Wouters, L., & Doreleijers, T. (2006). The ability of YSR scales to predict DSM/DISC-C psychiatric disorders among incarcerated male adolescents. *European Child and Adolescent Psychiatry, 15*, 88–96. doi:10.1007/s00787-006-0497-8

Wagner, M., Kutash, K., Duchnowski, A., & Epstein, M. (2005). The Special Education Elementary Longitudinal Study and the National Longitudinal Transition Study: Study designs and implications for children and youth with emotional disturbance. *Journal of Emotional and Behavioral Disorders, 13*, 25–41. doi:10.1177/10634266050130010301

Walker, H., & Severson, H. (1990). *Systematic screening for behavior disorders (SSBD).* Longmont, CO: Sopris West.

Walker, H. M., & Severson, H. (1992). *Systematic screening for behavior disorders* (2nd ed.). Longmont, CO: Sopris West.

Weisz, J. R., Sandler, I. N., Durlak, J. A., & Anton, B. S. (2005). Promoting and protecting youth mental health through evidence-based prevention and treatment. *American Psychologist, 60*, 628–648. doi:10.1037/0003-066X.60.6.628

Wilson, J. M. G., & Jungner, G. (1968). *Principles and practices of screening for disease.* Geneva, Switzerland: World Health Organization.

11

UNIVERSAL SCREENING OF ENGLISH LANGUAGE LEARNERS: LANGUAGE PROFICIENCY AND LITERACY

CRAIG A. ALBERS AND PAIGE L. MISSION

Much has been made of the increasing number of linguistically diverse students (hereafter referred to as English language learner [ELL] students) within schools throughout the United States. The changing demographics of our schools—particularly relating to ELL students—have drawn increasing media coverage and have resulted in legislation with specific implications for ELL populations, increasing recognition of the achievement gaps between many ELL and non-ELL students as well as the proliferation of materials that are intended to assist educators who work with ELL students. It is quite clear, however, that research examining issues relevant to ELL students continues to lag behind other education-specific priorities (e.g., Albers, Hoffman, &

The contents of this chapter were developed in part by a Grant Award (R305A100585) from the U.S. Department of Education, Institute for Education Sciences to Craig A. Albers, Thomas R. Kratochwill, and David Kaplan at the University of Wisconsin—Madison. The contents do not necessarily represent the policy of the U.S. Department of Education, and you should not assume endorsement by the federal government.

http://dx.doi.org/10.1037/14316-011
Universal Screening in Educational Settings: Evidence-Based Decision Making for Schools, R. J. Kettler, T. A. Glover, C. A. Albers, and K. A. Feeney-Kettler (Editors)
Copyright © 2014 by the American Psychological Association. All rights reserved.

Lundahl, 2009); one area that clearly illustrates the research gap between non-ELL and ELL students relates to the examination of universal screening procedures within ELL populations. Although academically based screening systems for nonlinguistically diverse students have been developed widely (e.g., see Chapter 6, Chapter 7, Chapter 8, and Chapter 9 in this volume) and are used frequently, less is known about culturally and linguistically appropriate screening systems and assessment tools. Thus, this chapter examines what is known and unknown regarding the universal screening of ELL students within the domains of English language proficiency (ELP) and literacy skills.

CHARACTERISTICS OF THE ELL POPULATION

Given the heterogeneity of ELL populations, any discussion regarding the implementation of universal screening procedures with ELL populations requires a thorough understanding of multiple variables, including relevant demographic characteristics. These characteristics include (a) ELL definition issues; (b) population estimates; (c) native languages; (d) achievement outcomes; (e) social, emotional, and behavioral outcomes; and (f) consequences associated with outcomes later in life.

Demographics of ELL Students

Definitions

Federal legislation, such as the No Child Left Behind Act (NCLB; Public Law 107-110, Part A, Sect. 9101 (25)(A-D)) of 2001, defines an ELL (referred to as limited English proficient) as

an individual—

(A) who is aged 3 through 21;
(B) who is enrolled or preparing to enroll in an elementary school or secondary school;
(C)(i) who was not born in the United States or whose native language is a language other than English;
 (ii)(I) who is a Native American or Alaska Native, or a native resident of the outlying areas; and
  (II) who comes from an environment where a language other than English has had a significant impact on the individual's level of English language proficiency; or
 (iii) who is migratory, whose native language is a language other than English, and who comes from an environment where a language other than English is dominant; and

(D) whose difficulties in speaking, reading, writing, or understanding
   the English language may be sufficient to deny the individual—
   (i) the ability to meet the State's proficient level of achievement on
      State assessments described in section 1111(b)(3);
   (ii) the ability to successfully achieve in classrooms where the lan-
      guage of instruction is English; or
   (iii) the opportunity to participate fully in society.

As will be described later in the discussion regarding the use of ELP measures, each state education agency is allowed to operationalize the definition of an ELL as they see appropriate. This approach results in variations among states regarding which students are considered ELL students, which students are entitled to language-related services, and how accountability indices are calculated. This also has implications for conducting universal screening with ELL students, as ELP is a critical variable to consider in interpreting data.

Population Estimates

Population estimates regarding the number of ELL students living within the United States, as well as the number of ELL students enrolled in public schools, are highly variable. Each estimate, however, tends to be consistent in two areas: (a) clearly, a significant number of ELL students are enrolled within public schools; and (b) the growth of ELL students within schools far outpaces the growth of students from other groups. Overall, the ELL population enrolled in U.S. public schools during the 2010–2011 academic year was approximately 4.5 million students (U.S. Department of Education, 2011a). Although the five largest states in terms of ELL enrollment (i.e., California, Florida, Illinois, New York, Texas) accounted for close to 2.9 million ELL students, approximately 67% of all schools within the United States had at least one ELL student enrolled (U.S. Department of Education, 2009). Nebraska and North Carolina, which are two states with relatively limited prior experience in providing services to ELL students, experienced ELL growth rates of 301% and 372% between 1996 and 2006 (Batalova, Fix, & Murray, 2006). Furthermore, U.S. Census Bureau (2011) estimates indicate that an even higher number of school-age individuals speak a language other than English at home, suggesting that the number of students enrolled in U.S. schools who may not be truly proficient in English is much higher than enrollment estimates. Finally, by 2030, estimates suggest that 40% of the school population will speak English as a second language (L2; U.S. Department of Education & National Institute of Child Health and Human Development, 2003). Consequently, schools that have not had ELL students to provide services to in the past are highly likely to have ELL students enroll in the near future.

Languages

Approximately 81% of the ELL students enrolled in U.S. public schools report Spanish as their primary language (Office of English Language Acquisition, Language Enhancement, and Academic Achievement for Limited English Proficient Students, 2012). The variety of languages spoken within U.S. schools is diverse, however, with more than 150 languages represented (U.S. Census Bureau, 2011). Although 43 states indicated Spanish to be the most frequent language spoken by ELL students, 7 states (i.e., Alabama, Hawaii, Maine, Montana, North Dakota, South Dakota, Vermont) have indicated that Spanish was not the most frequently spoken language by ELL students. For example, the most common language spoken by ELL students in Maine was Somali, whereas in North Dakota the most common language spoken by ELL students was Ojibwa. Thus, this heterogeneity within the ELL population requires that universal screening procedures be developed with more than just a consideration of Spanish-speaking students.

Achievement Outcomes

Data illustrate that as a group, ELL students generally display the lowest academic achievement scores and drop out of school at the highest rates of all public school students (McCardle, Mele-McCarthy, Cutting, Leos, & D'Emilio, 2005). These achievements gaps exist whether they are measured by state achievement tests (e.g., Abedi, 2004; Jimenez, 2004; Ruiz de Velasco & Fix, 2002) or national tests. For example, on the 2011 National Assessment of Educational Progress, fourth-grade ELL students scored 24 points below non-ELL students in math and 36 points below non-ELL students in reading. Gaps among eighth-grader students were even larger—41 points in math and 43 points in reading (U.S. Department of Education, 2011b). The most recent *Biennial Report to Congress on the Implementation of the State Formula Grant Program, 2006–2008* (Office of English Language Acquisition, Language Enhancement, and Academic Achievement for Limited English Proficient Students, 2012) indicated that the majority of states did not meet their annual measurable achievement objectives for increasing ELP, reading and English language arts, and math.

Behavioral, Social, and Emotional Outcomes

ELL status may place linguistic and other culturally diverse students at an elevated risk for emotional difficulties. For example, the U.S. Department of Health and Human Services (2001) emphasized that "Hispanic American youth are at significantly higher risk for poor mental health than white youth are by virtue of higher rates of depressive and anxiety symptoms, as well as higher rates of suicidal ideation and suicide attempts" (p. 11). Among other difficulties, anxiety in particular can negatively affect a child's ability to achieve proficiency in a new language (Hamayan & Damico, 1991), and some evidence indicates that anxiety about speaking English may even put some bilingual children at risk for such disorders as selective mutism (Esquivel & Keitel, 1990).

ELL students—particularly those who also are classified as immigrants—often are exposed to additional situations that are associated with mental health difficulties. These can include factors such as lifestyle changes and separation from family members who remained in their native country (Gopaul-McNicol & Thomas-Presswood, 1998). Children of migrant farmworker families may face specific challenges requiring professionals to consider their background (e.g., war or other trauma in their native country), language, and other factors that could be affecting sufficient acquisition of language (e.g., prejudice in the community; Henning-Stout, 1996). Schools may not be informed of a child's background history or the additional stressors that could affect the child (Albers, Mission, & Bice-Urbach, 2013).

The possibility for misidentification in ELL students is also an important consideration for social–emotional and behavioral assessment. ELL students may appear to have behavioral, social, or emotional issues because of language differences. Espinosa (2005) stated that "their ability to speak and understand English may be overestimated and their general cognitive and social abilities underestimated" (p. 849). This overestimation of English-speaking ability may be due to a lack of understanding among educators about the language acquisition process, with misdiagnosis and misidentification resulting from a lack of understanding of language ability and cultural factors. For example, a child's lack of interaction with other students or adults could be interpreted as a lack of appropriate social skills, anxiety regarding speaking in social situations, and so on, when in reality the child's failure to speak in social situations may be the result of limited listening and speaking proficiency in English. Therefore, careful consideration of language and cultural factors as they relate to the individual student is necessary to ensure an accurate consideration of social, emotional, and behavioral factors.

Consequences for Future Outcomes

A significant amount of research has suggested that the educational, occupational, economic, social, and health-related outcomes for first- and second-generation immigrants are significantly poor (Larsen, 2004; U.S. Census Bureau, 2004). These individuals not only tend to experience more academic difficulties but also experience disproportionately elevated rates of serious physical and mental health challenges, such as HIV/AIDS, asthma, diabetes, and infant mortality, as well as depression, anxiety, and suicidal behavior (U.S. Department of Health and Human Services, 2011). Despite these negative health outcomes, linguistically diverse individuals frequently are without health insurance that will cover the cost of medical or psychological care (U.S. Census Bureau, 2004). As a result, immigrant families as a group are more burdened by physical and mental health difficulties than any other ethnic or racial group in the United States as they often struggle to cope with debilitating conditions without many of the resources and support services that are more accessible to others (López, 2002). Thus, a prevention framework should consider high-quality education to be a protective factor for a wide variety of difficulties, and therefore preventing academic failure among language-minority students must be one of the leading priorities in today's school system. Universal screening is a critical component of such a prevention framework because it provides a formal data-based structure for identifying students who are in need of additional educational supports, as limited ELP not only often presents barriers to academic performance but also tends to delay the identification of learning and emotional difficulties that are hindering their progress.

CRITICAL COMPONENTS TO CONSIDER WITHIN A UNIVERSAL SCREENING SYSTEM FOR ELL STUDENTS

Abedi (2011) has reported that "language factors have a much more profound effect on ELL students than on native speakers of English" (p. 57). This inherent problem in universal screening tools, which largely have been developed for, validated on, and distributed across white middle-class populations, is based on cultural concerns. An overreliance on culture, which includes linguistic elements, to determine aspects of learning and development that are important to test threatens the usage of universal screening tools in such populations as ELL students. The language acquisition process, as experienced by bi- or multilingual students, differs from that of monolingual students. Rhodes, Ochoa, and Ortiz (2005) emphasized the importance of recognizing such differences. For example, students who are native English speakers receive nearly 22,000 hours of exposure to the English language before their formal schooling begins at age 5 years. Conversely, a student who speaks another language at home receives less than 4,000 hours of exposure to the English language. Recognizing that such a difference exists must be taken into account throughout the development and use of universal screening tools (Lembke, 2010). Responding to teacher, community, and family-based concerns throughout the implementation of screening procedures, as well as in the creation and standardization of both academic and social–emotional screening systems, will establish practices that more likely will be effective (Barrera, Corso, & Macpherson, 2003).

In an academic context, because positive student outcomes are highly associated with high-quality reading instruction at the classroom level, concerns regarding the lack of high-quality instruction for ELL students limit the extent to which screening practices can even presume that a lack of responsiveness to instruction exists (Haager, Calhoon, & Linan-Thompson, 2007). Fortunately, some evidence exists regarding the effectiveness of word-level instructional components with ELL students (e.g., explicit teaching of phonological awareness). Sustained concerns regarding the validity and acceptability of current curriculum-based measures (CBM) by teachers—particularly with ELL students—remains a significant point of contention that likely has thwarted the development of screening practices with ELL students (Haager et al., 2007). Although it is unclear whether research supports the inclusion of ELL students in the creation of progress-monitoring tools that are used for native English speakers, there is clearly a lack of evidence regarding the validity and usability of such progress-monitoring tools with ELL students. Regardless, in practice, such progress-monitoring tools as CBMs are used to track the responsiveness of ELL students to instruction as well as to other curricular activities.

Unlike universal screening procedures that are used for non-ELL students, the core characteristic of ELL students (i.e., lack of ELP) requires that all universal screening procedures incorporate consideration of academic ELP into the process. Although potentially many relevant variables and components are associated with the universal screening of ELL students, critical components consist of (a) academic language proficiency and (b) consideration of the instructional model being utilized.

Basic Interpersonal Communication Skills, Cognitive Academic Language Proficiency, and Academic Language Proficiency

ELP is a multidimensional construct consisting of various interrelated language components. These components are typically referred to as Basic Interpersonal Communication Skills (BICS), Cognitive Academic Language Proficiency (CALP), and academic language proficiency, each of which is described in more detail in the sections that follow.

Definitions

BICS and CALP were introduced by Cummins (1979), and were defined as the distinction between a person's linguistic conversational skills and the linguistic abilities that are required for academic success. The essential purpose of this distinction was to highlight the different time periods in which children, specifically immigrant children, develop conversational fluency for social interactions in their L2 in comparison to the more complex linguistic fluency in L2 that enables school success. Cummins (2008) predicted that BICS can be developed in approximately 2 years or more, whereas CALP—an academic level more comparable to that of a native speaker—may take as long as 5 years or more.

The BICS/CALP distinction has significant instructional implications for ELL students. A significant consequence for failing to understand the differences between BICS and CALP is the premature promotion of ELL students from English as a second language (ESL) classes into mainstream classes where they receive little to no linguistic support (Cummins, 1999). This frequently leads to academic failure, especially when teachers have a poor understanding of the difference between a student's ability to converse in English and his or her ability to navigate the cognitively demanding language used in textbooks and other classroom content. Another repercussion of this misunderstanding is the mislabeling of ELL students as having a specific learning disability when it is assumed that their English abilities are sufficient for valid psychological testing or typical academic achievement trajectories.

Despite the popularity of the BICS/CALP dichotomy, the work by Cummins (1999) has not been without criticism. For example, some have emphasized that academic language is diverse in that it envelops multiple and evolving literacies from unique disciplines and standards of discourse. This view leads to the notion that academia should be more tolerant to non-traditional varieties of expression. This view is also unrealistic, however, in that individuals who fail to develop CALP inevitably will be marginalized and penalized in academic settings. Scarcella (2003) rejected Cummins's perspective and the multiple literacies notion and presented an alternative view that academic language includes multiple, dynamic, interrelated competencies. She presented four discrete skills (reading, writing, speaking, and listening) across three dimensions (linguistic, cognitive, and socio–psychological). The linguistic dimension contains specific features of phonological, lexical, grammatical, sociological, and discourse knowledge. The cognitive dimension includes declarative and procedural knowledge, higher order thinking, strategy use, and metalinguistic awareness. The socio–psychological dimension has components surrounding social context and practices, such as typical beliefs, motivations, and behaviors. Scarcella's detailed explanations of these interrelated elements and dimensions of academic language must be further elaborated and developed to create a standard definition of academic language and academic language proficiency that can be used widely in classrooms, curricula, and assessments.

Thus, although obtaining academic language proficiency is perhaps the most critical variable associated with academic success (Francis, Rivera, Lesaux, Kieffer, & Rivera, 2006) for ELL students, there has been limited research regarding the concept of academic language, and the varying definitions illustrate the lack of consensus regarding what academic language actually consists of. Federal legislation (e.g., NCLB) considers academic language as a broad composite of oral communication skills, listening communication skills, reading skills, and writing skills; however, until there is greater agreement regarding specific components of academic language and the corresponding definition, practitioners should adhere to their state's definition of academic language, which usually is contained within their state ELP standards.

Language Growth

As made possible by the nationally mandated collection of academic English proficiency data for all ELL students, Cook, Boals, Wilmes, and Santos (2008) collected data on 12,836 ELL students from three states over the course of 3 years (2005–2007) that yielded important implications regarding targeted annual increases in the amount of children making progress in learning English and in attaining English proficiency. In general, their evidence emphasized one key finding that "lower is faster, higher is slower," meaning that lower grades and proficiency levels have faster growth with more students gaining proficiency levels annually and that higher grades and proficiency levels have slower growth with fewer students gaining proficiency levels annually. This implies that "one-size-fits-all" growth expectations across the continuum of ELP are not appropriate; rather, expectations should be tailored to students' proficiency and grade levels.

Slama (2012) completed a longitudinal analysis of academic English proficiency outcomes for adolescent ELL students and further refined the current knowledge regarding language proficiency growth trajectories by considering the impact of generational status. Results indicated that although U.S.-born ELL students began high school with greater levels of academic ELP than foreign-born ELL students, by the end of high school, levels of academic ELP were similar, despite the fact that U.S.-born ELL students already had spent more than 9 years in U.S. schools. Furthermore, both U.S.-born and foreign-born students continued to display relatively low levels of academic language proficiency throughout high school. Thus, according to Slama, the results suggest that the amount of time frequently reported as necessary to reach academic language proficiency probably is underestimated.

A number of moderator and mediator variables also have been identified that appear to be relevant in explaining the heterogeneity of ELL academic language proficiency growth trajectories. Examples include generational status, age, and previous education at arrival in the United States, instructional model at school, exposure to English outside of school, parents' educational attainment, degree of international and domestic mobility, acculturation into U.S. society, and socioeconomic status. Although the specific contributions of these variables still are being examined, it is clear that each of these variables is a logical contributor to first and second language experiences and academic motivation.

Instructional Approaches and Models

The three broad instructional *approaches* for providing academic services to ELL students include (a) ESL, (b) bilingual approaches, and (c) transitional approaches. According to the U.S. Department of Education (2012), ESL approaches emphasize the provision of instruction in English, whereas bilingual approaches utilize the student's native language to assist in developing English proficiency. In transitional approaches, students transition from a bilingual to an English-only approach after reaching a certain grade level. Instructional *models* are

> a specific set of instructional services or a fully developed curriculum designed to help English learners acquire proficiency and meet high academic standards . . . and serves as a rough blueprint that classrooms, schools and districts may follow as an implementation guide. (U.S. Department of Education, 2012, p. ix)

A wide number of instructional models are used throughout schools in the United States, including the more common models of (a) developmental bilingual education, (b) dual immersion, (c) structured English immersion, (d) transitional bilingual education, and (e) newcomer services.

Data suggest that bilingual approaches tend to produce more positive outcomes than ESL approaches; for example, the National Literacy Panel's meta-analysis of studies on the effectiveness of various instructional approaches reports that bilingual education models seem to have a positive, small to moderate effect on English reading outcomes (August & Shanahan, 2006). Recent research (e.g., Irby et al., 2010; Slavin, Madden, Calderon, Chamberlain, & Hennessy, 2011), however, suggests that the more critical factor might actually be the quality of the specific instructional practices and implemented curriculum. Thus, it becomes apparent that the specific instructional approach, model, and implementation quality are essential variables to consider when conducting literacy universal screening with ELL students.

LANGUAGE PROFICIENCY SCREENING WITH ELL STUDENTS

The identification of a student who is learning English as an additional language is critical for (a) meeting federal accountability requirements and (b) making appropriate decisions regarding placement, services, and monitoring purposes. Approaches to accomplish this identification include the use of home language surveys (HLS), parent language questionnaires (PLQ), and ELP assessments. States, however, use different ELP standards, use different definitions and criteria for determining ELP, and also have different exit criteria. Thus, there is no guarantee that a student who is considered an ELL in one state would be considered an ELL in a different state.

Home Language and Parent Language Surveys

Federal legislation (e.g., NCLB) requires that states identify all students who are learning English as an additional language. To accomplish this requirement, states implement a multiple-gate procedure for determining ELL status (for a thorough discussion of multiple gating, universal screening, and related issues, see Chapter 3 in this volume). As seen in Table 11.1, HLSs and PLQs are used as an initial language proficiency screening by each of the 50 states. If the responses to the HLS or PLQ indicate that a student may be considered as a non-native English-speaking student, the student then is administered a language proficiency measure for screening of English proficiency status.

Questions exist regarding the reliability and validity of HLSs and PLQs. For example, Bailey and Kelly (2010) suggested that the use of these surveys threatens the validity of the language identification process. In particular, the evidentiary basis of using these surveys has not been explored adequately; thus, it is possible that the use of HLSs and PLQs results in the failure to identify a student as a possible ELL (i.e., false negative), which deprives the student of legally entitled services and removes the school district from being held accountable for the student's progress in attaining ELP. The primary threat to the validity of HLSs and PLQs is that parental responses to the questions can be influenced by multiple factors, including (a) concerns regarding citizenship status, (b) concerns regarding possible discrimination because of their language status, and (c) the possibility that the parents are not able to understand the survey because of language differences. Thus, when determining whether to implement a universal screening process, or when interpreting universal screening data, it is essential to remember that some students actually may be non-native English-speaking students who simply have not been identified as such. Consequently, if there are questions regarding whether a student who was not determined to be an ELL actually should be considered as an ELL, the student's classroom teachers should be asked questions about the student that help determine whether his or her level of language proficiency is "surface-level proficiency" or "conceptual-linguistic proficiency," such as the preferred language used at home or the type of language programs that the child has been offered or has participated in (Scribner, 2002).

TABLE 11.1
English Language Proficiency Identification Procedures by State

State	HLS (H) or PLQ (P)	W-APT	AZELLA	ELDA	CELDT	LAS	CELLA	ELPA	LAB-R or LAB-RS	NYSESLAT	OTELA	TELPAS	UALPA	Qualification as ELL if—
AL	H	X												(a) PHL other than English, and (b) W-APT score
AK	P	X												(a) PHL other than English or if the student is an Alaskan Native, Native American, or a native resident from outlying areas and who comes from an environment where a language other than English has had a significant impact on the individual's level of English language proficiency, and (b) W-APT score
AZ	H		X											(a) PHL other than English, and (b) AZELLA score
AR	H			X										(a) PHL other than English, and (b) ELDA score
CA	H				X									(a) PHL other than English, and (b) CELDT score
CO	H	X												(a) PHL other than English, and (b) W-APT score
CT	H					X								(a) PHL other than English, and (b) LAS score
DE	H	X												(a) PHL other than English, and (b) W-APT score
DC	H	X												(a) PHL other than English, and (b) W-APT score
FL	H						X							(a) PHL other than English, and (b) CELLA score
GE	H	X												(a) PHL other than English, and (b) W-APT score

HI	H	X				(a) PHL other than English, and (b) W-APT score
ID	H				X	(a) PHL other than English, and (b) ELPA score
IL	H	X				(a) PHL other than English, and (b) W-APT score
IN	H			X		(a) PHL other than English, and (b) LAS score
IA	H		X			(a) PHL other than English, and (b) ELDA score
KS	H				X	(a) PHL other than English, and (b) ELPA score
KY	H	X				(a) PHL other than English, and (b) W-APT score
LA	H		X			(a) PHL other than English, and (b) ELDA score
ME	H	X				(a) PHL other than English, and (b) W-APT score
MD	H	X				(a) PHL other than English, and (b) W-APT score
MA	H	X				(a) PHL other than English, and (b) W-APT score
MI	H				X	(a) PHL other than English, and (b) ELPA score
MN	H	X				(a) PHL other than English, and (b) W-APT score
MS	H	X				(a) PHL other than English, and (b) W-APT score or a composite score of 4.9 or below on the Tier B form of the WIDA-ACCESS test
MO	H	X				(a) PHL other than English, and (b) W-APT score
MT	H	X				(a) PHL other than English, and (b) W-APT score

(continues)

TABLE 11.1
English Language Proficiency Identification Procedures by State (Continued)

State	HLS (H) or PLQ (P)	W-APT	AZELLA	ELDA	CELDT	LAS	CELLA	ELPA	LAB-R or LAB-RS	NYSESLAT	OTELA	TELPAS	UALPA	Qualification as ELL if—
NE	H			X										(a) PHL other than English, and (b) ELDA score
NV	H	X												(a) PHL other than English, and (b) W-APT score
NH	H	X												(a) PHL other than English, and (b) W-APT score
NJ	H	X												(a) PHL other than English, and (b) W-APT score
NM	H	X												(a) PHL other than English, and (b) W-APT score
NY	H								X	X				(a) PHL other than English, and (b) Language Arts Battery–Revised (LAB-R) or a Spanish language proficiency score on the LAB-Spanish (for Spanish-speaking students, who do not pass the LAB-R), and on the New York State English as a Second Language Achievement Test (NYSESLAT) for the purposes of placement.
NC	H	X												(a) PHL other than English, and (b) W-APT score
ND	H	X												(a) PHL other than English, and (b) W-APT score
OH	H										X			(a) PHL other than English, and (b) OTELA score
OK	H	X												(a) PHL other than English, and (b) W-APT score
OR	H							X						(a) PHL other than English, and (b) ELPA score

State						Identification criteria
PA	H	X				(a) PHL other than English, and (b) W-APT score
PR	H	X				(a) PHL other than English, and (b) W-APT score
RI	H	X				(a) PHL other than English, and (b) W-APT score
SC	H	X				(a) PHL other than English, and (b) ELDA score
SD	H	X				(a) PHL other than English, and (b) W-APT score
TN	H	X				(a) PHL other than English, and (b) ELDA score
TX	H			X		(a) PHL other than English, and (b) TELPAS score
UT	H				X	(a) PHL other than English, and (b) U-ALPA score
VT	H	X				(a) PHL other than English, and (b) W-APT score
VA	H	X				(a) PHL other than English, and (b) W-APT score
WA	X		X			(a) PHL other than English, and (b) WELPA score
WV	X	X				(a) PHL other than English, and (b) ELDA score
WI	X	X				(a) PHL other than English, and (b) W-APT score
WY	X	X				(a) PHL other than English, and (b) W-APT score

Note. AZELLA = Arizona English Language Learner Assessment; CELDT = California English Language Development Test; CELLA = Comprehensive English Language Learning Assessment; ELDA = English Language Development Assessment; ELPA = English Language Proficiency Assessment; HLS = Home-Language Survey; LAB-R = Language Arts Battery-Revised; LAB-RS = Language Arts Battery–Revised Spanish Version; LAS = Language Assessment Scales; NYSESLAT = New York State English as a Second Language Achievement Test; OTELA = Ohio Test of English Language Acquisition; PHL = primary home language; PLQ = Parent Language Questionnaire; TELPAS = Texas English Language Proficiency Assessment System; UALPA = Utah Academic Language Proficiency Assessment; WIDA ACCESS (W-APT) = World-Class Instructional Design and Assessment measure for Assessing Comprehension and Communication in English State-to-State for English Language Learners Placement Test.

ELP Screeners and Assessments

Once a student is identified as a possible ELL through parental completion of the HLS or PLQ, each of the states require that an ELP screener or assessment be administered; additionally, New York requires that standardized achievement test scores be considered. Thirty-one states currently are part of the World-Class Instructional Design and Assessment (WIDA) Consortium and thus administer WIDA's Assessing Comprehension and Communication in English State-to-State for English Language Learners ACCESS Placement Test (W-APT). The W-APT, which assesses the four language domains of listening, speaking, reading, and writing, is administered individually and takes approximately 60 minutes to complete. Results are used to assign an indicator of the student's ELP level (1–6) on the WIDA ELP standards and thus are used to determine the student's ELP classification and eligibility for English language services.

In states that are not members of the WIDA Consortium, a variety of ELP measures are utilized (see Table 11.1 for a complete list of these measures). All of these measures differ from ELP measures that were utilized before implementation of NCLB, as pre-NCLB measures were designed to measure a general language ability construct, as compared with post-NCLB measures, which are designed to assess academic language (Albers, Kenyon, & Boals, 2009).

Once identified as an ELL, federal legislation requires that all ELL students participate in annual ELP assessments. Scores obtained from these ELP assessments are used for accountability purposes and also for determining ongoing eligibility for language services. As the goal of these requirements is to facilitate the student's learning of English, the expectation is that the student eventually will be considered as proficient in English and will be exited from receiving language services. Each state, however, is allowed local flexibility in determining criteria for exit from language programming. States tend to require that four exit criteria are met, including the following: (a) obtaining a defined score on the state's language proficiency measure, which includes a specified composite score or a specific composite score combined with a minimum level of proficiency on certain domain scores (i.e., reading, writing, speaking, and/or listening); (b) obtaining a minimum level of performance on the state's academic achievement measure; (c) consulting with the student's parents; and (d) providing a teacher evaluation of the student's language proficiency. Additionally, certain states (e.g., Ohio, Rhode Island) have restrictions regarding the exiting from language services. For example, Ohio prohibits a student from being exited from language services before third grade, whereas Rhode Island prohibits students in kindergarten from being exited from services.

LITERACY SCREENING IN ELL STUDENTS

Although literacy screening systems are now used in many schools (see Chapter 6 and Chapter 7, this volume), these screening systems have not been fully explored and validated for use with ELL students. Although basic principles associated with universal screening practices can be applied in working with linguistically diverse students, questions remain around specific issues of validity and acceptability. Important changes include the current attempt to dismantle deficit thinking about these populations and the inclusion of culturally and linguistically diverse students in the initial validation of test protocols (Valencia, 2010). Taking such an ecological perspective in considering the acceptability, validity, and reliability of universal screening tools ultimately can help in informing the future use of these tools for supporting the advancement of instructional practices and curricular development and intervention work for the purpose of promoting student development (e.g., social–emotional, behavioral, academic) as well as addressing systemic issues.

The importance of considering contextual factors cannot be overlooked in implementing universal screening systems (Ikeda, Neeseen, & Witt, 2008); considering these contextual factors becomes even more significant when conducting universal screening with ELL students. Taking an ecological and behavioral approach in developing and applying assessment procedures therefore can be potentially useful for practitioners and researchers alike (Sheridan & McCurdy, 2005). Founded in Bronfenbrenner's ecological theory of development and influence, such a perspective allows for a comprehensive review of environmental influences as well as the extent to which the student fits within his or her given conditions. Ultimately, this perspective promotes the development of solution-focused data-based decision making. More specifically, such solutions serve the purpose of "build(ing) ecological systems that can support children, youth, schools and families by linking assessment to intervention, addressing . . . contextual variables, using a problem-solving framework, and focusing on outcomes" (Sheridan & McCurdy, 2005, p. 44). In the context of students that come from culturally and linguistically diverse backgrounds researchers must consider learning environments and parent and community perspectives, and both recognize and examine the cultural loading of assessment protocols (Rhodes et al., 2005).

Teacher Judgments of ELL Students' Literacy Skills

As discussed in Chapter 9 in this volume, teacher judgments of academic functioning appear to be a viable option within universal screening systems. The majority of studies that have examined the accuracy of teacher judgments, however, have been conducted with non-ELL students. Limbos and Geva (2001) conducted one of the few studies that examined the accuracy of rating scales, nominations, and teacher-expressed concerns in identifying ELL students experiencing reading difficulties. Results revealed that all of these forms of assessment demonstrated low sensitivity in identifying ELL students at risk for reading difficulties. Of the three types of teacher assessment, teacher-expressed concern evidenced in student scholastic records and during interviews was considerably less accurate than the others. These results suggest that it is crucial for school personnel to recognize that waiting for teachers to spontaneously voice concerns about the academic performance of ELL students is not an accurate screening measure. The researchers speculated that the teachers infrequently expressed concerns about the reading performance of ELL students because these students already are receiving services (e.g., L2 support); therefore, teachers may not have felt that reporting concerns was necessary. Also, teachers may have felt that the observed academic difficulty was a typical aspect of L2 development. Yet another speculation was that teachers felt inhibited to refer linguistically diverse students for evaluations because of the reported overrepresentation of minority students in special education. A related critical finding of this study was that children inaccurately identified as at risk for learning difficulties by teachers had lower oral language proficiency. Thus, it appeared that teachers inappropriately used a child's ELP to judge reading skills.

Curriculum-Based Measurement in English

Given the accumulating data supporting the psychometric properties and treatment utility (see Chapter 7 in this volume; Deno, 1985), CBM appears to be a promising tool for identifying learning difficulties within the ELL population. Researchers have studied the technical adequacy of CBM procedures to assess the reading skills of ELL students, and some (e.g., Baker & Good, 1995) have suggested that the use of CBM reading probes in English was as reliable and valid for bilingual second graders as for non-ELL students, with correlations between the oral reading probes and other assessments of comprehension ranging from .73 to .76. This was an important finding because although there is a strong research base supporting the link between oral reading fluency (ORF) and comprehension for non-ELL students (Deno, 1985; Hintze, Shapiro, Conte, & Basile, 1997), little is known about this relationship for ELL students. Teachers of ELL students have argued that the link between fluency and comprehension for students learning English is weak, asserting that their students often can decode texts in English without understanding what they are reading because of low levels of English proficiency (De Ramirez & Shapiro, 2006).

One obvious benefit of using CBM with ELL students is the ability to develop local norms that allow educators to compare an ELL student's current performance and ongoing progress to other ELL students, rather than to the performance of native English speakers (Albers et al., 2013). Although relatively little is known about the language and literacy developmental trajectories of ELL students (McCardle et al., 2005), studies have begun to investigate expected reading fluency growth trajectories. One group of researchers examined whether ORF growth rates between non-ELL students ($n = 97$) in general education classrooms and Spanish-speaking ELL students ($n = 68$) taught in a bilingual setting differed (De Ramirez & Shapiro, 2006). Results indicated that the non-ELL students read more fluently in English than the ELL students read in Spanish or English. Additionally, the ELL students' reading fluency in English and Spanish grew at a slower rate than the general education students. Educators must consider these differences when setting expected growth rates for their Spanish-speaking ELL students.

With increasing pressure to demonstrate adequate yearly progress on high-stakes assessments, researchers have tested the ability of CBM reading probes to predict student outcomes on these mandated state tests. Although most of these studies have been conducted with non-ELL students, Wiley and Deno (2005) examined the predictive validity of CBM across non-ELL and ELL students. Specifically, they looked at the ability of CBM maze and oral reading measures to predict performance on the reading portion of a state standards assessment administered in third and fifth grade. Contrary to the researchers' hypotheses, results indicated that the maze task was a better predictor of performance on the states standards test for fifth grade non-ELL students but that the CBM-ORF was a stronger predictor of performance for the ELL group at both grade levels. Thus, this research supported previous data substantiating the ability of CBM-ORF to predict performance on state achievement tests (e.g., Good, Simmons, & Kame'enui, 2001; Hintze & Silberglitt, 2005). These results are an important contribution to the literature because, contrary to the beliefs held by many educators that ORF does not measure a student's ability to comprehend text, this research demonstrated that ELL students who performed more quickly and accurately on the probes scored better on the high-stakes assessment that required text comprehension. The researchers, however, only reported correlational data, thereby failing to analyze predictive indices, such as sensitivity and specificity. Additionally, they did not examine differences in the predictive validity of CBM-ORF across language proficiency levels.

Thus, the critical issue in need of examination is whether CBM reading procedures are appropriate for use with ELL students. In particular, one unanswered question regarding the use of CBM with ELL students relates to the examination of CBM data with ELP considered to be a continuous variable (i.e., specific ELP levels) instead of as a dichotomous variable (i.e., non-ELL vs. ELL). Prior guidelines and recommendations regarding cut scores for ELL students failed to consider ELP as a continuous variable and likewise failed to consider the type of instructional model that was being used with these students. This later issue is also significant; for example, it is unknown what the ORF trajectory should look like for a first-grade ELL who has been provided instruction only in Spanish as part of a developmental bilingual education model. Failure to consider ELP levels and the instructional model likely would result in incorrect decisions being made regarding the progress (as measured by changes in scores) of ELL students.

These issues further illustrate the importance of (a) identifying universal screening and progress-monitoring measures to more accurately identify ELL students at risk for reading difficulties and (b) testing the psychometric properties of these measures across language proficiency levels. Unfortunately, the examination of differences in performance on screening measures across English language abilities rarely, if ever, has been incorporated into research designs to date. Additional research is needed to look at expected learning trajectories in the ELL population. This research should include larger sample sizes of ELL students, different native languages, a wider range of age-groups, and examination of skills across ELP levels. Supported by such data, CBM assessments could play an even more important role in helping educators identify ELL students evidencing reading difficulties that are atypical from those experienced by the majority of students acquiring ESL.

Curriculum-Based Measurement in Spanish

The *Indicadores Dinamicos del Exito en la Lectura* (IDEL; Good, Bank, & Watson, 2003) and the AIMSweb Spanish Reading CBM, which are Spanish versions of the DIBELS and AIMSweb probes, respectively, were developed to assist in making academic decisions about students who speak Spanish as their primary language. Although minimal reliability and validity information regarding both measures is available, the IDEL has been reported to have strong alternate form reliability for the ORF probes administered to students in first through third grade (range = 0.87–0.94; Baker, Cummings, Good, & Smolkowski, 2007). Additionally, criterion-related validity of the IDEL-ORF measures with the Woodcock-Muñoz Bateria-R Combined Scores of Amplia Lectura was reported to be .79 (Watson, 2004; Woodcock & Muñoz-Sandoval, 1996).

Currently, educators have few resources to guide decisions regarding whether to administer CBM in English or Spanish to native Spanish-speaking students. Such decisions require not only research examining the predictive validity of the multiple measures but also information about how the validity differs across ELP levels. Furthermore, guidelines do not exist for how to appropriately interpret scores across these multiple measures. On the basis of what we currently know regarding the acquisition of English proficiency, combined with what we know regarding dual language learners who have language proficiency and literacy skills in their native language, the recommendations provided in Table 11.2 are proposed guidelines given the limited knowledge base regarding the universal screening of language minority students. As can be seen in the Table 11.2, there are multiple possible combinations of language proficiency and risk status on CBM in reading (CBM-R), including those in Spanish and English. Caution should be used, however, when following these recommendations, as more empirical work needs to be done in this area.

CASE EXAMPLE: USING CBM-R IN ENGLISH IN SCHOOL SETTINGS

To further emphasize and clarify the use of CBM-R as a universal screening measure with ELL students, while considering the impact of specific ELP levels and types of instructional models, a brief example of a school that uses CBM-R as a universal screening measure is provided.

Mountain View Elementary School is a dual-immersion language school in which the population of students is approximately 60% ELL students (native Spanish-speaking students) and 40% native English speaking. As a dual-immersion language school, the school's goal is to develop literacy in both Spanish and English; to accomplish this goal, kindergarten instruction is 90% in Spanish, 80% in Grade 1, 70% in Grade 2, 60% in Grade 3, and 50% in Grades 4, 5, and 6.

After administering the AIMSweb English and Spanish CBM-R at the fall benchmark, the school's intervention planning team (IPT) examined the data. The team's purpose was to identify all students who were at risk based on these measures. The IPT identified one student in particular who had scores that were of concern to the team members. Alante was a third-grade student whose ACCESS for ELLs scores indicated that his ELP level was a 2, which is considered to be at the "beginning" level. Before third grade, Alante attended school in Mexico. Scores located within his file indicated that he was considered to be proficient in the Spanish language.

The benchmarking data indicated that his performance on the AIMSweb Spanish CBM-R placed him within the minimal risk category, suggesting that he had developed early literacy skills in Spanish. His AIMSweb (English version) scores portrayed a different story, however, as his ORF score was 21 words read correctly per minute. The IPT had to determine how to interpret these scores. Their first step was to examine Alante's scores in relation to the national norms provided by AIMSweb; his ORF of 21 placed him in the bottom 3% of students at his grade level.

Considering that Alante was (a) identified as being only at the beginning levels of ELP, (b) was exposed to literacy instruction exclusively in Spanish

TABLE 11.2

Interpretation of ELP in Spanish and English and Risk Status
on CBM-R Measures in Spanish and English

Spanish CBM-R risk status	English CBM-R risk status	Interpretation[a]
Proficient in Spanish language, proficient in English language		
No/minimal risk	No/minimal risk	• No/minimal risk • Ongoing progress monitoring
No/minimal risk	At risk	• Likely not at risk due to acquiring literacy skills in native language • Continue progress monitoring to determine risk status or whether more time is needed to acquire English literacy skills • Consider adding supplemental literacy intervention to facilitate English literacy
At risk	No/minimal risk	• Likely not at risk due to acquiring language proficiency in both languages and acquiring English literacy skills • Ongoing progress monitoring • If in bilingual/dual language program, consider providing supplemental Spanish literacy intervention
At risk	At risk	• Likely at risk as did not acquire literacy skills in either native or non-native language, yet has language proficiency in both native and non-native languages • Continue progress monitoring to determine risk status • Consider adding supplemental literacy intervention to facilitate English literacy
Proficient in Spanish language, not proficient in English language		
No/minimal risk	No/minimal risk	• No/minimal risk • Ongoing literacy progress monitoring • Monitor ELP development
No/minimal risk	At risk	• Likely not at risk due to acquiring literacy skills in native language • Continue progress monitoring to determine risk status or whether more time is needed to acquire English literacy skills • Monitor ELP development • Consider adding supplemental literacy intervention to facilitate English literacy
At risk	No/minimal risk	• Currently minimal risk due to obtained English literacy skills • Ongoing progress monitoring • Monitor ELP development • If in bilingual/dual language instruction, consider providing supplemental Spanish literacy intervention

TABLE 11.2

Interpretation of ELP in Spanish and English and Risk Status
on CBM-R Measures in Spanish and English   (*Continued*)

Spanish CBM-R risk status	English CBM-R risk status	Interpretation[a]
At risk	At risk	• Likely at risk as did not acquire literacy skills in either native or non-native language • Continue progress monitoring to determine risk status or whether more time is needed to acquire English literacy skills • Monitor ELP development • Consider adding supplemental literacy intervention to facilitate Spanish and/or English literacy
Not proficient in Spanish language, proficient in English language		
No/minimal risk	No/minimal risk	• No/minimal risk due to English language and literacy proficiency • Ongoing progress monitoring
No/minimal risk	At risk	• Likely not at risk due to acquiring literacy skills in native language • Likely needs additional time to acquire English literacy skills • Ongoing progress monitoring • Consider adding supplemental literacy intervention to facilitate English literacy
At risk	No/minimal risk	• Likely not at risk due to acquiring ELP and English literacy skills • Ongoing progress monitoring
At risk	At risk	• Likely at risk as did not acquire literacy skills in either native or non-native language, yet is considered to be proficient in English language • Continue progress monitoring to determine risk status or whether more time is needed to acquire English literacy skills • Consider adding supplemental literacy intervention to facilitate English literacy
Not proficient in Spanish language, not proficient in English language		
No/minimal risk	No/minimal risk	• Minimal risk due to acquiring literacy skills in native and non-native languages; however, lack of proficiency in either language is a concern • Ongoing progress monitoring • Monitor ELP development
No/minimal risk	At risk	• Minimal risk due to acquiring literacy skills in native language; however, lack of proficiency in either language is a concern

(*continues*)

TABLE 11.2

Interpretation of ELP in Spanish and English and Risk Status
on CBM-R Measures in Spanish and English   (*Continued*)

Spanish CBM-R risk status	English CBM-R risk status	Interpretation[a]
At risk	No/minimal risk	• Ongoing progress monitoring • Monitor ELP development • Consider adding supplemental literacy intervention to facilitate English literacy • Some risk due to only acquiring literacy skills in non-native language; lack of proficiency in either language is a concern
At risk	At risk	• Ongoing progress monitoring • Monitor ELP development • Likely at risk as did not acquire literacy skills in either native or non-native language, and is not proficient in either language • Continue progress monitoring to determine risk status or whether more time is needed to acquire English literacy skills • Consider adding supplemental literacy intervention to facilitate English literacy

Note. CBM-R = curriculum-based measures in reading; ELP = English language proficiency.
[a]Interpretation can vary by grade level, instructional program, specific ELP levels, mobility, and so on.

while attending school in Mexico, and (c) experienced limited English literacy instruction in third grade at Mountain View Elementary School as part of the dual-language immersion program, the IPT determined that using national norms that did not include consideration of these factors would not be appropriate. Instead, they determined it would be better to use local school norms for guidance in how to interpret his performance.

The school then considered whether to use local norms that provided non-ELL versus ELL norms, or whether to use local norms developed for each ELP level at each grade level. If they used the non-ELL versus ELL norms illustrated in Figure 11.1, Alante's performance continued to be significantly below the performance of other ELL students, as the mean ORF was approximately 62 words read correctly per minute. Conversely, if the IPT used local norms developed for specific ELP levels, his ORF of 21 would place him above the average ORF of other students at the same ELP level. Thus, the IPT determined that since Alante was (a) proficient in the Spanish language, (b) displayed early Spanish literacy skills, and (c) was not proficient in the English language, that he was likely in the process of obtaining ELP and needed time to obtain additional instruction in English literacy. Consequently, the IPT determined that they would continue to progress monitor his English literacy skills and monitor his

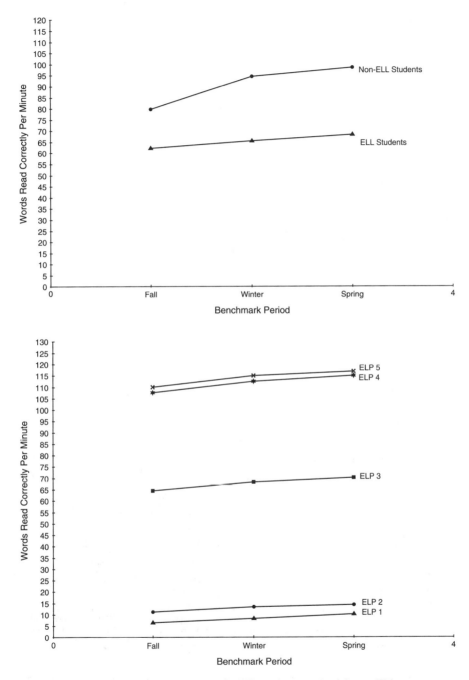

Figure 11.1. Local oral reading fluency (AIMSweb) norms by (a) non-ELL versus ELL students and (b) specific ELP levels.

ELP growth. If his trajectories in either domain failed to show growth at future benchmarks, they then would recommend additional instructional and intervention services.

CONCLUSION

Unfortunately, there is clearly a lack of validated screening measures that can be used in ELL populations. Perhaps more disturbing, however, is that there is a lack of consensus regarding how to most appropriately conduct universal screening with ELL students, or whether it should even occur at all. Future research clearly is needed in the identification and establishment of valid and effective screening systems for ELL students in schools. The evidence supporting the benefit of early intervention, the impact of early intervention on ELL students, and the negative academic outcomes faced by many ELL students is unequivocal; the status quo is no longer acceptable, and as such, a call for more research in this area is warranted.

REFERENCES

Abedi, J. (2004). The No Child Left Behind Act and English language learners: Assessment and accountability issues. *Educational Researcher, 33*, 4–14. doi:10.3102/0013189X033001004

Abedi, J. (2011). Assessing English language learners: Critical issues. In R. Basterra, E. Trumbull, & G. Solano-Flores, G. (Eds.), *Cultural validity in assessment: Addressing linguistic and cultural diversity* (pp. 49–71). New York, NY: Routledge.

Albers, C. A., Hoffman, A., & Lundahl, A. (2009). Journal coverage of issues related to English language learners across student-service professions: School psychology, special education, speech-language pathology, and counseling. *School Psychology Review, 38*, 121–134.

Albers, C. A., Kenyon, D., & Boals, T. (2009). Measures for determining English language proficiency and the resulting implications for instructional provision and intervention. *Assessment for Effective Intervention, 34*, 74–85. doi:10.1177/1534508408314175

Albers, C. A., Mission, P. L., & Bice-Urbach, B. J. (2013). Considering diverse learner characteristics in problem-solving assessment. In R. Brown-Chidsey & K. J. Andren (Eds.), *Assessment for intervention: A problem-solving approach* (2nd ed., pp. 344–360). New York, NY: Guilford Press.

August, D., & Shanahan, T. (Eds.). (2006). *Developing literacy in second-language learners: Report of the National Literacy Panel on language-minority children and youth.* Mahwah, NJ: Erlbaum.

Bailey, A. L., & Kelly, K. R. (2010). *The use and validity of home language surveys in state English language proficiency assessment systems: A review and issues perspective.* White paper prepared for the U.S. Department of Education for the Evaluating the Validity of English Language Proficiency Assessments project.

Baker, D. L., Cummings, K. D., Good, R. H., & Smolkowski, K. (2007). *Indicadores Dinámicos del Éxito in la Lectura (IDEL): Summary of decision rules for intensive, strategic, and benchmark instructional recommendations in kindergarten through third grade* (Tech. Rep. No. 1). Eugene, OR: Dynamic Measurement Group.

Baker, S. K., & Good, R. (1995). Curriculum-based measurement of English reading with bilingual Hispanic students: A validation study with second grade students. *School Psychology Review, 24,* 561–578.

Barrera, I., Corso, R. M., & Macpherson, D. (2003). *Skilled dialogue: Strategies for responding to cultural diversity in early childhood.* Baltimore, MD: Brookes.

Batalova, J., Fix, M., & Murray, J. (2006). *Measures of change: The demography and literacy of adolescent English language learners.* Washington, DC: Migration Policy Institute.

Cook, G. H., Boals, T., Wilmes, C., & Santos, M. (2008). *Issues in the development of annual measurable achievement objectives for WIDA Consortium states* (Working Paper. No. 2008-2). Madison: Wisconsin Center for Education Research.

Cummins, J. (1979). Cognitive/academic language proficiency, linguistic interdependence, the optimum age question and some other matters. *Working Papers on Bilingualism, 19,* 121–129.

Cummins, J. (1999). *BICS and CALP: Clarifying the distinction.* Retrieved from http://www.eric.ed.gov/PDFS/ED438551.pdf

Cummins, J. (2008). BICS and CALP: Empirical and theoretical status of the distinction. In B. Street & N. Hornberger (Eds.), *Encyclopedia of language and education* (2nd ed., pp. 71–83). New York, NY: Springer Science.

Deno, S. L. (1985). Curriculum-based measurement: The emerging alternative. *Exceptional Children, 52,* 219–232.

De Ramirez, R., & Shapiro, E. S. (2006). Curriculum-based measurement and the evaluation of reading skills of Spanish-speaking English language learners in bilingual education classrooms. *School Psychology Review, 35,* 356–369.

Espinosa, L. M. (2005). Curriculum and assessment considerations for young children from culturally, linguistically, and economically diverse backgrounds. *Psychology in the Schools, 42,* 837–853. doi:10.1002/pits.20115

Esquivel, G. B., & Keitel, M. A. (1990). Counseling immigrant children in the schools. *Elementary School Guidance and Counseling, 24,* 213–221.

Francis, D., Rivera, M., Lesaux, N., Kieffer, M., & Rivera, H. (2006). *Practical guidelines for the education of English language learners: Research-based recommendations for instruction and academic interventions.* Portsmouth, NH: RMC Research Corporation, Center on Instruction.

Good, R. H., Bank, N., & Watson, J. M. (Eds.). (2003). *Indicadores dinámicos del exito en la lectura.* Eugene, OR: Institute for the Development of Educational Achievement.

Good, R. H., Simmons, D. C., & Kame'enui, E. J. (2001). The importance and decision-making utility of a continuum of fluency-based indicators of foundational reading skills for third-grade high-stakes outcomes. *Scientific Studies of Reading, 5,* 257–288. doi:10.1207/S1532799XSSR0503_4

Gopaul-McNicol, S., & Thomas-Presswood, T. (1998). *Working with linguistically and culturally different children: Innovative clinical and educational approaches.* Needham Heights, MA: Allyn & Bacon.

Haager, D., Calhoon, M. B., & Linan-Thompson, S. (2007). English language learners and response to intervention: Introduction to special issue. *Learning Disability Quarterly, 30,* 151–152. doi:10.2307/30035560

Hamayan, E. V., & Damico, J. S. (1991). Developing and using a second language. In E. V. Hamayan & J. S. Damico (Eds.), *Limiting bias in the assessment of bilingual students* (pp. 40–75). Austin, TX: Pro-Ed.

Henning-Stout, M. (1996). Que podemos hacer? Roles for school psychologists with Mexican and Latino migrant children and families. *School Psychology Review, 25,* 152–164.

Hintze, J. M., Shapiro, E. S., Conte, K. L., & Basile, I. (1997). Oral reading fluency and authentic reading material: Criterion validity of the technical features of CBM survey-level-assessment. *School Psychology Review, 26,* 535–553.

Hintze, J. M., & Silberglitt, B. (2005). A longitudinal examination of the diagnostic accuracy and predictive validity of R-CBM and high-stakes testing. *School Psychology Review, 34,* 372–386.

Ikeda, M., Neeseen, E., & Witt, J. (2008). Best practices in universal screening. In A. Thomas & J. Grimes (Eds.), *Best practices in school psychology* (5th ed., pp. 103–114). Bethesda, MD: National Association of School Psychologists.

Irby, B., Tong, F., Lara-Alecio, R., Mathes, P., Acosta, S., & Guerrero, C. (2010). Quality of instruction, language of instruction, and Spanish-speaking English language learners' performance on a state reading achievement test. *TABE Journal, 12,* 1–42.

Jimenez, R. (2004). More equitable literacy assessment for Latino students. *Reading Teacher, 57,* 576–578.

Larsen, L. J. (2004). The *foreign-born population in the United States: 2003* (Current Population Reports, 20-551). Washington, DC: U.S. Census Bureau.

Lembke, E. (2010). The use of curriculum-based measurement with diverse student populations. *Reading and Writing Quarterly, 26,* 285–288. doi:10.1080/10573569.2010.500247

Limbos, M. M., & Geva, E. (2001). Accuracy of teacher assessments of second-language students at-risk for reading disability. *Journal of Learning Disabilities, 34,* 136–151.

López, S. R. (2002). Mental health care for Latinos: A research agenda to improve the accessibility and quality of mental health care for Latinos. *Psychiatric Services, 53*, 1569–1573. doi:10.1176/appi.ps.53.12.1569

McCardle, P., Mele-McCarthy, J., Cutting, L., Leos, K., & D'Emilio, T. (2005). Learning disabilities in English language learners: Identifying the issues. *Learning Disabilities Research and Practice, 20*, 1–5. doi:10.1111/j.1540-5826.2005.00114.x

Office of English Language Acquisition, Language Enhancement, and Academic Achievement for Limited English Proficient Students. (2012). *Biennial report to Congress on the implementation of the Title III state formula grant program, school years 2006–07 and 2007–08*. Washington, DC: Author.

Rhodes, R., Ochoa, S. H., & Ortiz, S. O. (2005). *Comprehensive assessment of culturally and linguistically diverse students: A practical approach*. New York, NY: Guilford Press.

Ruiz de Velasco, J., & Fix, M. (2002). *Limited English proficient students and high-stakes accountability systems*. Washington, DC: Urban Institute.

Scarcella, R. (2003). *Academic English: A conceptual framework* (Tech. Rep. No. 2003-1). Irvine: University of California, Linguistic Minority Research Institute.

Scribner, A. P. (2002). Best assessment and intervention practices with second language learners. In A. Thomas & J. Grimes (Eds.), *Best practices in school psychology IV* (pp. 1485–1499). Bethesda, MD: National Association of School Psychologists.

Sheridan, S. M., & McCurdy, M. (2005). Ecological variables in school-based assessment and intervention planning. In R. Brown-Chidsey (Ed.), *Assessment for intervention: A problem solving approach* (pp. 43–64). New York, NY: Guilford Press.

Slama, R. B. (2012). A longitudinal analysis of academic English proficiency outcomes for adolescent English language learners in the United States. *Journal of Educational Psychology, 104*, 265–285. doi:10.1037/a0025861

Slavin, R. E., Madden, N., Calderon, M., Chamberlain, A., & Hennessy, M. (2011). Reading and language outcomes of a multiyear randomized evaluation of transitional bilingual education. *Educational Evaluation and Policy Analysis, 33*, 47–58. doi:10.3102/0162373711398127

U.S. Census Bureau. (2004). *Current population survey: Annual social and economic supplement*. Immigration Statistics Staff, Population Division. Washington, DC: Author.

U.S. Census Bureau. (2011). *2011 American community survey*. Washington, DC: Author.

U.S. Department of Education. (2009). *U.S. Department of Education, National Center for Education Statistics, schools and staffing survey: Public school, BIE school, and private school data files*. Washington, DC: National Center for Education Statistics.

U.S. Department of Education. (2011a). *Common core of data: Local education agency universe survey, 2010–11, version provisional 2a*. Washington, DC: National Center for Education Statistics.

U.S. Department of Education. (2011b). *National Assessment of Educational Progress, 2011 reading assessment*. Washington, DC: National Center for Education Statistics.

U.S. Department of Education. (2012). *Language instruction educational programs (LIEPs): A review of the foundational literature*. Washington, DC: Office of Planning, Evaluation, and Policy Development; Policy and Program Studies Service.

U.S. Department of Education & National Institute of Child Health and Human Development. (2003). *National symposium on learning disabilities in English language learners: Symposium summary*. Washington, DC: Author.

U.S. Department of Health and Human Services. (2001). *Executive summary. Mental health: Culture, race, and ethnicity—A supplement to mental health: A report of the Surgeon General*. Washington, DC: Author.

U.S. Department of Health and Human Services. (2011). CDC health disparities and inequalities report—United States, 2011. *Morbidity and Mortality Weekly Report, 60*(Suppl.), 1–113. Retrieved from http://www.cdc.gov/mmwr/pdf/other/su6001.pdf

Valencia, R. (2010). *Dismantling contemporary deficit thinking*. New York, NY: Routledge.

Watson, J. (2004). *Examining the reliability and validity of the Indicadores Dinámicos del Exito en la Lectura (IDEL): A research study*. Unpublished doctoral dissertation, University of Oregon.

Wiley, H. I., & Deno, S. L. (2005). Oral reading and maze measures as predictors of success for English language learners on a state standards assessment. *Remedial and Special Education, 26*, 207–214. doi:10.1177/07419325050260040301

Woodcock, R. W., & Muñoz-Sandoval, A. F. (1996). *Bateria Woodcock-Muñoz: Pruebas de aprovechamiento—rivisada* [Woodcock-Johnson III Tests of achievement]. Itasca, IL: Riverside.

INDEX

Abbott, R., 59
Abedi, J., 280
Abilities, as latent traits, 86–87
Academic and social behavior screening,
    223–243
    availability of intervention following,
        236–237
    broadband, 226, 228–232, 237–241
    case example of, 237–241
    framework for, 227–228
    future directions for, 241–243
    models supporting, 223–224
    narrowband, 228–229
    past measures for, 224–226
    technical adequacy of, 232–236
Academic engaged time (AET), 51
Academic language proficiency, 281–283
Academic outcomes
    of English language learner students,
        278, 282
    with poor behavioral and emotional
        risk outcomes, 250
    screening scores linked to, 43
Accuracy, 234–235
Achenbach, T., 53
Achenbach, T. M., 53, 228
Achenbach System of Empirically
    Based Assessment (ASEBA), 252
Active informed consent, 264–266
Adelsheim, S., 129
ADHD (attention-deficit/hyperactivity
    disorder), 228, 231
Advocacy, 133–134
AET (academic engaged time), 51
AIMSweb, 176, 181, 185, 294, 295
Albers, C. A., 13, 26, 28, 122, 235,
    240, 257
Alcohol abuse and dependency, 266
Alphabetic knowledge, 144–145
Alternate form reliability, 95, 96, 102
American Educational Research
    Association, 6
American Psychological Association,
    6, 127
Antisocial behavior, 56, 60–61

Anxiety, 251
Appropriateness, evaluating screening
    based on, 13
Area under the curve (AUC), 106,
    210–213
Argument-based approach to validity,
    100–107
Asarnow, J. R., 259
ASEBA (Achenbach System of Empiri-
    cally Based Assessment), 252
Assessment
    formative, 10, 12
    legislation supporting, 130
    standards-based, 103
    timed vs. untimed, 217
    web-based technology for, 67–68
At-risk students, 127, 174–175, 225.
    See also Suicide risk screening
Attention-deficit/hyperactivity disorder
    (ADHD), 228, 231
AUC (area under the curve), 106,
    210–213
August, G. J., 53

BACESS (Brief Academic Competence
    Evaluation Screening System), 122
Baglici, S. P., 202
Bailey, A. L., 285
Baker, S., 207
Bandura, A., 224
Barbaranelli, C., 224
BASC-2 (Behavior Assessment System
    of Children-Second Edition), 251
BASC-2 BESS. See Behavioral
    Assessment for Children,
    Second Edition-Behavioral and
    Emotional Screening System
Basic Interpersonal Communication
    Skills (BICS), 281–282
BBR scales. See Brief behavior rating
    scales
Behavioral and emotional risk (BER)
    screening, 249–267
    and academic outcomes, 250
    available methods for, 251–252

(BER) screening, *continued*
    definitions of risk for, 252
    and error in classification, 257
    major dimensions of, 256
    method selection and measurement
        issues with, 253–256
    newfound interest in, 249
    for social behavior. *See* Academic
        and social behavior screening
    standards for, 266–267
    universal, 257–265
    uses of, 5
Behavioral Assessment for Children,
    Second Edition-Behavioral and
    Emotional Screening System
    (BASC-2 BESS)
    function of, 225
    multiple-gate screening with, 262
    overview of, 251–254
    sample protocol, 261
    scores on, 239, 256
Behavioral checklists, 228
Behavioral outcomes, of English
    language learner students,
    278–280
Behavioral problems and disorders
    academic outcomes with, 250
    identifying students at risk for, 225
    interventions for, 243
    National Research Council
        research on, 6
    systematic screening for, 253–254
    and Systematic Screening for
        Behavior Disorders,
        49–51, 253
Behavior Assessment System of
    Children-Second Edition
    (BASC-2), 251
BER screening. *See* Behavioral and
    emotional risk screening
BICS (Basic Interpersonal Communi-
    cation Skills), 281–282
*Biennial Report to Congress on the
    Implementation of the State
    Formula Grant Program,* 278
Bilingual instructional approaches, 284
Binet, Alfred, 3, 80
Binet-Simon scale, 3–4
Boals, T., 283

Brief Academic Competence Evaluation
    Screening System (BACESS), 122
Brief behavior rating (BBR) scales, 49,
    55–57, 60
Briggs-Gowan, M. J., 129
Broadband screening, 226, 228–232,
    237–241
Bronfenbrenner, U., 291
Brown, M. M., 264
Burns, M. K., 184
Buros Institute, 81

Caldarella, P., 61
California Healthy Kids Survey
    (CHKS), 264
California Mental Health Department,
    54–55
CALP (Cognitive Academic Language
    Proficiency), 281–282
Cantwell, D. P., 259
Caprara, G. V., 224
Carlson, G. A., 259
Carter, A. S., 129
Case, R., 207
Castell, William, 249
Catalano, R., 59
Categorical approach, to screening, 51
Catts, H. W., 147
CBM-R. *See* Curriculum-based
    measurement in reading
CBMs. *See* Curriculum-based measures
CCSS (Common Core State Standards),
    209, 215
CELF Preschool-2 (Clinical Evaluation
    of Language Fundamentals-
    Preschool, 2nd Edition), 154
Centers for Disease Control and
    Prevention, 264
Chafouleas, S. M., 56, 60, 239
Change agents, 112, 113, 117, 132
Change scores, 97
Charlebois, M., 49, 57, 59, 60
Chartier, M., 265
Child Behavior Checklist, 251
Children's Learning Institute, 150
CHKS (California Healthy Kids Survey),
    264
Christ, T. J., 28
Chu, B. C., 120, 121

Cicchetti, D. V., 235, 240
CIRCLE-Phonological Awareness,
    Language, and Literacy System+
    (C-PALLS+), 147–148, 150–152,
    156–157
Clarke, B., 213
Classical test theory (CTT), 13, 87–88,
    93–94
Classification, 257
Classwide problems, with reading,
    184–186
Clinical Evaluation of Language
    Fundamentals-Preschool,
    2nd Edition (CELF Preschool-2),
    154
Codding, R., 202
Cognitive Academic Language
    Proficiency (CALP), 281–282
Coie, J. D., 258
Coladarci, T., 230
Collaborative for Academic, Social,
    and Emotional Learning, 225
Common Core State Standards
    (CCSS), 209, 215
Communication process (screening
    implementation), 112, 114
Comprehension, 145
Computer-Based Assessment System
    for Reading, 176
Concurrent validity
    of C-PALLS+, 151–152
    in criterion model of validation, 98
    of Get Ready to Read! Revised, 149
    of Individual Growth and Develop-
        ment Indicators, 154–155
Conditional probability analysis,
    8, 235
Conduct Problems Prevention Research
    Group, 52, 58, 61, 258
Construct model for validation, 99
A Consumer's Guide to Analyzing a Core
    Reading Program, 39
Content model for validation, 99
Continuous improvement, 22–24
Convergent validity, 53
Cook, C., 56
Cook, G. H., 283
Core school programs, 23, 25
Cowen, E. L., 267

C-PALLS+. See CIRCLE-Phonological
    Awareness, Language, and
    Literacy System+
Criterion model of validation, 98–99
Cronbach, L. J., 48
Cronbach's alpha, 96
Crosby, R., 53
CRtIEC agency, 159
CTT. See Classical test theory
Culture, language learning and, 280
Cummins, J., 281, 282
Curriculum-based measurement in
        reading (CBM-R)
    function of, 88, 89
    validity of, 95, 99, 101–103, 106
Curriculum-based measures (CBMs)
    for English language learner students,
        281, 292–295
    for reading skills screening, 175–176,
        190
Curriculum sampling, 209
Cut scores
    for academic and social behavior
        screening, 234
    in behavioral and emotional risk
        screening tools, 257
    for mathematics screening,
        213–214, 217
    setting of, 9

Data (screening), 29–35
    decisions based on, 24
    instructional changes with, 31–32
    leadership decisions using, 26
    management of, 31
    and professional development, 30,
        32–34
    review of, 31
    systematic use of, 23–24
    uses of, 21
Davis, N. O., 129
DBR (direct behavior rating) scales,
    53–54
DBR-SI (Direct Behavior Rating-Single
    Item Scales), 239
DEC (Division of Early Childhood), 159
Decisions
    data-based, 24, 26, 34–35
    innovation, 115

Decisions, *continued*
  instructional, 20–21
  and validity, 103–106
Decision study (D-study), 89–90
Decision threshold, 106–107
Demaray, M. K., 230
Deno, S. L., 185, 224, 293
Depression, 251, 252
Depression screening, 114–115,
    117–118, 266
Developing Skills Checklist (DSC), 148
Developmental issues, with multiple
    gating, 57
Developmental Pathways Screening
    Program, 263
Development and evaluation of screening
    systems
  development and documentation
    of measures in, 83–86
  and methods of administering tests,
    107
  problems arising in, 79–80
  psychometric theories relevant to.
    See Psychometrics
  steps in, 83–85
  test review and selection in, 81–82
  validation of test for. *See* Validity
Dever, B. V., 256, 260, 264
Diagnostic decisions, 95
DIBELS, 294
Difference scores, 97
Dimensional approach, to screening, 51
DiPerna, J. C., 226–228
Direct behavior rating (DBR) scales,
    53–54
Direct Behavior Rating-Single Item
    Scales (DBR-SIS), 239
DiStefano, C. A., 256, 258, 264
Division of Early Childhood (DEC),
    159
Documentation, of screening measures,
    83–86
Dodge, K. A., 259
Domain score, 102
Dowdy, E., 256, 264
Downing, S. M., 83
Dropout, school, 19
Drumond anti-social scale, 56, 60
DSC (Developing Skills Checklist), 148

D-study (decision study), 89–90
Dual immersion language programs,
    284, 295
Duerr Evaluation Resources Inc., 54–55
Duncan, G. J., 200
DuPaul, G., 119
DuPre, E. P., 123, 125
Durlak, J. A., 123, 125, 225
Dymnicki, A. B., 225
Dynamic Indicators of Basic Early
    Literacy Skills, 152, 176. *See also*
    Individual Growth and Develop-
    ment Indicators

Early Childhood Assessment (report), 145
Early childhood education, 143–144
Early childhood literacy screening,
    141–164
  current approaches to, 145–147
  future directions for research on,
    163–164
  and language development, 144–145
  as preventative intervention, 142–143
  professional development for, 162–163
  program improvements affecting,
    159–161
  research and theoretical foundations
    of, 161–162
  review of existing measures for,
    147–156
  setting context for, 158–159
Early Childhood Longitudinal Study-
    Kindergarten, 200
Early Literacy Index, 149
Early Reading First, 143
Early reading skills screening, 171–193
  aligning curriculum and practice
    with, 175
  case example, 183–186, 188–192
  identifying classwide problems with,
    184–186
  identifying intervention targets with,
    188, 190–191
  identifying students at risk with,
    174–175
  identifying supplement services
    needs with, 186–188
  measures used for, 175–182
  prevention with, 171–172

procedures for, 182–183
psychometric adequacy of tools
from, 173
Early Screening Project, 61
Easy CBM, 176, 209, 214
Eating disorder screening, 266
EBDs. *See* Emotional or behavioral
disorders
Eckert, T., 119
Ecological theory of development and
influence, 291
Education
special. *See* Special education
universal screening in. *See* Universal
screening in education
Educational Measurement, 83, 100
Education of All Handicapped Children
Act, 53
Elliott, S. N., 122, 224, 226–227, 230,
231
ELL students. *See* English language
learner students
ELP. *See* English language proficiency
Emotional or behavioral disorders
(EBDs)
case study of identifying, 63–67
identification of, 61
Emotional outcomes, of English language
learner students, 278–280
Engagement, as predictor of academic
success, 226–228
English as a second language (ESL)
classes, 282, 284
English language learner (ELL) students,
275–300
academic achievement of, 278, 282
behavioral, social, and emotional
outcomes of, 278–280
case example, 295, 298–300
defined, 276–277
instructional approaches and models
for helping, 284
language acquisition process in, 280
and language components, 281–284
language proficiency screening with,
284–290
literacy screening with, 291–298
population estimates of, 277
primary languages spoken by, 278

English language proficiency (ELP),
276–278
as multidimensional construct, 281
screening tools for, 284–290
ESL (English as a second language)
classes, 282, 284
Espinosa, L. M., 279
Evaluation
of implementation, 133
of screening systems. *See* Development and evaluation of
screening systems
Evidence-based instruction, 20
Evidence-based medical policy, 59
Expressive One Word Picture Vocabulary
Test, 151

Fact retrieval math screening measures,
206
Fagley, N. S., 120, 121
False-negative outcomes
in behavioral and emotional risk
screening, 257
in multiple gating, 57, 59–60
and validity, 104–105
False-positive outcomes
in multiple gating, 57, 59–60
tolerance for, 120–121
and validity, 104–105
Feeney-Kettler, K. A., 235, 240
Findell, B., 199
First Step intervention program, 61
Fixsen, D. L., 115, 116
Fletcher, J. M., 5, 19
Flynn, J. M., 230
Forman, S. G., 120, 121
Formative assessment, 10, 12
Foster, E. M., 259
Francis, D. J., 5, 19
Francis, G., 231
Fuchs, L. S., 207, 209
Furlong, M. J., 264

Gagnon, C., 49
Gates-MacGinitie Reading Test, 182
Gating, multiple. *See* Multiple gating
Generalizability study (G-study), 89–90
Generalizability theory (GT), 89–90,
93–95

Gersten, 202n1

Get Ready to Read! Revised (GRTR-R) screening measure, 147–149, 156–157

Geva, E., 291–292

Gibbons, K. A., 184

Gleser, G. C., 48

Glover, T. A., 13, 26, 28, 235, 240, 257

Goodman, A., 256

Goodman, R., 256

Greenberg, M. T., 258

Gresham, F., 56, 57, 60, 71

Grills, A. E., 259

Group-administered comprehension assessments, 182

GRTR-R (Get Ready to Read! Revised) screening measure, 147–149, 156–157

Grumet, J. G., 264

G-study (generalizability study), 89–90

GT (generalizability theory), 89–90, 93–95

Guidance counselors, 114

Guidelines for Evaluating a Comprehensive Core Reading Program, 40

Hall, G. E., 115

Handbook of Test Development, 83

Hart, B., 144

Hawkins, J. D., 59

Head Start, 143, 148

Hill, K., 59

Hill, L. G., 258

Hintze, J. M., 43, 107, 213

HLS (home language surveys), 285–289

Hoagwood, K., 56

Hoge, R. D., 230

Home language surveys (HLS), 285–289

Hord, S. M., 115

ICC (item characteristic curves), 90–92

IDEIA (Individuals with Disabilities Education Improvement Act), 6, 223

IDEL (Indicadores Dinamicos del Exito en la Lectura), 294

IDGIs 2.0 (Individual Growth and Development Indicators, Version 2.0), 148, 152–157

IEP (Individualized Educational Program), 187

IIF (item information function), 92

Illinois Children's Mental Health Act, 127

Immigrants, 280–282. See also English language learner students

Implementation, 111–134
components of, 112–115
factors related to success of, 123–128
roles in, 133, 134
stages of, 115–118
steps in, 131–134
studies of factors affecting, 119–122
tips for, 128–131

Implementers, of screening, 112–115, 124–126

Indicadores Dinamicos del Exito en la Lectura (IDEL), 294

Individual Growth and Development Indicators, Version 2.0 (IDGIs 2.0), 148, 152–157

Individualized Educational Program (IEP), 187

Individuals with Disabilities Education Improvement Act (IDEIA), 6, 223

Inferences, 80

Informal reading inventories (IRIs), 174–175

Informant selection, 258–260

Informed consent, 264–266

Initial sound fluency (ISF), 176

Innovation (screening implementation), 112, 114, 123–125

Innovation decisions, 115

Institute of Medicine, 56

Instruction
bilingual approaches to, 284
and data screening, 31–32
evidence-based, 20
Tiers One and Two, 201, 250
Tier Three, 201

Instructional decisions, 20–21

Intelligence, 86

Internal consistency
of academic and social behavior screening tools, 233
of behavioral and emotional risk screening tools, 255, 256

of early childhood literacy screening
    tools, 148, 149, 151
overview of, 95, 96
Interrater reliability
    of academic and social behavior
        screening tools, 233, 238
    acceptable, 37
    of letter-sound fluency, 179
    of mathematics screening tools, 209
    of Maze tool, 181
    overview of, 95, 96
    of phoneme segmentation fluency, 178
Intervention(s)
    early childhood literacy screening as,
        142–143
    First Step intervention program, 61
    following academic and social
        behavior screening, 236–237
    multitiered response to. *See* Multitiered
        response-to-intervention [RTI]
    for reducing problem behaviors, 243
    stemming from early reading skills
        screening, 188, 190–191
Intervention-sensitive instruments,
    55–57
Invernizzi, M., 129
Iowa Test of Basic Skills, 182
IRIs (informal reading inventories),
    174–175
IRT. *See* Item response theory
ISF (initial sound fluency), 176
Item characteristic curves (ICC), 90–92
Item information function (IIF), 92
Item response theory (IRT), 13, 84,
    90–94, 258

Jenkins, J., 43
Johnson, E., 213
Johnston, C., 259
Jones, D., 259
Jones, S., 255
Jordan, N. C., 207
Journal of School Psychology, 13

Kalberg, J. R., 14
Kamphaus, R. W., 264
Kane, M. T., 94, 100
Kappa coefficients, 106
Kelly, K. R., 285

Kettler, R. J., 122, 134, 235, 240
Kilgus, S. P., 53, 54, 239
Kilpatrick, J., 199
Klin, A., 235
Koch, G., 238
Kosterman, R., 59

Landis, J. R., 238
Landry, Susan, 150
Lane, K. L., 14, 255, 262
Language acquisition, 280
Language development, 144–145
Language proficiency
    academic, 281–283
    English. *See* English language
        proficiency [ELP]
Larivee, S., 49
Latent trait, 86–87
Latent variables, 87
Leadership, 24–26
Learning disability in mathematics
    (MLD)
    indicators of, 200
    types of difficulties with, 209
Leblanc, M., 49
Legislation
    No Child Left Behind. *See* No Child
        Left Behind Act [NCLB]
    relating to English language learner
        students, 283, 285, 290
    supporting assessment, 130
Lei, P., 228
Letter naming fluency (LNF), 178–179
Letter-sound fluency (LSF), 179
Levitt, J., 56, 70, 71
Likelihood ratio, 214–215
Limbos, M. M., 291–292
Literacy screening, 291–298. *See also*
    Early childhood literacy screening;
    English language learner (ELL)
    students
LNF (letter naming fluency), 178–179
Lochman, J. E., 52, 61, 258
Locuniak, M. N., 207
Loeber, R., 52, 60
Lonigan, C. J., 149
Los Angeles Unified School District,
    259–260
LSF (letter-sound fluency), 179

MacDonald, A., 53

Magnitude comparison (mathematics screening), 203, 205

Malecki, C. K., 224, 231

Manifest variables, 87

MAP-R. *See* Measures of Academic Progress for Reading

Marquez, B., 68

Marsalowicz, A. J., 120

Mathematics screening, 199–217
  current approaches to, 201–209
  future directions in, 215–217
  increased interest in, 199–200
  likelihood ratio for, 214–215
  purpose of, 200–201, 209–210
  reporting of area under the curve with, 210–213
  setting of cut scores for, 213–214, 217

Math skills, of English language learner students, 278

Mattison, R. E., 259

Maze screening tool, 181–182

McConaughy, S., 53

McCurdy, M., 291

Measures of Academic Progress for Reading (MAP-R), 182, 188, 190

Mental health screening, 266. *See also* Behavioral and emotional risk (BER) screening

Mental health systems, 56

Mental Measurements Yearbook, 81

Menzies, H. M., 14

Merrell, K., 47

Messick, S., 99

Miller, D., 119

Mirkin, P. K., 185

MLD. *See* Learning disability in mathematics

Monitoring Basic Skills Progress system, 209

Moore, E., 129

Morabia, A., 235–236

Morgan, G., 256, 258

Morgan, R. J., 200

Motivation, 19, 226–228

MTSS (multitiered systems of supports), 172–173, 183–184

Muir Gray, J. A., 14

Multiple gating, 47–72
  in behavioral and emotional risk screening, 260, 262–263
  case study, 62–67
  critical features of, 48–51
  defined, 47, 48
  and emerging web-based assessment technology, 67–68
  future directions for, 71–72
  and intervention-sensitive instruments, 55–57
  methodological issues with, 57–61
  procedural variations in, 51–55
  recommendations for, 68–71

Multiple number proficiency math screening measures, 206–209

Multitiered assessment approaches, 56

Multitiered response-to-intervention (RTI), 19–44
  actions and procedures for successful use of data in, 29–35
  case example of, 35–42
  comprehensive mental health systems in, 56
  continuous improvement in, 22–24
  future needs for, 42–44
  high-quality instructional decisions in, 20–21
  leadership and planning for systems-level decision making in, 24–26
  selecting screening tools in, 26–29
  universal screening within, 5–6, 121–122, 142

Multitiered systems of supports (MTSS), 172–173, 183–184

Murray, C., 259

NAEYC (National Association for Education of Young Children), 159

Naquin, G., 62

Narrowband screening, 228–229

National Academies, 252, 263

National Academy of Sciences Committee on Development Assessment and Outcomes for Young Children, 145

National Assessment of Educational Progress, 278

National Association for Education of Young Children (NAEYC), 159
National Center on Response to Intervention (NCRTI), 6–7, 81, 176
National Council on Measurement in Education, 6
National Governors Association, 215
National Institute of Mental Health, 127
National Literacy Panel, 284
National Reading Panel (NRP), 175, 190
National Research Council (NRC), 6, 175
NCLB. *See* No Child Left Behind Act
NCRTI. *See* National Center on Response to Intervention
NCTM Focal Points, 209, 215, 216
Negative likelihood ratio, 214–215
Negative predictive value (NPV)
   of academic and social behavior screening tools, 234
   acceptable values for, 10, 11
   of behavioral and emotional risk screening tools, 258
   calculation of, 8
   classification based on, 105
   of SSIS-PSG measure, 239
Nelson, P. M., 28
Nese, J., 213
New Freedom Commission on Mental Health, 127
Nix, R., 259
NKT (number knowledge test), 206, 207
NMAP, 215
No Child Left Behind Act (NCLB)
   definition of English language learner in, 276–277
   evidence-based practices implemented with, 223
   grants for identifying at-risk children from, 127
   language ability measures in, 290
   requirements of, 6
Nonsense word fluency (NWF), 179–180, 190
Norming, 89, 292
NPV. *See* Negative predictive value
NRC (National Research Council), 6, 175
NRP (National Reading Panel), 175, 190

Number competency measures, 201–202
Number knowledge test (NKT), 206, 207
Number sense brief (screening measure), 206
NWF (nonsense word fluency), 179–180, 190

Oakes, W. P., 14
Observations (generalizability theory), 89
Observed scores, 89, 102
Ochoa, S. H., 280
O'Connell, M. E., 252
Okamoto, Y., 207
Ollendick, T. H., 231, 259
Oral language development, 144
Oral reading fluency (ORF), 180–181, 183, 187, 190–191, 292–294
Oregon Social Learning Center, 58, 59
ORF. *See* Oral reading fluency
Ortiz, S. O., 280
Oswald, P. D., 231

PAM (pupil assistance model), 62–67
Parallel reliability. *See* Test-retest reliability
Parent language questionnaires (PLQs), 285–289
Parents
   consent for screening from, 265, 266
   judgments by, 231–232
Passive informed consent, 264, 265
Pastorelli, C., 224
PBIS. *See* Positive behavior intervention and supports
Peabody Picture Vocabulary Test—4th Edition (PPVT-4), 154
Pearson product-moment correlation. *See* Reliability coefficient
Peer social behavior (PSB), 51
Permissions, for screening, 264–265
Person-based perception, 80
Phi coefficients, 106
Philips, B. M., 149
Phoneme segmentation fluency (PSF), 178
Phonological awareness, 144, 151. *See also* CIRCLE-Phonological Awareness, Language, and Literacy System+ (C-PALLS+)

PLQs (parent language questionnaires), 285–289
PMT (web-based screening system), 68
Policy, 6, 59, 126–127
Positive behavior intervention and supports (PBIS), 56–58, 67, 71
Positive likelihood ratio, 214–215
Positive predictive value (PPV)
    of academic and social behavior screening tools, 234, 235
    acceptable values for, 10, 11, 235
    of behavioral and emotional risk screening tools, 257–258
    calculation of, 8
    classification based on, 105
    of SSIS-PSG measure, 239, 240
PPRA (Protection of Pupil Rights Amendment), 264
PPV. *See* Positive predictive value
PPVT-4 (Peabody Picture Vocabulary Test—4th Edition), 154
Predictive validity
    with academic and social behavior screening tools, 234
    of behavioral and emotional risk screening tools, 253, 256
    of C-PALLS+, 151–152
    function of, 98–99
    of Individual Growth and Development Indicators, 154–155
    of mathematical screening measures, 205, 207
    overview of, 8–11
    and selecting screening tools, 27, 43
Predictors, 61
Preschool Comprehensive Test of Phonological Processing and Print Awareness, 152
Prevention, 171–172. *See also* Intervention(s)
Primary implementers, of screening, 113–115, 125
"Probes" (academic monitoring), 224
Problem identification, assessments as means for, 79
Professional development
    and continuous improvement, 23
    for early childhood literacy screening, 162–163

future directions for research on, 44
    and screening data, 30, 32–34
Program champions (stakeholders), 125
Program developers, 133
Prosocial behaviors, 224–225
Protection of Pupil Rights Amendment (PPRA), 264
PSB (peer social behavior), 51
PSF (phoneme segmentation fluency), 178
Psychodiagnostik (Hermann Rorschach), 4
Psychologists, school. *See* School psychologists
Psychometrics, 86–94
    applications of, 93–94
    classical test theory, 87–88, 93–94
    contemporary, 107
    generalizability theory, 89–90, 93–95
    item response theory, 90–94
    latent trait and theory, 86–87
    of tools assessing early reading skills, 173
    utility of, 81
Pupil assistance model (PAM), 62–67

Raffle, A. E., 14
Rahbar, M. H., 230
Raines, T. C., 264
Reading
    curriculum-based measurement in. *See* Curriculum-based measurement in reading [CBM-R]
    early childhood literacy. *See* Early childhood literacy screening
    and English language learner students, 278
    motivation needed for, 19
    National Research Council research on, 6
Reading screening instruments, 43
Realmuto, G., 53
Receiver operating characteristic (ROC) analysis, 60, 210–213, 235–236
Recognition and Response agency, 159
Reid, E. L., 228
Reliability. *See also specific types of reliability*
    of academic and social behavior screening tools, 233

of behavioral and emotional risk
screening tools, 249, 254–256
classical notions of, 95–97
of C-PALLS+, 151
defined, 95
of English language learning
measures, 294
of Get Ready to Read! Revised
measure, 149
of Individual Growth and Development Indicators, 154
of mathematic screening tools, 209
for reading skills screening tools,
176–181
Reliability coefficient, 95, 233
Response-to-intervention (RTI)
with behavioral and emotional risk
screening, 249
common models for, 201
Individual Growth and Development Indicators in, 152
literacy screening in, 159–160, 162
mandated use of, 127
multitiered. See Multitiered response-
to-intervention [RTI]
phases of, 235
prevention with, 172
Reynolds, C. R., 267
Reynolds, W. M., 119
Rhodes, R., 280
Richardson, M., 61
Riley-Tillman, T. C., 119, 239
Risley, T., 144
ROC analysis. See Receiver operating
characteristic analysis
Rogers, E. M., 115, 116, 123–125
Rohde, P., 59
Romanelli, L., 56
Rorschach, Hermann, 4
RTI. See Response-to-intervention
Rubin, M., 129
Ruchkin, V., 255

Saka, N., 56
Sample-dependent behavior
(classical test theory), 88
Santos, M., 283
Scarcella, R., 282
Schellinger, K. B., 225

School psychologists, 114–115, 117,
119–121, 242
School psychology, 43, 236
Schoolwide Positive Behavior Support,
242
Schwab-Stone, M., 255
Science, technology, engineering, and
mathematics (STEM), 199
Screening: Evidence and Practice
(A. E. Raffle & J. A. Muir Gray),
14
Screening, history of, 3–4. *See also*
Universal screening in education
Screening, Identification, and Monitoring
System (SIMS), 49n1
Screening data. *See* Data (screening)
Screening tests and tools, 6, 26–29.
See also specific tests and tools
SDQ (Strengths and Difficulties Ques-
tionnaire), 251–256
Secondary implementers, of screening,
113, 114
Seeley, J. R., 59, 60
Seethaler, P. M., 207
Self-efficacy, 125
SEM (standard error of measurement),
95, 97–98
Semantic interpretations (validity),
100–102
Sensitivity (validity)
of academic and social behavior
screening tools, 234
acceptable values for, 11, 235
and area under the curve, 106
of behavioral and emotional risk
screening tools, 257
calculation of, 8
classification based on, 105
of C-PALLS+, 151
with early literacy screening,
146–147
of Get Ready to Read! Revised, 149
of Individual Growth and Development Indicators, 155
of mathematic screening tools, 214
of SSIS-PSG measure, 239
Severity, in multiple-gating approaches,
57
Severson, H., 58, 60, 62, 64

Sharkey, J. D., 264
Shaywitz, B. A., 5, 19
Shaywitz, S. E., 5
Sheridan, S. M., 291
Showalter, D., 235
Silberglitt, B., 107, 213
Simon, Theodore, 3
SIMS (Screening, Identification, and Monitoring System), 49n1
Single-proficiency math screening measures, 201–206
Skill-based screenings, 5
Skinner, B. F., 249
Slama, R. B., 283
Snow, C. E., 145
Social behavior screening. *See* Academic and social behavior screening
Social skills, 226–228, 278–280
Social Skills Rating Scale-Teacher (SSRS-T), 231
Social system (screening implementation), 112, 114, 125
Spanish curriculum-based measurement, 294–298
Sparta (ancient Greece), 3
Spearman, C., 87
Spearman-Brown prophecy formula, 96
Special education, 6, 161, 292
Specificity (validity)
    of academic and social behavior screening tools, 234
    acceptable values for, 10, 11, 235
    and area under the curve, 106
    of behavioral and emotional risk screening tools, 257
    calculation of, 8
    classification based on, 105
    of C-PALLS+, 151
    with early literacy screening, 146–147
    of Get Ready to Read! Revised, 149
    of Individual Growth and Development Indicators, 155
    of mathematic screening tools, 214
    of SSIS-PSG measure, 239
SRSS. *See* Student Risk Screening Scale
SSBD. *See* Systematic Screening for Behavior Disorders

SSIS-PSG measure, 237–241
SSIS-RS measure, 240
SSRS-T (Social Skills Rating Scale-Teacher), 231
Stakeholders, 113–115, 124–125
Standard error of measurement (SEM), 95, 97–98
Standardization
    of data collection, 34
    of screening systems, 266–267, 280
Standards-based assessment, 103
Standard setting, 103–104
Standards for Educational and Psychological Testing
    and cut scores, 155
    screening assessment defined by, 79
    standard error of measurement in, 98
    test evaluation guidelines in, 83
    validity evidence in, 100, 234
Stanford-Binet scale, 3–4
State standards, 209
STEM (science, technology, engineering, and mathematics), 199
Stice, E., 59
Stiggins, R., 192
Stigma, 129
Strategic counting math screening measures, 205, 206
Strengths and Difficulties Questionnaire (SDQ), 251–256
Student Risk Screening Scale (SRSS), 251–252, 254, 255
Student self-report judgments, 231
Study skills, 226–228
Stuebing, K. K., 5, 19
Subsystems (screening implementation), 114
Suicide risk screening
    community and government sponsorship of, 266
    implementation of, 114–115, 117–120, 122, 129
Supplemental services, for early reading skills, 186–188
Suprasystems (screening implementation), 112, 114, 126–127
Surveillance, of risk, 263–264
Sustainability, 133
Swafford, J., 199

Systematic Screening for Behavior
    Disorders (SSBD), 225
    broad use of, 253
    case study of, 61–67
    construction of, 58
    future recommendations for using,
        68–71
    multiple-gate screening with,
        260, 262
    overview of, 49–51
    web-based version of, 67–68
Systematic Screenings of Behavior to
    Support Instruction (Lane, Menzies,
    Oakes, and Kalberg), 14
Systems-level decision making, 24–26
Systems support, 130–131

Taylor, R. D., 225
Teachers
    attitudes and perspectives of, 122
    efficacy of, 125
    judgments of academic and social
        behavior by, 230–232
    and literacy screening, 159
    as primary implementers of screening,
        113, 114
Technical adequacy, 13
Technical assistance, 127–128
TerraNova, 213
Test information function (TIF), 93
Test of Preschool Early Literacy
    (TOPEL), 149, 154
Test-retest (parallel) reliability
    of academic and social behavior
        screening tools, 233, 238
    calculation of, 233
    of early reading skills screening tools,
        178–180
    of mathematics screening tools, 207
    overview of, 95, 96
Test review and selection, 81–82
Tier 1 instruction, 201, 250
Tier 2 instruction, 201, 250
Tier 3 instruction, 201
TIF (test information function), 93
Timed assessments, 217
Timing, of screening, 263
TOPEL (Test of Preschool Early Literacy),
    149, 154

Training, for screening implementation,
    127–128, 134
Trait
    defined, 100
    latent, 86–87
Transitional approaches, for English
    language learner students, 284
Treatment services, 236–237. *See also*
    Intervention(s)
Triannual screening, 97
True-negative outcomes, 104–105
True-positive outcomes, 104–105
True score model (classical test theory),
    87–88
True scores, 233
Tyron, G., 202

Universal screening in education, 4–12
    for behavioral and emotional risk,
        257–265
    costs and benefits of implementing, 44
    definitions of, 4, 6–7
    as formative assessment, 10, 12
    guidelines for evaluating, 13
    increase in policy emphasis on, 6
    within multitiered response-to-
        intervention framework, 5–6
    predictive validity of, 8–11
    stages in, 4–5
Universe score, 102
University of New Orleans (UNO),
    62–67
Untimed assessments, 217
U.S. Department of Education, 284
U.S. Department of Health and Human
    Services, 278
Usability, evaluating screening
    based on, 13

Validity, 94–107
    of academic and social behavior
        screening tools, 233–236
    argument-based approach to, 100–107
    of behavioral and emotional risk
        screening tools, 249, 254–256
    classical notions of, 98–99
    concurrent. *See* Concurrent validity
    of English language learning
        measures, 294

Validity, *continued*
    of mathematic screening tools, 209
    predictive. *See* Predictive validity
    of reading skills screening tools, 173,
        174, 176–181, 192
    reliability evidence for, 95–98
    types of, 94
VanDerHeyden, A. M., 214, 215
Vander Stoep, A., 263
Van Hemel, S. B., 145
Vermeiren, R., 255
Volkmar, F., 235
Volpe, R. J., 56, 227

Walker, H., 58, 60, 62, 64
Walker-McConnel Scale of Social
        Competence and School
        Adjustment, 54–55
Walkup, J., 120, 121
Web-based assessment technology, 67–68
Weissberg, R. P., 225
Weist, M. D., 129–131
Welsh, M. E., 239

Wentzel, K. R., 224
WIDA (World-Class Instructional
        Design and Assessment)
        Consortium, 285
Wiley, H. I., 293
Wilmes, C., 283
Woodcock-Johnson III (math screening),
        207
Woodcock-Muñoz Bateria-R Combined
        Scores of Amplia Lectura, 294
World-Class Instructional Design
        and Assessment (WIDA)
        Consortium, 285
Wrobel, G., 129
Wyatt, M. A., 149

Yeaton, P., 68
Young, B., 61
Young, E., 61
Young, K., 61

Zhang, F. F., 235–236
Zimbardo, P. G., 224

ABOUT THE EDITORS

Ryan J. Kettler, PhD, is an assistant professor of school psychology in the Graduate School of Applied and Professional Psychology at Rutgers, The State University of New Jersey. He earned his doctorate in educational psychology from the University of Wisconsin–Madison in 2005. Dr. Kettler's research on data-based decision making in education has been funded externally and has yielded more than 40 publications. He is currently a coprincipal investigator of the School System Improvement Project, funded by the U.S. Department of Education, as well as the website editor of the research registry of the Society for the Study of School Psychology.

Todd A. Glover, PhD, is a research associate professor at the Nebraska Center for Research on Children, Youth, Families, and Schools at the University of Nebraska–Lincoln. His research and publications focus on school-based screening, academic and behavioral supports for students at risk, and response to intervention. Dr. Glover is the principal or coprincipal investigator of ongoing grant projects funded by the U.S. Department of Education's Institute for Education Sciences and the Nebraska Department of Education. He is also director of research operations for the National Center for Research on Rural Education.

Craig A. Albers, PhD, is an associate professor of educational psychology in the School Psychology Program and is the chairperson of the Interdisciplinary Prevention and Intervention Sciences Program at the University of Wisconsin–Madison. He earned his doctorate in educational psychology at Arizona State University in 2002. Dr. Albers has received multiple U.S. Department of Education and Institute of Education Sciences research and training grants associated with implementation of response-to-intervention models. He is a member of the Society for the Study of School Psychology and serves as an associate editor for the *Journal of School Psychology.*

Kelly A. Feeney-Kettler, PhD, is a consultant in educational psychology in Basking Ridge, New Jersey. She earned her doctorate in educational psychology from the University of Wisconsin–Madison in 2008. Dr. Feeney-Kettler developed the Preschool Behavior Screening System to promote the early identification of children at risk for mental health problems. She was recognized by Division 16 (School Psychology) of the American Psychological Association with an outstanding dissertation award. She also has been recognized as an Early Career Scholar by the Society for the Study of School Psychology.